Awakening Albion

From Cornwall to East Anglia – walking together as a mindful community

Edited by
Jane Bottomley
Sarah Bowen
Jonathan How
Gerry Jacobson
Graham Joyce
Lynne Merryland

Coherent VISIONS

First published
2009
Coherent Visions
BCM Visions
London
WC1N 3XX

ISBN-13
978-0-9524396-8-4
ISBN-10
0-9524396-8-9
Paperback

Typesetting, Design & Layout
Jonathan How
www.coherentvisions.com

Illustration Sequence
Jane Bottomley
www.janebottomley.com

Distribution
Edge of Time Ltd
BCM Edge
London
WC1N 3XX
www.edgeoftime.co.uk

Awakening Albion
www.awakeningalbion.com

Acknowledgements

Written Contributions
Sarah Bowen
Dixey Brooks
Carolin Comberti
Geoff Dixon
Danu Fox
Rhian Hill
Jonathan How
Justine Humphrey
Gerry Jacobson
Graham Joyce
Melanie Long
Lynne Merryland
Sarah Partridge
Tess Redshaw
Steve Seekings
Ian Woodcock
Melody Wright

Tanka
Gerry Jacobson

Drawings
Jane Bottomley
Dixey Brooks
Ruth Morgan

Photographs
Sarah Bowen
Marion Fanning
B'anna Federico
Jonathan How
Nate Smith
and many others

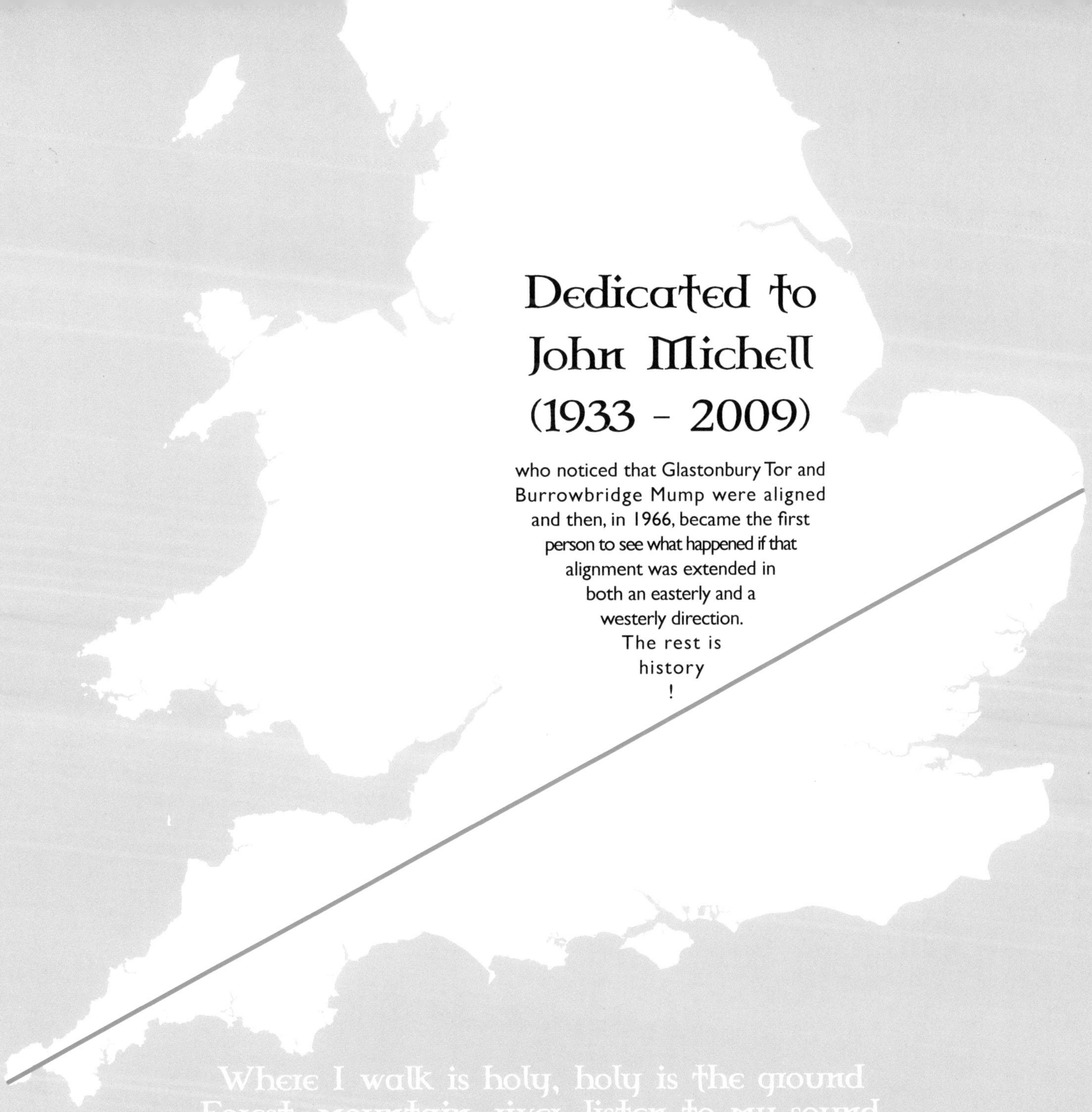

Dedicated to John Michell (1933 - 2009)

who noticed that Glastonbury Tor and
Burrowbridge Mump were aligned
and then, in 1966, became the first
person to see what happened if that
alignment was extended in
both an easterly and a
westerly direction.
The rest is
history
!

Where I walk is holy, holy is the ground
Forest, mountain, river, listen to my sound
Great Spirit circles all around me
Great Spirit circles all around me

Foreword

Twenty five years ago I was inspired by my mentor, John Michell, to find out a little more, if I could, about the Michael Line. John has recently left the planet and I can see him stomping around the Elysian Fields happily guiding the current heirarchy on new ways of thinking.

I took his work seriously and spent a fascinating six months working with the complex and beautifully co-ordinated energies of the Michael Line. In the end I could find that special signature, a unique blend of a large band of frequencies, like a vast musical chord, even when blindfolded at night in a closed van.

Following that weaving line, visiting ancient sites, hills and churches was a magical experience. For the first eighteen months I was aware of a number of strange unsolved anomalies, and an indefinable feeling of puzzlement that I was not being allowed to see the full picture.

At Avebury on a May day sunrise the Management must have reckoned it was time to show this bumbling pupil that life was not quite so simple, and tweaked my senses up a notch. They introduced me to Mary, the balancing energy that, of course, I should have realised was necessary for the harmony nature requires for her existence.

Back to the beginning at Carn Lês Boel, working with Mary, many of the anomalies were resolved and led to a realisation that the discoveries were perhaps a major breakthrough to a clearer understanding of the way earth energies work,

I could never have guessed, and am extremely humbled to find, that some 25 years later a very special group of people would get together and tune to the wonderful caduceus of energy formed by the two lines as they visit sacred places across the country. Not only were they to work in resonance with these ancient frequencies but spend weeks in deeper and deeper appreciation of the profound effects earth energies have on human behaviour.

I was close to tears when I had the privilege of meeting the group on the second evening of the journey. My contribution was over and they were just beginning a great adventure.

I have seen the first drafts of the book and have to say how immensely pleased I am that the group commitment comes through on every page. It is a unique concept. Layout, text, photographs, exquisitely executed, beautifully expressive black and white drawings combine with an honesty which is totally refreshing.

My heartfelt congratulations and best wishes to everyone involved in the journey.

Hamish Miller

Albion,
The Wounded Being We Inhabit

The giant's flesh became the soil.

The giant's bones became rocks and stones.

The giant's blood became the springs and streams and lakes and the blue waters of the wide sea.

The dome of the giant's skull became the great dome of the sky that stretches high above our heads.

The giant's brains became the white scudding clouds.

One eye became the sun, the other the moon.

The giant's breath became the wind that lifts the hair from our foreheads.

And we, the people, treading the skin of the world beneath the vast dome of the sky, we are its dreams.

Some say the wounded, sleeping being we inhabit is called Albion.

It is the grandfather of all the grandfathers, the grandmother of all the grandmothers.

We are its dreaming and its skin holds the memory of all that it has dreamed in the past.

Adapted by storyteller Hugh Lupton from the 12th century Icelandic 'Prose Edda', by Snorri Sturluson

Prologue

The Awakening Albion Walk was organised by Lynne Merryland and Graham Joyce, and took place during May and June 2008. The initial inspiration goes back 25 years. In 1983 I took part in 'A Walk For Life', an 11 week journey from Faslane, near Glasgow, to Greenham Common, near Newbury, Berkshire, both being military bases with nuclear weapons. At a time of mass demonstrations against such weapons, a basic purpose of that walk was to take a 'peace camp' on the road, combining protest with living in community. It was a transformational experience; to walk as an intentional community through so much of the British landscape left me with powerful memories and a desire to offer others something similar.

Some years later, a book called *The Sun and the Serpent* introduced me to new ways of perceiving the land. By Hamish Miller and Paul Broadhurst, it detailed the dowsing of two intertwining paths of earth energy running from Cornwall to Norfolk along the Michael Leyline, which they named the Michael and Mary Lines. I discovered surprising personal connections: that my birthplace and childhood home in East Anglia both lay on these energy lines, and indeed that I'd spent much of my life traveling to and fro along them. I also learnt about Albion. In his introduction to that book, the author John Michell told of a mural he had once painted, of the giant Albion lying across southern England, feet in Cornwall and head in East Anglia. The Michael/Mary Lines and their crossing or node points could thus be seen as the major meridian lines and chakras of this earth giant. I was getting a sense of a vast mythic landscape, and the thought that this might be the journey I wished to make.

I already knew that Albion was an early name for Britain. From a study of William Blake, I discovered that he had written about Albion, who he saw both as the spirit of the land itself and as an Everyman figure. Blake created his own version of the ancient myth, that our inner wounding is mirrored by the creation of a damaged landscape around us. He saw that the process of healing necessarily involved a shift from intellectual comprehension alone, connecting also with our emotional responses to the world, as well as with the creative imagination. Feeling our deep connection with each other and all of life, awakening to community and a sense of the sacred, could lead to social and ecological restoration.

This discovery of Blake's writings about Albion related to work I had been doing. Over the past 15 years or so I have helped with organising Creative Arts Camps in East Anglia. The content of these has varied, but an underlying theme has been that they offer people a gateway into the experience of being in community in nature. The camps seem to meet a core biological need, to live, if only for a short while, in a way more natural to humans. They serve to restore a sense of belonging in the world, our deep ecology. It was at a camp with a theme of walking the land that Lynne and I first considered organising this Walk. We could take a camp on the road and walk across the country. Thus the Awakening Albion Walk was conceived.

That camp was in autumn 2005. We worked together through that winter, planning for the Walk to occur the following summer, but for various reasons were forced to postpone the project. A year passed, then in spring 2007 Lynne decided she was going to make her own pilgrimage by vehicle, and invited me along. Immediately the Universe lent a helping hand by providing a full set of OS maps from Cornwall to Wiltshire (50p each in my local charity shop); magic was in the air! During that journey we visited many of the sites mentioned in *The Sun and the Serpent* and generally got a sense of the land. It was a powerful time; I remember us feeling both inspired and overwhelmed at the thought of organising a walk over such a distance.

During the summer I spent two weeks studying OS maps of southern England, including those supplied by Hamish Miller showing the Michael and Mary earth energy lines, and created a provisional walking route and a list of villages to visit for campsites. In October 2007 Lynne and I drove from Norfolk to Cornwall with the intention of finding these night stops for the Walk on the return journey. Arriving in the Lands End area I remember well the anxiety and doubt I felt; having given ourselves only two weeks to sort out over forty campsites, success seemed unlikely. Yet even before we began knocking on doors, there were miracles and signs of encouragement. It being a Sunday, we decided not to start work till the next day, but instead to enjoy visiting some of the holy wells and other sacred sites we'd discovered on our spring trip. That afternoon at Boscawen-un stone circle we met a local family who, curious about our project, were able to provide leads for the first two sites. The next day, on the morning we walked to Carn-lês-Boel, the headland meeting point of the two Serpent energy lines, we were excited by the sighting of two snakes. It felt a powerful omen; magic was in the air again. This sense of encouragement continued when a meeting later that day (on unrelated business) led to our third campsite.

Some sites proved harder to find than others, and there were return trips to the west country, but overwhelmingly there was a sense of flow to the process, of being supported by Spirit, and of repeatedly experiencing, in Lynne's words, 'the kindness of strangers'. Often there was a need just to get out of our own way. During one occasion early on, after having arranged a number of night stops in various farmers' fields, we were repeatedly directed to a local campsite. At that point I still had a personal prejudice against 'proper' sites, so went there with some reluctance. It was a powerful lesson and a great delight to be proved so wrong. It was a small sheltered meadow beside a tumbling stream, with basic facilities. Arriving there on the Walk, we had the place to ourselves, except for a couple in a camper-van who were also exploring the Michael/Mary Lines!

Our requests for assistance were repeatedly met with friendliness, generosity and support. For some sites there was a fee, but others were offered to us for free, or in return for a donation to a local charity. Further synchronicities occurred, and I mention a few here to give a flavour of the process. Looking at Hamish's maps in Cornwall, I was drawn to a farm that lay between the energy lines, at a point where they ran close together and parallel to each other. Enquiring in the village shop about camping, I was immediately directed to that farm, where I received an enthusiastic welcome. In Devon, as we drove towards an inn, I joked that I'd only stop if someone were standing outside, and as we arrived, there indeed was a man, a friend of the owner, seemingly waiting for us. Again we were willingly offered camping there. Some days after we'd left Cornwall, we received an unexpected phone call that provided a site just where one was needed, breaking an overly long day's walk into two easier ones. In Suffolk the managers of a National Trust property that did not allow camping surprised themselves by offering us a beautiful campsite in their parkland estate. Visiting our last stop, I went to the local boatyard to discover if our group could be ferried across the river. Having been directed to the quay of the one person who might help us (a man who lived on the marsh side of the river and only went out once or twice a week), I arrived just as he was getting into his boat to go home; a few minutes earlier or later and the meeting would not have happened.

Reflecting on the process of organising the campsites, and noticing the number of synchronicities that occurred, I see how these increased my sense of trust, relieving initial fears and doubts. Positive responses early on boosted my self-confidence, and as I grew more at ease with discussing our project, that undoubtedly helped to gain further support along the way. I experienced a shift into a sense of service to the Walk, which enabled me to get out of my own way, allowing me to become less prejudiced as to who I approached. Having a simple and straightforward request certainly helped, and perhaps the nature of our venture, as a community pilgrimage, tapped into some subconscious ancestral memory that evoked support. There was definitely a powerful and growing sense for Lynne and myself that this project was meant to happen. We ended up making the return journey, and arranging most of the sites, in 11 days!

Back in Norfolk, I remained focussed on the sites and route, as well as writing most of the website material, while Lynne took on much of the other work, creating an information booklet, arranging insurance, and taking bookings. With her address including 'HQ' in the postcode, it seemed natural that it should become so. A room in her home became the Walk office, with a large map of the route on one wall, a growing list of walkers on the other, and a stack of folders. We worked hard that winter, but with an underlying sense of service, bringing the sacred into our work with a lit candle and time sitting in council. A highpoint came when we received our first booking, from Gerry in Australia, for a full-time place – it was happening!

Throughout the process we received unexpected help. From a summer meeting came an offer to create a website: many thanks for that to Julie for all her tireless work, and also to Geoff for invaluable business help and advice. Both offered enthusiastic support before, during and after the Walk. When my vehicle was written off in an accident, Alex, who had developed a growing interest in the Walk, offered his van instead; appropriately already named 'Albion' from the plate he'd fixed to the front.

Hamish Miller, who had dowsed the Michael and Mary earth energy lines 20 years earlier, was supportive throughout, providing maps, offering encouragement, and even giving a generous donation to support the project. We met Hamish during the Walk. Sitting around the fire in council that evening, we each shared our reasons for joining the Walk. When Hamish spoke, it was inspiring to see how visibly moved he was to know that we were making this pilgrimage. Whilst various individuals had made this journey before, this was the first time that there had been a community walking pilgrimage. It seemed this was a culmination of his dream as well.

Graham Joyce

In the early 2,000s I met Graham at several community camps, talked about his ideas on his New Jerusalem project and my long held dream to walk from East Anglia to Avebury. Eventually the idea of a walking community emerged.

In March 2007 I had a real pull to follow the trail as told by Paul Broadhurst and Hamish Miller in their book *The Sun and the Serpent*. "I'm going next Sunday, you coming?" Graham did. We left in the old bus, drove to Hopton, the start of the Michael/Mary leyline. We dropped in at a friend's labyrinth for equinox celebrations and were given a royal send off. Rattling on down the line we stopped at Silbury, visited the Swallowhead Spring, thence to the Hurlers. In Cornwall we discovered Carn Lês Boel, watching as the sun poured out on the sea. After a few days exploring we were off following the line east. Wonderful days full of promise.

We met regularly after that. Lighting a candle and holding hands before the day's work and, at the end, a few minutes of reflection and thanks, blowing it out to close, became the structure for what was to become an obsession over the next year. Meetings unfolded, lead to long talks, jokes, fun, heads crammed with ideas. Eventually the walk structure evolved – Graham mastering maps, and site finding; me on organisation of what to take, etc.

October and we set off once again in the bus – very different this time. The hard work of finding sites started at 7am and ran to 7 or 8pm when we slept, starting again next day. Learning to look and listen for the clues to the next site, being well guided to each place. Then revising the next day's walk, constant work for Graham. Each night every lead was noted and logged. We returned with two-thirds of the sites found. We were amazed. A few weeks on Graham hunted for the remaining sites. Sites varied from friends' gardens to the National Trust permitting camping on their land. We are grateful to these open minded people who let a motley crew of pilgrims use their land for small remittance, charitable donation or just out of kindness.

Julie and Geoff helped greatly, setting up a website for us. Christmas came and our first booking from Gerry, full time and from Australia! Then more – each bringing a thrill of excitement. Days were spent list making, letter writing, phone calls and e-mails. All too soon the last frantic days slipped by, with one site falling through and a few still to be confirmed, we packed.

So with loaded Transit and trailer we set off. We made camp in a field near Lands End and set up Graham's beautiful new yurt he'd made for the walk. Then we walked out to Carn Lês Boel and closed the organisation with a simple ceremony. Heading back to camp we awaited the walkers' arrival ...

Lynne Merryland

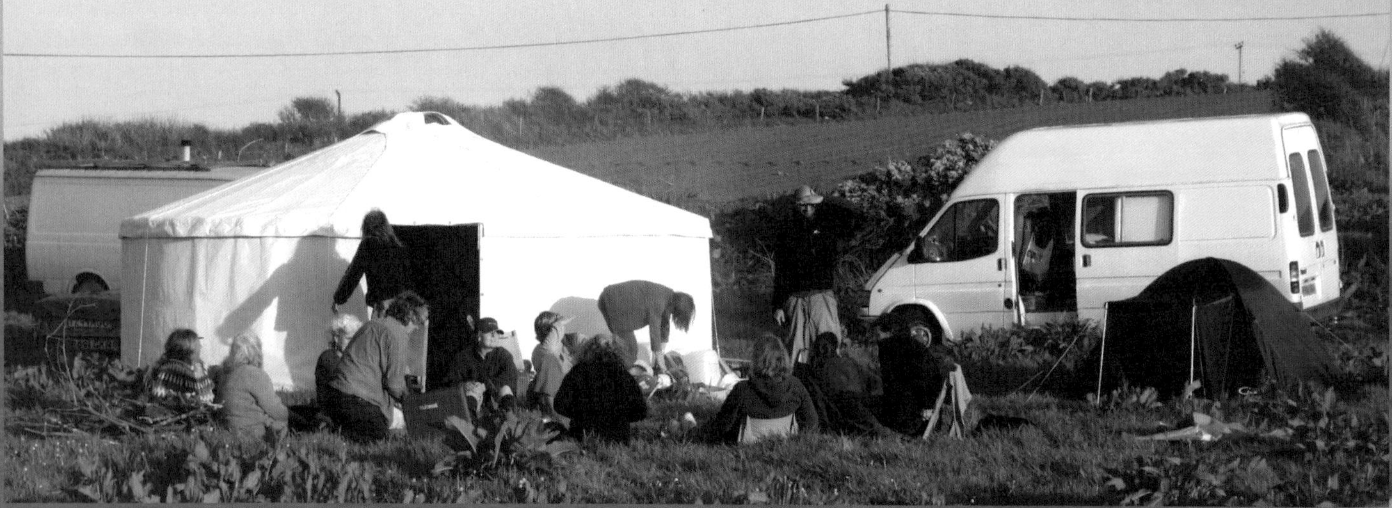

Day 0

Polgigga to Carn-Lês-Boel

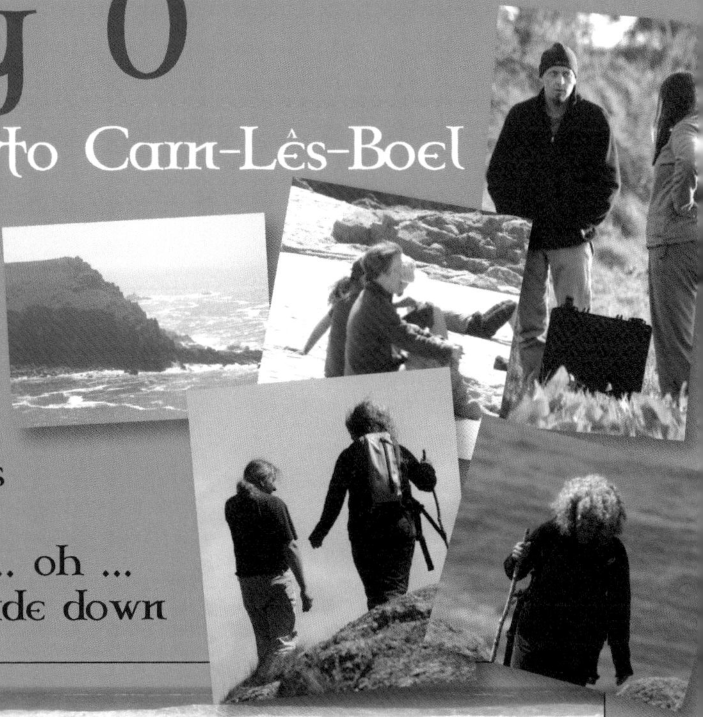

Walked to beach, washed in sea, rinsed mouth out with sea-water, that was the first time in my life that it was done purposely, ate fresh seaweed. Giant cave. Walked to Lands End, a great coastal path. Saw seals in sea. Too many tourists. Chips and Earl Grey tea. Walked back. Early night.

SS

So beautiful to wake up in a field. I opened up the zip and sat taking in the green, the lush grass, the bird song. A mist was here first thing. I felt overwhelmed with joy and filled up with emotion to realise that I will wake up in a field and sleep close to the earth for 50 days and nights! Celia brought me tea in bed, what a lovely woman! We ate porridge for breakfast in the yurt, then sat in a circle and at the moment we all held hands the sun came out.

ML

jetlagged
aussie opens his eyes
in a fog
north is south and ... oh ...
oh ... the sky is upside down

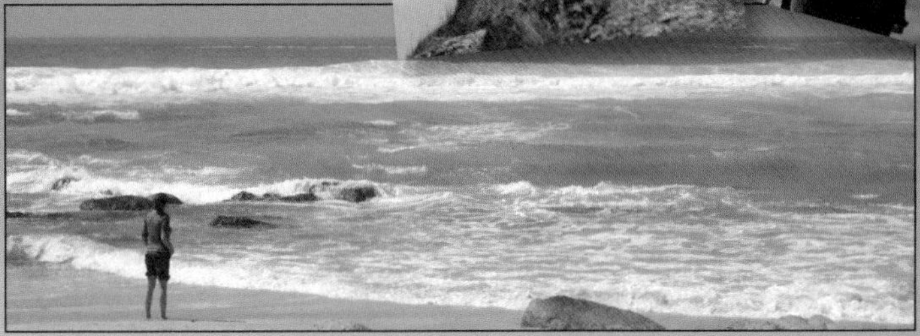

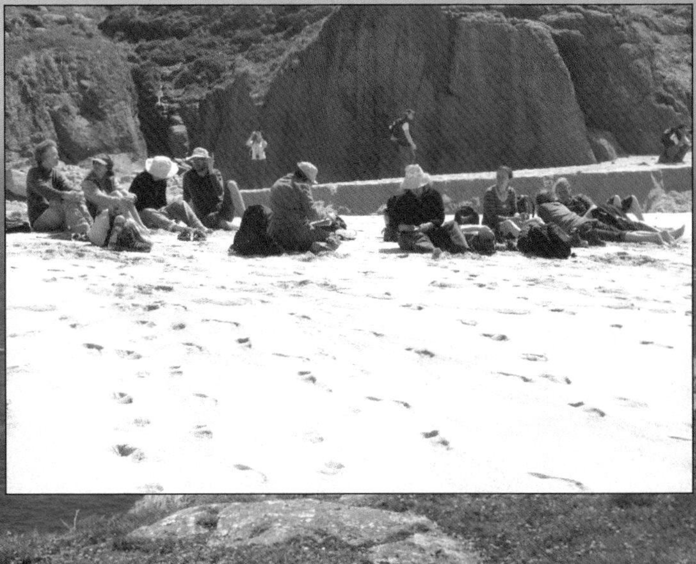

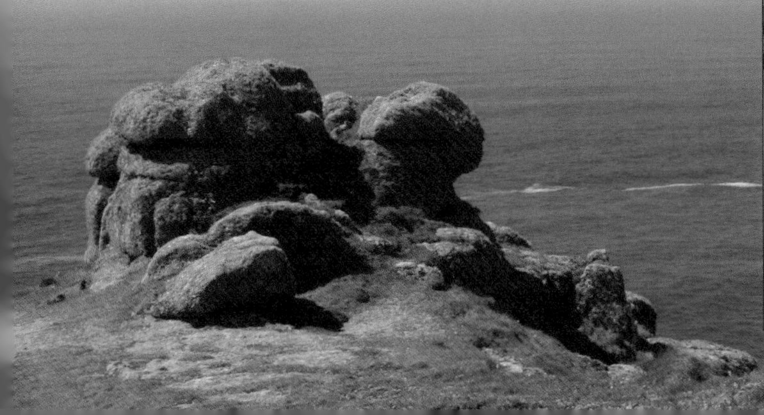

We got up when it was still dark and processed through quiet hedgerows to the headland. Jupiter and a few stars lit the dark blue sky. At the headland, Carn-Lês-Boel it was cold, the fog rolled in, and the foghorn was calling out to sea. People visited us. Ian with his guitar. We huddled together on the rock, taking turns in the middle for warmth, we sang and hummed and the glorious sun appeared in the East, illuminating the path we will take. I wept.

I felt my first love for this community, smiling round at them fondly. I watched the sun through the mist, red, pink, green, blue and purple: vivid colours swam around him. I made tea in flasks for everyone, doing a bit of service for the community drew them and I closer together. I feel more knitted in this morning.

Together we captured the Beltane sunrise, using a crystal ball and cramp balls (fungus from dead trees such as ash and beech and silver birch), also known as King Alfred's Cakes. The rays of the sun lit the fungus, Alex used tinder to feed the smoulder, I lit a candle from the small fire, then we lit two paraffin lanterns. We will try and carry the flame across the country! ***ML***

grey mist
descends on the
headland ...
the sea gets wilder
dragons bare their teeth

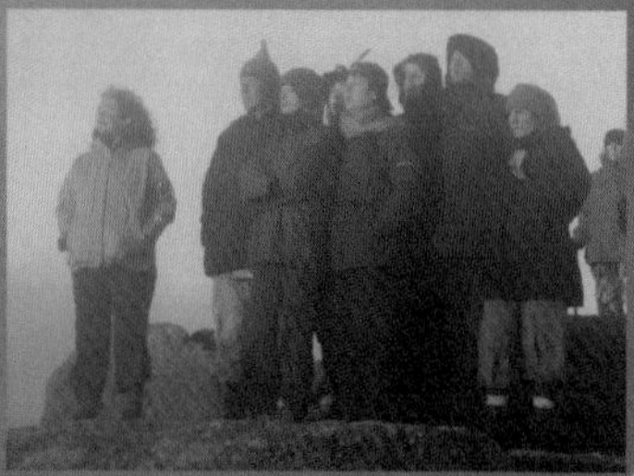

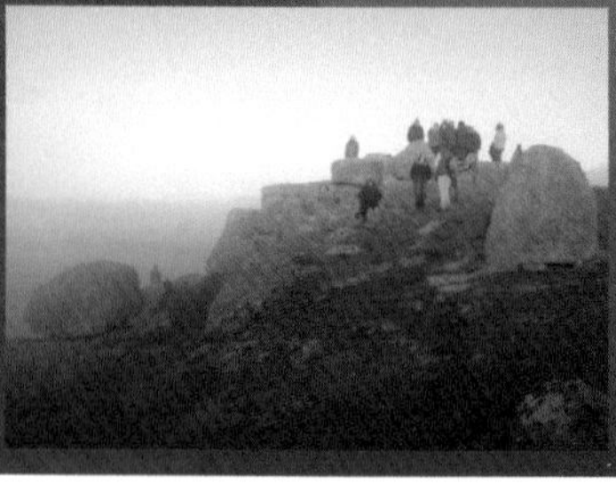

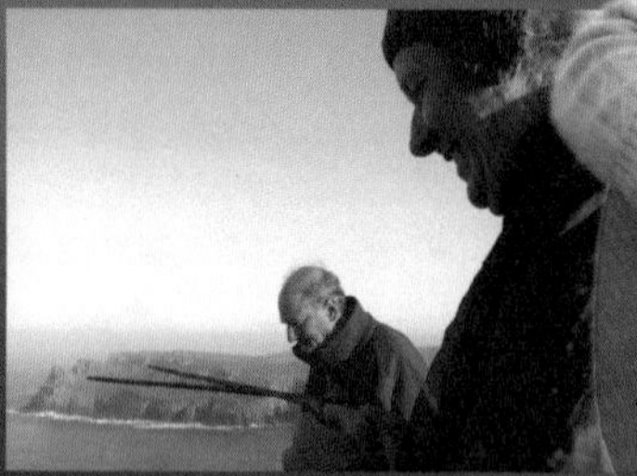

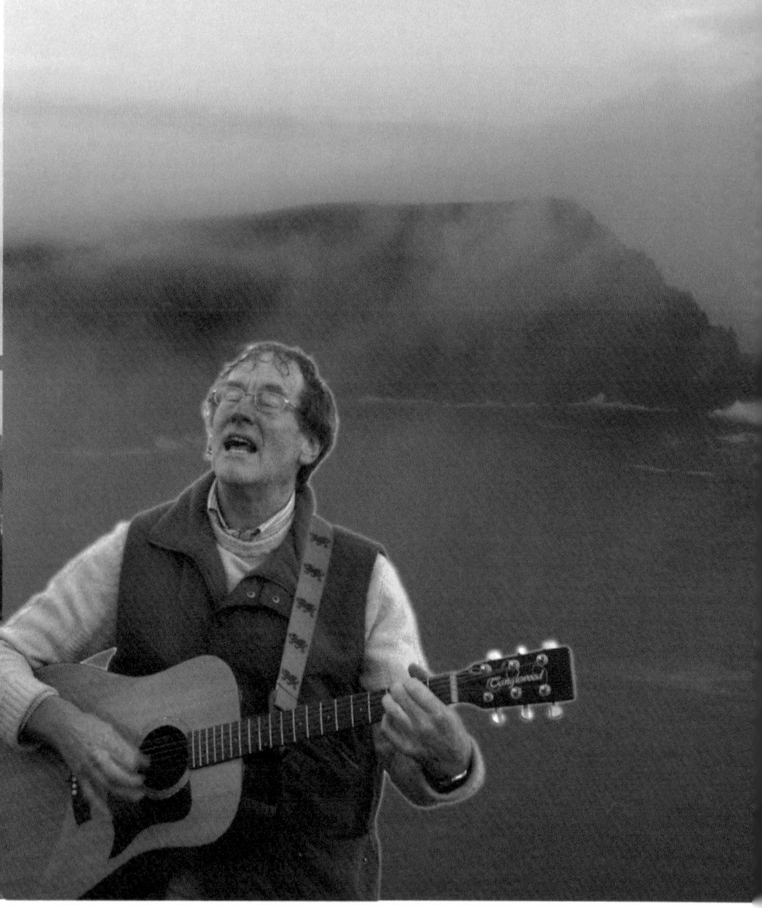

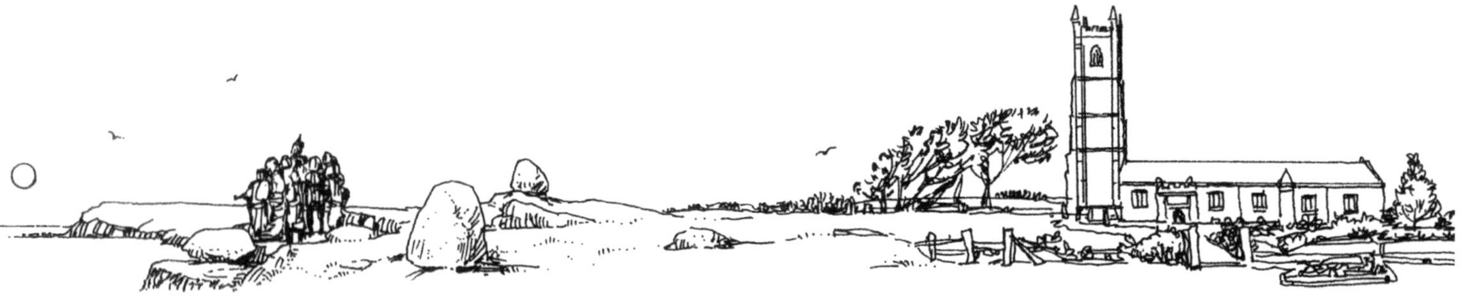

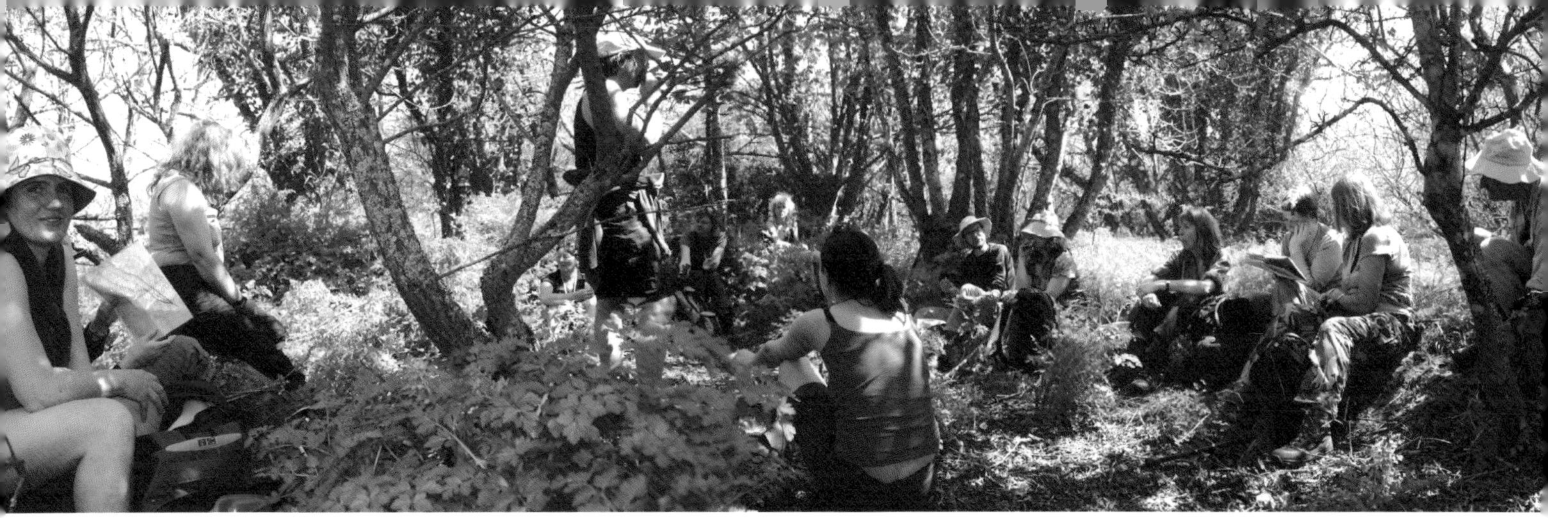

Map read and walk my way to Kerris along lanes and woods over field on field of silvered grass; they call it Paradise, they are not wrong, that valley quiet and cool in the day's heat. Clear water runs over my feet and bluebells cast a haze of healing blue. ***LM***

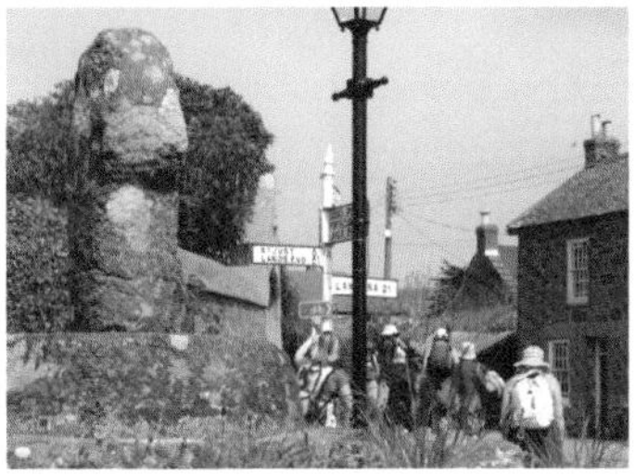

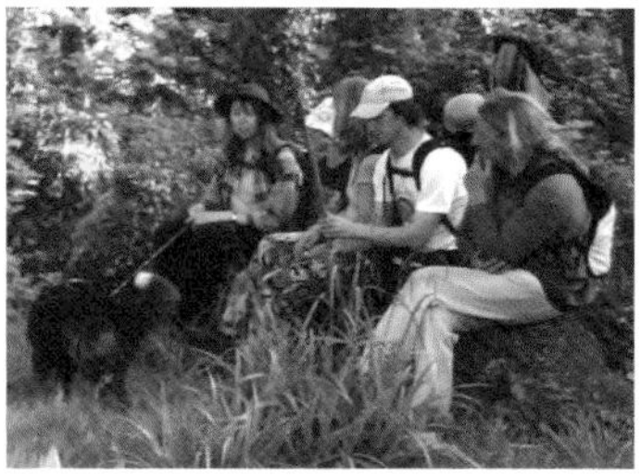

Walk begins. Bluebells and loads more beautiful flowers. Smells. Vistas. Stone Circle. Met Frank (local GP) who guided walk to next camp. Caught sun. Very tired. Early night. Lots of new people to get to know. Visitors. Guest walkers. So many nice happenings. Everybody really friendly. ***SS***

Day 1 Carn-Lês-Boel to Kerris

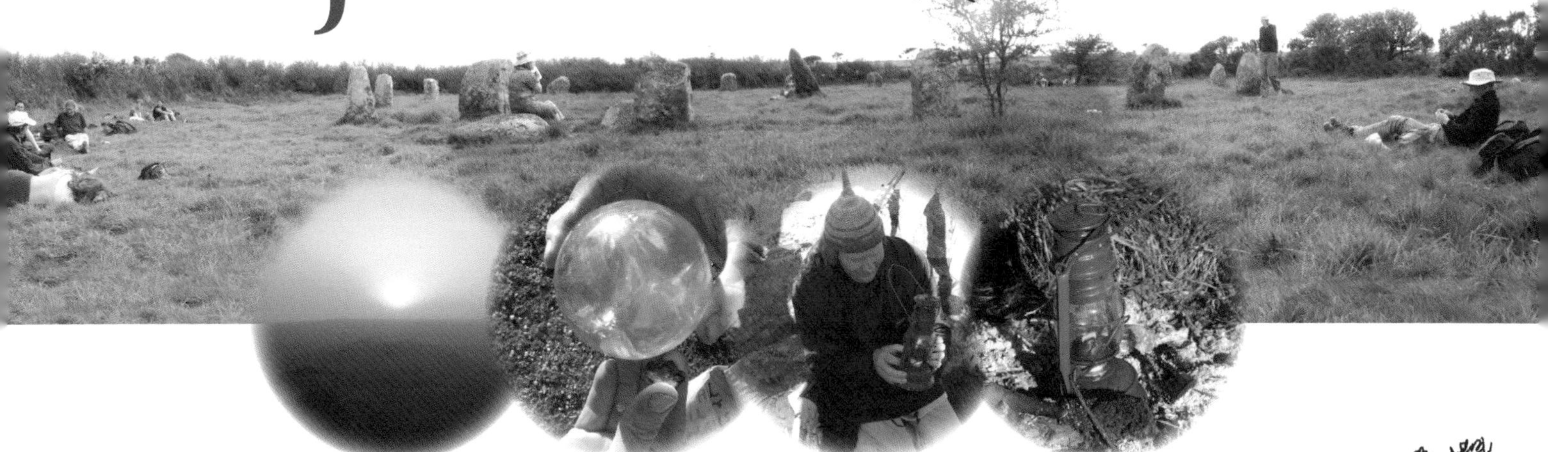

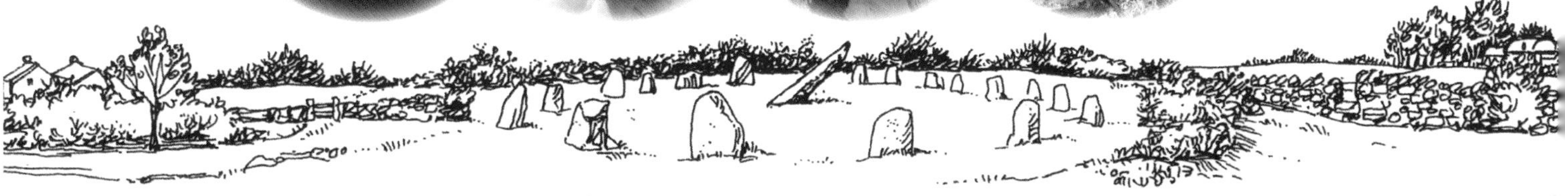

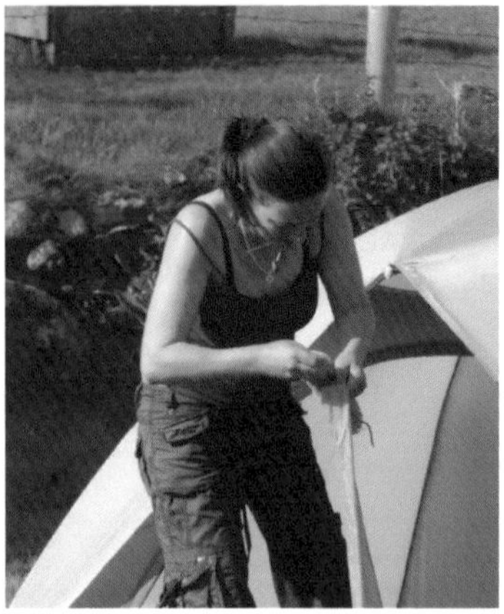
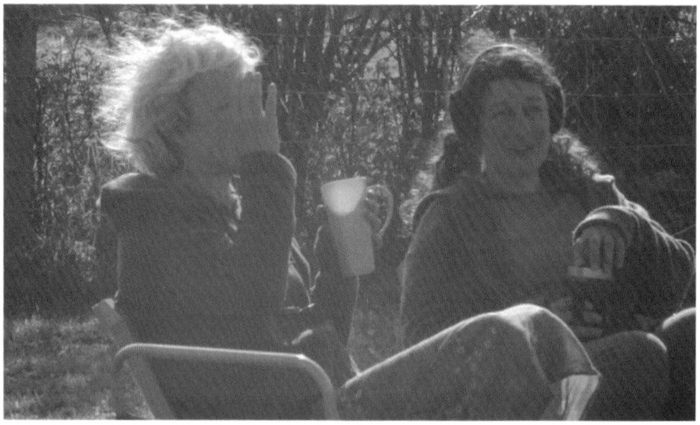
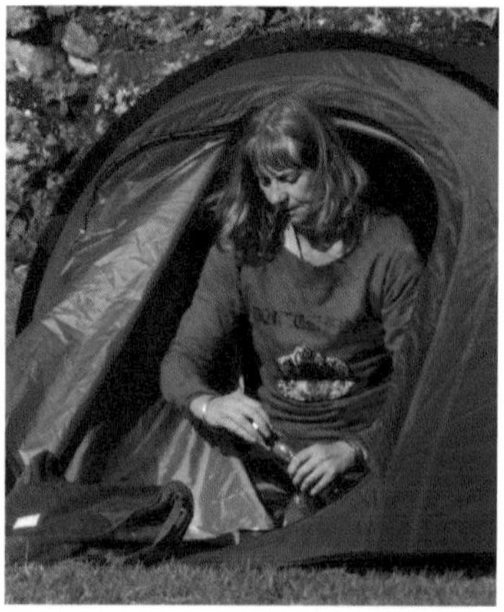

Day 2

Kerris to Townshend

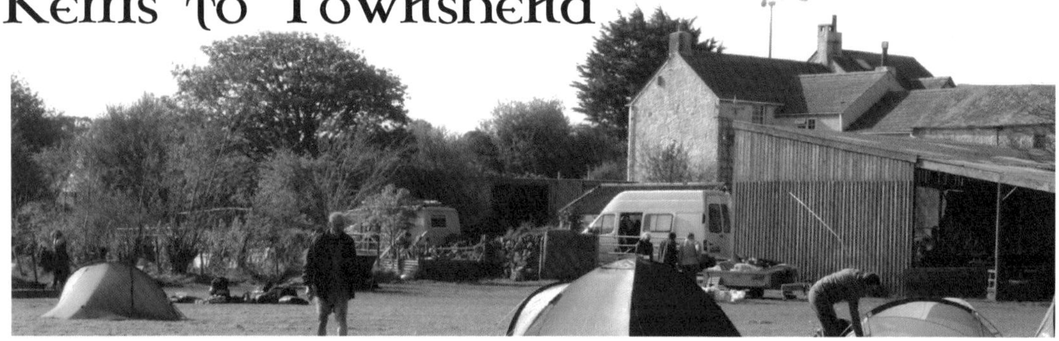
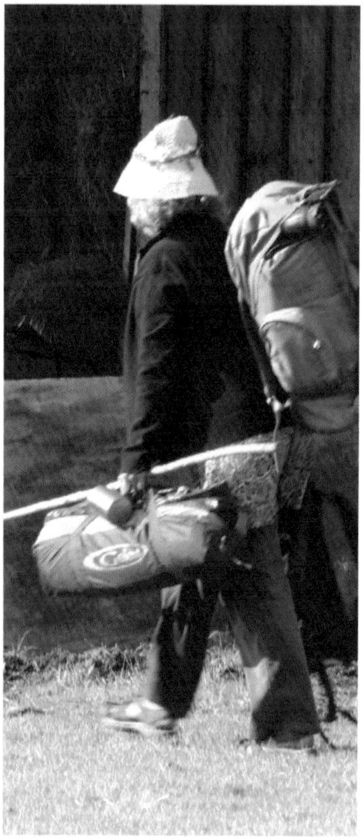
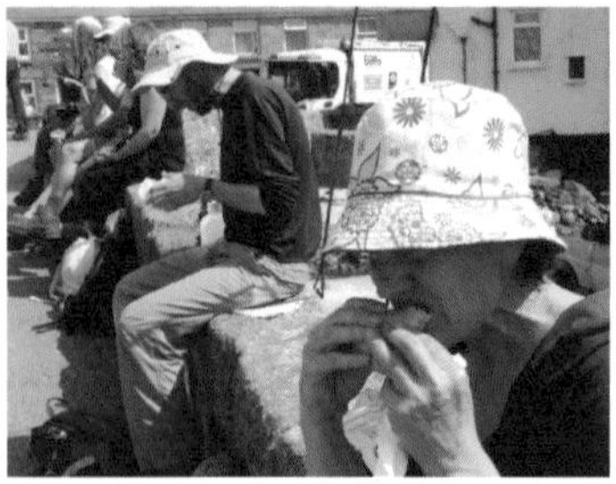

Newlyn to Penzance. Pastie with Alex. Swam in sea, not quite up to knees, naked of course. Walked to St Michaels Mount via the causeway, tide coming in fast, had to run there and back, just made it, sea up to knees by the time we got back, ran with Graham, we just had to do it. Great fun! Continuing on, very hot, came upon river, once again stripped off and jumped in, swam a bit, same depth as sea.

SS

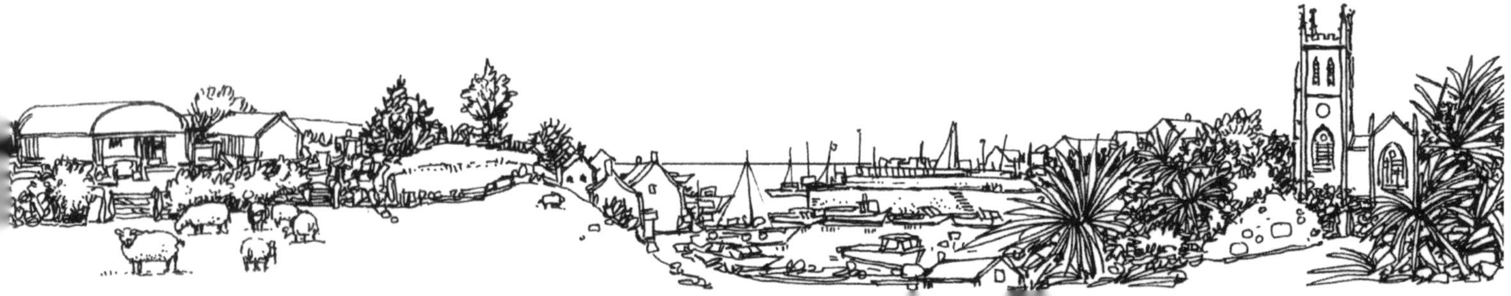

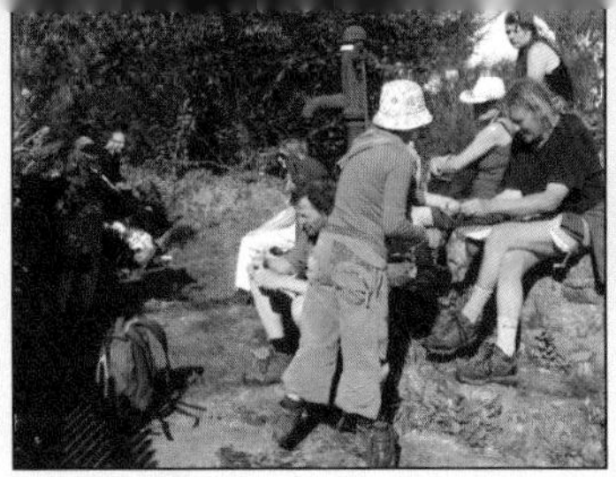

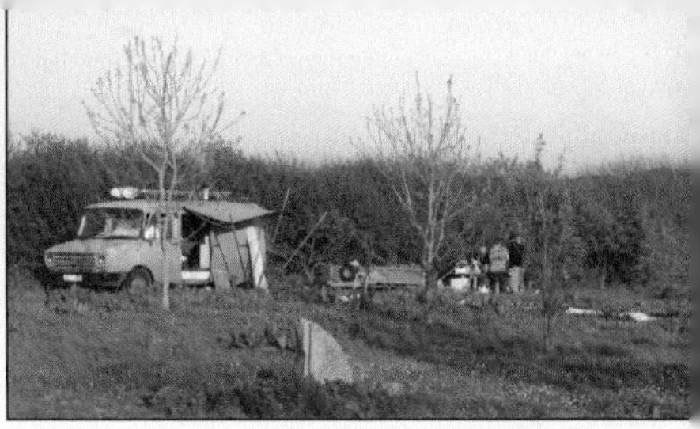

Today and yesterday we have at times struggled to find the esoteric footpaths. Having traversed ploughed fields and barbed wire barriers we had reached a dead-end between Keep Out signs and a sharply declining wooded slope. The map suggested we were really close to our destination. Hip-hop was rising up through the trees from the valley below. I hooted out the Australian "coo-ee" taught to me by Gerry. We heard a hoot back. I shouted out that we were lost and the distant voice called up the directions down the steep slope. He said he would meet us by the stream. We tumbled down the slope to be greeted by six feet of red-headed, tattooed man. He fetched a wooded pallet to make a bridge for us to cross. He is living off grid in that valley and installs solar panels for others who also aspire to be free from energy dependency. He was funny and friendly and kind and I wanted to pull off my boots and live happily ever after. But dinner was cooking in Dr Dan Rainbow's field up the hill ... so we said farewells and thank-yous to this St Christopher. ***SB***

campfire ...
circle of my longing ...
smoke swirls
starlit pilgrims
share their stories

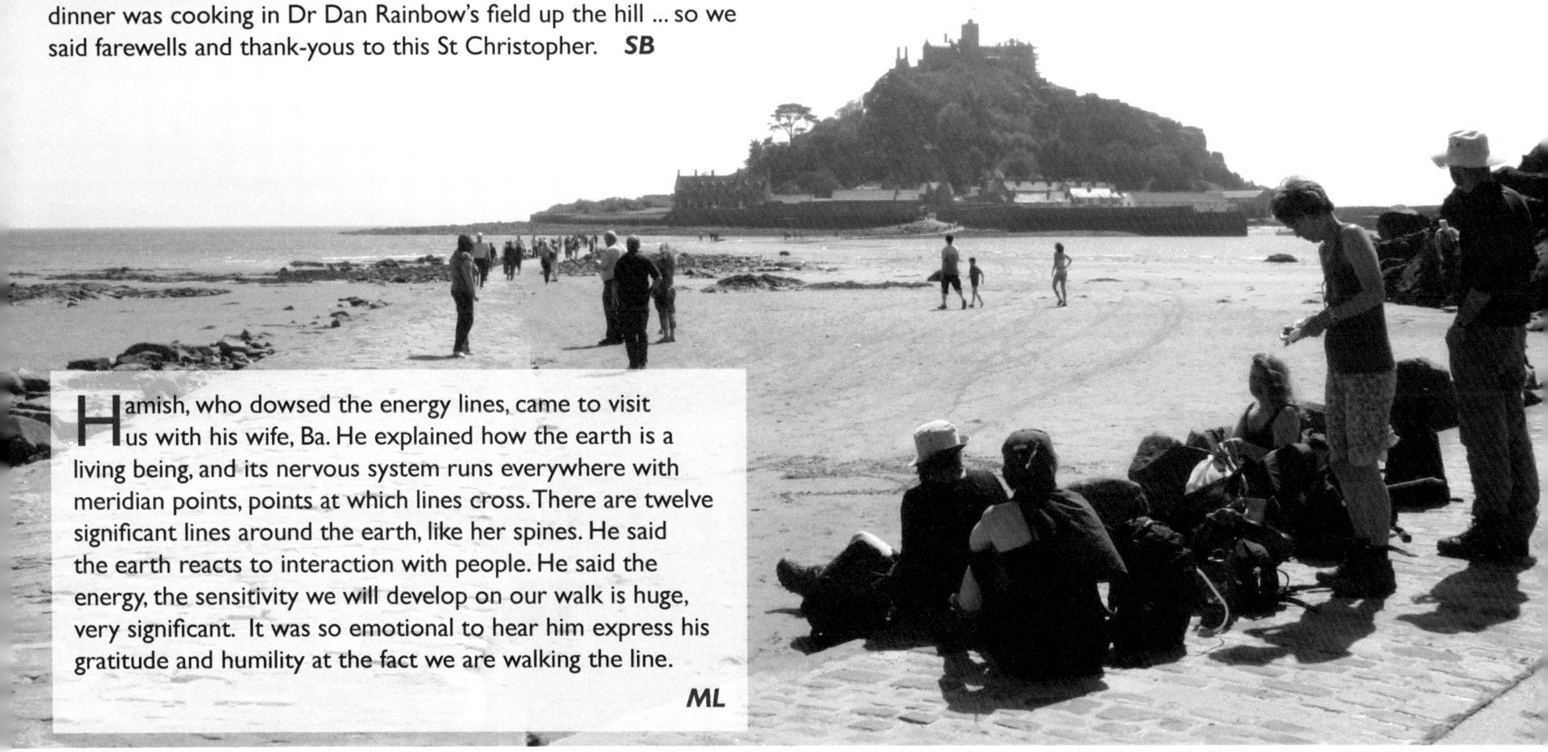

Hamish, who dowsed the energy lines, came to visit us with his wife, Ba. He explained how the earth is a living being, and its nervous system runs everywhere with meridian points, points at which lines cross. There are twelve significant lines around the earth, like her spines. He said the earth reacts to interaction with people. He said the energy, the sensitivity we will develop on our walk is huge, very significant. It was so emotional to hear him express his gratitude and humility at the fact we are walking the line.

ML

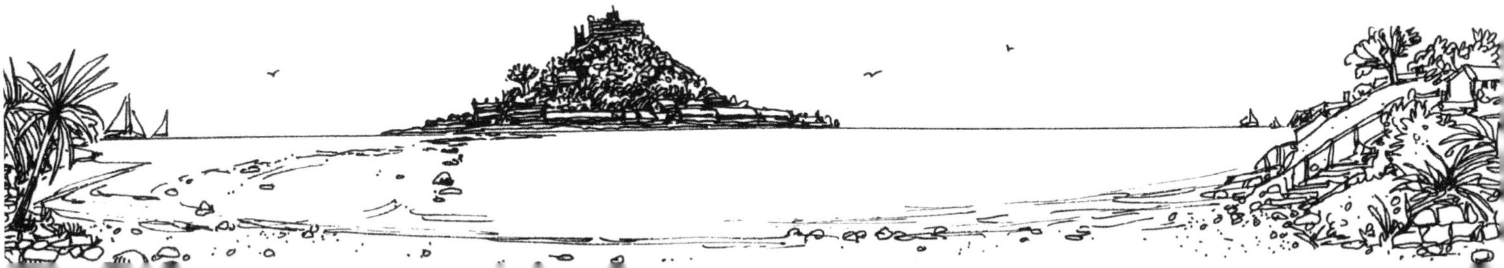

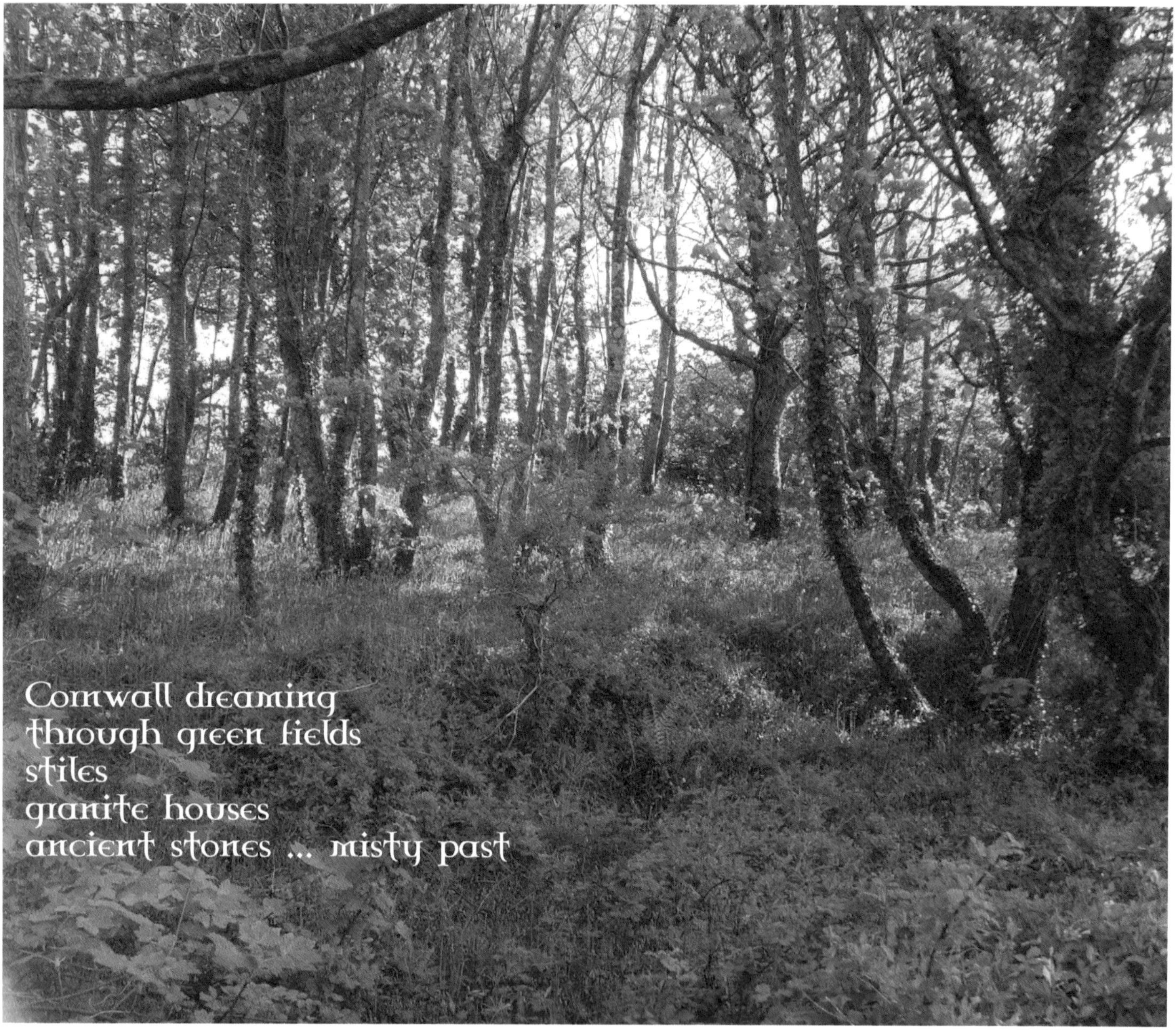

Cornwall dreaming
through green fields
stiles
granite houses
ancient stones ... misty past

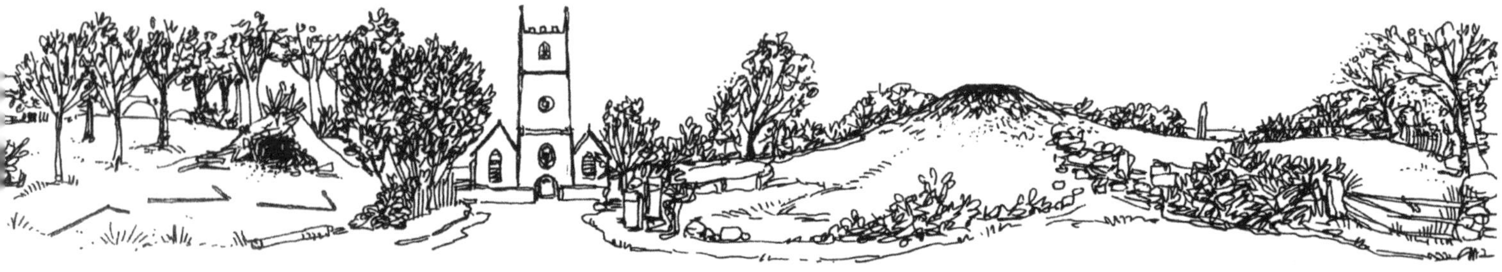

Another day of glorious sunshine, it was very hot today, and a long way. I feel tired but strong. We blessed the space with song before we left this morning and Jonathan left, he will be back. I saw a lot of frisky cows (scary) and horses and plenty of barking dogs dashed out to see us pass through their farms. A friendly man filled my water bottle from the hose he was washing his car with. I filled it again from a hose on the side of a cow shed. I spotted a Jack Russell blissfully rooting in rabbit holes.

I felt a strong magic down an exquisite little lane, lined with gnarled old trees, bluebells and high stones, the sunlight danced on the new leaves, and for the first time I think I sensed the Mary Line. We spotted an amazing wrought iron shaped cartwheels gate, and a bearded tree, then we went through a farm covered in cow shit! Lakes of it! Yuck! I learnt about new plants, the last few days – plantain, sorrel, pennywort (tasty). We went past a farm with 20 cats today and ate pickled onions in the churchyard of the wild god.

We are camping in the garden of the lovely Steve and Lesley in Perrenwell. They just cooked us a fabulous meal. They have two friendly cats. ***ML***

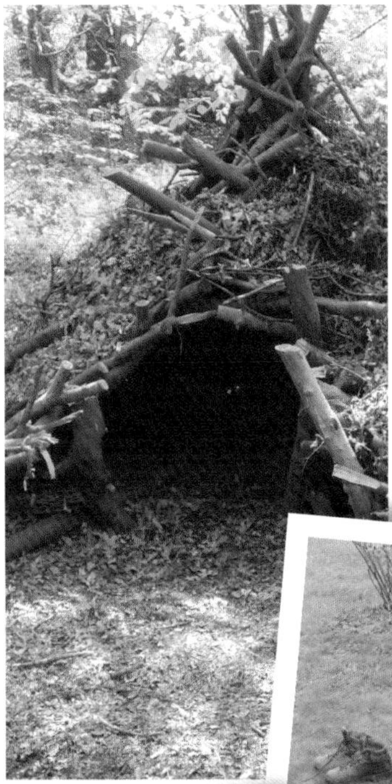

Longest walk, 16 miles? Beautiful flowers everywhere. Water wheel, 22 feet across, largest in Cornwall. Bathed feet in stream. Van forgot lunch. Camped in Steve and Lesley's garden, they also cooked us a fantastic meal, so, so kind and friendly. Alex, Mel and I ran the last couple of hundred yards to their home.

SS

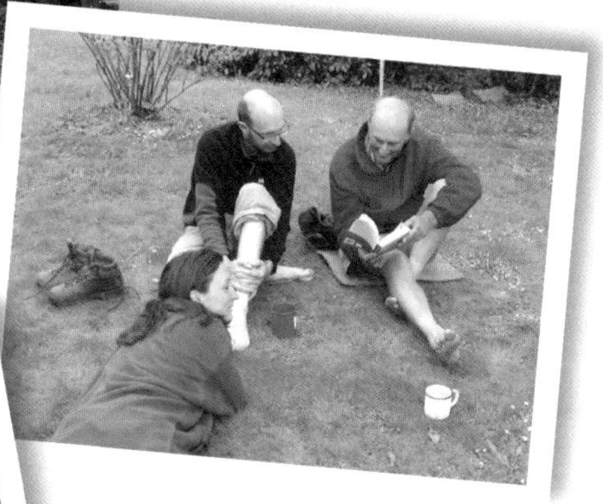

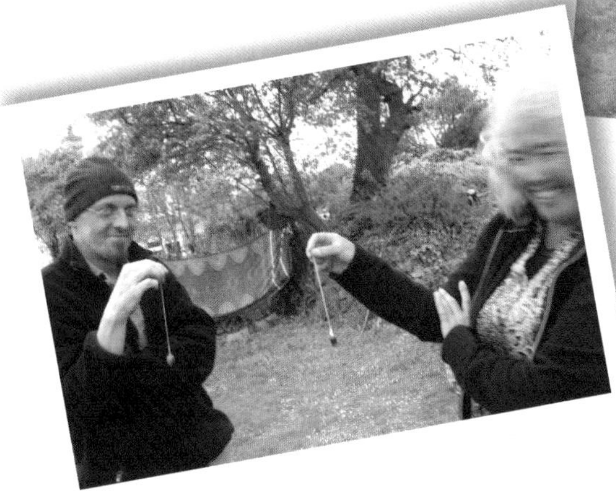

In Steve and Lesley's peaceful, welcoming garden tonight. A real haven – very glad to get here after long walk today. Magic woodlands, flowers, bogs and gigantic stone stiles.

RH

Day 3 Townshend to Perrenwell

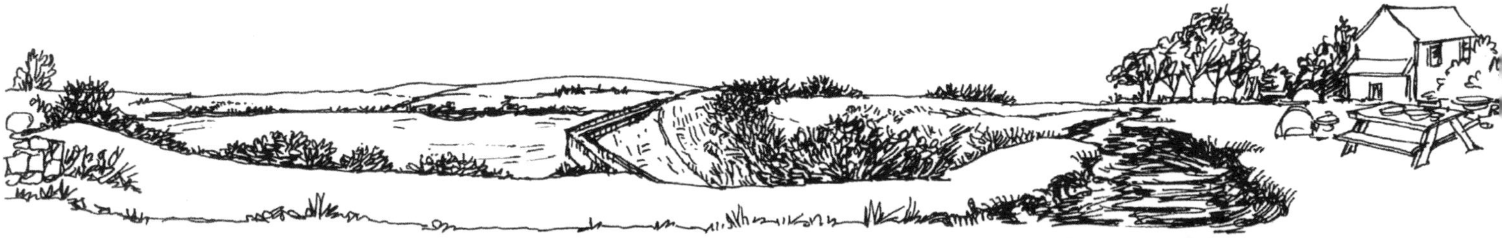

Day 4 Perrenwell to Treworga

I hear
the sound of silence
deep
within ... it's dark
I breathe ... my heart beats

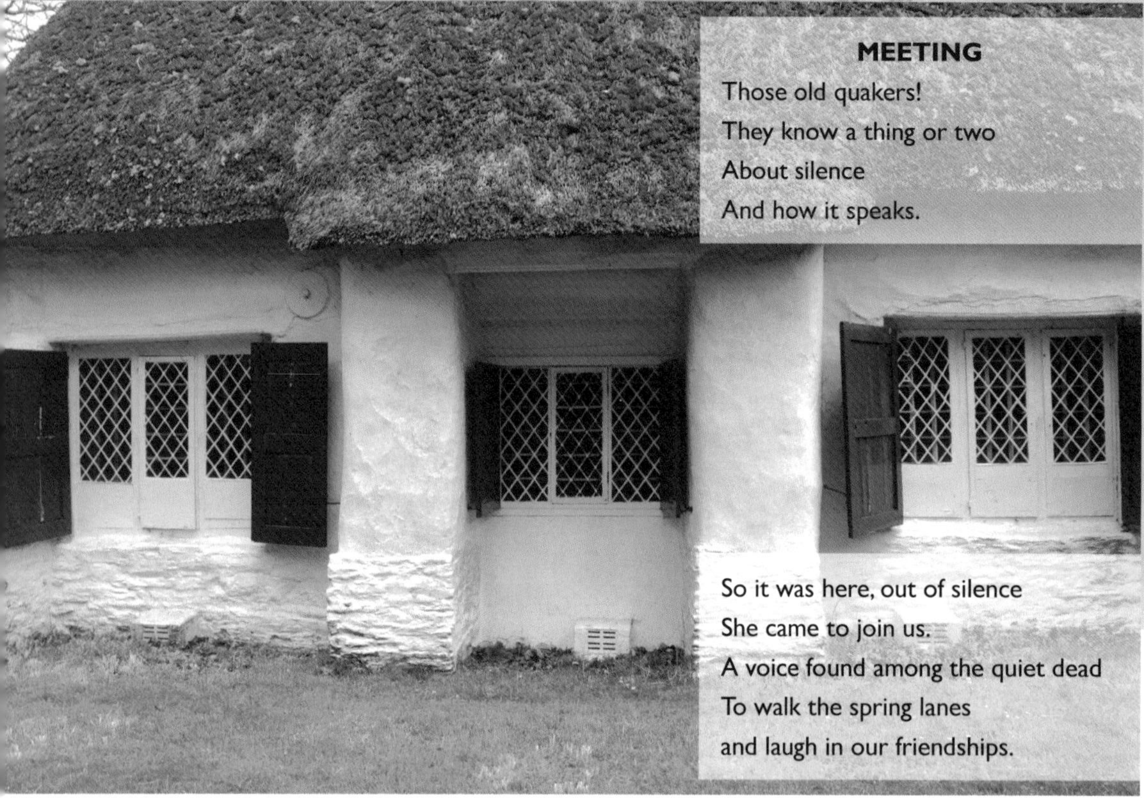

MEETING

Those old quakers!
They know a thing or two
About silence
And how it speaks.

So it was here, out of silence
She came to join us.
A voice found among the quiet dead
To walk the spring lanes
and laugh in our friendships.

The meeting house was called Come to Good. I remember it as being made of entirely natural things, wood-crooked and arched, whitewashed walls, stone flags, thatched roof. It stood in grass and there were trees and a path down to a burial place. Was it raining? ***MW***

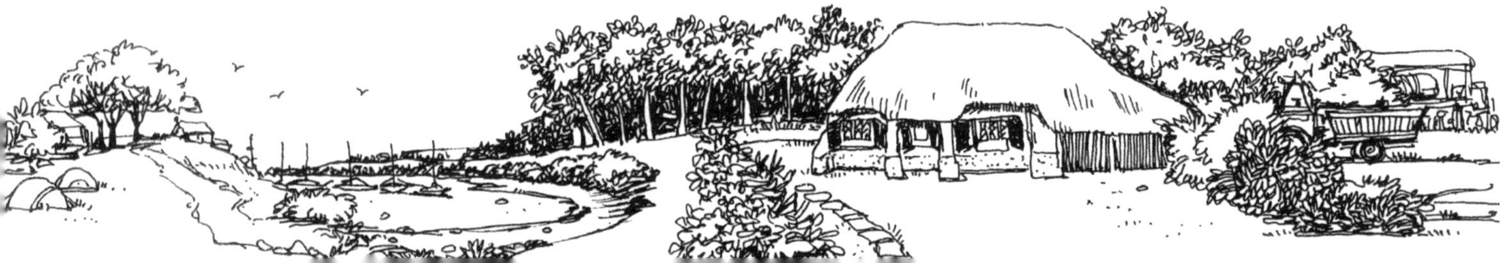

We left the quiet of the meeting house … and then … and then up a lane and round the corner an ancient pub "The Punchbowl and Ladle". I couldn't believe it … the song had been in my head for weeks "Give me the punch ladle I'll fathom the bowl ..!" ever since the folk festival at Easter ... and we had sung it one morning loading the van and stowing Carolin's precious brass bowl. And the pub sign with five bucolic farmers singing merrily ... I fell about and had to be rescued from passing traffic ...! ***GJ***

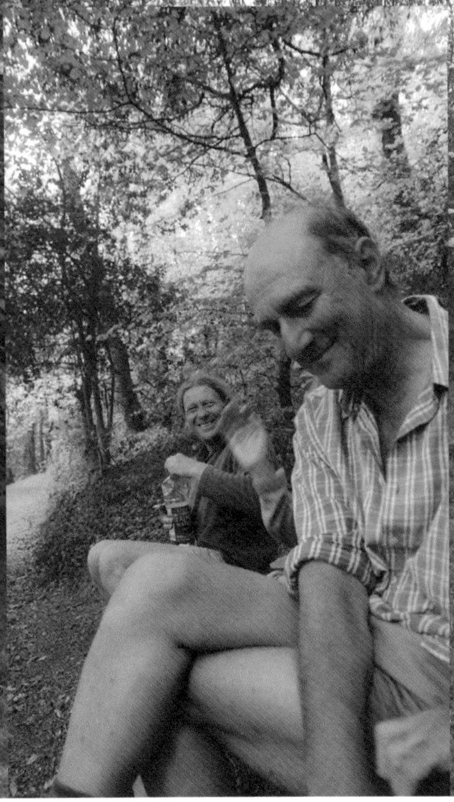

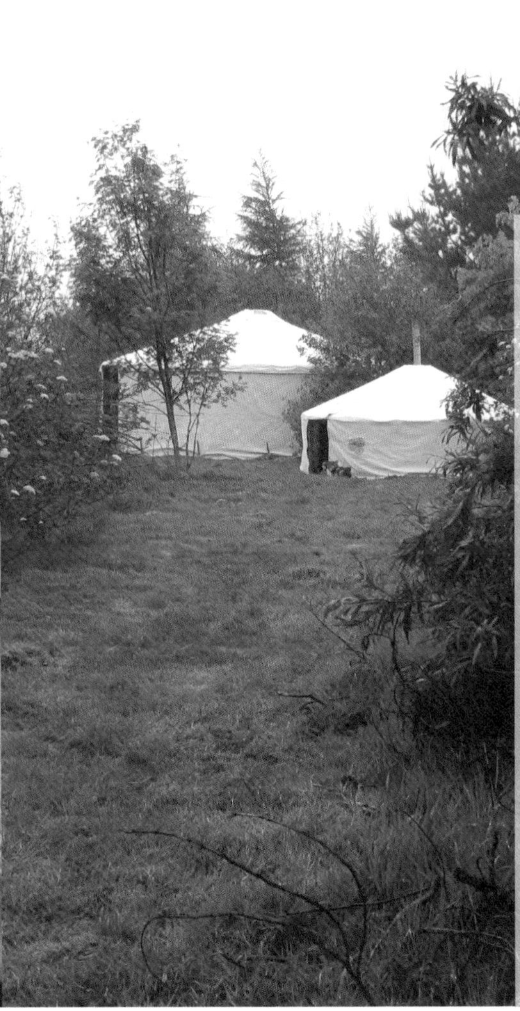

We've had a short day's walking, only about 12 miles. I felt a bit quiet and tired this morning. It was nice to wake up in Steve and Lesley's garden. They made us weybread (pilgrim's fare) for our journey. We went through some gorgeous beech woodland … stopped at a little Quaker meeting house, in a village called Come-to-Good, it was a lovely thatched simple place, we sat in silence and Melody shared about the death of her daughter Rosie and her grief. There were prayer flags written by children. One said "I like to dress up as a policeman"! Ha! We crossed the River Fal on King Harry's Ferry, pulled across on chains. I had a lovely chat with Tess. Tonight we have put up the big yurt, cos it's raining a bit and also the yurt sauna. Lovely … had a good sweat, fine singing.

ML

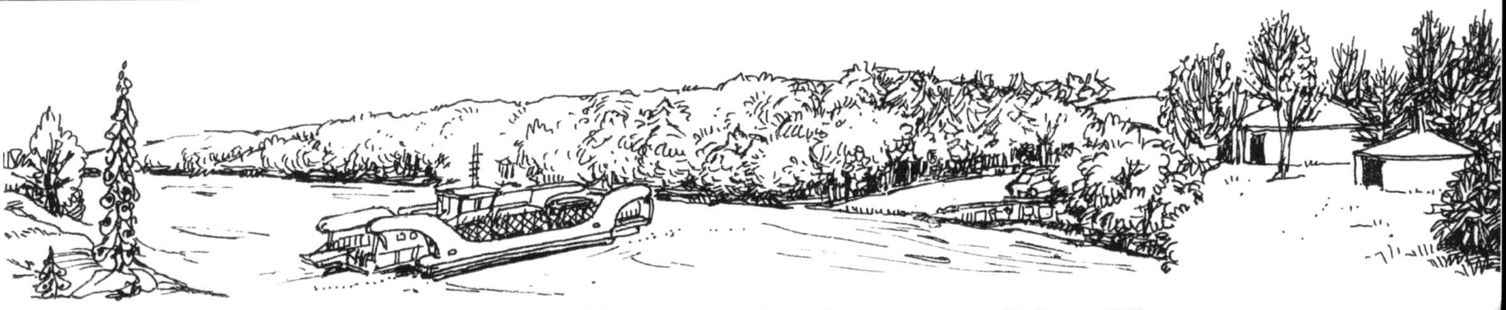

the leylines
cross – pilgrims dance
in the vortex
a pony watches –
is it Michael … or Mary?

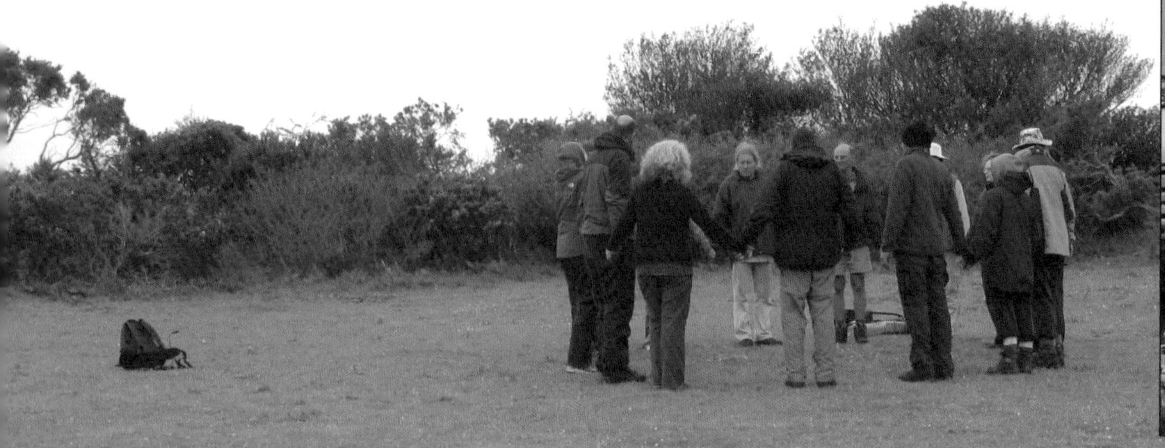

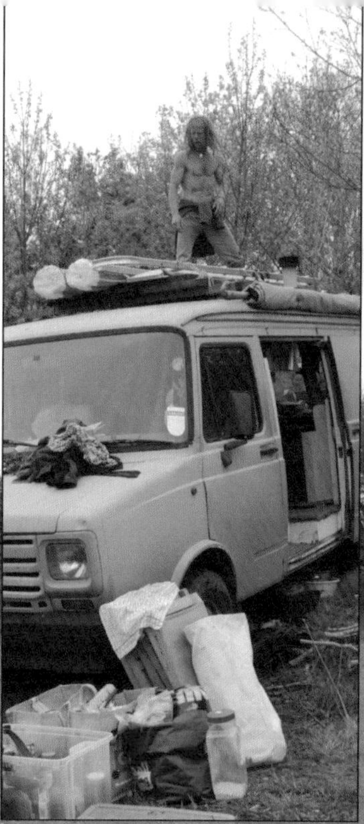

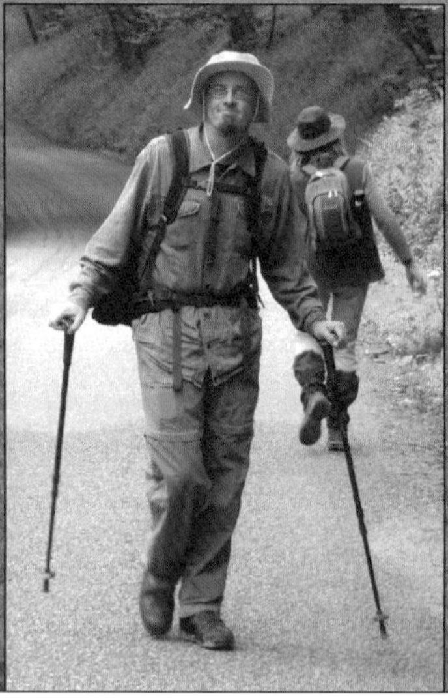

What a roller coaster day! Felt so sad this morning. Packed up in the wet and drove off in the van with Lynne and Jan. It felt good to be in a jitter wagon again! We found our way to the site. I dug a round fire pit. The ground here at Resugga is so rocky! We set up the kitchen. Then Jan and I went off hunting. We found a fab farm shop, then got horribly lost on the way back. Also the van was making a funny smell. I amazed myself with how calm I felt. Once we finally found our way home, I felt an enormous wave of happiness! Set up my tent, went wooding and sawed all the firewood. I cooked the rice and buried the compost with Gerry.

After a lovely tea we visited Resugga Iron Age hill fort, next to our field. I had a go with the dowsing rods and was stunned to sense an amazing energy. I stood, then sat, then lay in it, while it swirled my whole body, a lovely interaction with the Earth, awakening the kundalini!! I am happy. ***ML***

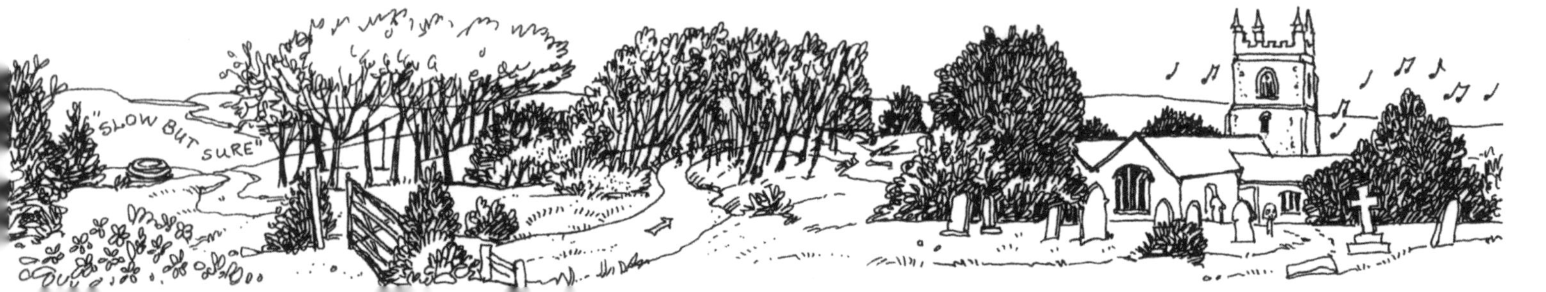

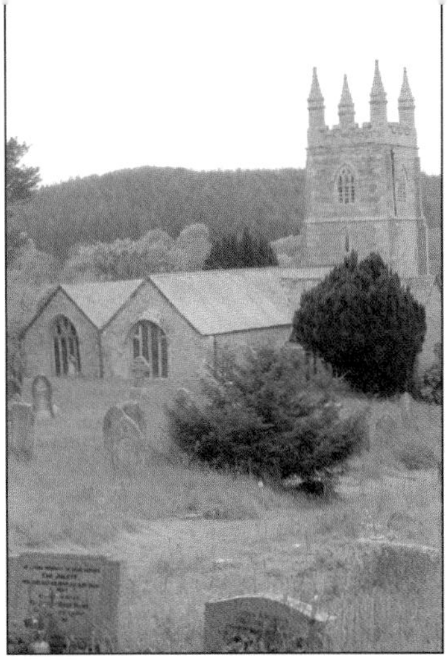

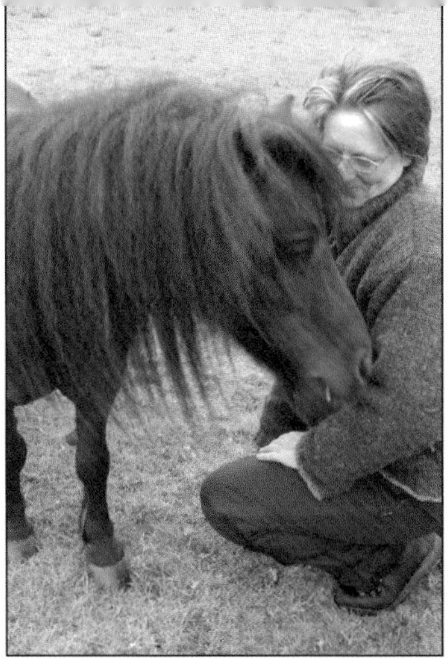

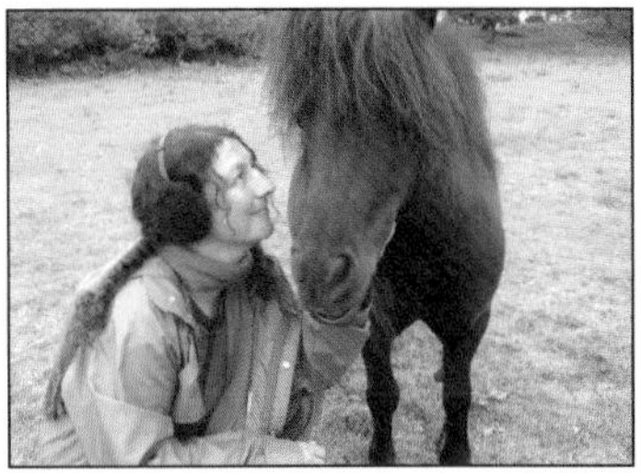

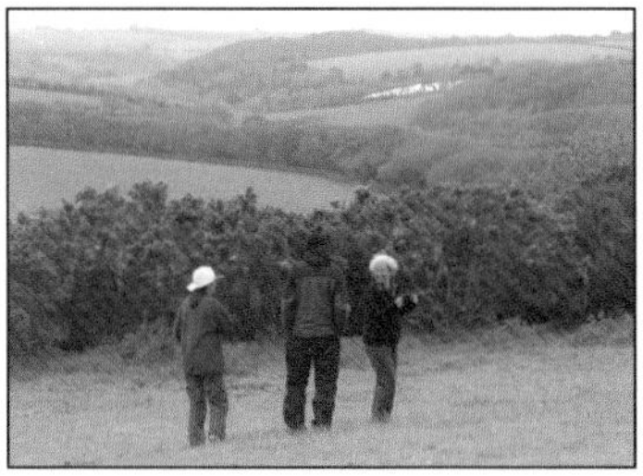

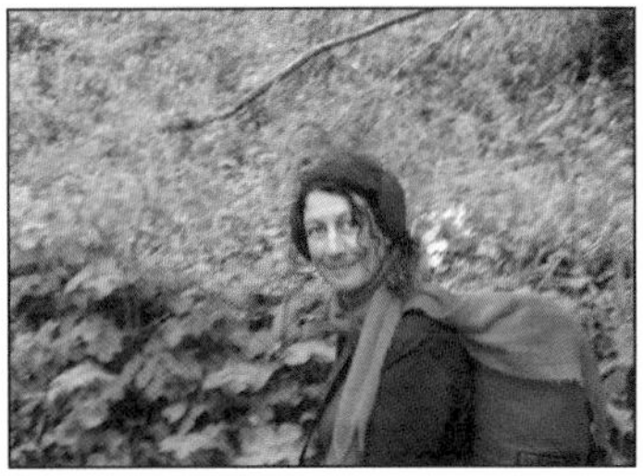

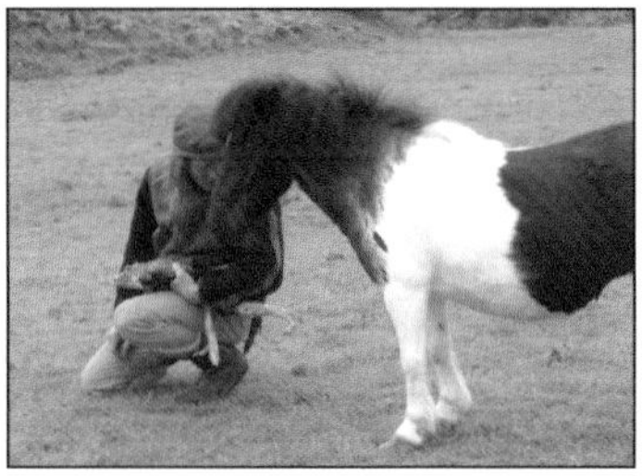

We all went into Resugga hillfort last night. Did some singing and dancing. Becoming aware of these earth energies flowing and intertwining, meeting and crossing.

RH

Today I learned that my dear friend Liana has died ...

SB

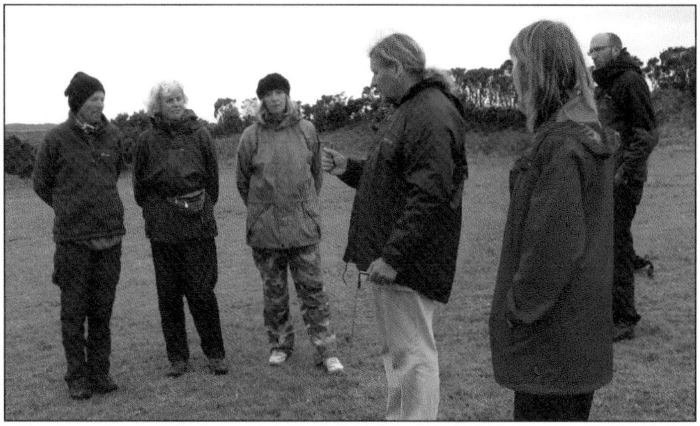

Up early, early, take down yurt and sauna. I think it was wet. Everywhere you walked, triggered off the mint, which was growing all over the site, the smell, oh, the air was just full of it, I loved it. Gentle walk for lunch at Creed Church, where beautiful singing was being recorded. After … up …up … down and up to the hillfort. Walked back with Alex.

SS

Day 5 Treworga to Coombe

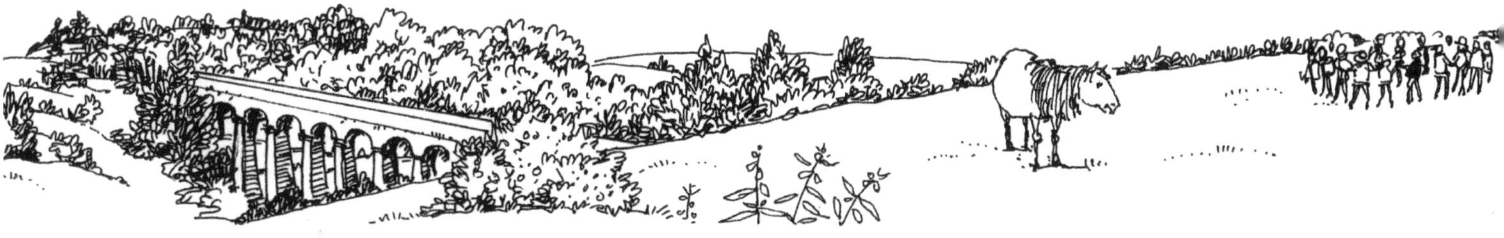

Day 6 Coombe to Luxulyan

misty ridge ...
tall chimneys dream
among slag dumps
and old workings
the wounded dragon sleeps

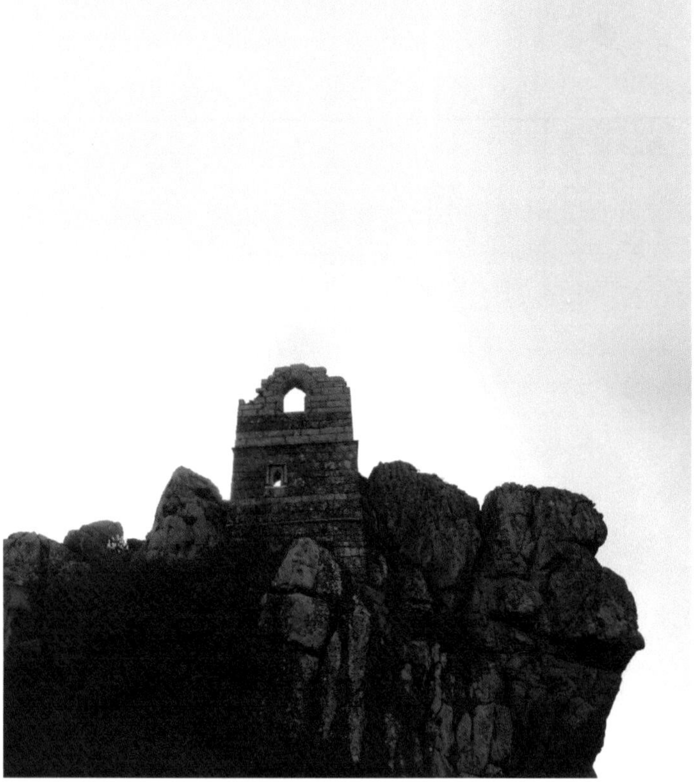

I am tired today and my ankle and heel were hurting like crazy this morning. I walked slow and alone for a few miles. Then we all met for lunch at Chapel Well and sat in the stone druids' seat, I felt a bit grumpy. Soon cheered up in the afternoon, we explored some old abandoned industrial works and saw two sweet baby goats, tethered and jumping on and off the roof of their tin hut. I have shared more about me with some of the community, opened up a bit more, got vulnerable! ***ML***

In the afternoon Janey, Celia and I continued up the hill out of St Austell, along the busy road that seemed to exist exclusively for men in vans with go-faster stripes. Up up we walked. Through the dazzling industrial landscapes of the the open cast china clay mines ... We continued on to Roche a little town of new builds, with funny transient energy as if no one settles here, they just pass through. We walked up to Roche Rock, where a 14th Century hermitage and an ancient chapel dedicated to St Michael are built on top of a 100ft rock outcrop. It was the only place of interest in that grim little town and felt rather sinister to me. The view from the top was over flat land covered in new build bungalow estates with the clay mine moonscapes beyond them. Once a refuge for the tragic lovers Tristan and Iseult, Roche Rock is now evidently a refuge for bored teenagers who take their alco-pops and cheap cider up there to have sex. The place was littered with broken glass and abandoned underwear. Janey and Celia heroically cleared away as much as they could carry. ***SB***

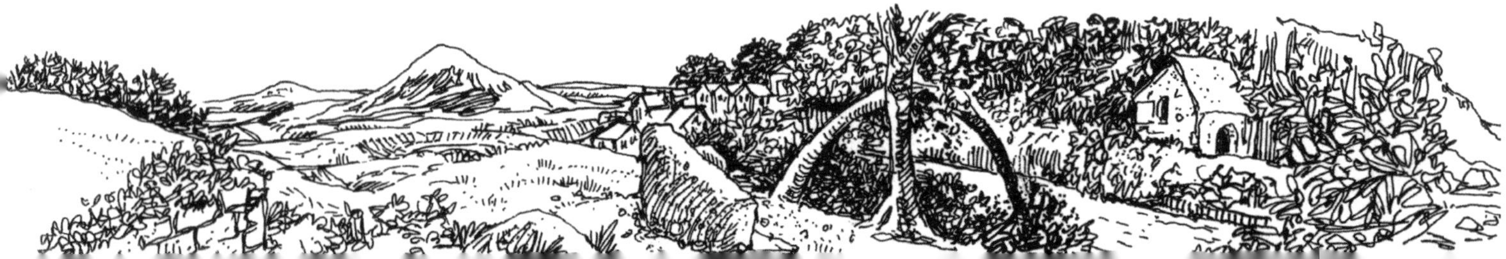

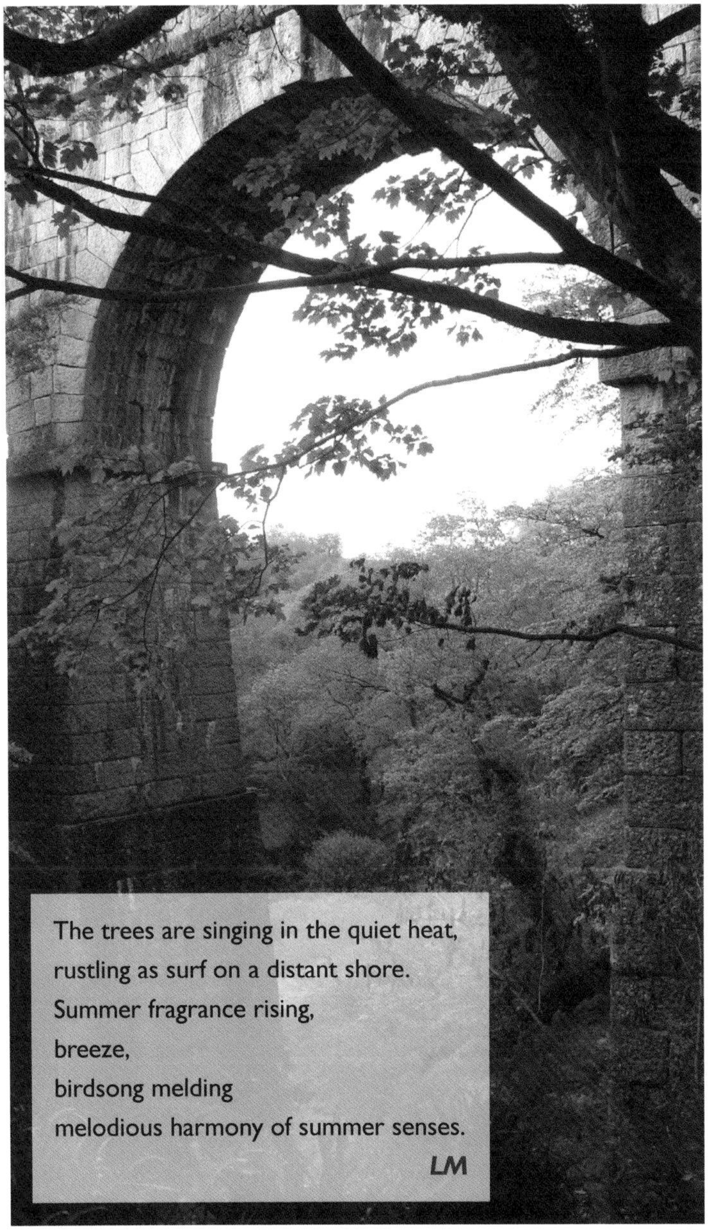

The trees are singing in the quiet heat,
rustling as surf on a distant shore.
Summer fragrance rising,
breeze,
birdsong melding
melodious harmony of summer senses.
LM

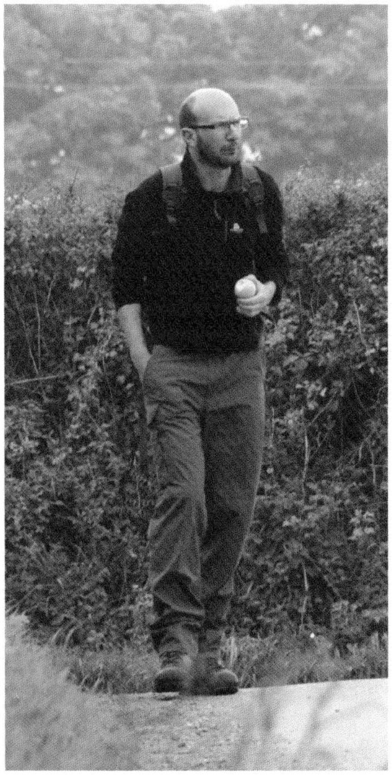

Walked to and climbed up Roche Rock (ancient hermitage) with Alex. They say that you will feel no fear climbing down the old iron ladders down from the rock. This seemed true. Long hot day, passed awesome china clay works. A rare ice-cream from a village shop. Washed feet in clear stream at end of walk. ***RH***

Site crew day: Nate and B'Anna and me in grey van, known as 'Albion'. Went to St Austell for pastie, then chips. Shopped for glue to fix Nate's boot sole. Then to campsite at farm. Fresh milk, rock cakes and tea. What a welcome from Martin and family at the farm house, so kind and welcoming. Mega-helpful, friendly family. Twixt the two lines, St Michael and St Mary. Dug fire pit and loo trench. First laundry session! First night of music making. Great! ***SS***

Am camping in the most beautiful valley I have ever seen! For two nights! Would love to be here with Paul and Poppy too. It is called the Luxulyan Valley. Gorgeous beech trees, huge boulders, sweeping bright green meadows, carpets of blue bells, fast flowing river Par, rushing over rocks, an old viaduct/aquaduct with the little canals, called leats, flowing horizontally. Am so pleased to be here two nights. Decided it is too wet to sleep out, saw a shooting star, we have been drumming, playing instruments and singing around the campfire. It feels that because it is rest day tomorrow everyone is more relaxed. None of us are brilliant musicians, but it was good to have the courage to sing, play and drum a little. As I lay in bed I can hear the drumming and the river rushing. Lovely dinner, mince and mash and cabbage, real comfort food. There is a rock here which is apparently the second biggest in Europe. ***ML***

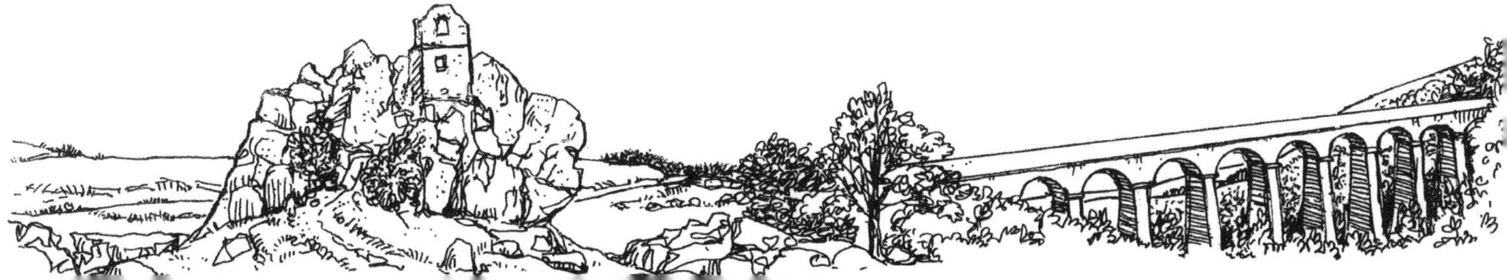

washing
my socks in stream song
cold hands
bluebells ... violets
stone bridge gathering moss

night surrounds us
fire warms us slowly
smokes us
huddling together
passing the cup round

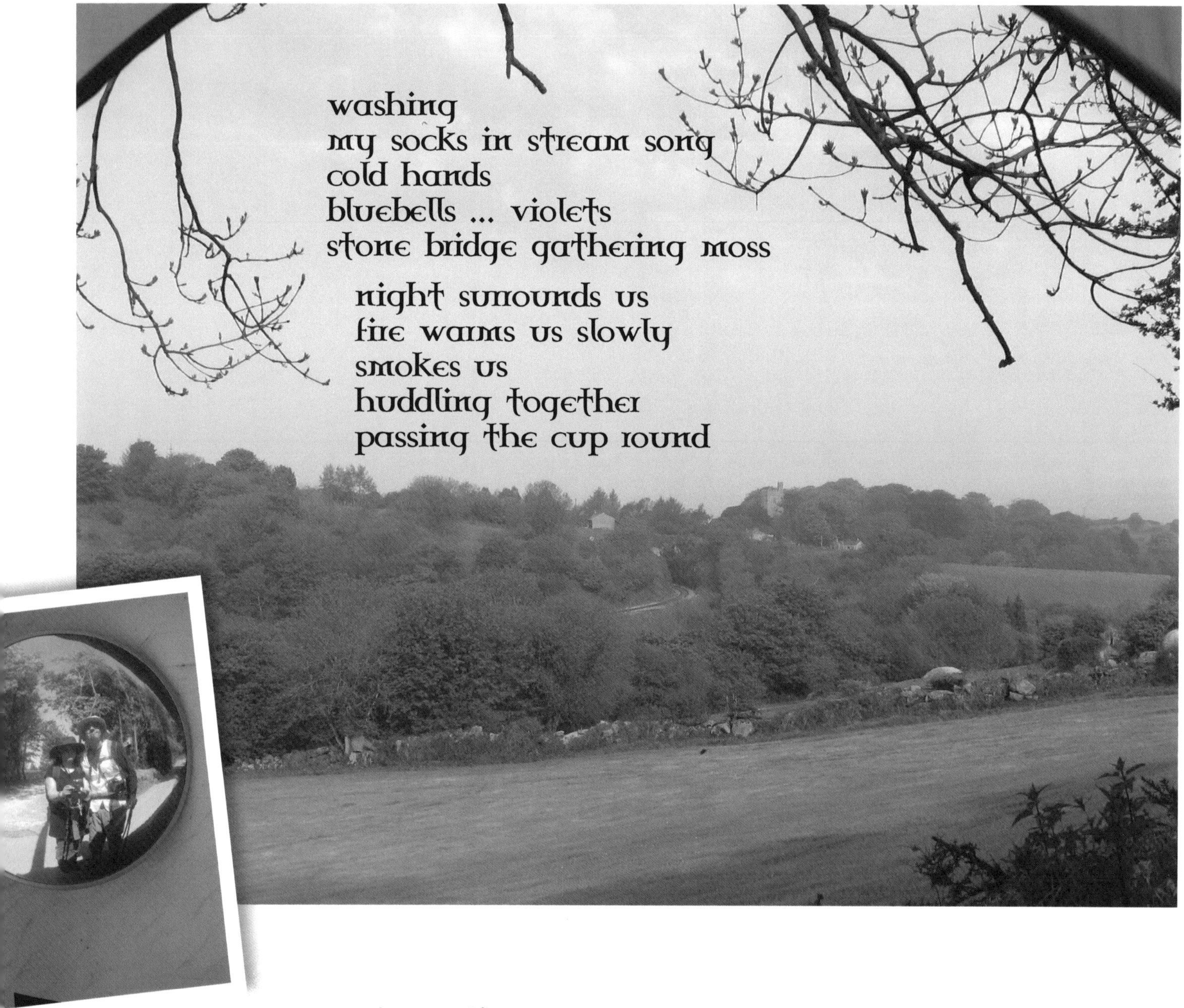

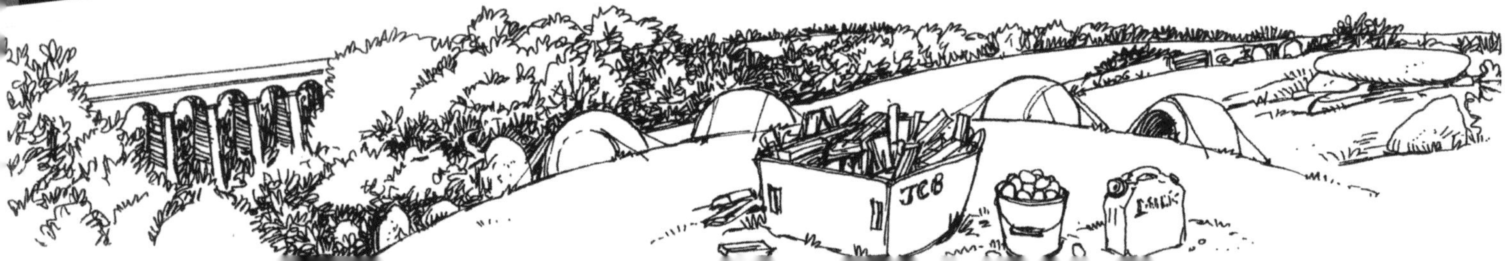

Day 7
Rest Day at Luxulyan

Rest day! Felt like heaven to wake up, open the zip on my tent to see the misty valley then drift off into dreams again. When I woke later I washed and tumbled all my clothes in the red barrel washing machine and squeezed them through the mangle. Found a linen prop, a stick from the hedge, and hung my washing in the breeze. This morning, the farmer, Martin, brought us 5 gallons of fresh milk and a bucket of eggs. I washed myself and my hair under a big rock in cold water from the trough and my skin felt blissful!

I explored Luxulyan valley alone, climbed into the cupped branches of an old beech tree and dreamed and thought. I walked barefoot in the woods and met Graham crossing the aquaduct; I saw a mouse living by the wall. We walked along the upper leat, looking for dipper birds, in peace. I was struck again how amazing it is that I am here, and feeling balanced and not overly self obsessed! Looked at the old water wheel which used to power trams I think, and crush rocks.

I sat in the middle of the River Par on a rock and read *The Sun and the Serpent*. Some little boys were leaping and shouting, I leapt around and paddled too. After a fab tea of home made burgers, Steve and I visited the second largest boulder in Europe, just up the hill from our site! Huge, powerful, granite boulder, balanced on the earth, hovering almost. We sat underneath it, cave like. In the cavern underneath was a huge penis-shaped rock!!

ML

Beautiful camp in lush sloping field. Generous, kindly farmer. Milk, logs and lots of goodwill.

RH

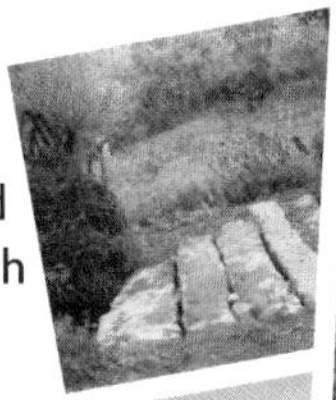

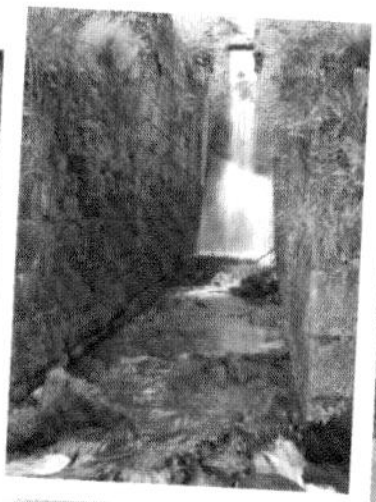

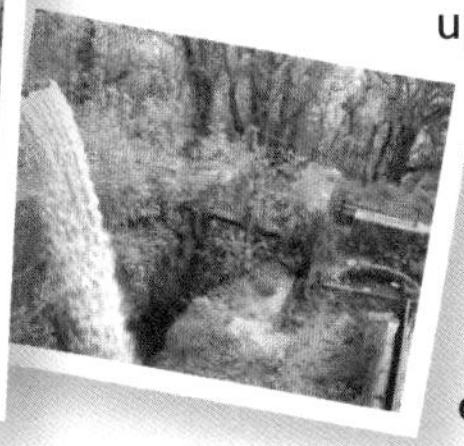

I feel content, grubby, connected, alone, confident, anxious, joyful ... I need to let go of some ego stuff ... and just let it be and let me be whoever I might be ... the journey is about belonging and this is the most important thing ... acceptance in the circle ... I'm enjoying my fitness and the tuning in to countryside ...

Down the valley found a sacred grove of beech trees and bluebells and caught up with writing ... nearby was a rubbished campsite and I restored it as best I could and then back to our camp. The valley is an old mining area with leats, now proclaimed a heritage site, and there is a sense that the woodland can be restored and is looked after... but there are notices about vandalism at the church and near the historic leats ...

GJ

I joined the walking snake for just seven days with the intention of singing the land as I went. It was the best week of the year and one with many gifts. It began with ... Turtle Dreaming ...! We walked up the hill to the largest boulder in Europe. There in the beginning of the trees was the rock, a leviathan of a rock, or a turtle sleeping, having finally come to rest. The trees lay their branches on her back as she tells of a time long ago, when today's stars were being born and planet earth was awash with mighty oceans. She knew the currents and tides of primeval forces and dark skies filled with bright explosions of light and fire. And she was brought here to rest and lay her eggs, scattered now in the fields around. Ancient, ancient memories. As I sit on the shiny quartz I drop into her, and sing in recognition of her antiquity. The beginnings of time. The beginning of my walk with Albion. Around me, lichen covered rocks, small plants, discarded acorn and hazelnut shells, I feel I have come home to a nomadic way of life and I think of my love and leaving and wish he could be here to experience the peace I feel. I remember all the things we've done and how I've loved him.

DF

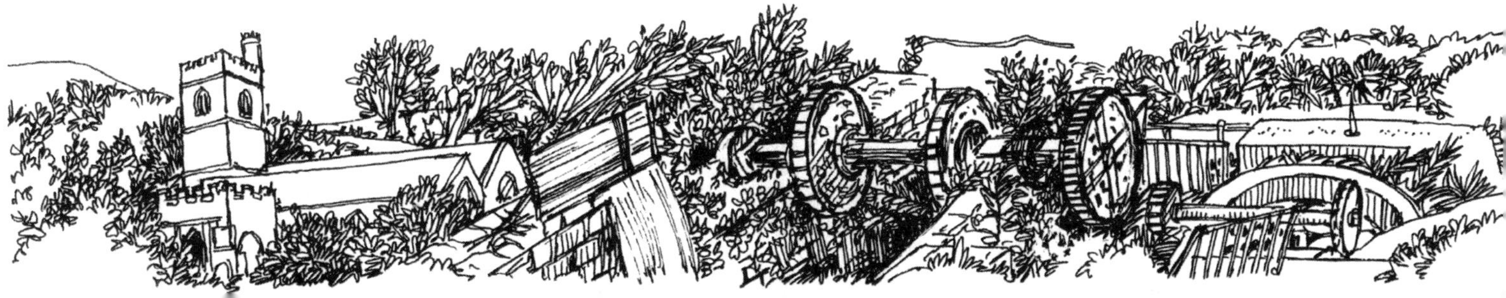

Day 8
Luxulyan to Trenant

My first day was a gruelling sixteen miles in full sun, with the hitherto 'leader' having a day off and doing site crew instead! There was in fact no leader each day but a very nifty system of arrows being left by those at the front and picked up by those at the back.

So I felt a little unnerved and hurried for most of the day but I still loved it, despite my feet complaining and gaining blisters from very old walking boots. So at about mile twelve I decided not to risk the rest of the week and called the support crew to ask for a pick up. Joined by an old friend on the walk we dozed in a field, and I felt relieved to find it was fine to take a rest, fine not to be in competition with oneself or the rest of the group. We were driven into camp with feet saved, a victory for common sense.

What a camp! I'd been there the previous summer and it's a beautiful place, a small stream as a trickling boundary and that night a bright half moon in the sky. While the others prepared for a sweat in the amazingly quickly erected sweatlodge/sauna I sat by the fire and another song roared out of me. It was joyous and in praise of all that was in that moment. Later I had the privilege of listening to the others singing as they cleansed and again I was at peace. ***DF***

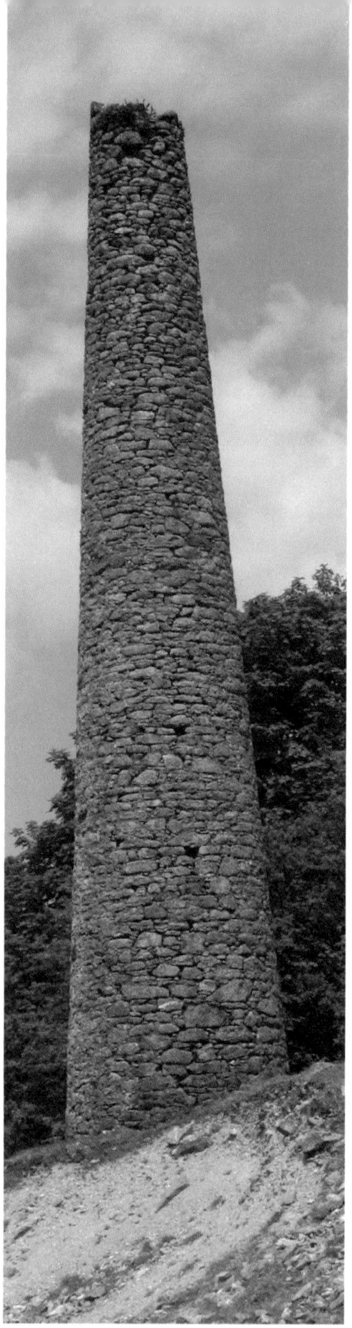

Today I was crewing with Jan. We drove the van up to some burial mounds where we met the walkers for lunch. It was a really hot day and we couldn't find shade, so put umbrellas over the food to try and keep it cool until the others arrived. The walk was a 16-miler so everyone was really glad to see us. Feeding the pilgrims involves throwing down a groundsheet by the side of the road then piling up the bread, cheese, salad, chutney, crisps etc. Ravenous walkers pile in, first come first serve, licking the knife clean for the next person. It's a health hazard of a meal! We've just had another sweat in the yurt pitched this evening right next to a little river where we could dunk ourselves in cold water. I offered prayers for Liana who I feel is floating around in a very good mood, curious and amused. I see her laughing. Camping tonight in a little site on the edge of Bodmin. Tonight is also the first night I've got into my sleeping bag and not felt cold! Probably due to the sweat and the dip in the river. I hear big dogs barking in the distance. The Yeth Hounds on Bodmin perhaps. ***SB***

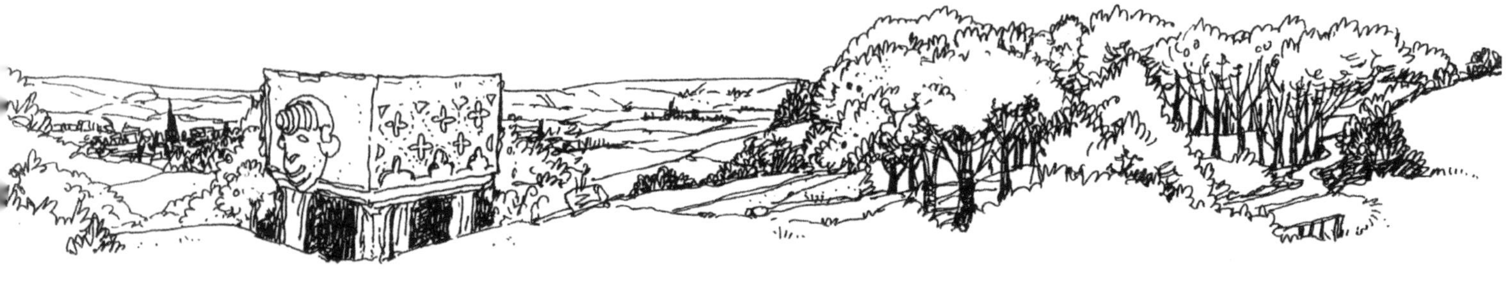

approaching
the kissing gate
I manoeuvre
to be between X and
Y who I really like

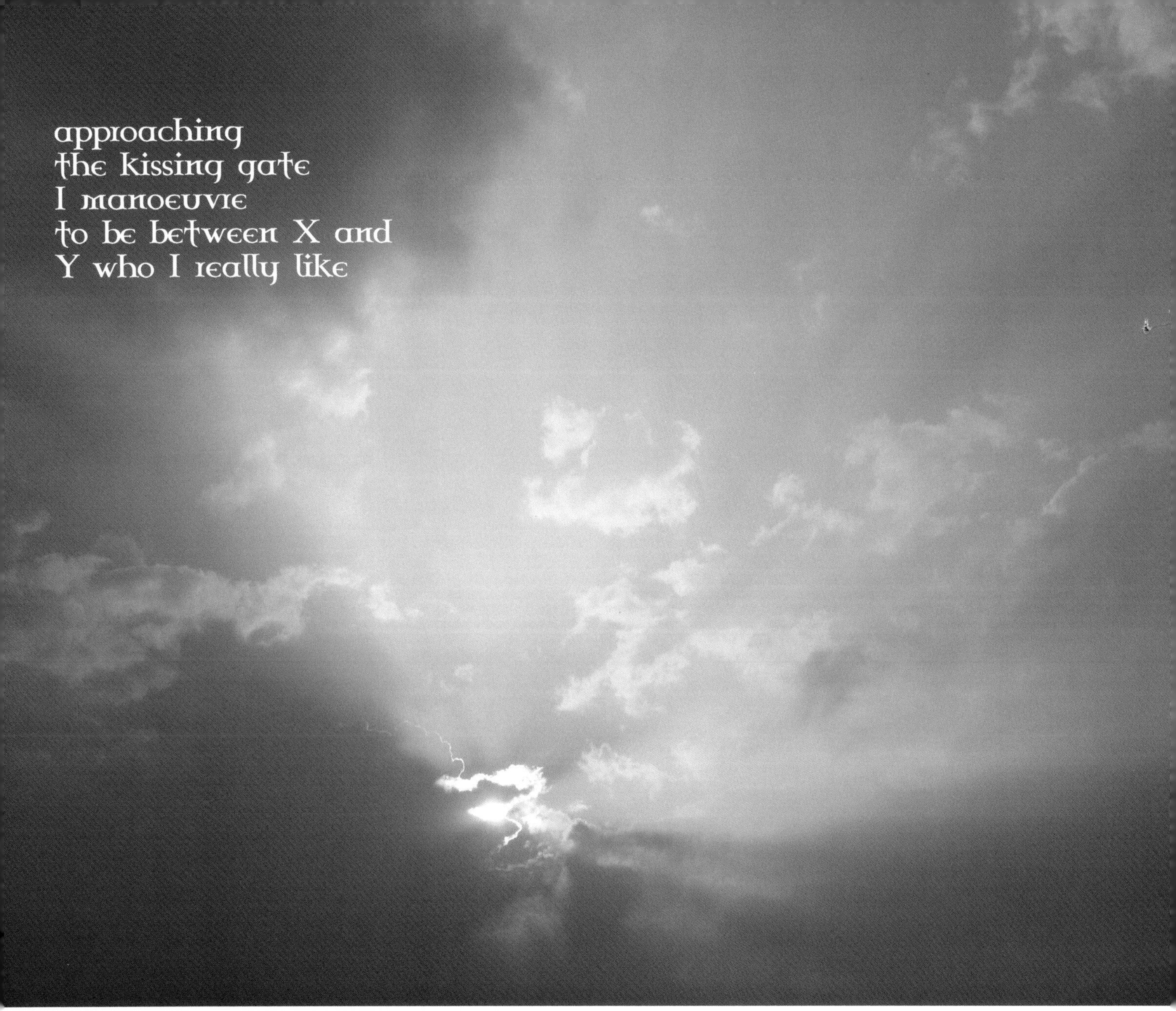

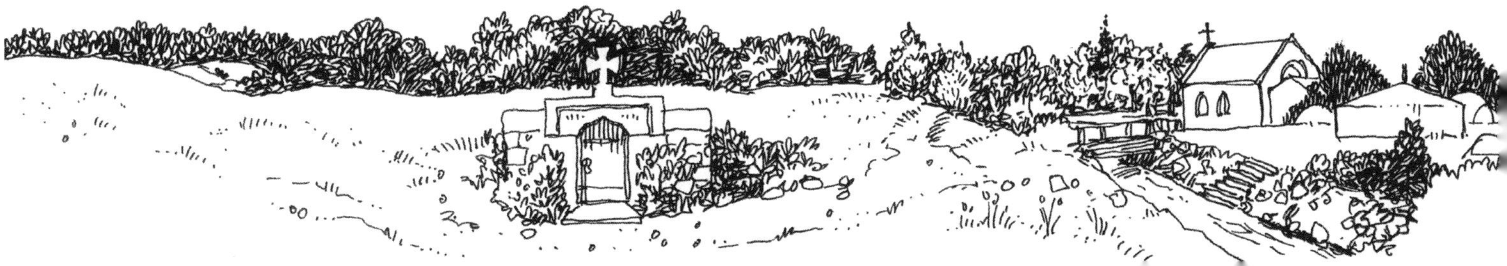

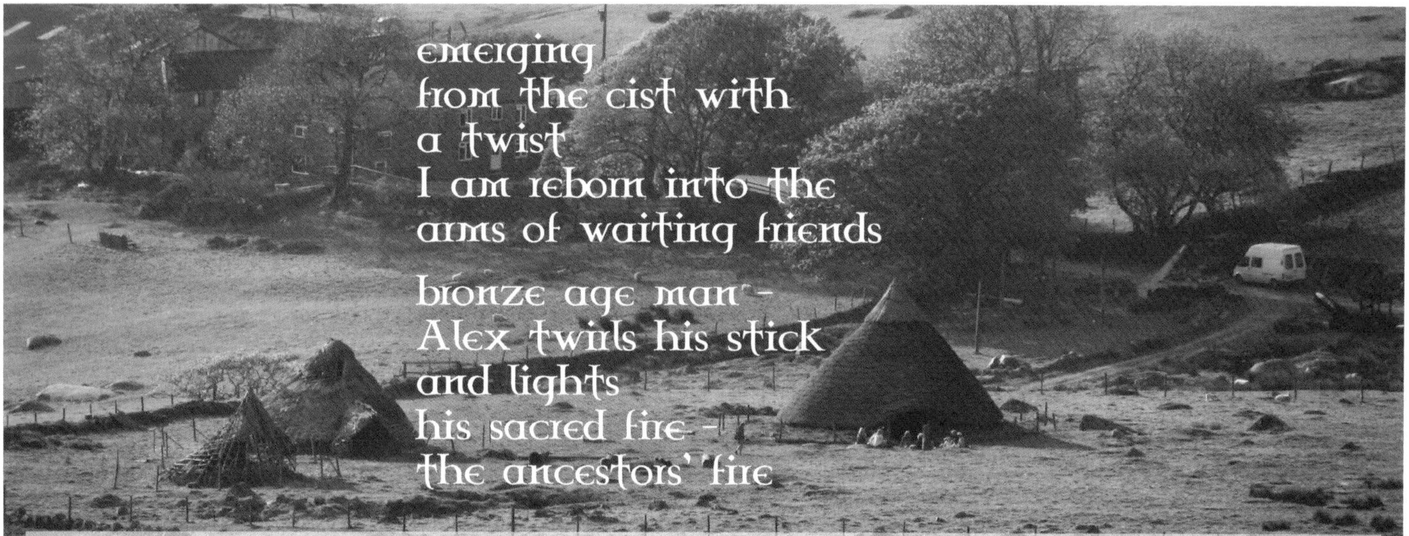

emerging
from the cist with
a twist
I am reborn into the
arms of waiting friends

bronze age man –
Alex twirls his stick
and lights
his sacred fire –
the ancestors' fire

The next day was a more leisurely amble via Golitha Falls to St Cleer, where we were so generously nurtured with cups of tea and cakes in the local community centre. The Mary Line was very evident here, everything was flourishing, people were prospering and doing good things. It was a very positive, cared for place. After that we went from Trethevy Quoit, up through the old mine workings to the Hurlers and the Cheesewring and Twelve Mens Moor. The weather was beautiful and as we crested the brow of the carn, down below was one of the most beautiful sights ever. Nestled in the valley in the sunny twilight haze were three Bronze Age round houses. The sight took one back to their time. No roads, cars, artificial lights – just the land stretching for miles and small dwellings, here and there, unobtrusive, part of the land itself. To complete the perfection a deer down below moved its way across the boulders blissfully unaware of our presence as we made our way down the tracks. I was greeted by a newcomer to the group who came out of the huts looking as if she belonged there herself, a girl from way back then. We slept to the sound of sheep, lambs, cows and summer breezes and again I was at peace.

DF

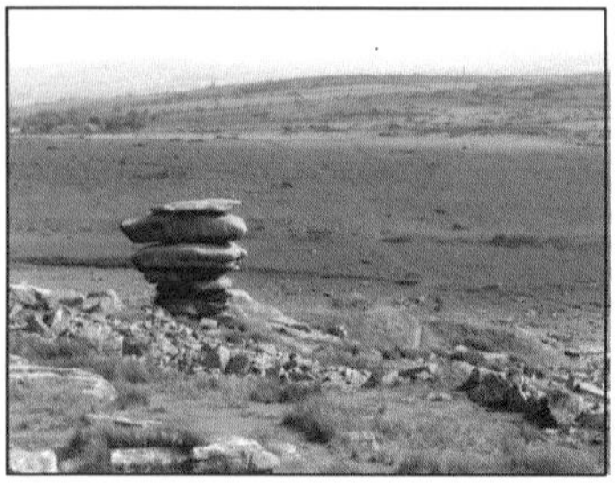

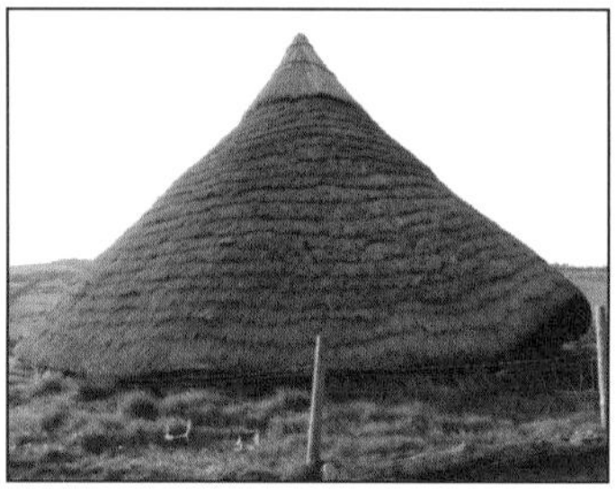

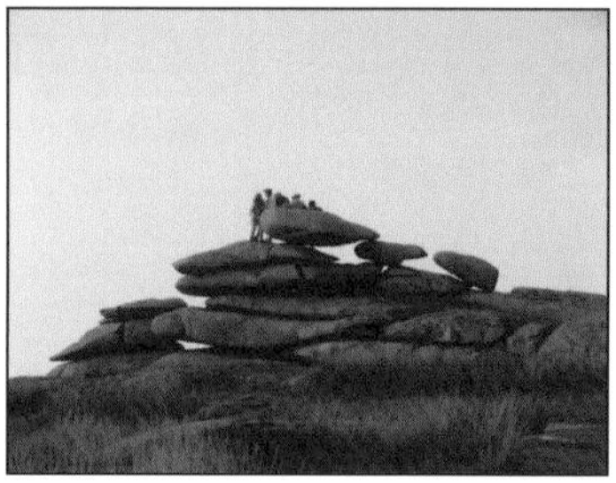

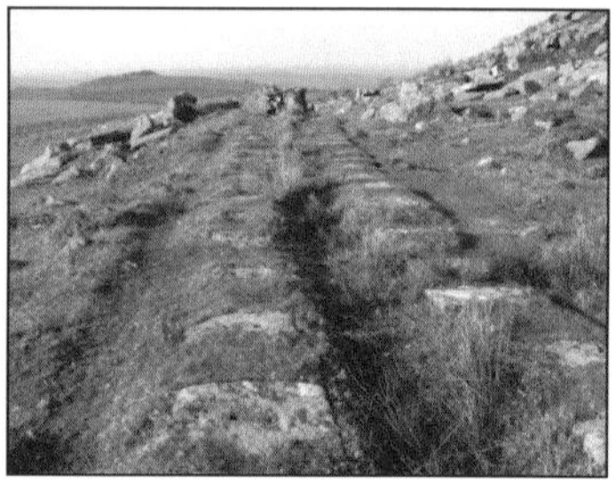

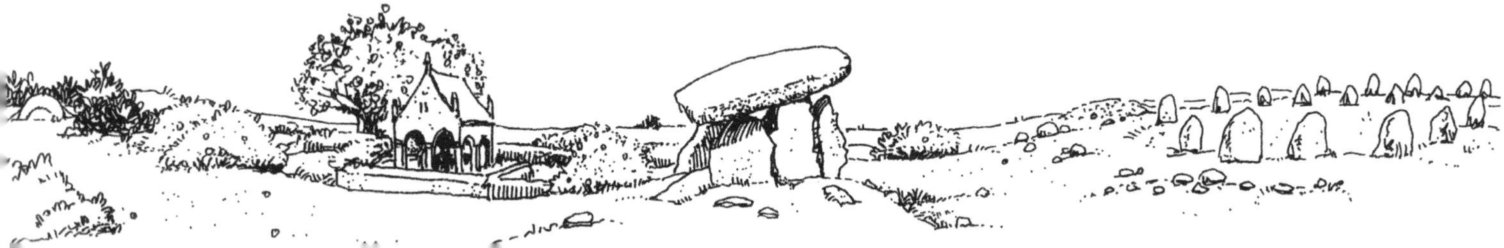

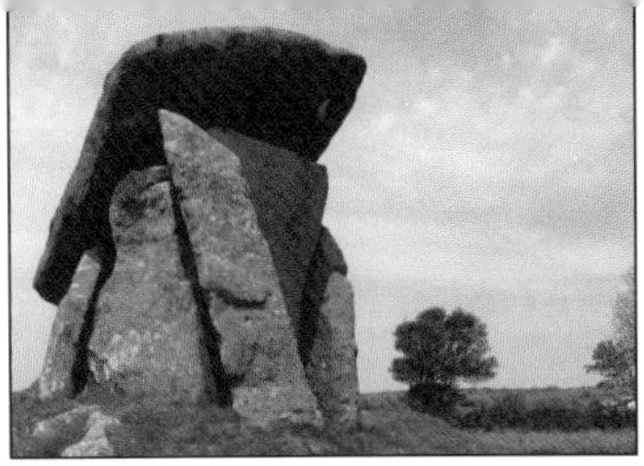
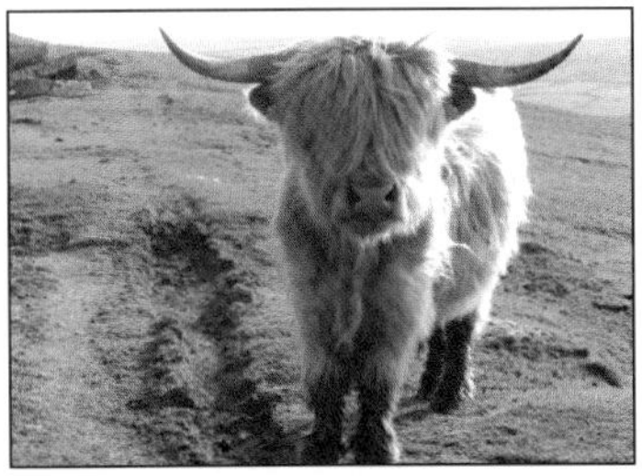
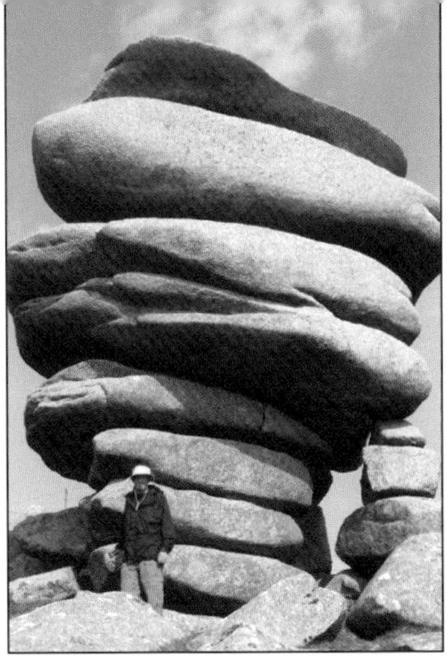
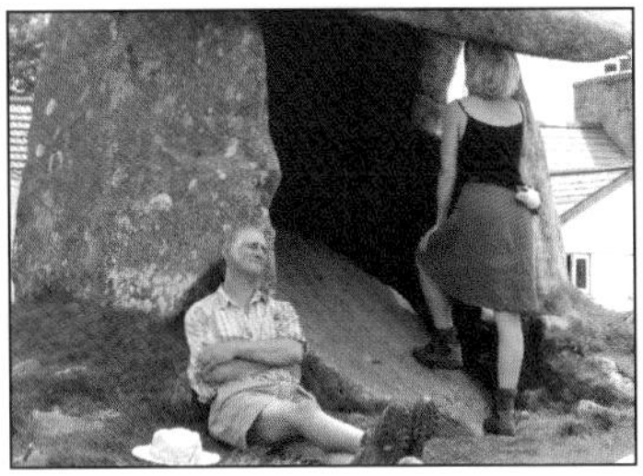
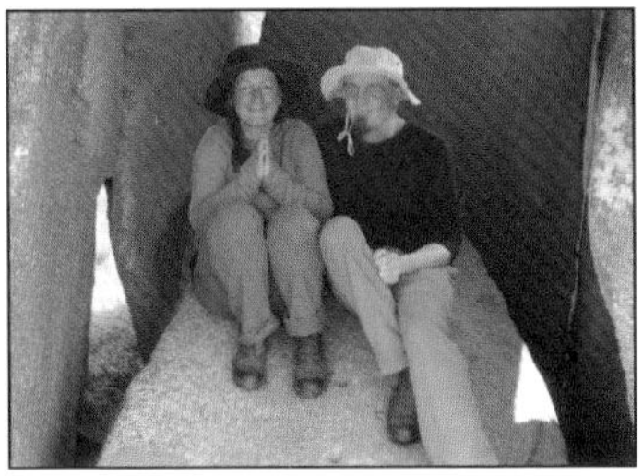

Left camp 9.25am. 10 miles. Gentle walking along lanes, footpaths, bridleways, fields and roads. Great sensations, pastie in churchyard, Norman doorway with arched chevrons. The church rooms were offering free tea, coffee, and cake, even gluten free cake, we made donations, amazing!

Holy well, made of stone. Cure for Madness and Blindness, couldn't get to try it out!

Crow's Nest pub, had some beer, plenty of names of people who were hanged here or nearby. Sore right heel. Heard my first cuckoo of the year, heard it all day, I think it followed me. Lunch at edge of Bodmin Moor. Burial mounds and stone circles, three in a row. Cist, giant stones on each other, corkscrewed into earth, golden cup found here, used by one of England's kings as a shaving mug! We all went in, Mel, B'Anna and me and I think Graham as well, then the others went in. Ravens flew over, one shed a feather and Mel tracked it down, amazing. Loads more of Moor!!! Bronze Age replica roundhouses, in the distance, looking down on them from high up, incredible view. Sat there for a while, it was absolutely brilliant. Alex made fire with his bow and spindle like in ancient times, beautiful, in the roundhouse where we had dinner, followed by stories then bed, 10.55pm. ***SS***

Walked on my own a lot today. Up on to Bodmin Moor. Explored the rocks around the Cheesewring. Lay on a large, sloping platform of rock that looked like a launching pad to fly into the valley below. Hot sun and strong wind and long views of our path. Finally over to the Bronze Age roundhouse. Wonderful place. Alex lit the 'wyld fire' in a flash! We soon had a blaze. We sang, ate food, listened to some tales around the fire. Everyone tired. Slept like a log. ***RH***

Day 9
Trenant to North Hill

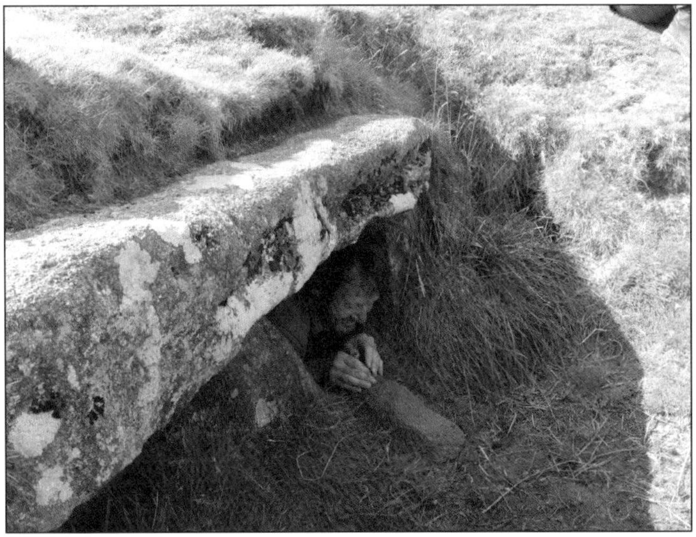

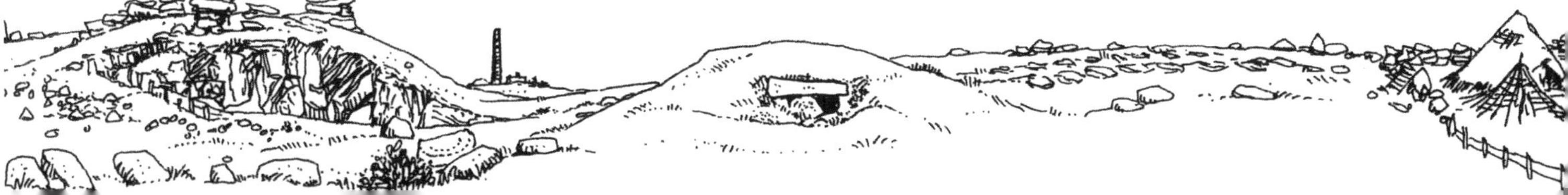

Day 10

North Hill to Trekenner

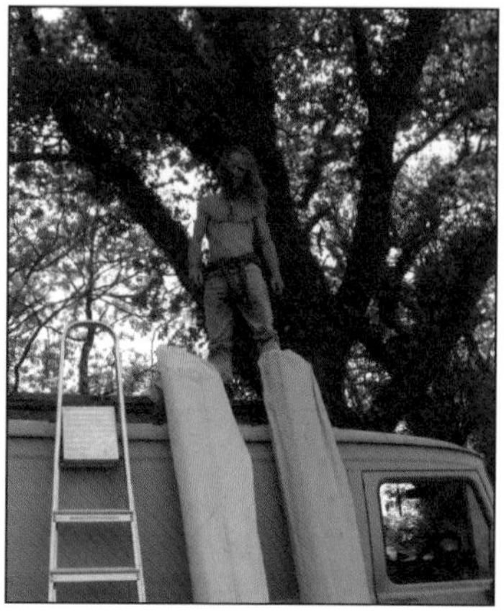

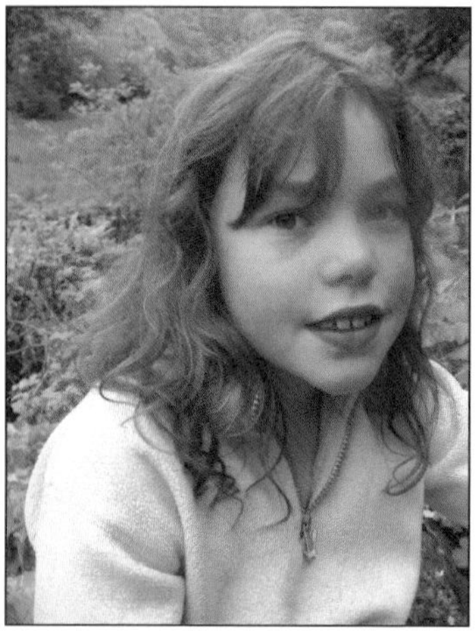

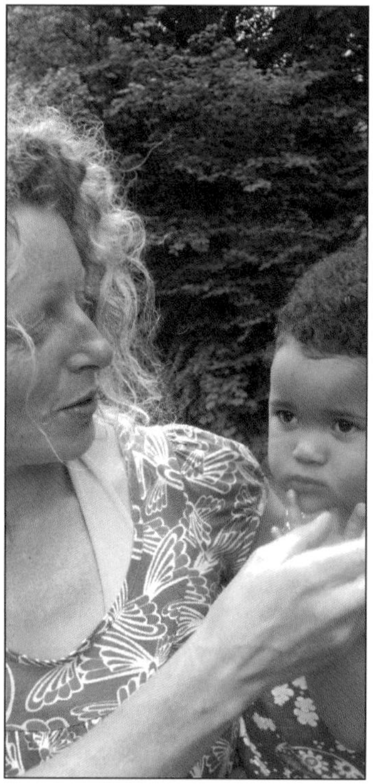

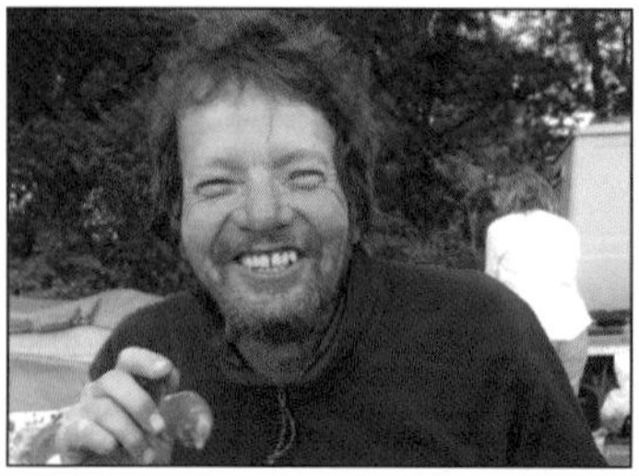

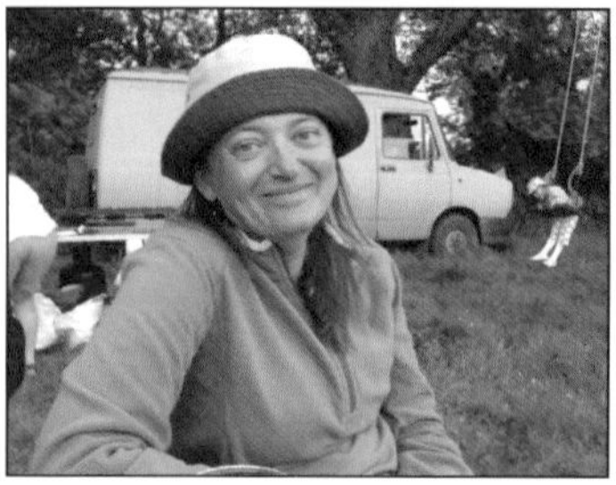

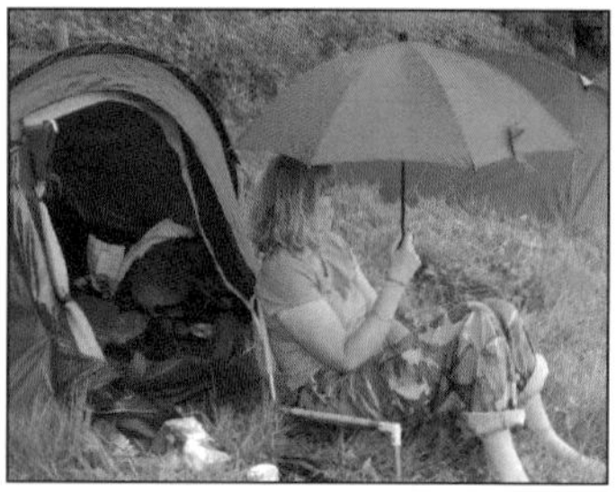

Cuckoo alarm call. Gentle walk off Moor. Little rain, waterproofs drill. Set free trapped/caged Magpie with Leighsa. Walked straight through to campsite. Wow! The walk was full of sensations. Then had lunch. Fell asleep after lunch as soon as I had put up my tent, which by the way is pretty good. Pouring with rain right now 11.45pm, in bed. Sleeping bag great sitting up, writing, headlamp on head and hood of sleeping bag over my head as well. Just got in, very heavy rain for the last two hours, might be in all night.

Been drumming with half a dozen locals, including the owners of the field, with djembés, what a night, I was in heaven, the yurt was full, people dancing, whooping it up, real party atmosphere, absolutely brilliant. ***SS***

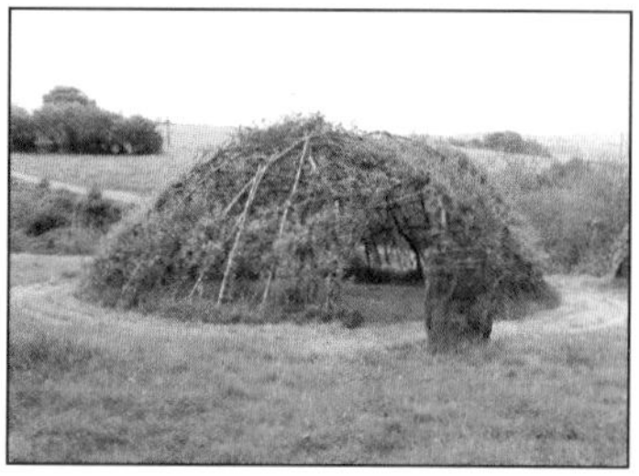

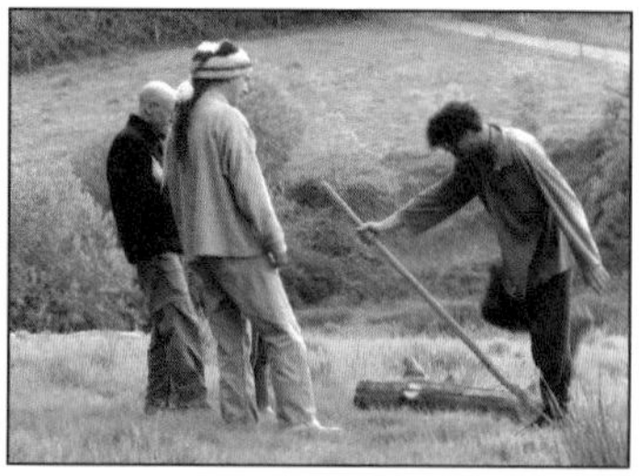

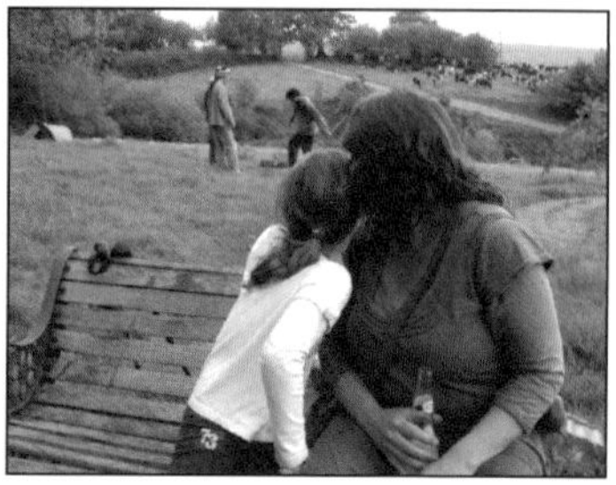

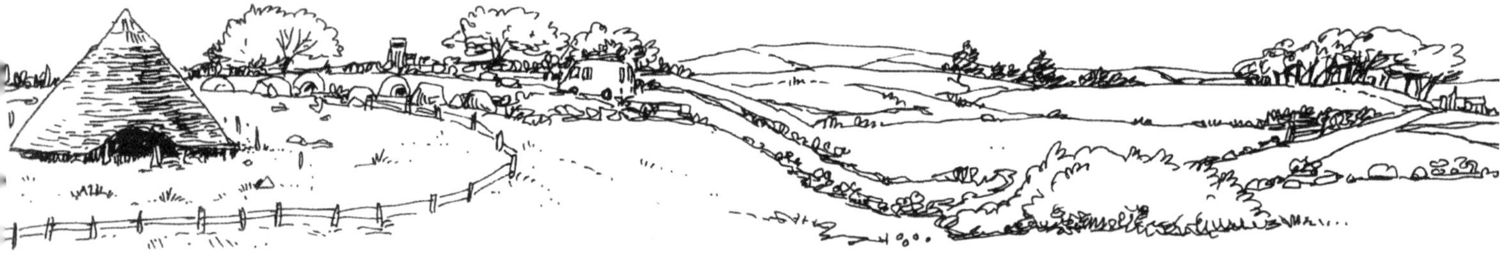

Thunder, lightning and lots of rain and fire.
Drums and dancing in the yurt.
Rain and drums blend as I go to sleep. ***RH***

Looking back I could see the landmarks, the china clay hills of St Austell, near where we had camped on the first night and it seemed a long way and yet we had walked it. It was possible and I realised my sense of distance was starting to change. The way I looked at the landscape was beginning to bring a feeling that it is possible to walk long distances and actually it's not as far as the eye might have one believe. It might take two days but it's possible. And with that came hope, hope for a future when we may not be able to use our present modes of transport and we will need to use foot and hoof again and that it will be possible, even preferable! ***DF***

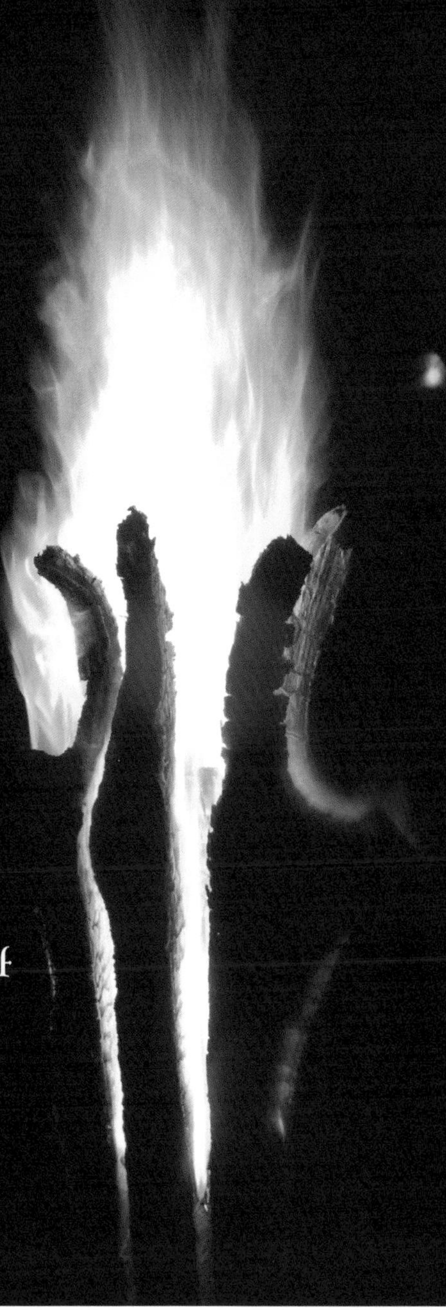

grey evening
yurt drumming
fire sculpture ...
all night rain
drumming on the tent roof

grey morning
after the rain
leaves drip ...
the land is green
the tea is brewing

I am in bed, it's raining really hard and the tent is leaking a bit. Hopefully it will hold out most of the rain. We are at Trekenner, at a farm. We have been partying tonight. I did some fun, wild dancing with lovely Jenny, who arrived today with Simon, from Bristol. Friends of the people who own this land came to drum and play. It was wild.

Short walk today, about 10 miles and quite easy terrain. One field of frisky bullocks tried to herd us, by running round us in circles, we shooed them away by running at them. We saw a magpie caught in a trap and Steve and Leighsa let him free. I think I forgot to write that one day last week we stopped at a village pump and when I pushed the handle a little blue tit flew out. I put a sign on the pump to warn other people he was nesting in there. Today I felt grumpy. Some people picked up a dead rabbit, slung it over their shoulders on a stick and brought it home to eat. I don't like this. When I'd put up my tent, I played the guitar and sang till I felt better. Spotted some beautiful butterflies today, little blue, an orange leopard print one, a small white with grey markings. ***ML***

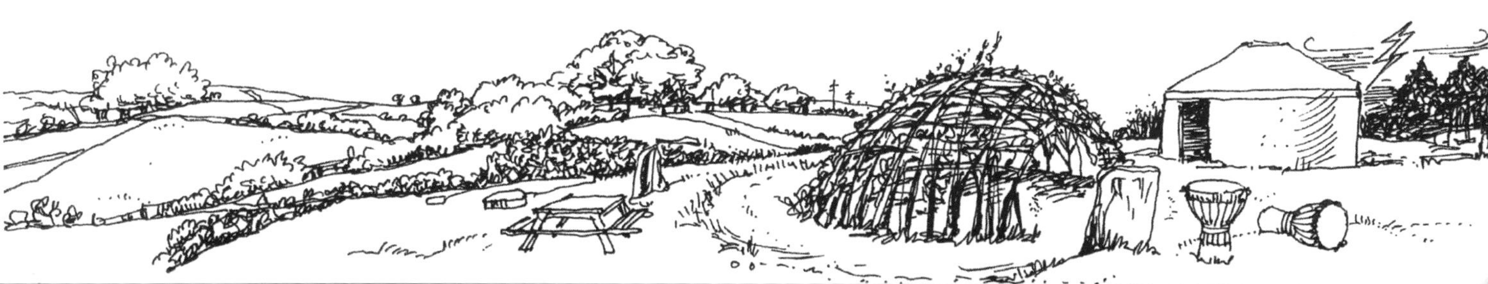

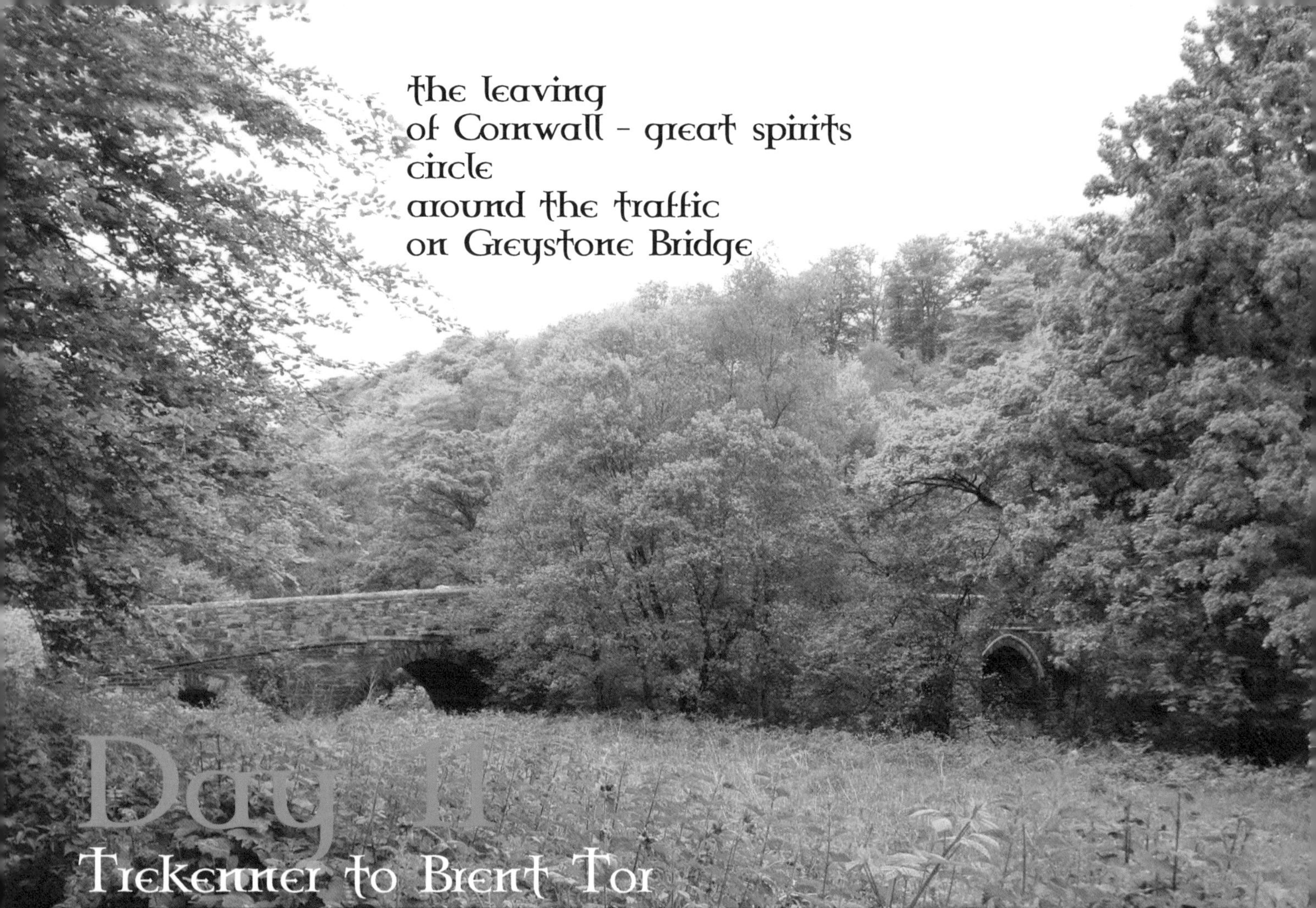

the leaving
of Cornwall - great spirits
circle
around the traffic
on Greystone Bridge

Day 11

Trekenner to Brent Tor

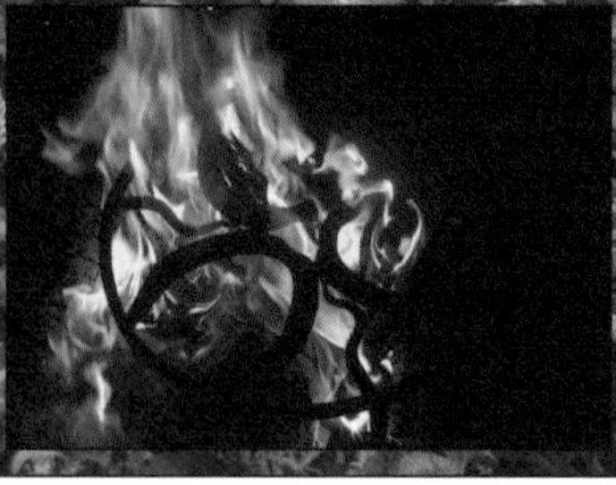

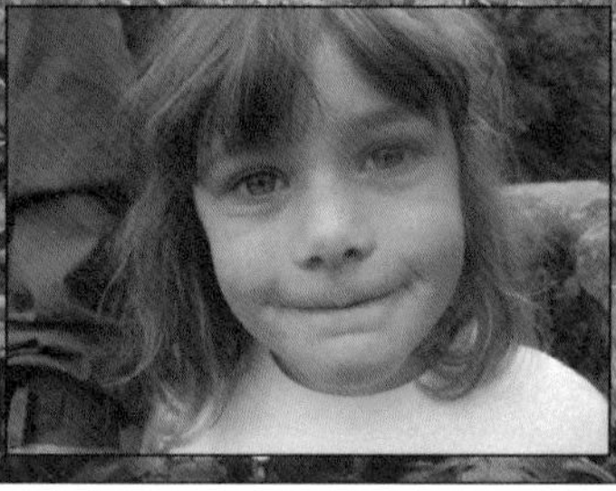

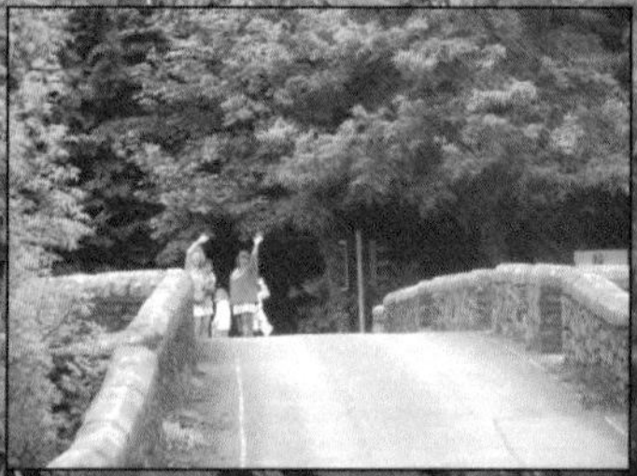

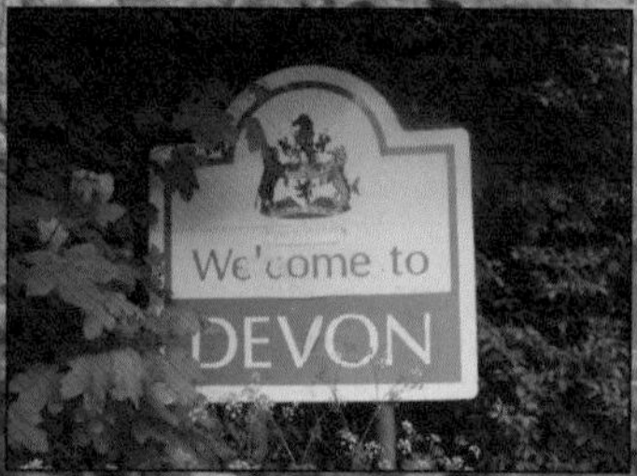

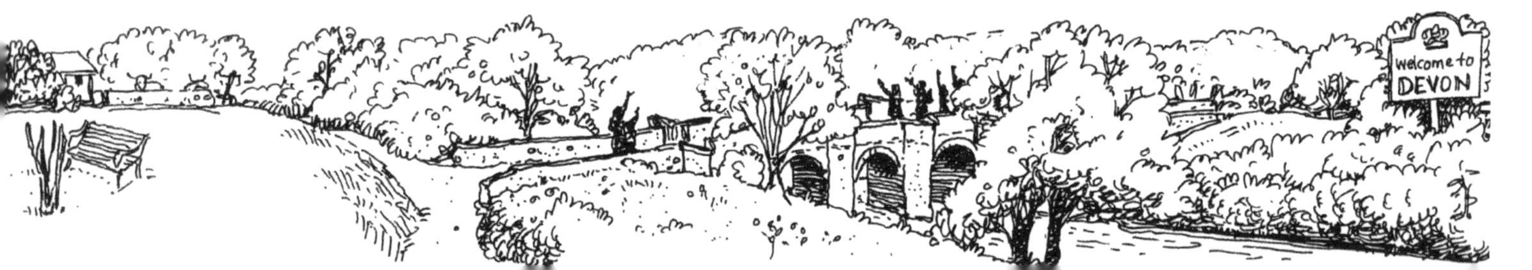

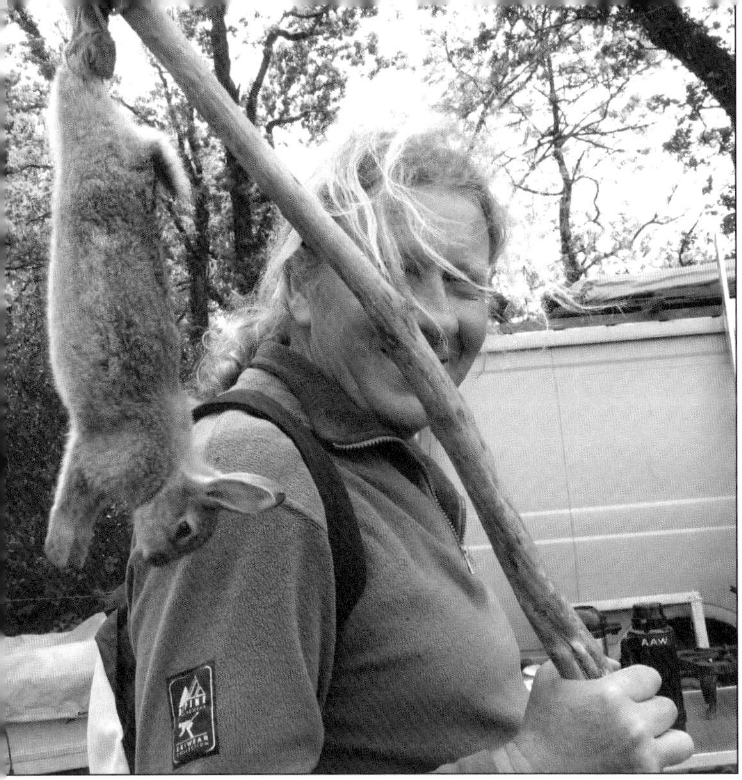

It's in the churches and chapels that I feel the energy is concentrated ... when I'm alone in these places I feel the deep resonance of centuries of devotion ... in the stone circles I feel the energy as more diffuse, perhaps softened by the sun and the rain and the distance back in time since they were used for ritual and worship. ***GJ***

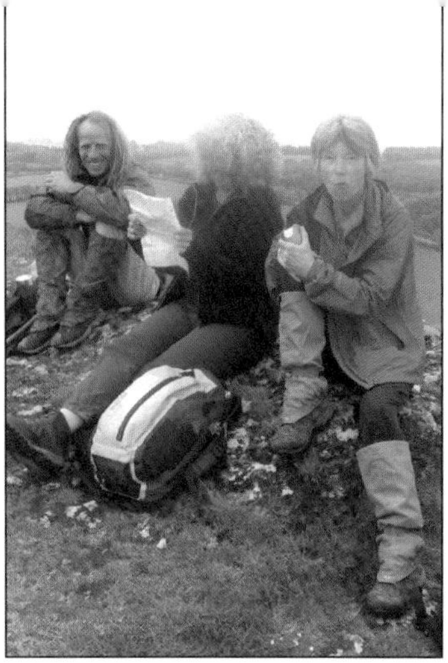

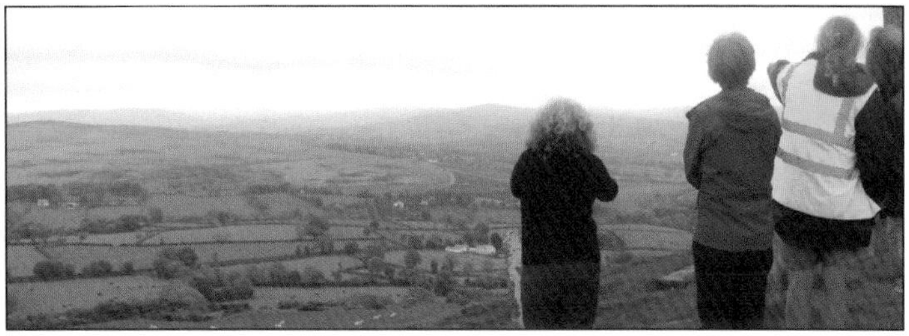

Brent Tor: We shared our next field with an ex-pub and an inquisitive young horse and that night I dreamed of a karmic lift shaft coming straight out of the Tor going up to a place where you could access the Akashic Records and see where and when you'd met other people before in past lives. An interesting place! ***DF***

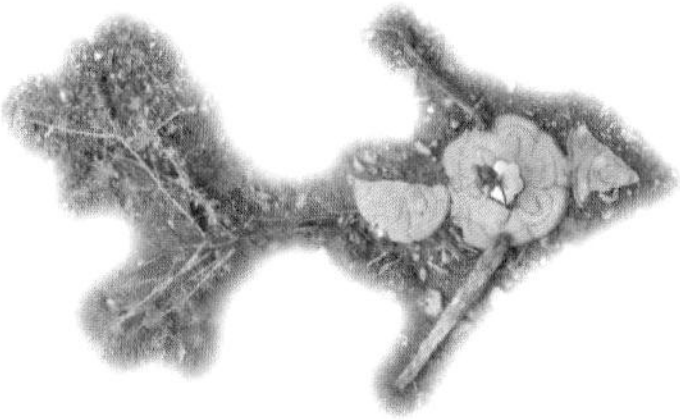

Brent Tor

Mist shrouded mount of Christendom

Overlay your pagan forbears

Bestride the land

From shore to shore

Michael, Mary and St George

LM

The walk was a good one today, with our hosts from last night walking with us to the bridge that divides Devon from Cornwall. It was very moving saying goodbye as they waved us over the border. It felt mythical and mysterious as if we were living in parallel worlds; one here in 2008 and one on another plane, outside of time, in the place of myth and legend. It was quite a remarkable feeling noted by several of the pilgrims.

On the other side of the river the feeling was quite different. We walked up and up and up the very steep Felldownhead Hill, leaving behind the land of plenty. Our first encounter with the locals was when we stopped for a water break at the top of Felldownhead, next to the cyder brewery. A women with dramatic red hair and heavily penciled brows sneered down at us from an open window. We have left the country of Cornwall and are now in England. The change in ambience is reflected in the change of weather. ***SB***

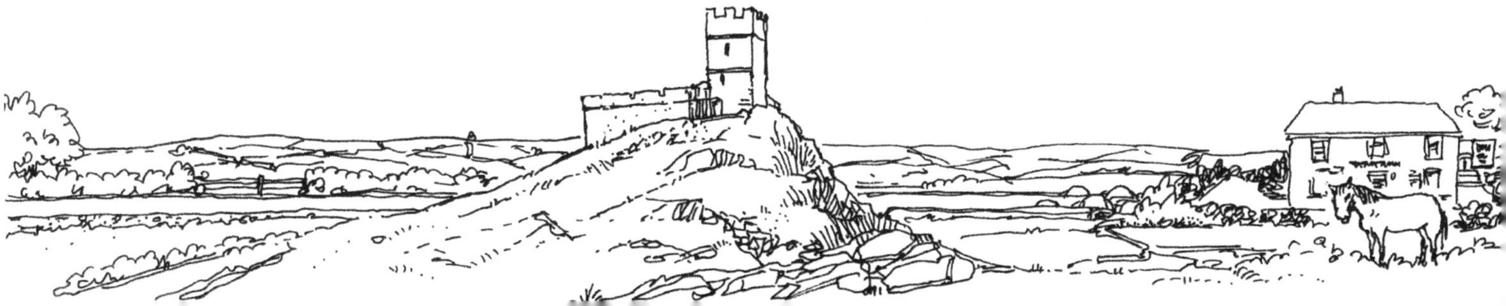

Coming into the softer energies of Devon was a delight. The lanes and fields were so green, filled with bluebells, birdsong, magpies and herds of charging bullocks. As we dropped down to the Tavy river I could feel the Mary line singing again and we stopped there, ahead of schedule, for a repose and the songs came rushing through me again as I sat on the stones in the river. As we came up to the church, still ahead of schedule, we decided to explore inside and the local church organist was there practising. I wondered if he might indulge me by playing Amazing Grace so I could have a sing. He was delighted and that was it. For forty five minutes we sang all the hymns we could muster accompanied by a very surprised but happy organist. Gerry danced and sang around the church and we were totally carried away by the moment, singing without a care in the world. It was wonderful. The energy and vibrancy of the Mary Line came straight through us and out in song. I'll never forget it. **DF**

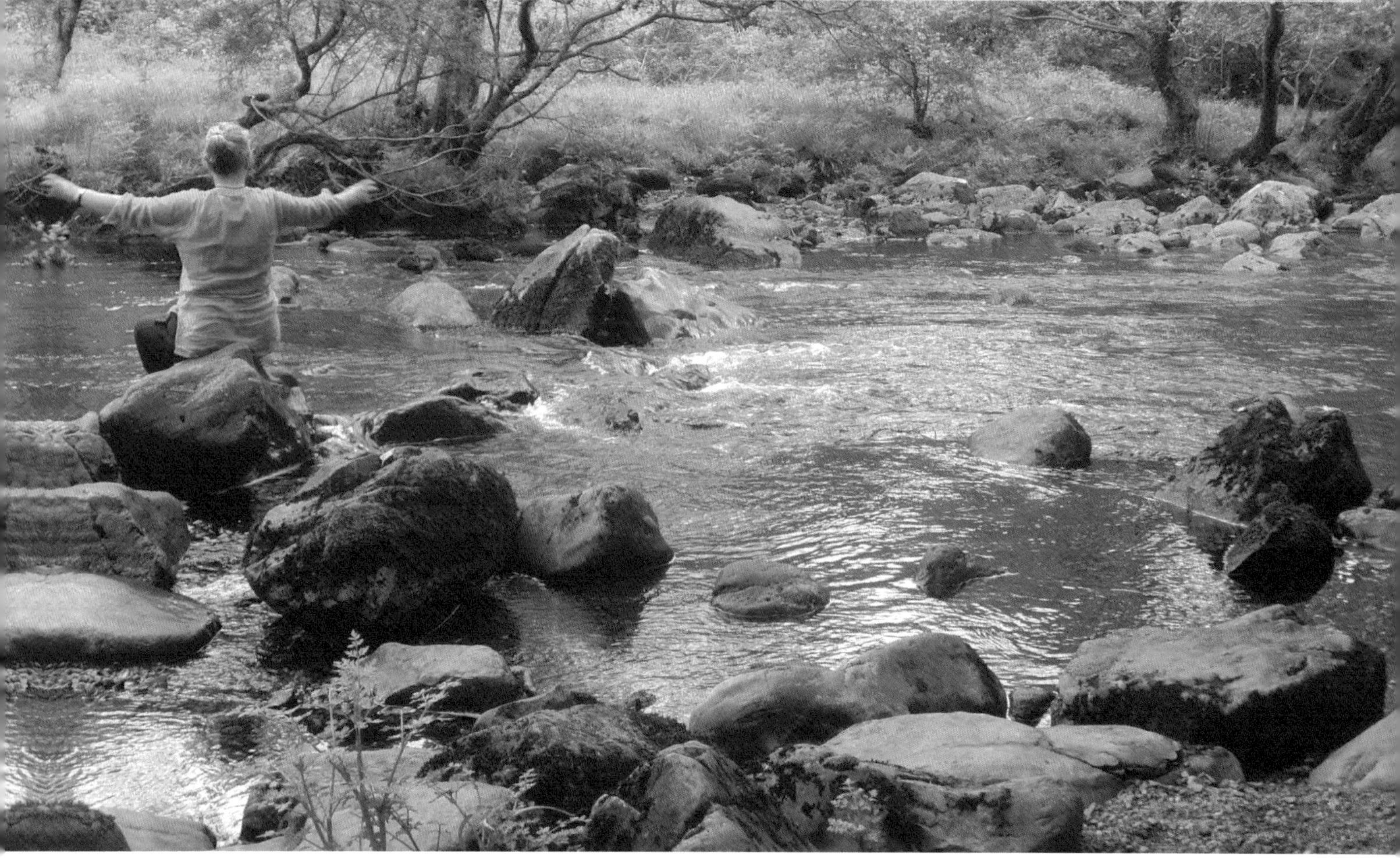

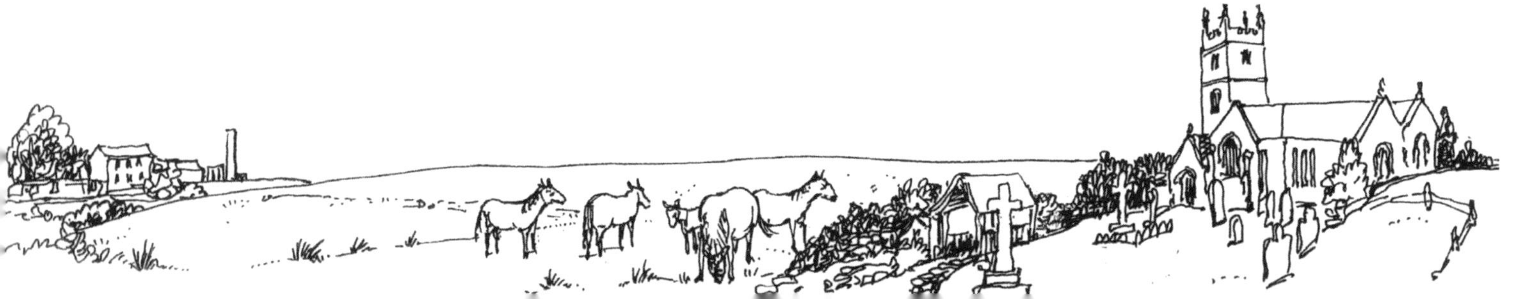

Day 12 Brent Tor to Two Bridges

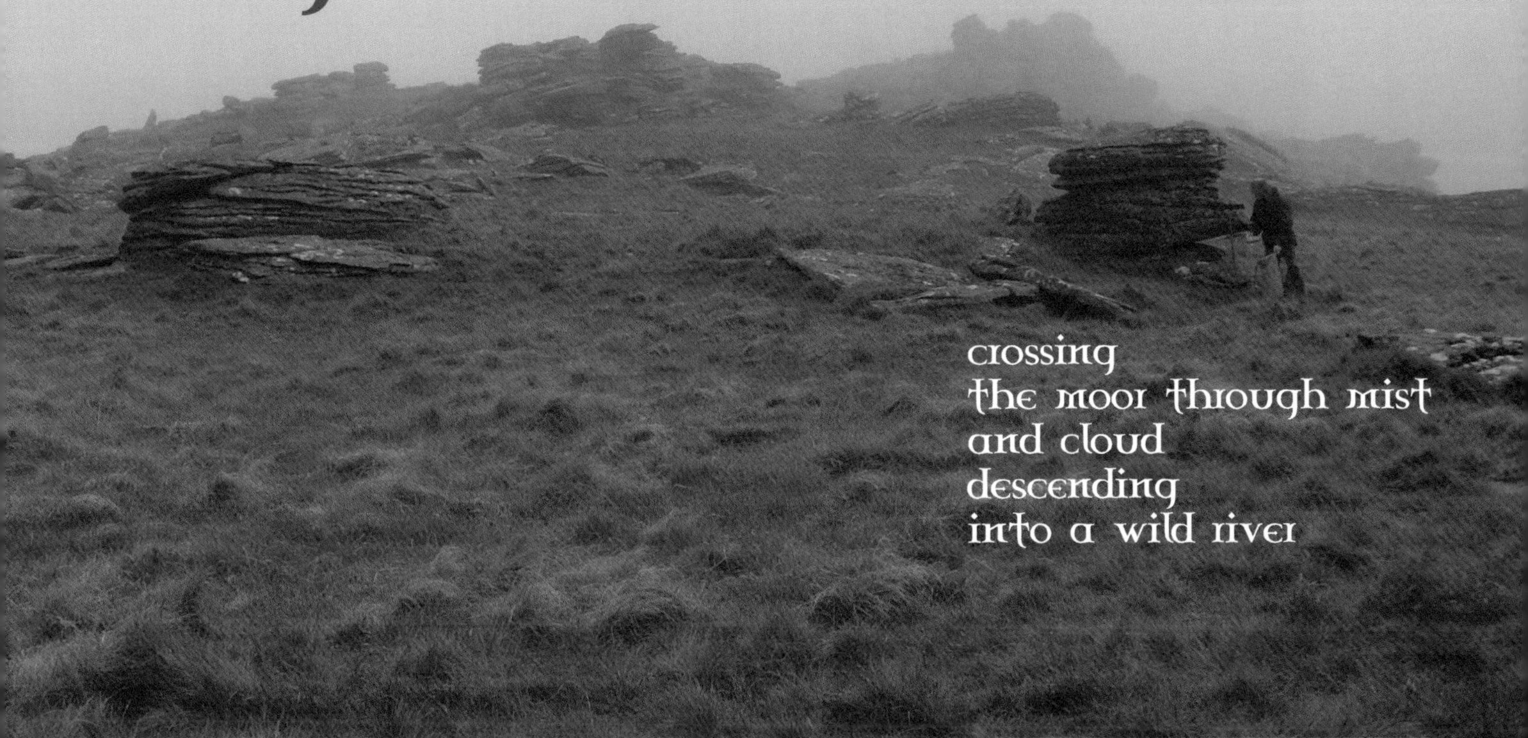

crossing
the moor through mist
and cloud
descending
into a wild river

Off over Dartmoor. Mist 50 yards visibility. One bluebell, stones, bogs, cracked earth, very tricky terrain. Pretty freaky! Long long walk, giant rocks appear, giant trees just out of the blue. One by one, walking in line, thirteen moor walkers, with map and compass. We needed them both! My compass came in full use for the first time in several years. It was just totally the best exposure to the wilderness. ***SS***

Setting up camp at Bear Down Farm on the edge of Dartmoor today. Rushing stream, dripping trees and waterfalls. Very wet day. Ended up singing my heart out in the rain. 'Oh, Great Spirit!' Did find some firewood and lit a fire. Dipped in the peaty brown river. Welcomed the tired, wet walkers in from their long, fog-laden walk on Dartmoor. Later on, steaming in a warm yurt, we celebrate Janey's birthday with her family. Cake and Cava! ***RH***

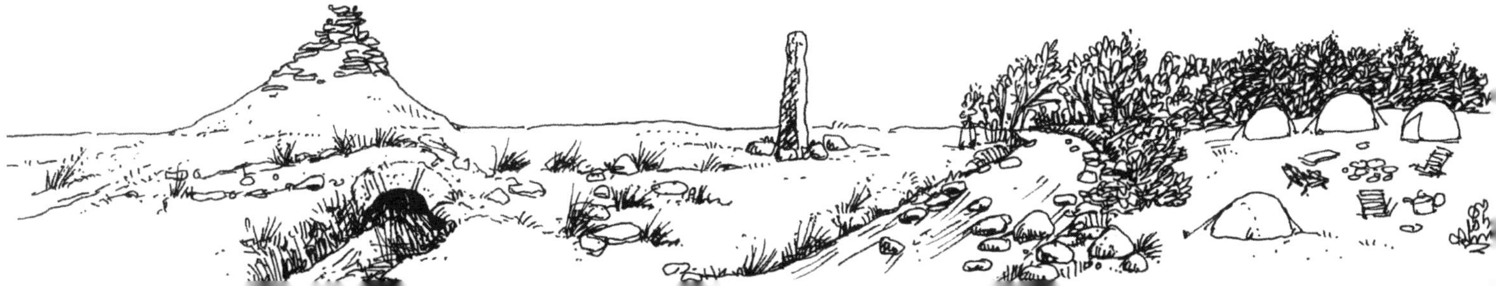

wind drops ...
the high country stills
around me
the stones stand still ...
my mind wanders

finding comfort
in the circle
of stones
comfort in the
circle of people

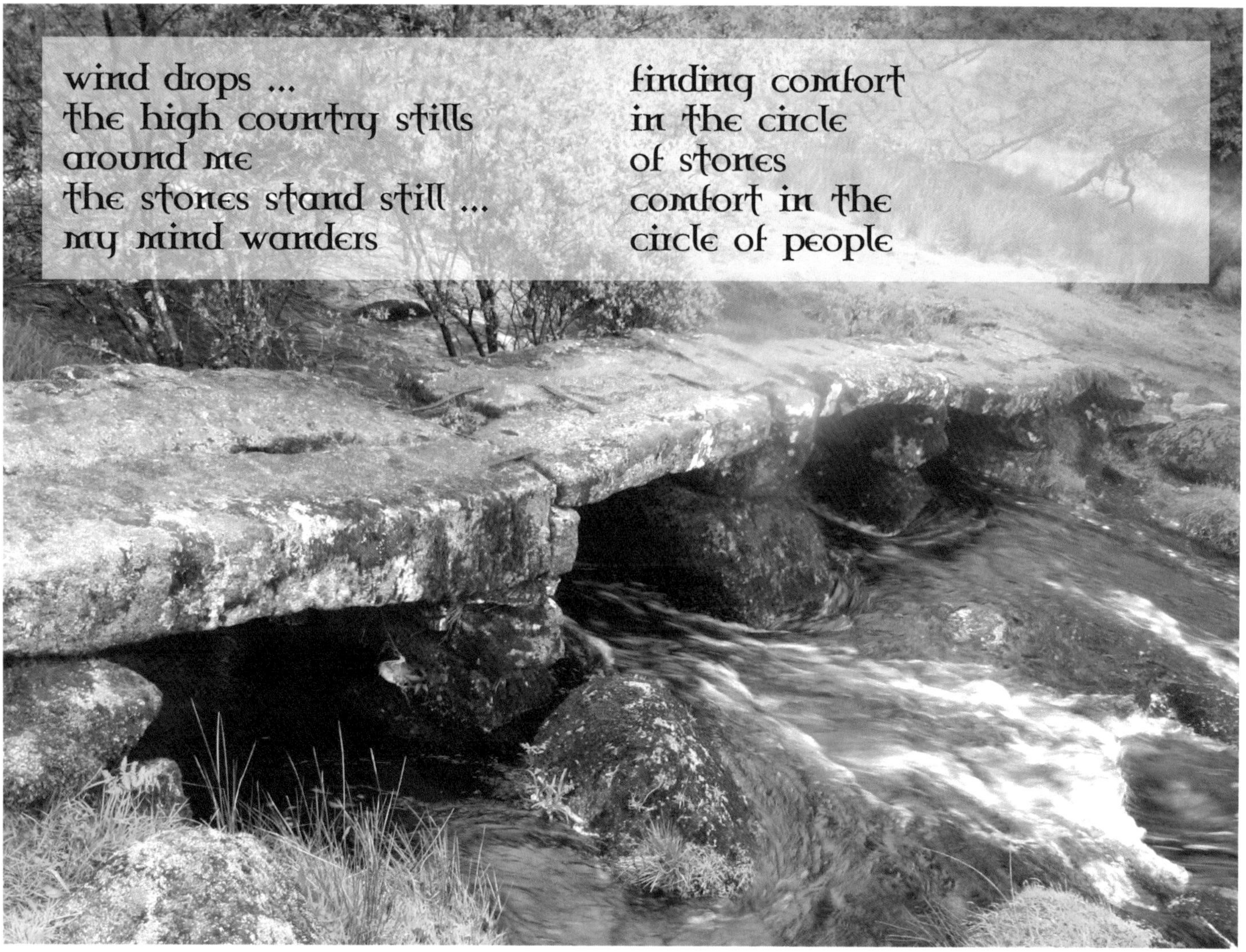

Day 13 Two Bridges to Chagford

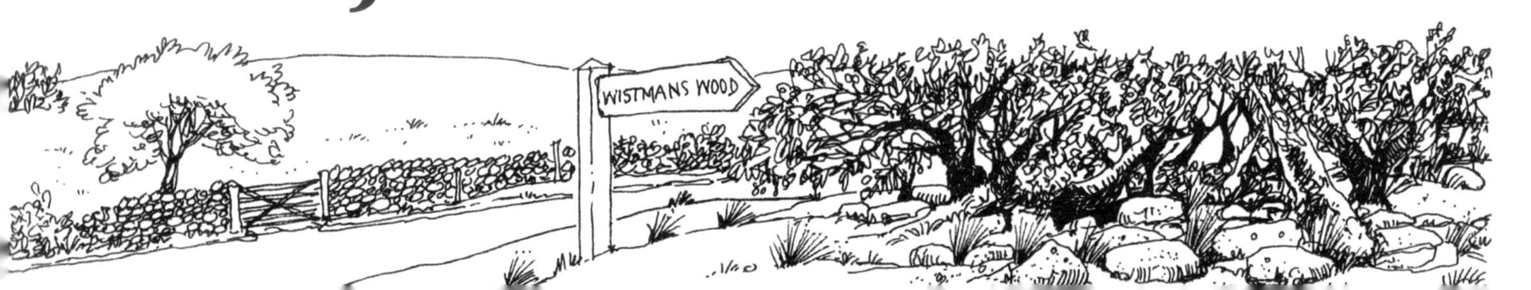

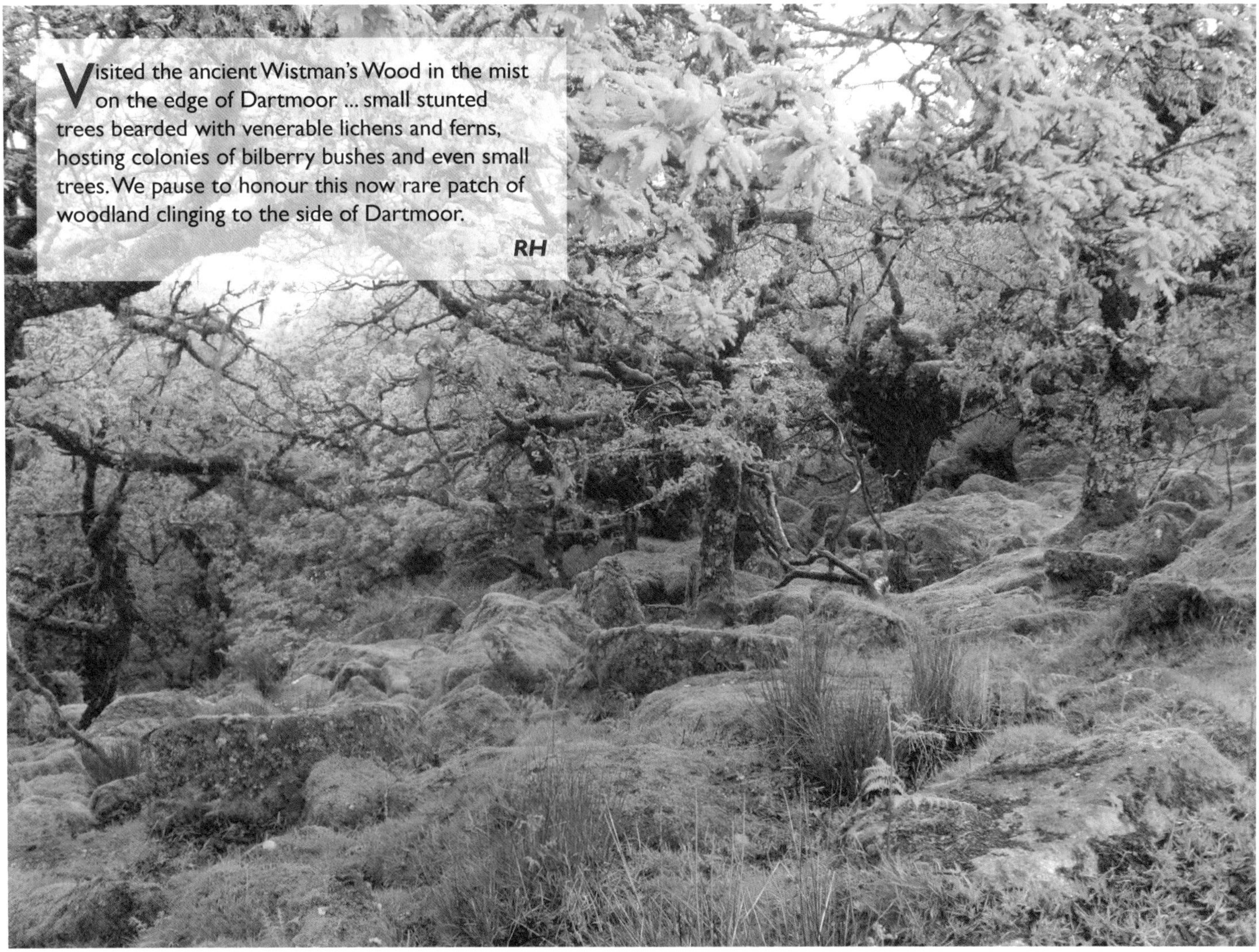

Visited the ancient Wistman's Wood in the mist on the edge of Dartmoor ... small stunted trees bearded with venerable lichens and ferns, hosting colonies of bilberry bushes and even small trees. We pause to honour this now rare patch of woodland clinging to the side of Dartmoor.

RH

On my penultimate night I began to feel so sad at the thought of leaving the group. I felt like this way of travelling was the most natural thing in the world and I loved it, and I knew the group would move on and I would go back to a more static existence, less simple, more structured with less time for just being and walking. ***DF***

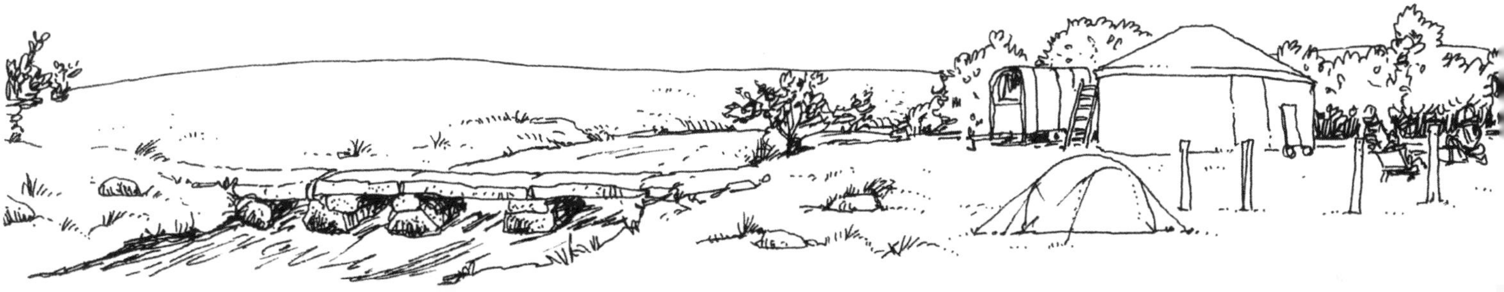

Day 14

I realised by the second week of the walk that my back (I have a degenerative scoliosis) was going to give me considerable agro and that I was not going to be able to walk every inch of the way like the nimble leaders I envied, who always stayed at the front of the line every day. So my journey was a slower and more reflective one in which I took time to spend at each crossing point and country church where the energies were at their strongest and made grateful use of the relief vehicles when backache restricted walking. ***CC***

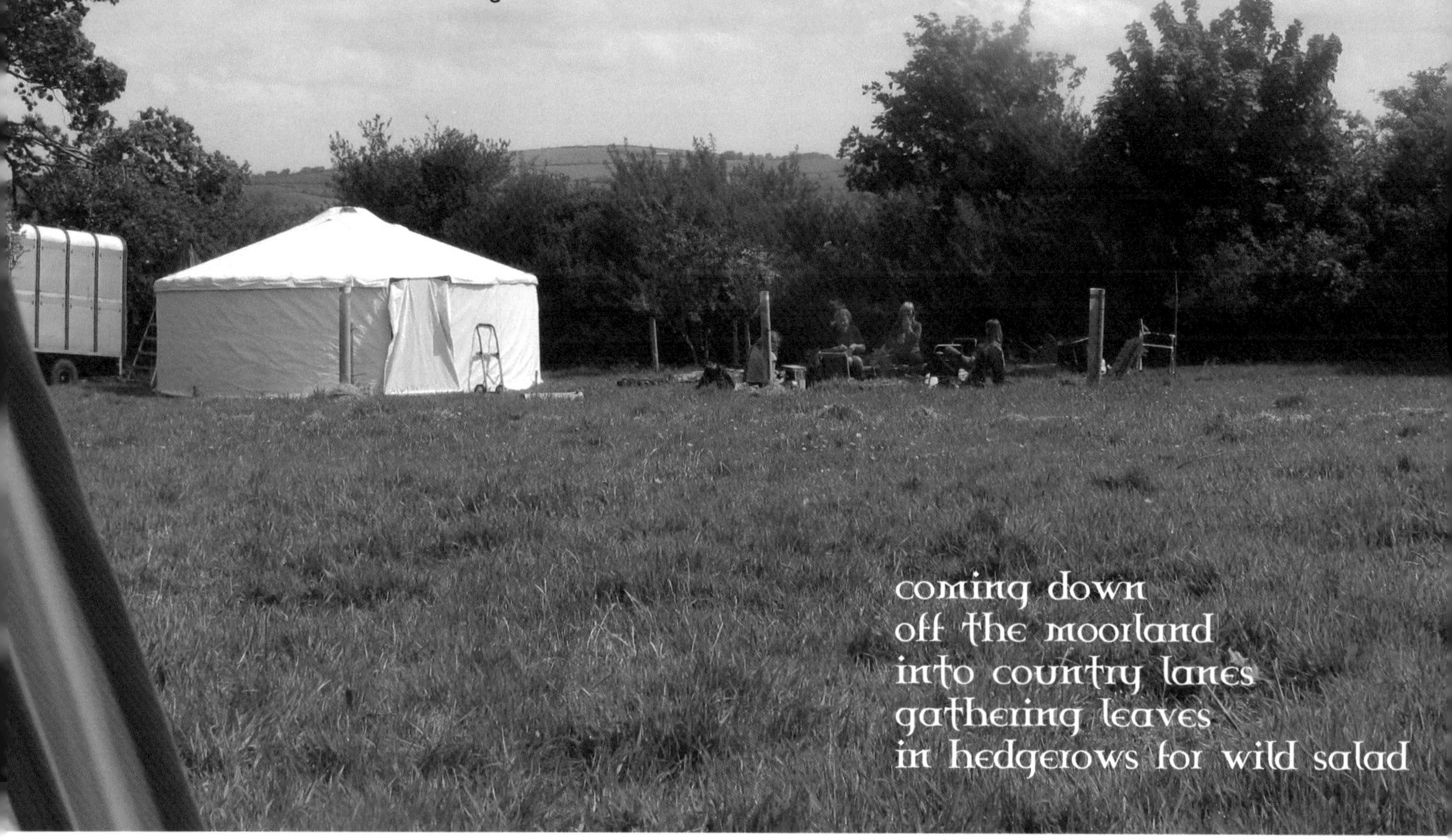

coming down
off the moorland
into country lanes
gathering leaves
in hedgerows for wild salad

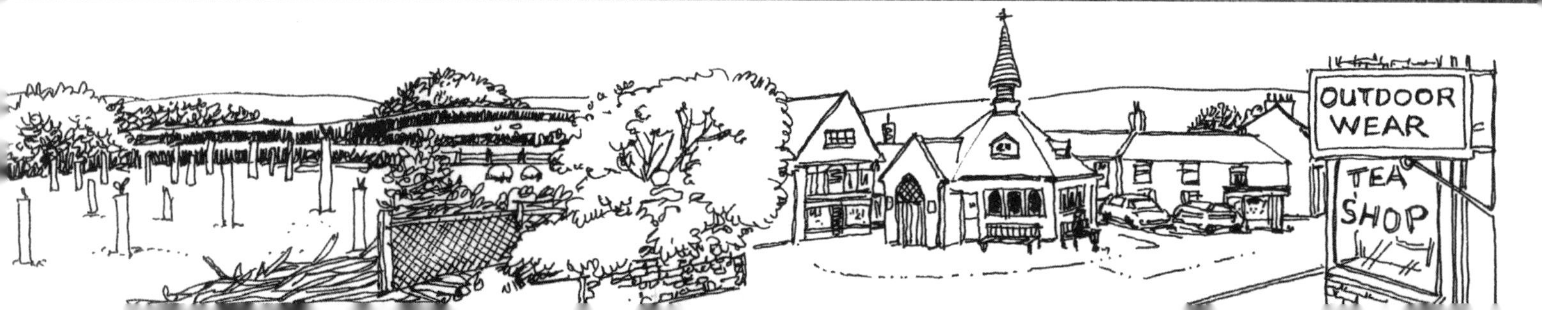

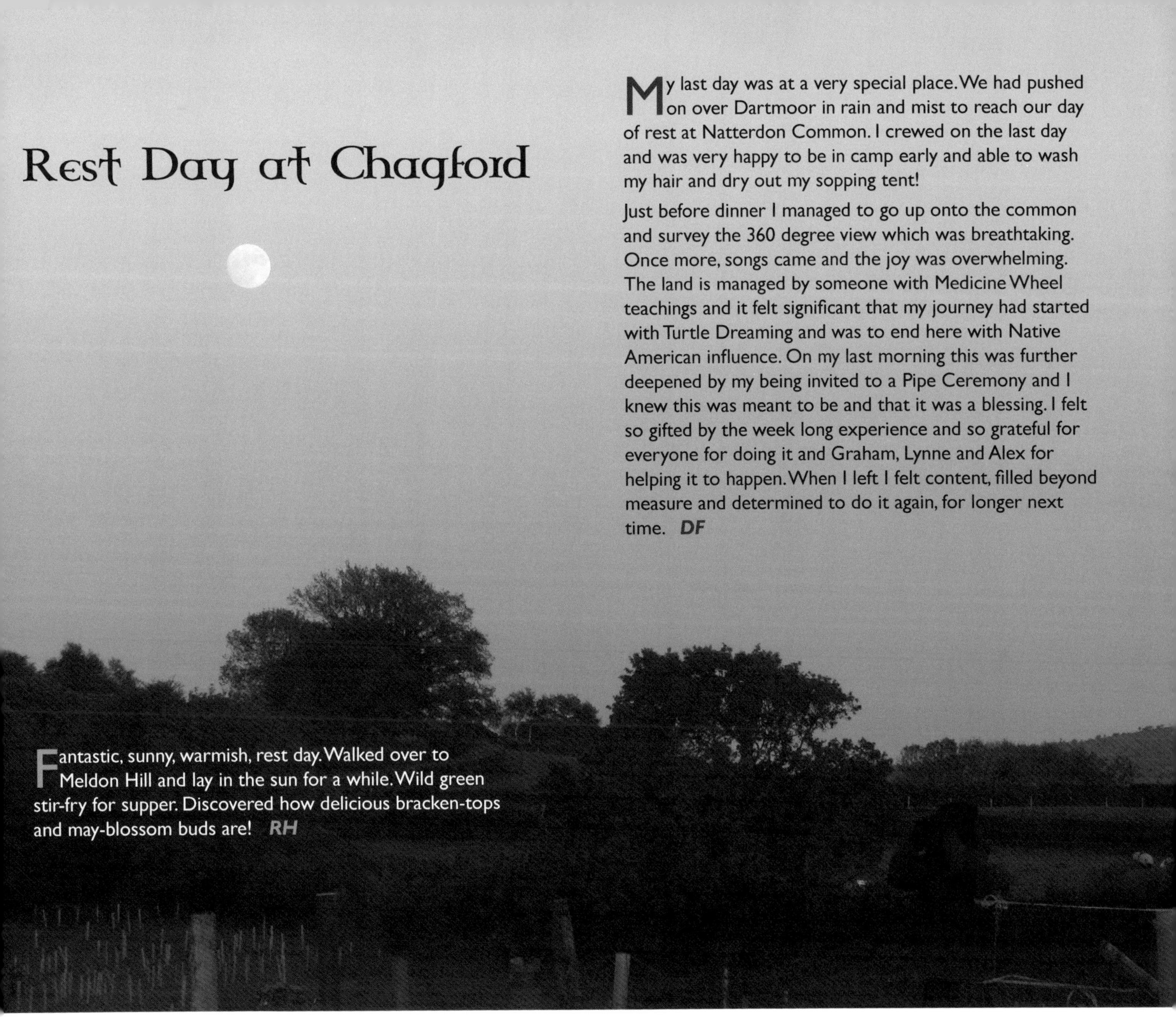

Rest Day at Chagford

My last day was at a very special place. We had pushed on over Dartmoor in rain and mist to reach our day of rest at Natterdon Common. I crewed on the last day and was very happy to be in camp early and able to wash my hair and dry out my sopping tent!

Just before dinner I managed to go up onto the common and survey the 360 degree view which was breathtaking. Once more, songs came and the joy was overwhelming. The land is managed by someone with Medicine Wheel teachings and it felt significant that my journey had started with Turtle Dreaming and was to end here with Native American influence. On my last morning this was further deepened by my being invited to a Pipe Ceremony and I knew this was meant to be and that it was a blessing. I felt so gifted by the week long experience and so grateful for everyone for doing it and Graham, Lynne and Alex for helping it to happen. When I left I felt content, filled beyond measure and determined to do it again, for longer next time. ***DF***

Fantastic, sunny, warmish, rest day. Walked over to Meldon Hill and lay in the sun for a while. Wild green stir-fry for supper. Discovered how delicious bracken-tops and may-blossom buds are! ***RH***

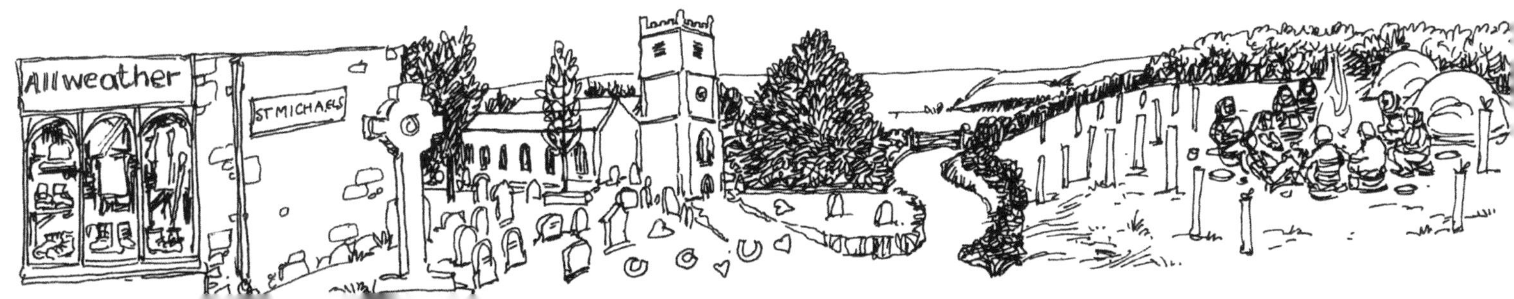

Day 15 Chagford to Uton

Cook Coo! Wake up Pee! 5.00 am Tired, feels like we all need a bit more rest. Beautiful sunny morning. Turned round head in doorway in sun one hour then up. Clotted cream in porridge with honey, yummy!

Morning walk alongside river 6-7 miles. Cream tea before lunch by river bridge. Lunch in field. Fisherman swearing, lost salmon. Such a great river walk. Ups, downs, rocks, steps and handrails. Afternoon lanes, tracks, footpaths and bridleways. Saw my first orchid, after being shown so many.

Camp by lake fishery. Nice old lady (the owner) rides around on a quad bike. Geese fight off intruders (other geese). Nate's fire-ball Initiation to Burning Man (a festival in the California desert). Chocolate. Finished malt (a bottle of Scotch single malt whiskey) bought and shared by a few pilgrims. Bed. 11.00. Full Moon. ***SS***

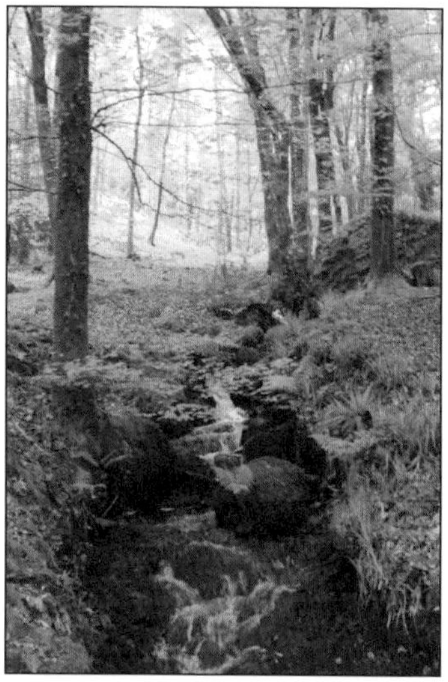

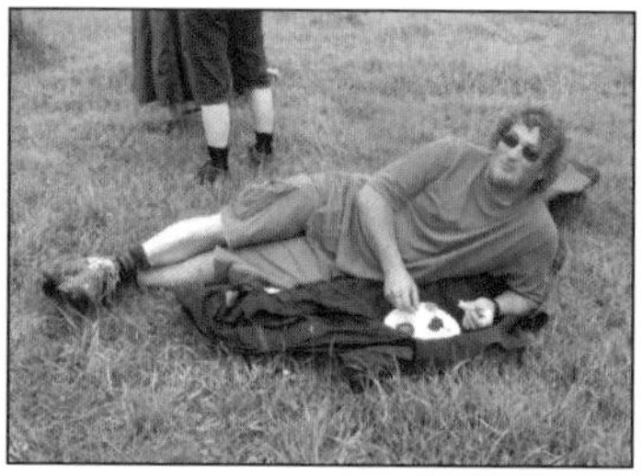

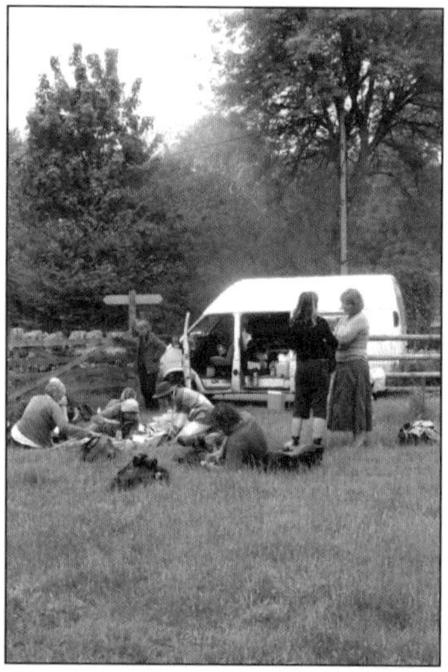

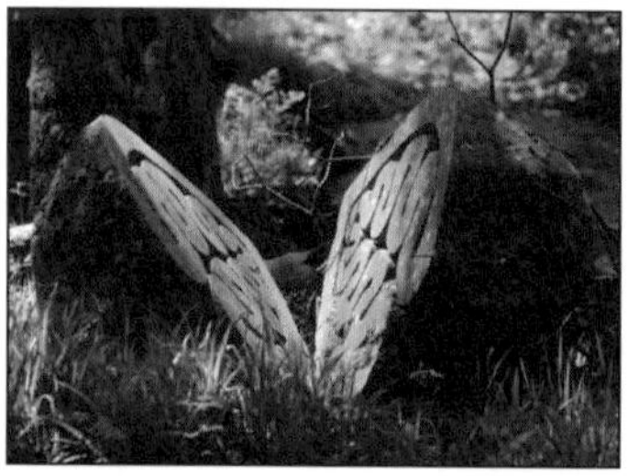

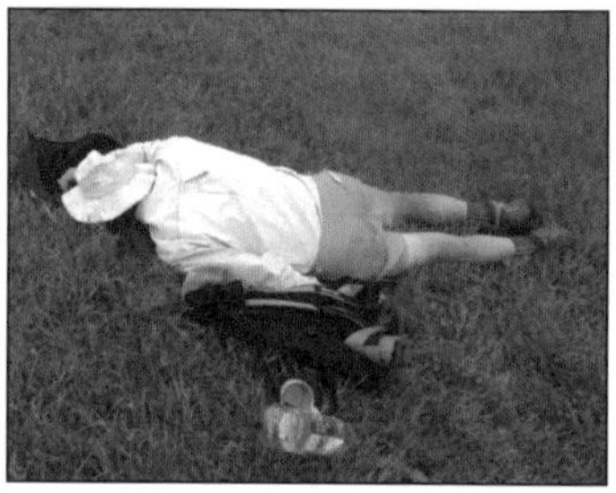

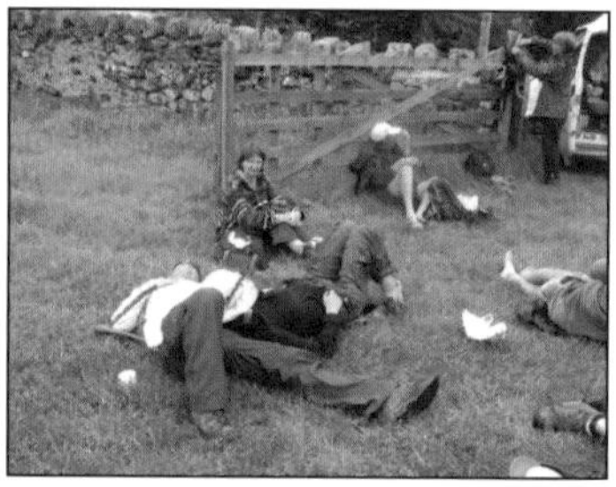

Another fine day! When we left Jeremy's land this morning he smudged us with frankincense, using feathers, a beautiful kingfisher's feather. It was heavenly to walk down his hill, through leafy lanes again.

Walked along the River Teign, a beautiful riverside path. I saw dippers! Feeding their babies, who hopped and dipped and flapped their wings. I saw two big brown and orange hairy caterpillars. We walked along a squelchy mud path and across little wooden bridges.

We had a cream tea at Fingle Bridge Inn, and saw lots of tiny fishes and also tadpoles in puddles. I saw orchids, common cow wheat, foxgloves, cow parsley and lots of buttercups. It was lovely to spend time with Paul.

We are on a campsite with fishing lakes, in Uton, around the fire laughing. We also had a fire spectacular! Nate made a fire-work out of wire wool, and as the full moon rose over the hills, accompanied by the haunting sound of the bull roarer, Steve spun a huge circle of sparks in the night sky. ***ML***

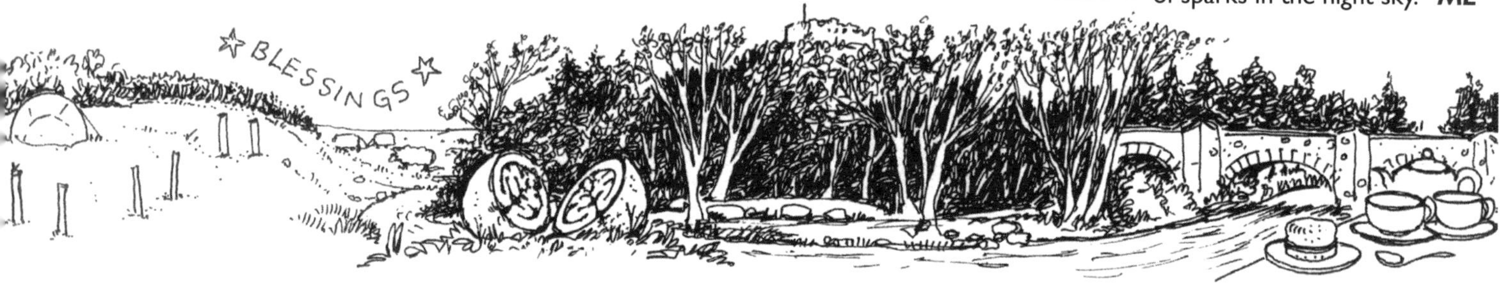

rolling green hills
thatched cottages –
am I
walking through
a picture postcard?

Setting up camp by fishponds today. Showered and drying by fire, boiling kettle for walkers' tea. Home-made firework extravaganza tonight as full moon rises. **RH**

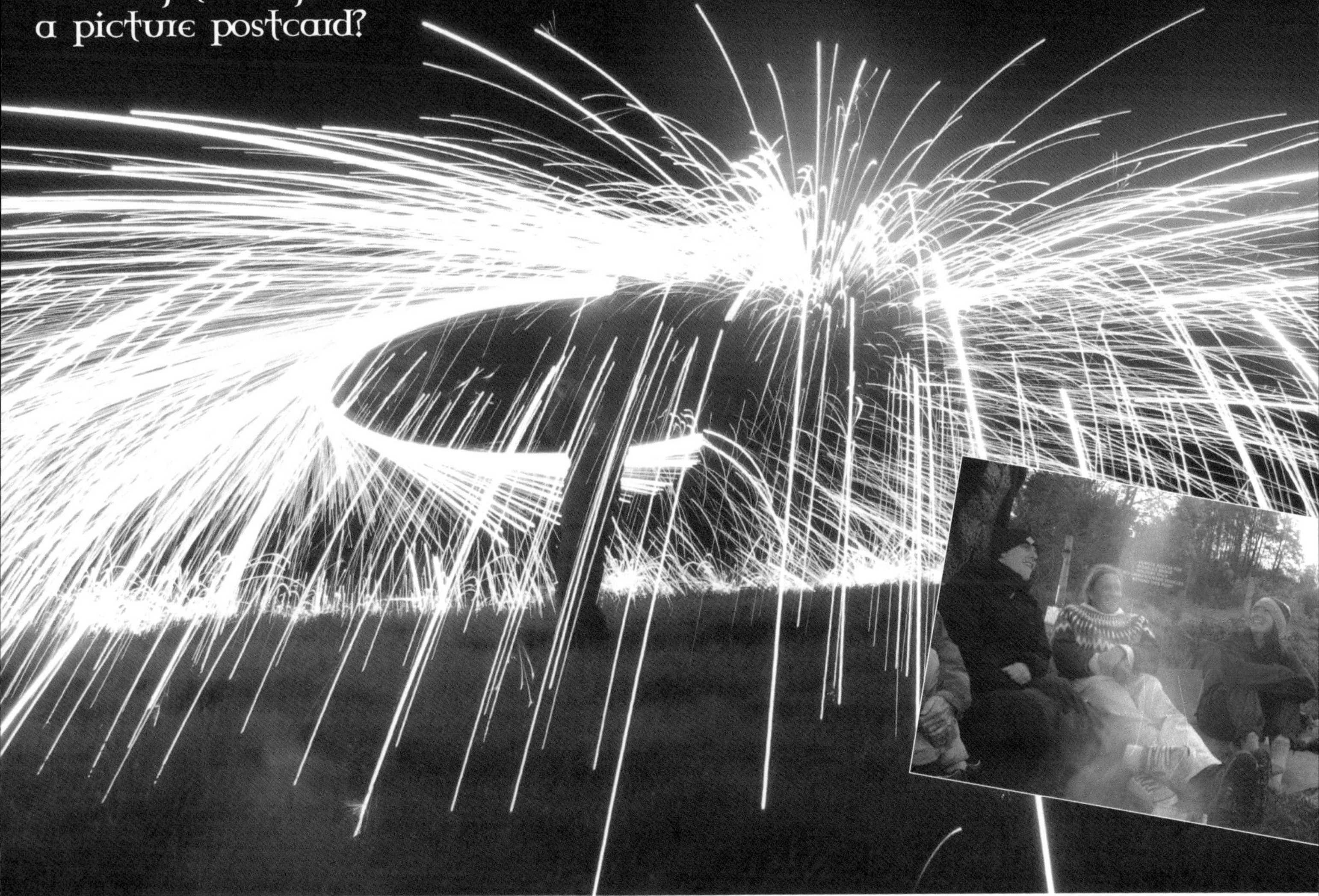

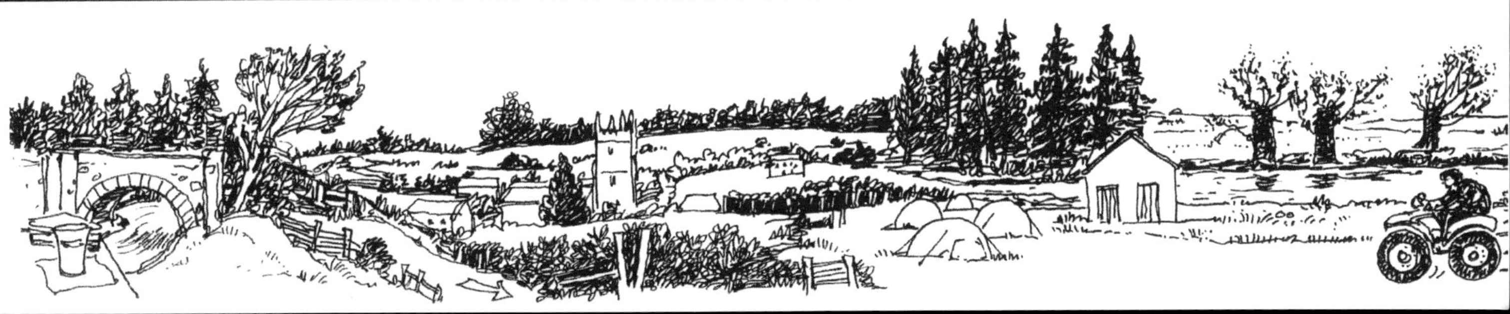

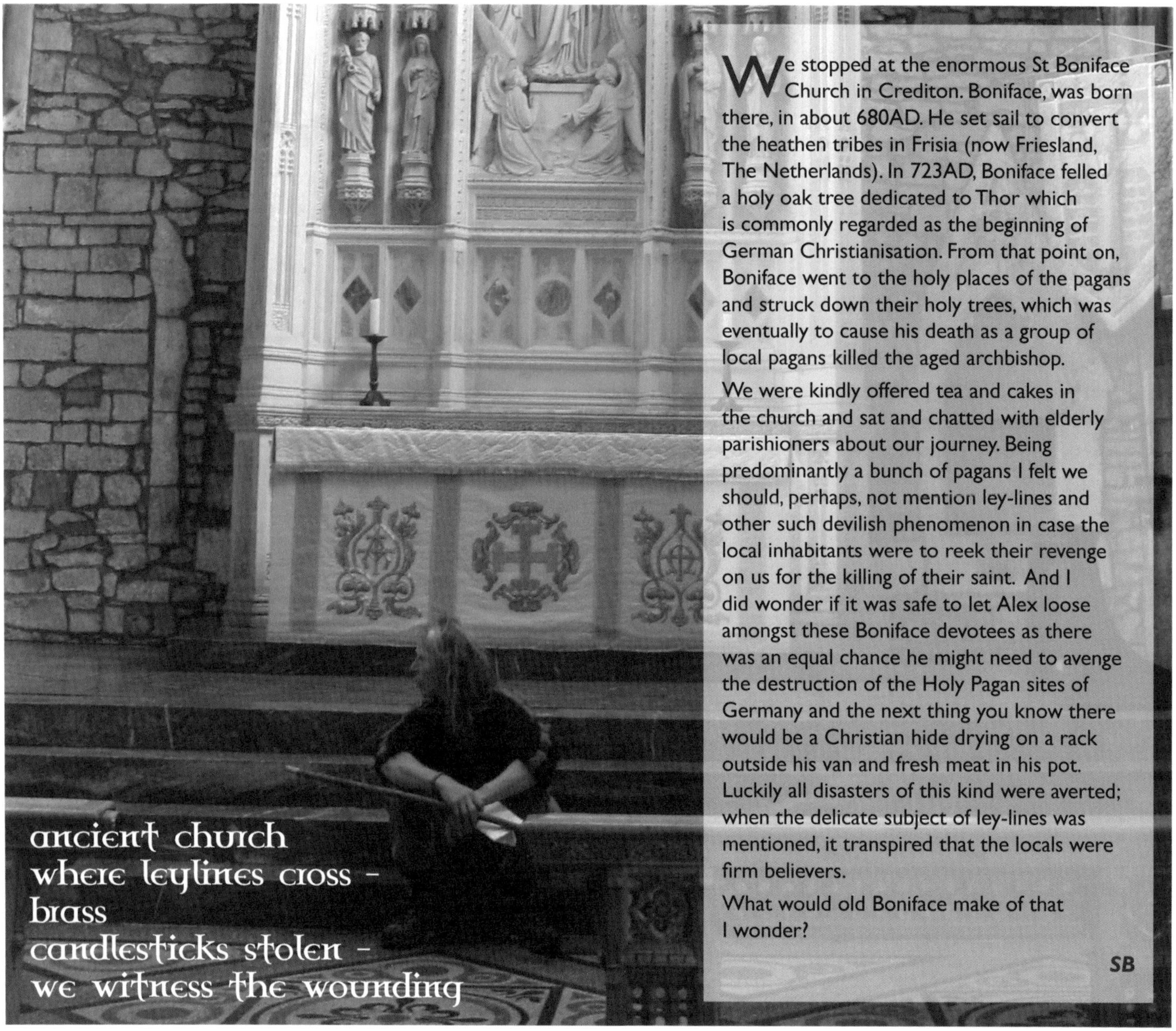

We stopped at the enormous St Boniface Church in Crediton. Boniface, was born there, in about 680AD. He set sail to convert the heathen tribes in Frisia (now Friesland, The Netherlands). In 723AD, Boniface felled a holy oak tree dedicated to Thor which is commonly regarded as the beginning of German Christianisation. From that point on, Boniface went to the holy places of the pagans and struck down their holy trees, which was eventually to cause his death as a group of local pagans killed the aged archbishop.

We were kindly offered tea and cakes in the church and sat and chatted with elderly parishioners about our journey. Being predominantly a bunch of pagans I felt we should, perhaps, not mention ley-lines and other such devilish phenomenon in case the local inhabitants were to reek their revenge on us for the killing of their saint. And I did wonder if it was safe to let Alex loose amongst these Boniface devotees as there was an equal chance he might need to avenge the destruction of the Holy Pagan sites of Germany and the next thing you know there would be a Christian hide drying on a rack outside his van and fresh meat in his pot. Luckily all disasters of this kind were averted; when the delicate subject of ley-lines was mentioned, it transpired that the locals were firm believers.

What would old Boniface make of that I wonder?

SB

ancient church
where leylines cross -
brass
candlesticks stolen -
we witness the wounding

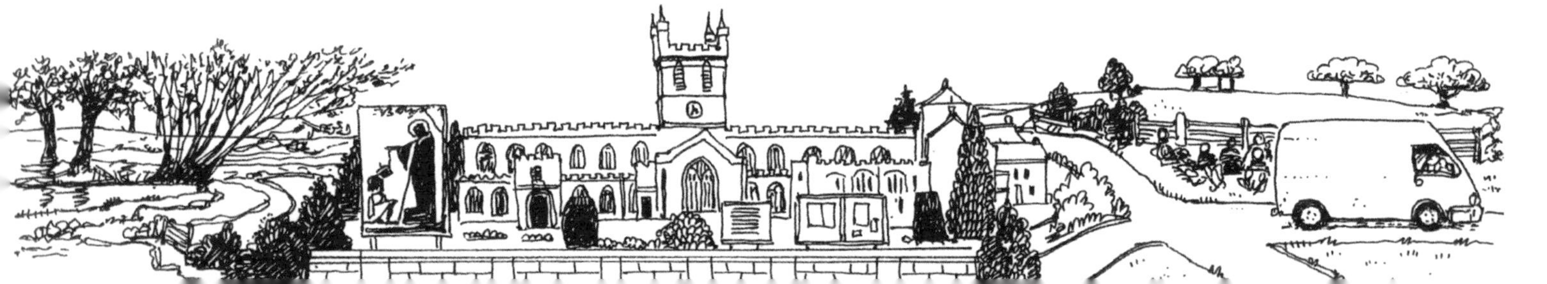

Day 16 Uton to Bickleigh

A fine day. Started walking into Crediton, but found my ankle is really painful, looked round in the church where the Michael and Mary lines cross, but couldn't really get into it as was worried about my ankle. It made me cry, the combination of pain and disappointment at thinking I could not walk. Lynne helped me with arnica, ibuprofen, lavender cream, paracetamol and her staff and I walked on. Felt not present, and in a fuzzy dream state until just before lunch. We ate lunch in the sheep field of a big manor house estate. The soil is so red and beautifully rich here. We found a bright whitey, green spider. There were some huge hills to walk down this afternoon. We had a tea break at Cadbury Castle, an Iron Age Hill Fort, surrounded by trees and beautiful rolling hills. Fantastic!! Got a bit lost and went through a cow field and farm yard, the farmer came out and was not too thrilled, but helped us find our way. We walked past delightful Bickleigh Castle and we are camping in a buttercup field at Bickleigh Mill. ***ML***

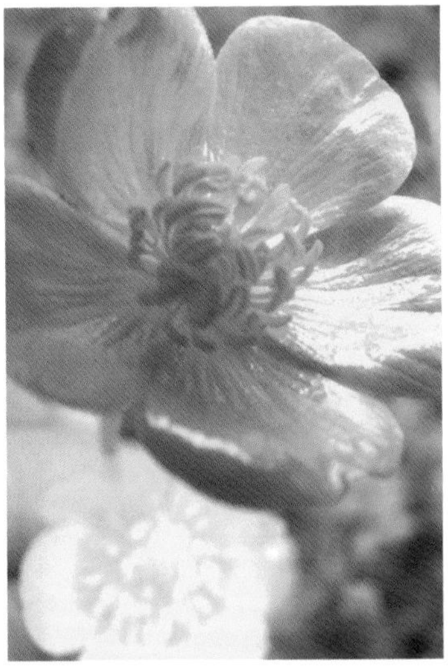

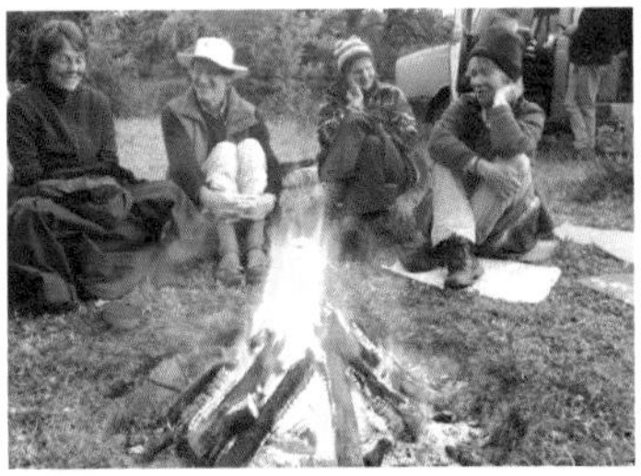

Sunshine. Turned around laid in doorway ¾ hour, sheer delight. Simon left today after take-down. Nice day's walking. Sunny, windy, cool and hot. Avenue of lime and chestnut. Mel: ankle pain, but like a true pilgrim, she battled on. Amazing. Lunch: wait 10 minutes at crossroads. Gerry went back in White 'Awakening' after lunch.

Nice church organ. Coffee, cake, biscuits, made donations. Walking up, up, up and down, really big hills. Made our own way, decision time, go by road or make new path. Down across fields over fences into woods, over more fences, downhill through mud, loads of it, very tricky. Rhian, Alex and I wait and watch as the followers made their way through the mess, we did laugh. We had left arrows and markers so they knew it was the only way forward. Melody and Sarah went by road.

Continuing: over narrow swing bridge two planks wide with hand rails just above knee height. One by one we crossed the wide river, the bridge was very springy, wicked, freaky but amazing. 1½ miles walk down old railway track to site. Nice walk for poo! over/under bridges.

Quiet drumming with Nate and yes Ian came to visit us and played didge, brought gifts of re-proofing coats and jackets. What a hero! Such a lovely man! B'Anna is the Chocolate Goddess! Nice kissing gates like yesterday. 11.00 goodnight. ***SS***

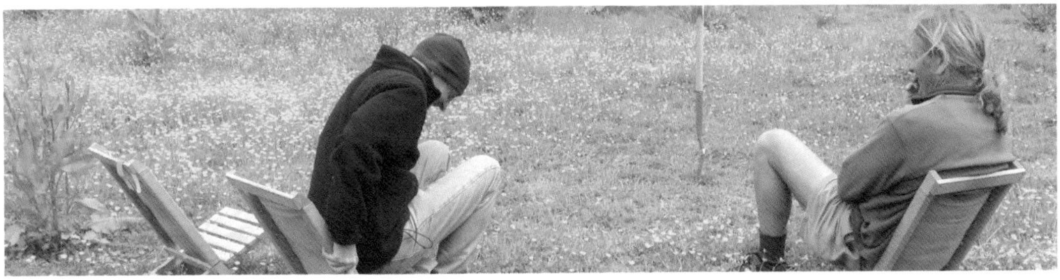

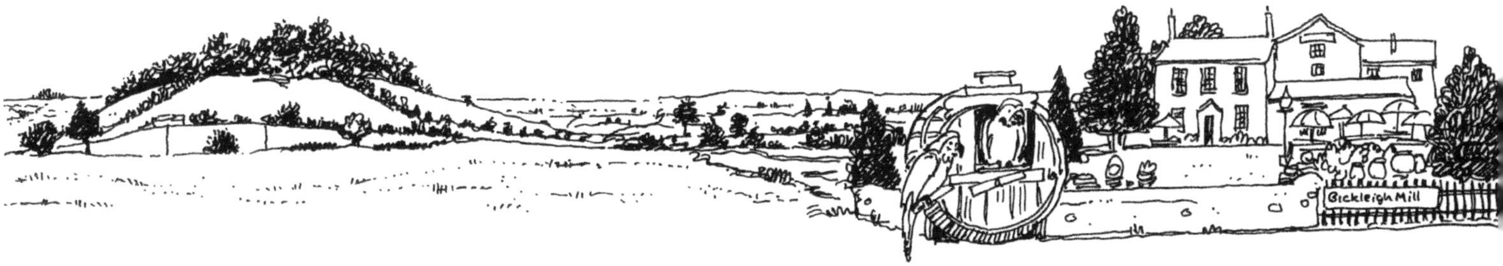

Day 17

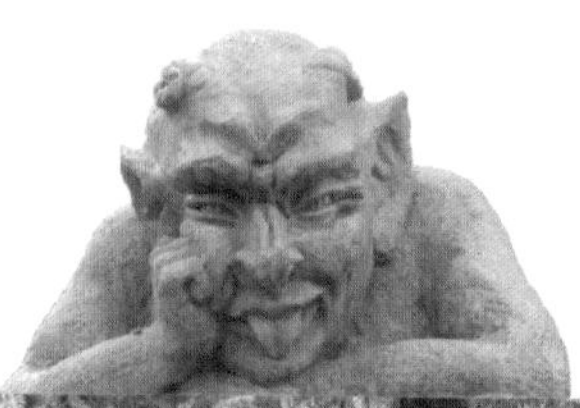

Bickleigh to Appley

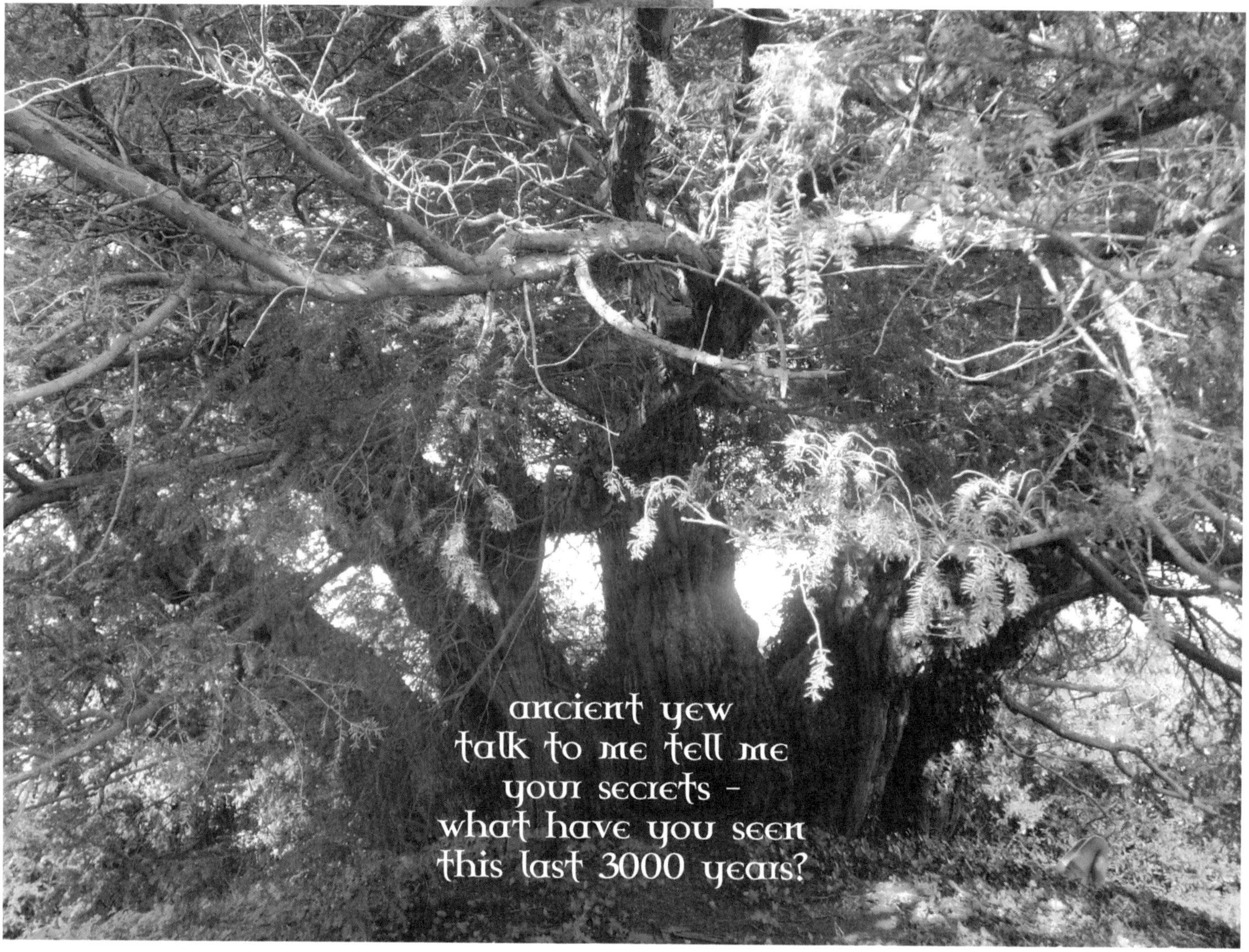

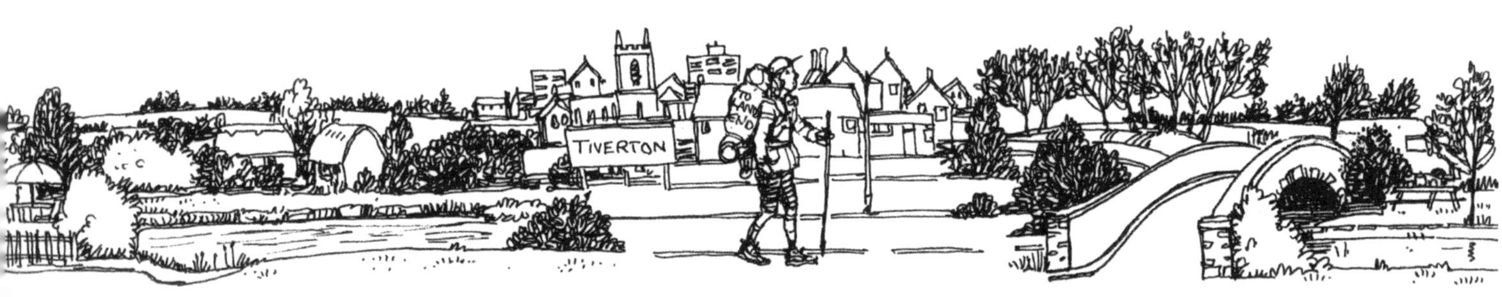

WILD FOOD STIR-FRY

– may blossom buds (unopened)

– bracken tops (furled and just unfurling)

– young nettle tops

– dock leaf tops

– young comfrey leaves

– young dandelion leaves

– sorrel leaves and tops

– wild garlic (ransoms) leaves

Stir fry in large frying pan over open fire. Add garlic with a little oil before greens and buds. Stir fry quickly until just tender and still green. Add seasoning, share and enjoy RH

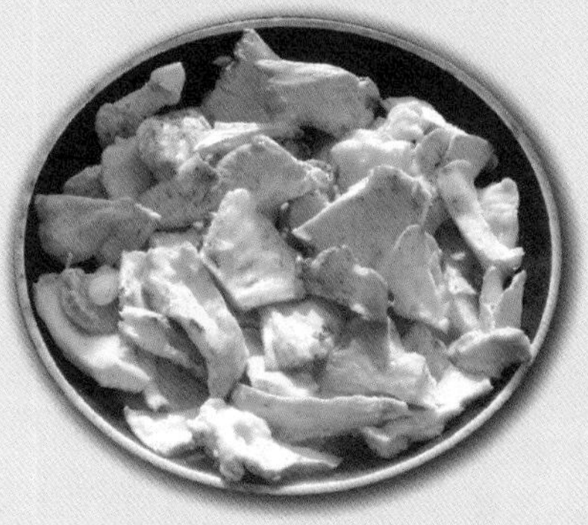

I pushed myself to walk through the afternoon, wanting to see the oldest tree in England, the yew at Ashbrittle, 3800 years old ... getting tired in the late afternoon we were grateful for a pilgrims' miracle ... passing a house at Kytton Barton we were offered a cup of tea in the lovely garden of Richard and Tess ... and in conversation discovered mutual friends and connections with our mob ... ***GJ***

Am tired and happy. This is Jan's place at Appley. It is a beautiful circle mown into a meadow with a fire pit and proper compost loos. The fire is gorgeous and we shared under the stars. Vegetable in cheese sauce and banoffee pie for tea, plus hedgerow pickings fried in a pan – bracken tops, sorrel, may flowers, nettles, docks and other yummy things. We walked far today, about 17 or 18 miles, all along the River Exe, a wide meanderer. We found 'Chicken in the Woods' fungus, bright orange and good to eat. Then along the canal, the Grand Western, I saw a kingfisher on the river and swans, goslings, ducks, coots and moorhens on the canal. We saw a horse-drawn barge with a black and white dog lying on its brightly painted top. We visited the Ashbrittle Yew, a grand old yew tree in a churchyard, estimated to be 3,800 years old! Mature when Stonehenge was being used. I lay on the earth next to it and wondered at its new shoots, surging from its ancient trunks. What an amazing life!! ***ML***

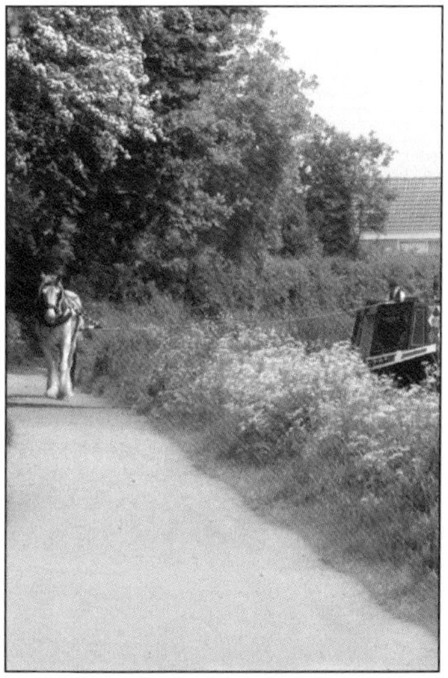

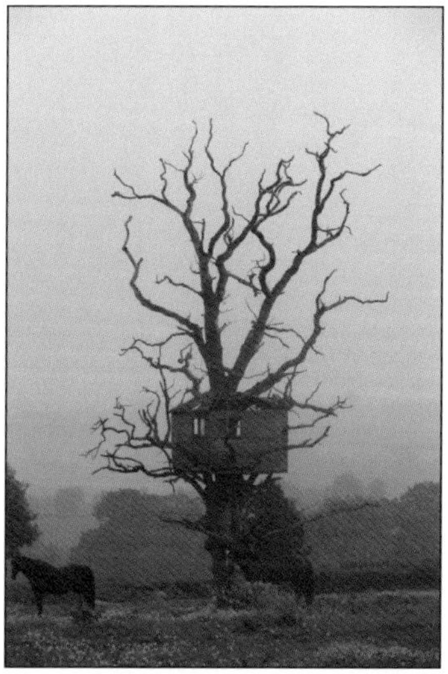

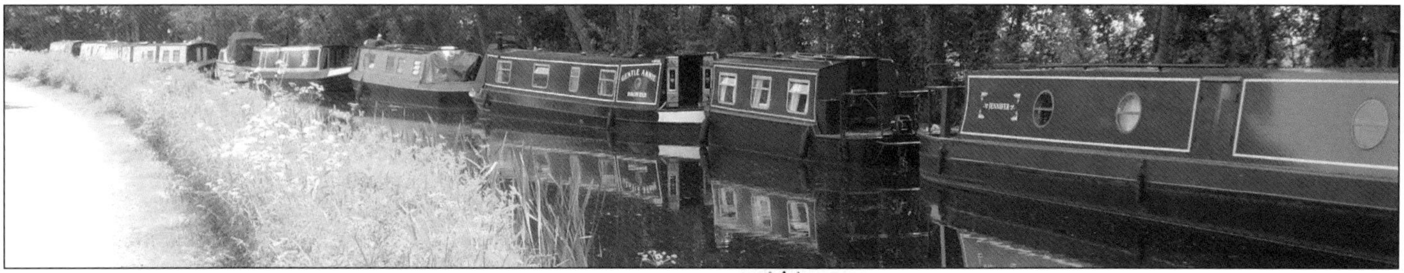

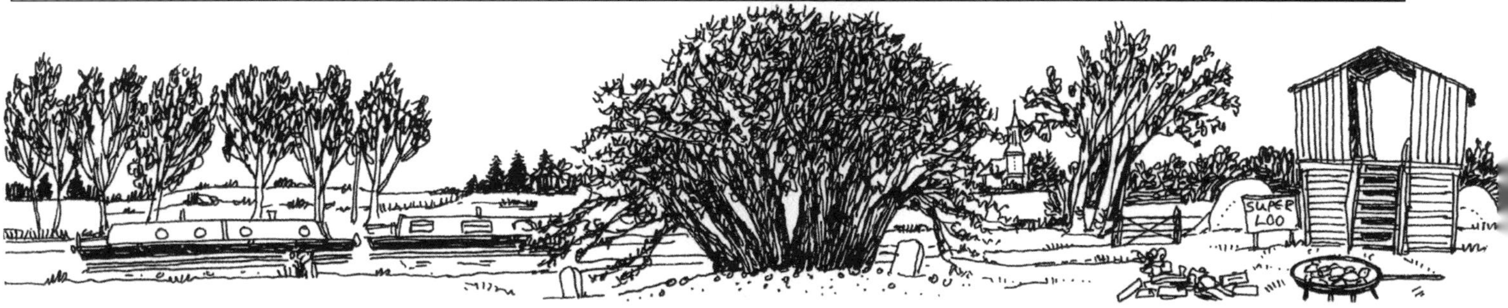

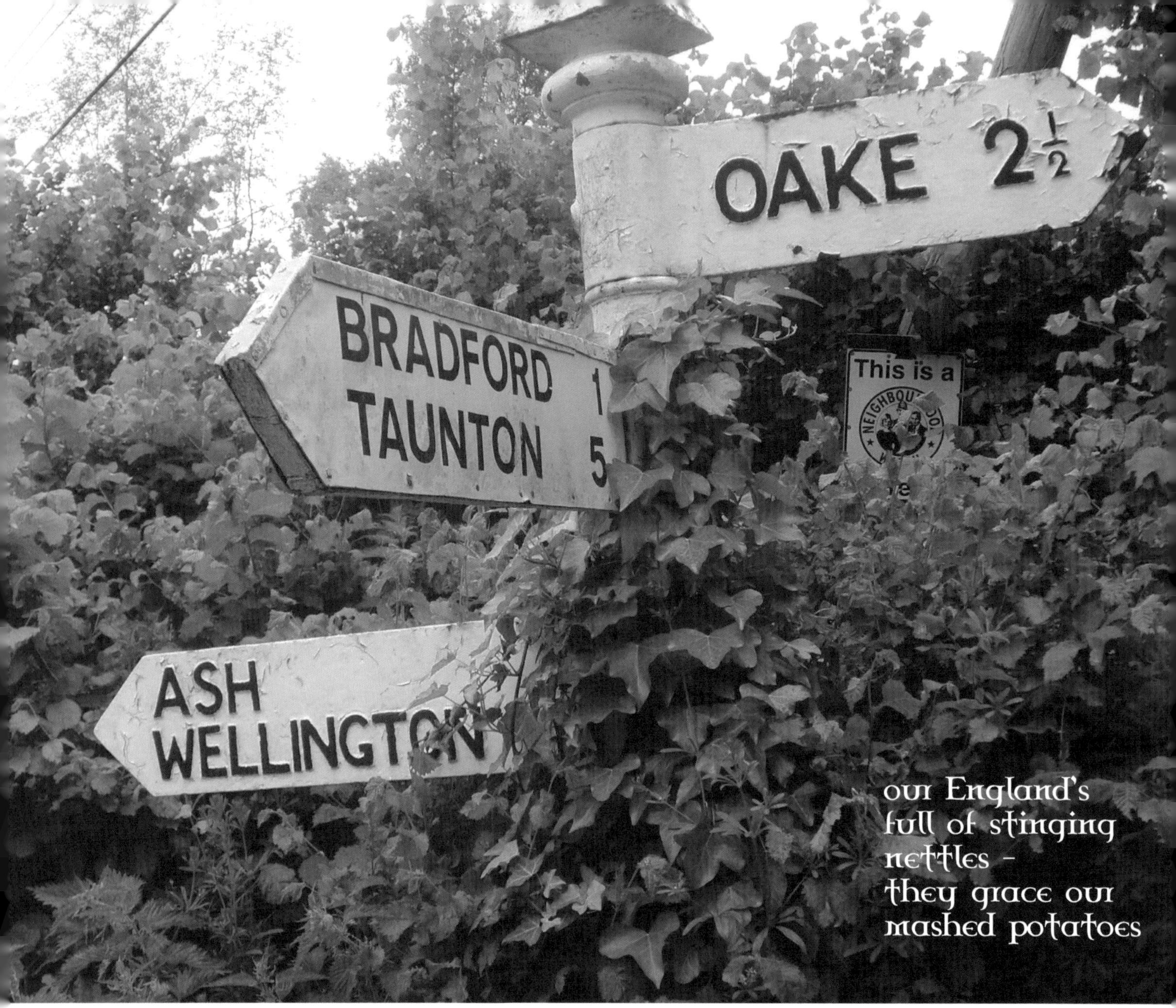

our England's
full of stinging
nettles -
they grace our
mashed potatoes

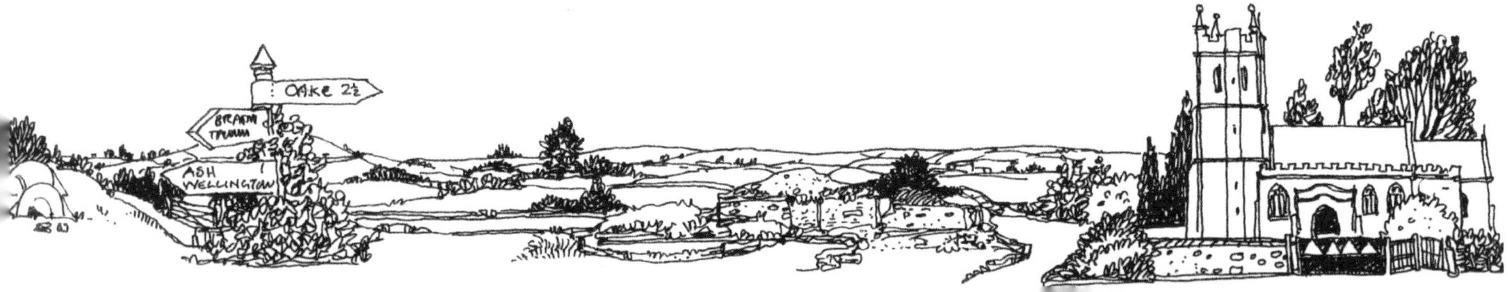

Day 18 Appley to Pitminster

Mel, a wood nymph of the forest
Ivy crowned, dark hair shining
Barefoot walker
Silver stream strider
Forging forward to sea
and home and man

LM

Walked along an old canal derelict for 100 years and filled in with some ponds and old lock structures ... some adventures with barbed wire, a railway crossing, oxbows in the River Tone ... the last section that I walked with Steve and Melody was confusing, the map didn't seem to fit the country ...! ***GJ***

Wet take down! Tight boots. Sore heel. Two loos. Long walk to vans. Tried a little bit of 'Chicken in the Woods' fungi. White with yellow underneath half-plate size on tree in layers. Tasted just like dry breast of chicken. That was part of breakfast for those who were brave enough to try it or mad enough, I think one could trust the judgement of our fellow pilgrims. Alex cooked it again for dinner with potatoes, onions and loads of hedgerow food.

Dry canal walk rather nice (dry, meaning empty of any water) in parts, then no trace of it, then old empty dry locks. Loads of kissing gates. Bridges. Over M5. Rivers, streams and brooks. Oxbow lakes. Over main line railway tracks, two-way tracks, the London-Penzance line. Freaky! I think it was just Gerry and I on this stretch of the walk! Brampton on Tone for lunch by church wall. Carpet tiles to sit on. Kettle crisps, made in Norwich. Banoffee Pie leftovers. Mel made flask of tea for us for the afternoon walk. Drank it at Trull church. The church was locked, Graham particularly wanted us to see the inside, we were all a little disappointed to say the least. He did try to find the Vicar but alas no luck.

Lovely singing round fire. Graham crashed and missed dinner. Loads of chocolate. Great Loos in woods at site. Had to use trowel for second time (Sacred Trowel for digging Poo hole). Very handy. 10.35 good night. ***SS***

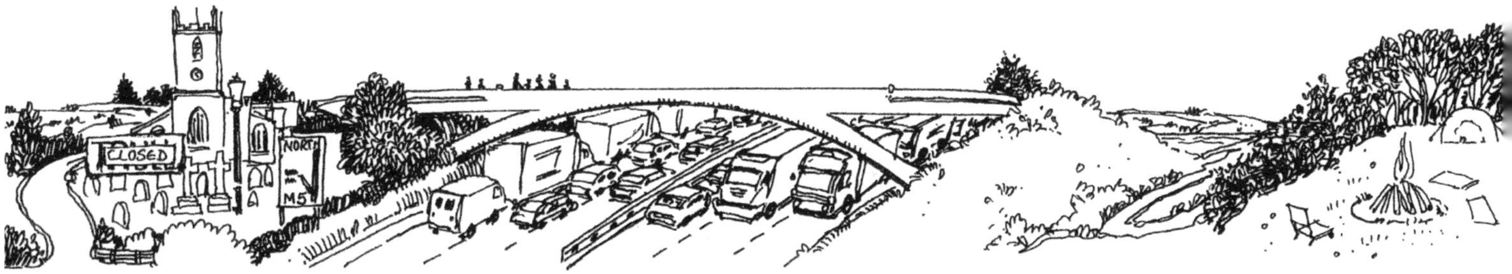

Day 19 Pitminster to Staithe

The afternoon had a different character ... intended to be a water walk we followed the canal for a while, then the River Tone until the footpath disappeared into waist-high nettles ... four of us went over a field and jumped a dyke to get on to a country lane and out of trouble ... later followed the river again then lanes in to the camp ... ***GJ***

No rush, Albion crew day. Alex, Miriam and me. To Burrow Mump. Nice campsite. Drove a couple of miles in the opposite direction before realising. Mare and foal. Dug fire pit, gathered wood, big sawing session. Alex, Miriam and I went in white 'Awakening' to Mump. Climbed up, had a cup of tea (Alex's flask), peace pipe! Alex and Miriam could see Glastonbury Tor. Sarah back from London. Lynne left for eight days. Mel out on the tiles, visiting old friend. Nate Willow Whistle. 10.30 bed. ***SS***

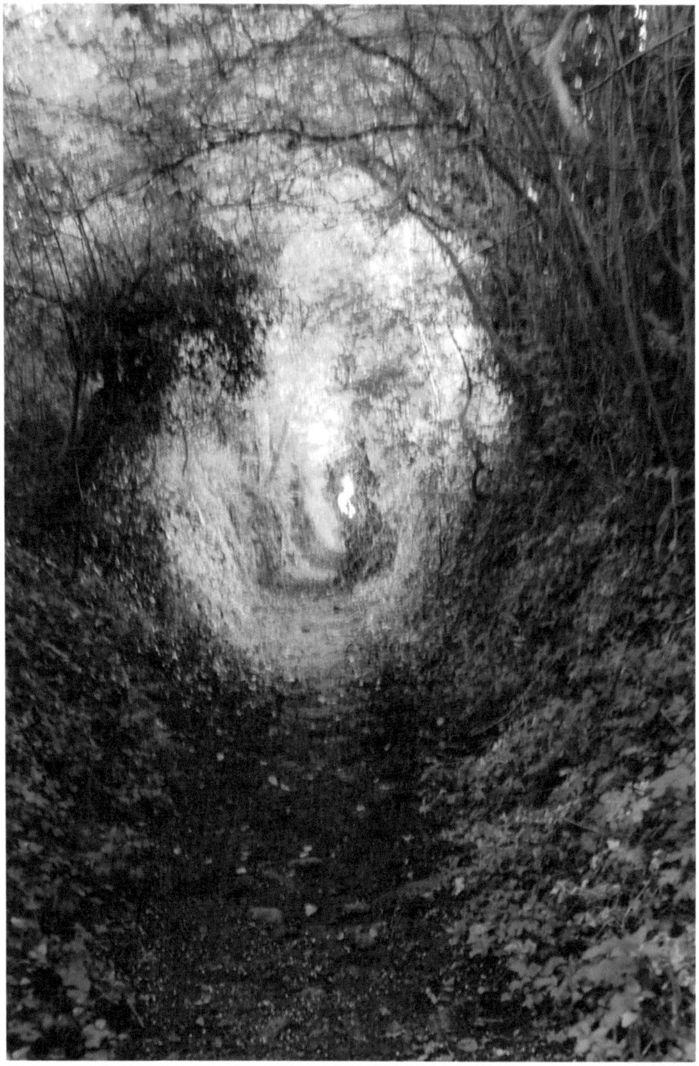

Walked a half day today, through lots of farmers' fields, wheat and barley. Stopped at some churches. Felt irritable and picky at people. Visited Burrow Mump in the afternoon, with Carolin and Graham.
We talked about the beauty, peace and timelessness of the Somerset Levels behind us, contrasted with the seeming "peak oil", splashed on the front of the newspapers in a garage where we stopped. I would like to ignore media hype and think of the coming changes to our life style as a result of the end of oil supplies, as a positive and healing thing.

Heard woodpeckers today. I saw a big red deer, a stag, standing drinking at the river last night. Magnificent. Lovely campsite, we are at Staithe. There are two little ol' dogs. One stole a fox skull out of Alex's truck! Ha!

ML

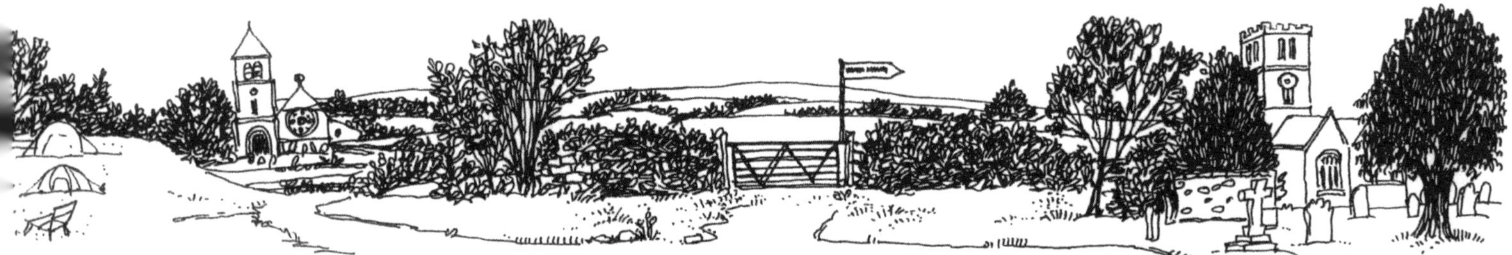

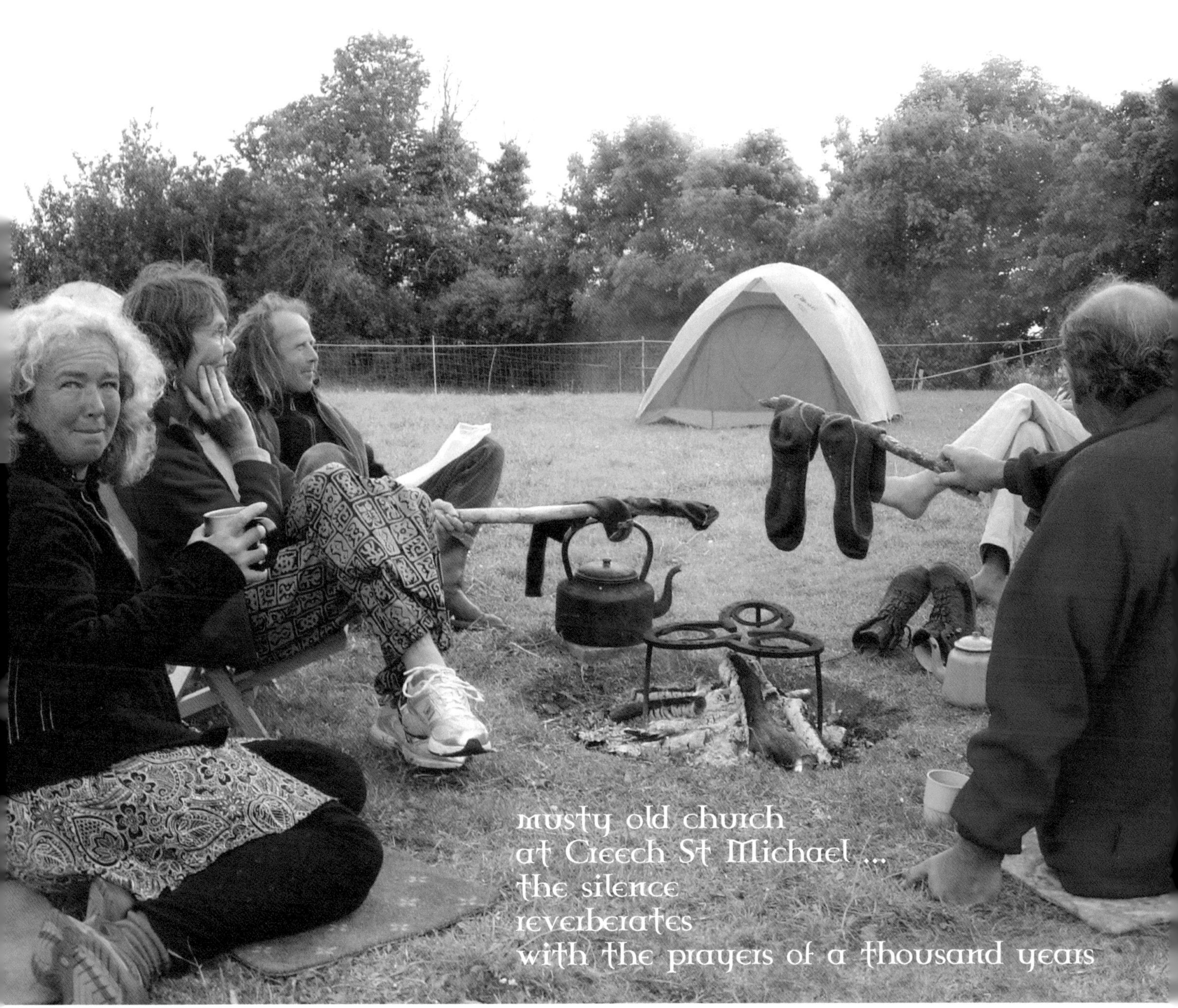

musty old church
at Creech St Michael ...
the silence
reverberates
with the prayers of a thousand years

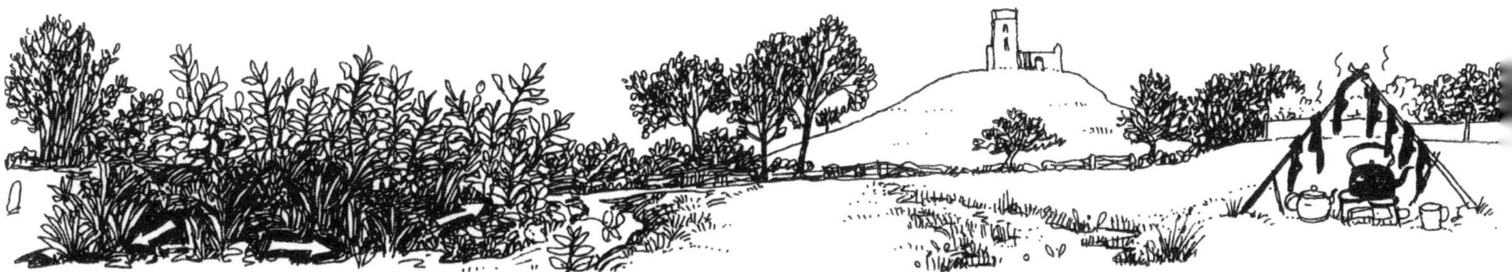

green field
scattered tents
campfire ashes
pilgrims sleep ... sun rises
somewhere in Somerset

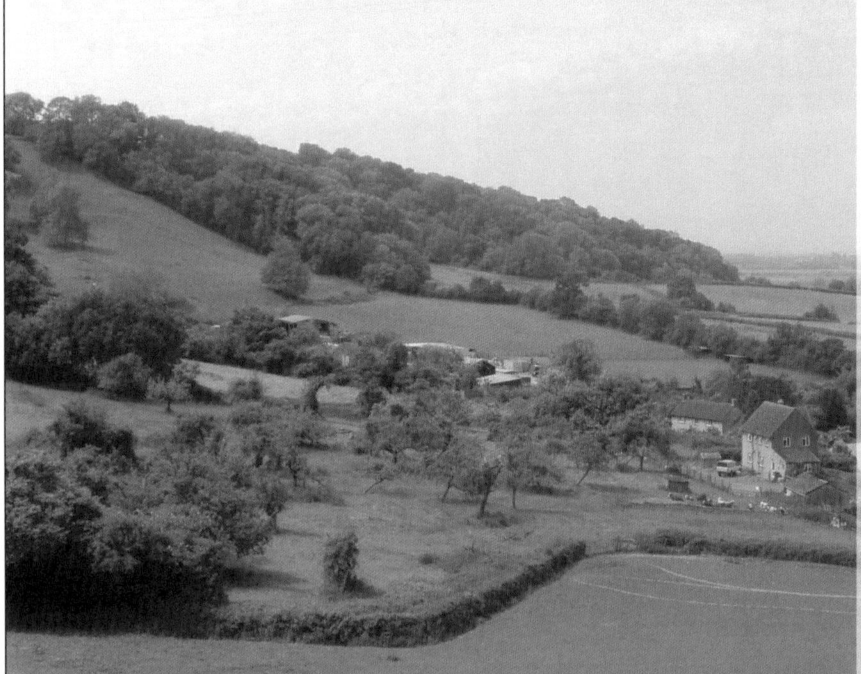

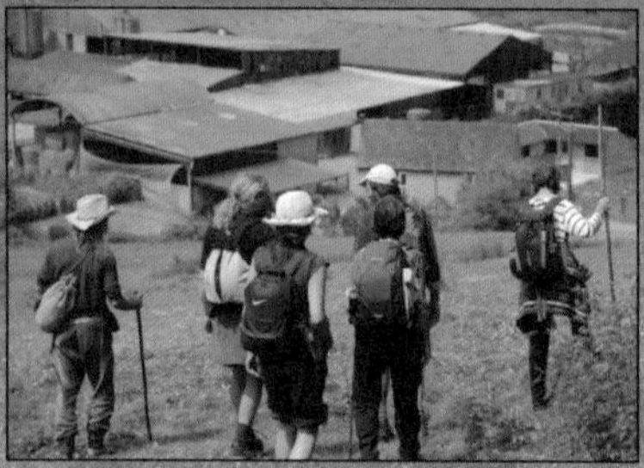

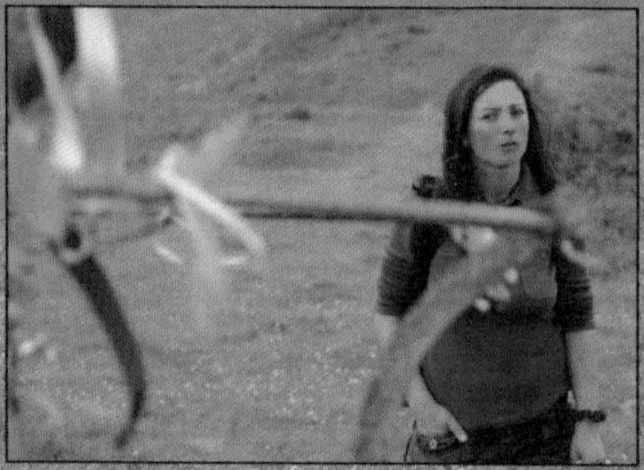

This morning when we left the farm, the lovely little tan and white Jack Russell dog who was biting at Christine's gaiters, followed us for a good mile, and I walked her back. I felt absurdly pleased to see that everyone had waited for me. Some people were hiding in the shelter of a hollow tree. I think it was a willow, or maybe an ash. From that moment on I felt loved and loving all day.

We walked through boggy woods and saw a white butterfly orchid. We walked across the Somerset levels, sprinkled with buttercups, along the old drovers' roads. We walked through fields with huge bulls in them, and through an estate, Sharpham Park, which is organic and has rare breeds: alpacas, white park cattle, hebridean and manx loghtan sheep.

I got some nice compliments from people in our community today, I feel proud and affirmed and cared for. Melody left today and I felt a wrench of sadness. Some new people came: Geoff, Julie, their sons Jim, Max and Harry, Ruth, Lois, Kieran and I think some others too. Big group!

Walked up "Weary-all" or Worral Hill, where the Glastonbury Thorn stands, it is all decorated with ribbons. Apparently Joseph of Aramethea stuck his staff in the ground and the thorn tree grew. I thought it looked like a bit of a poor old thing. Had fun today, laughing with Steve, Graham and Alex. Waded through big nettles!

ML

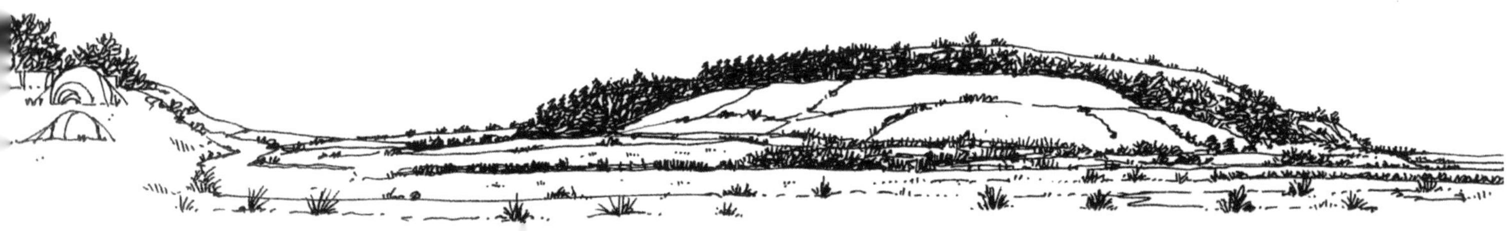

Day 20 Staithe to Glastonbury

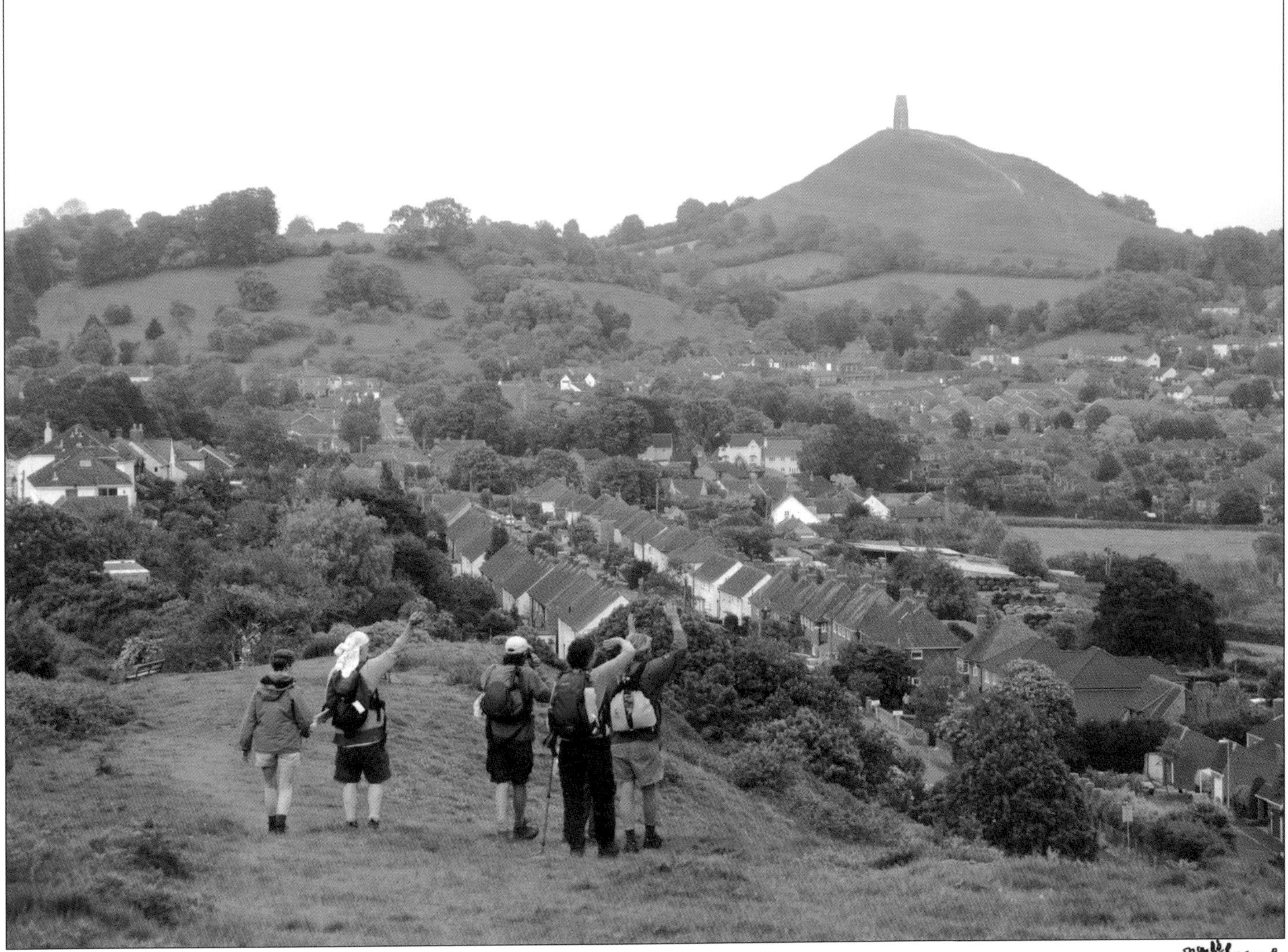

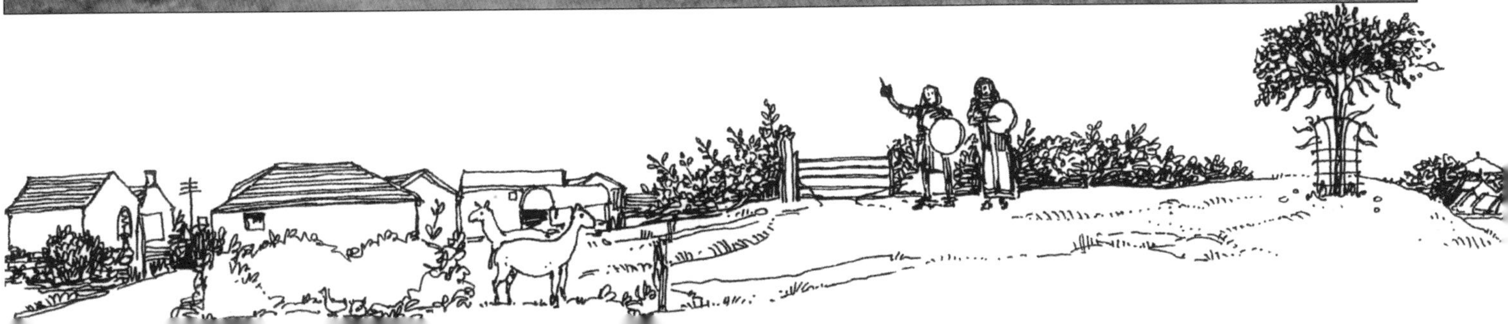

Day 21

Rest Day at Glastonbury

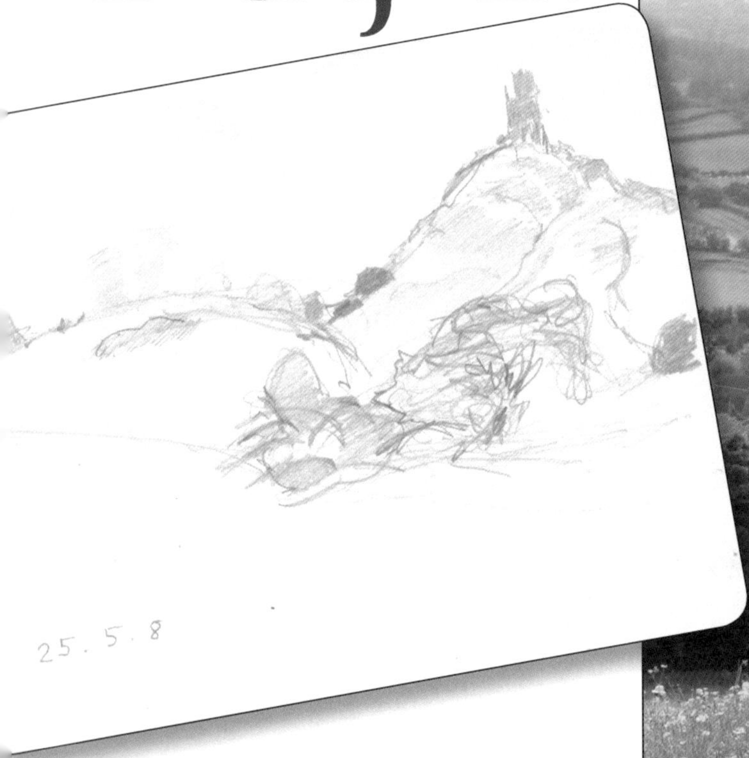

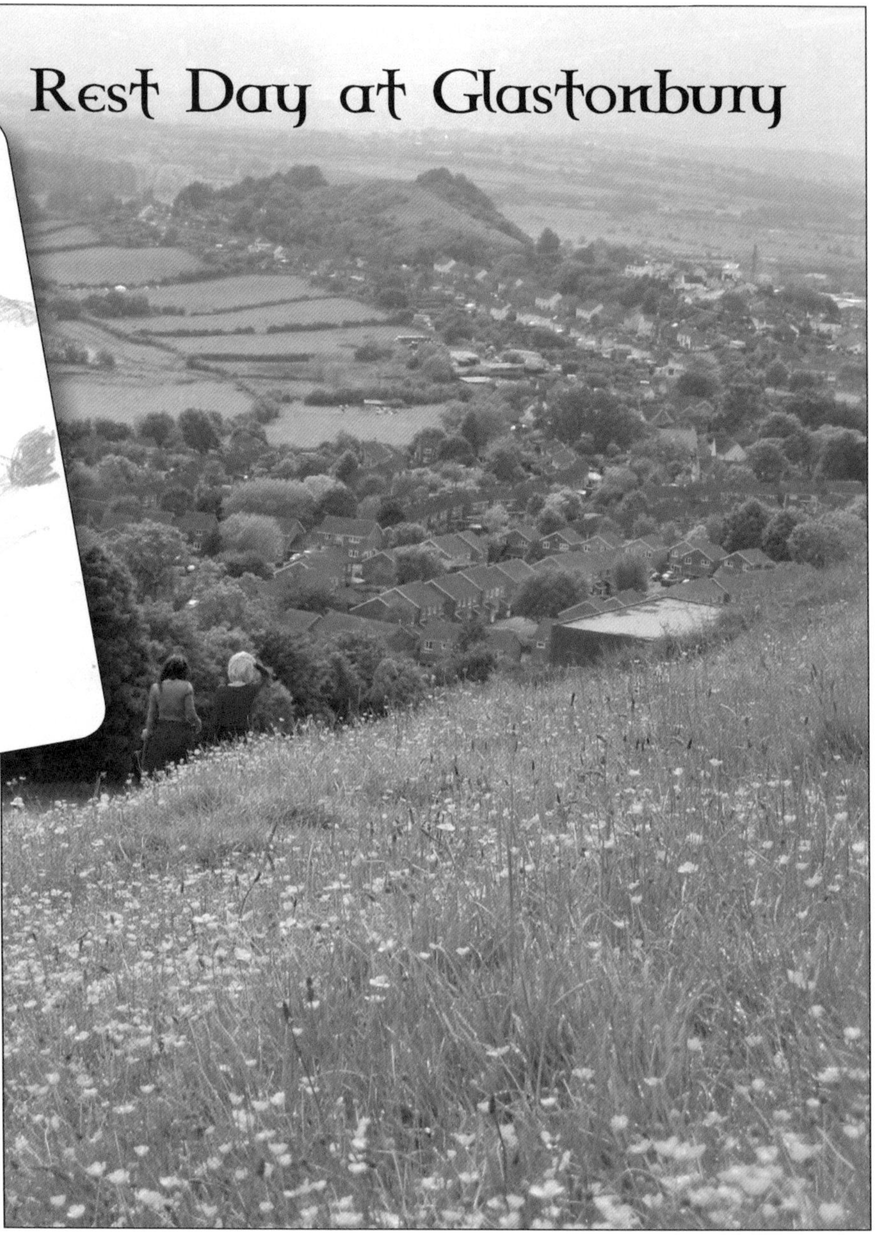

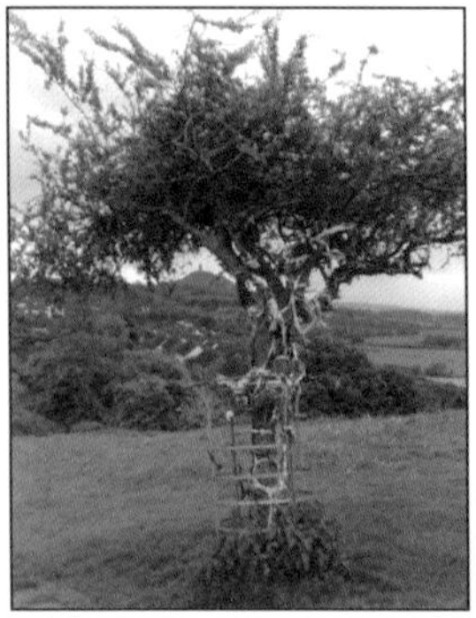

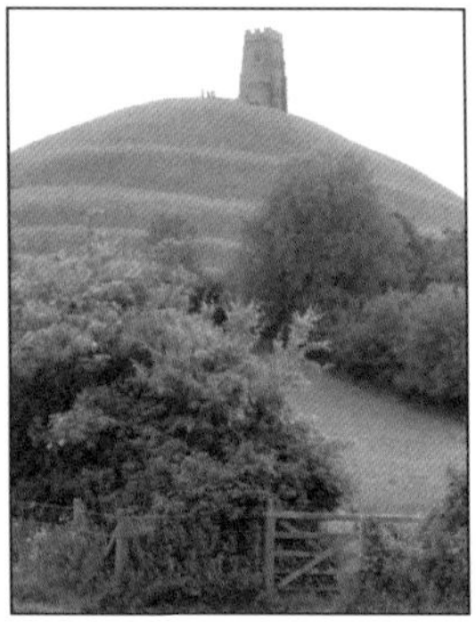

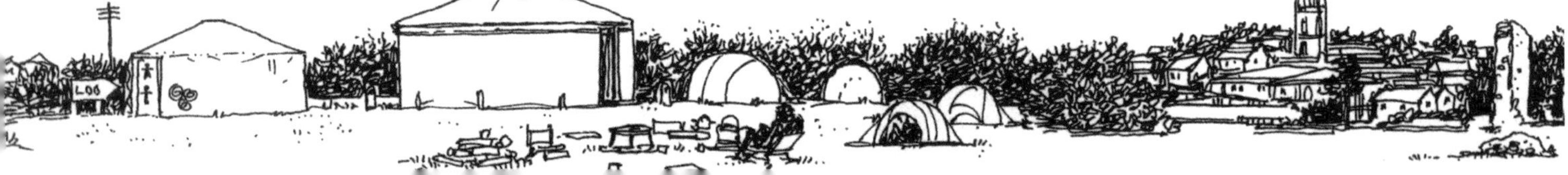

What a night. Strong winds and heavy rain. Wet morning. Up 9.00am. Tea, straight back to bed. It's great to have a cup of tea in bed in the morning. First on walk. Yeah. Three weeks. Amazing! Day of rest. Went into the town of Street with Mel and Carolin to do the laundry. It took hours, had a little stroll and bought some toffees. Went to Sainsbury's then home. Chilled out until dinner. Very gentle. Christine left. She was very generous. She left me a micra towel, blister plasters and essential oils for everyone and a rucksack for Graham to borrow. And not forgetting chocolate and Kendal mint cake, what a sweetheart! Nick arrived (mens' lodge member). Cathy arrived. Busy, Busy. Ian came to visit. Nate shows how to make Willow Whistle. I must learn, practice so I can show Melody whom I promised. I could hear a Rave going on in the distance on the wind. Loud thunder. A touch of heavy rain. Hot toddy (scotch, lemon and hot water) made by Alex. Time for sleep. 11.05pm.

SS

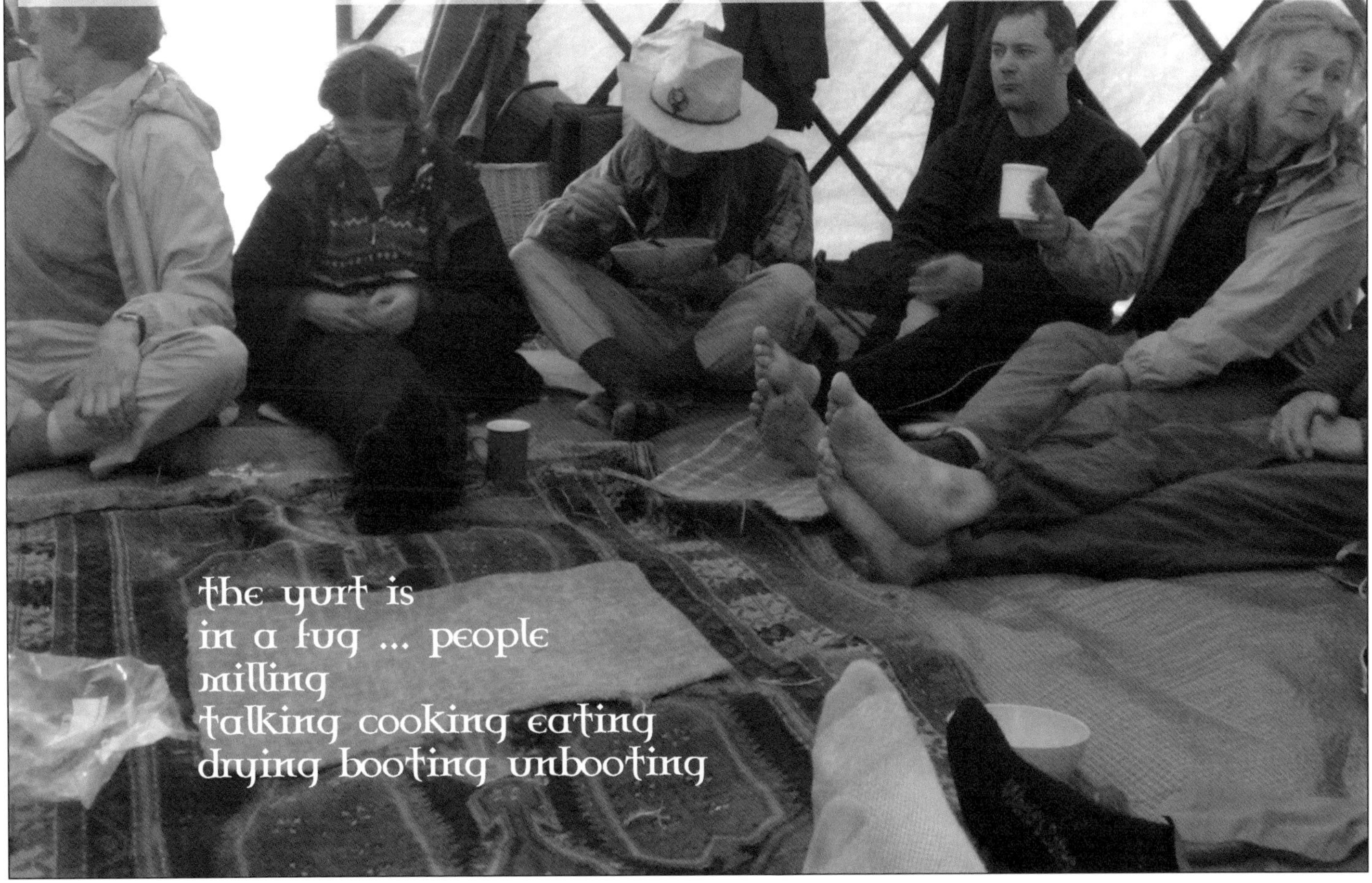

the yurt is
in a fug ... people
milling
talking cooking eating
drying booting unbooting

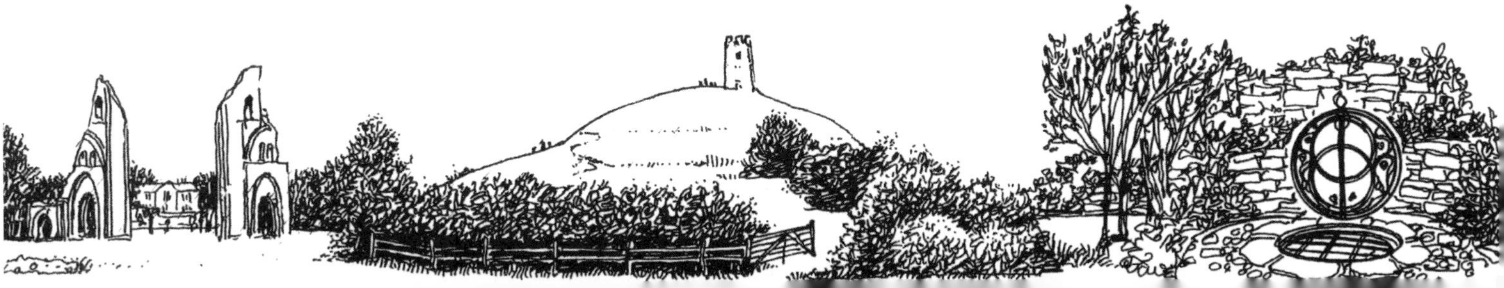

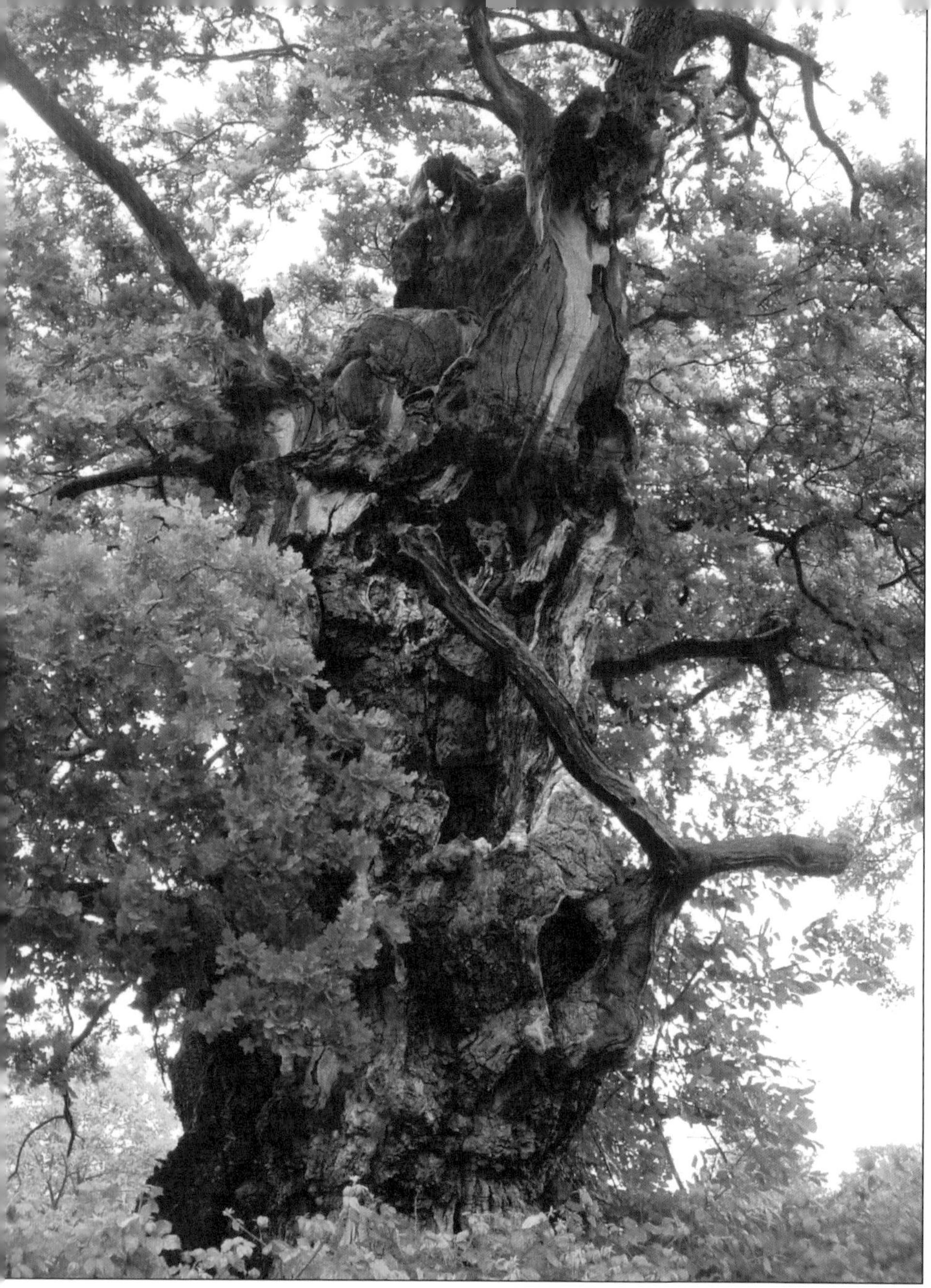

It was a really windy day today generating the most difficult walking conditions we have experienced so far. The day started with the challenge of striking the camp including both yurts, in strong winds and rain, then carry all the gear up the field, up a slippery muddy slope and past the house quietly so as not to disturb the meditators and onto the van parked ¼ a mile away on the street. The weather conditions meant packing everything wet and consequently everything is damp this evening.

Once packed, we set off to Glastonbury Tor. The wind was fierce as we climbed in a line with heads down and jaws set against the driving rain. The wind was so strong at the top we could actually lean against it as it drove through the arches of St Michael's Tower. We made our way down the north east side of the Tor, all the time battling with the wind as it attempted to blow us over the edge of the hill, passed two ancient oaks at the bottom called Gog and Magog and into the parallel world of Avalon. We walk in these hazardous conditions, for what seemed like eons, on constant alert for the falling branches and precarious electric cables.

SB

Five of us stopped at the Poachers Pouch at Chelynch for tea and to warm up by the fire ... we then proceeded to get thoroughly lost ... no arrows to follow ... had some vague ideas of where the campsite was but they were wrong ... it was misty ... some lovely walking through woodland and saw deer ... am I ever really lost?

GJ

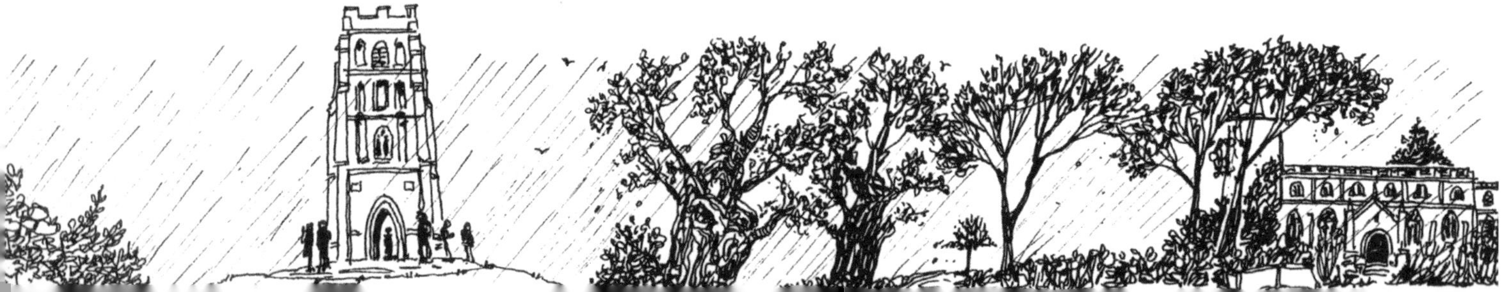

cold rain drives
the Somerset levels
tramping on ...
wind in my face
hands in my pockets

we're lost –
no arrows point
the way
the map is obscure
the campsite uncertain

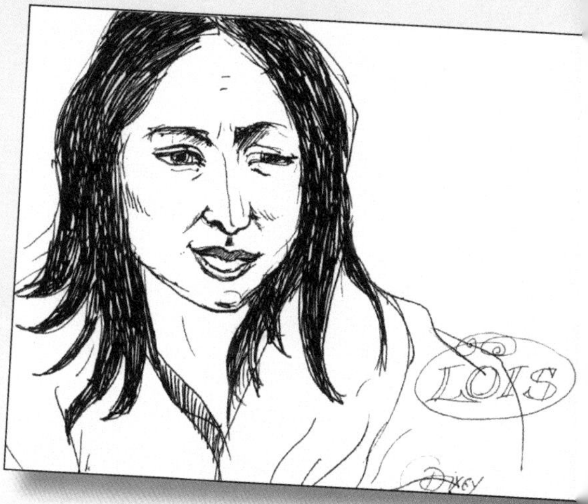

Day 22 Glastonbury to Cranmore

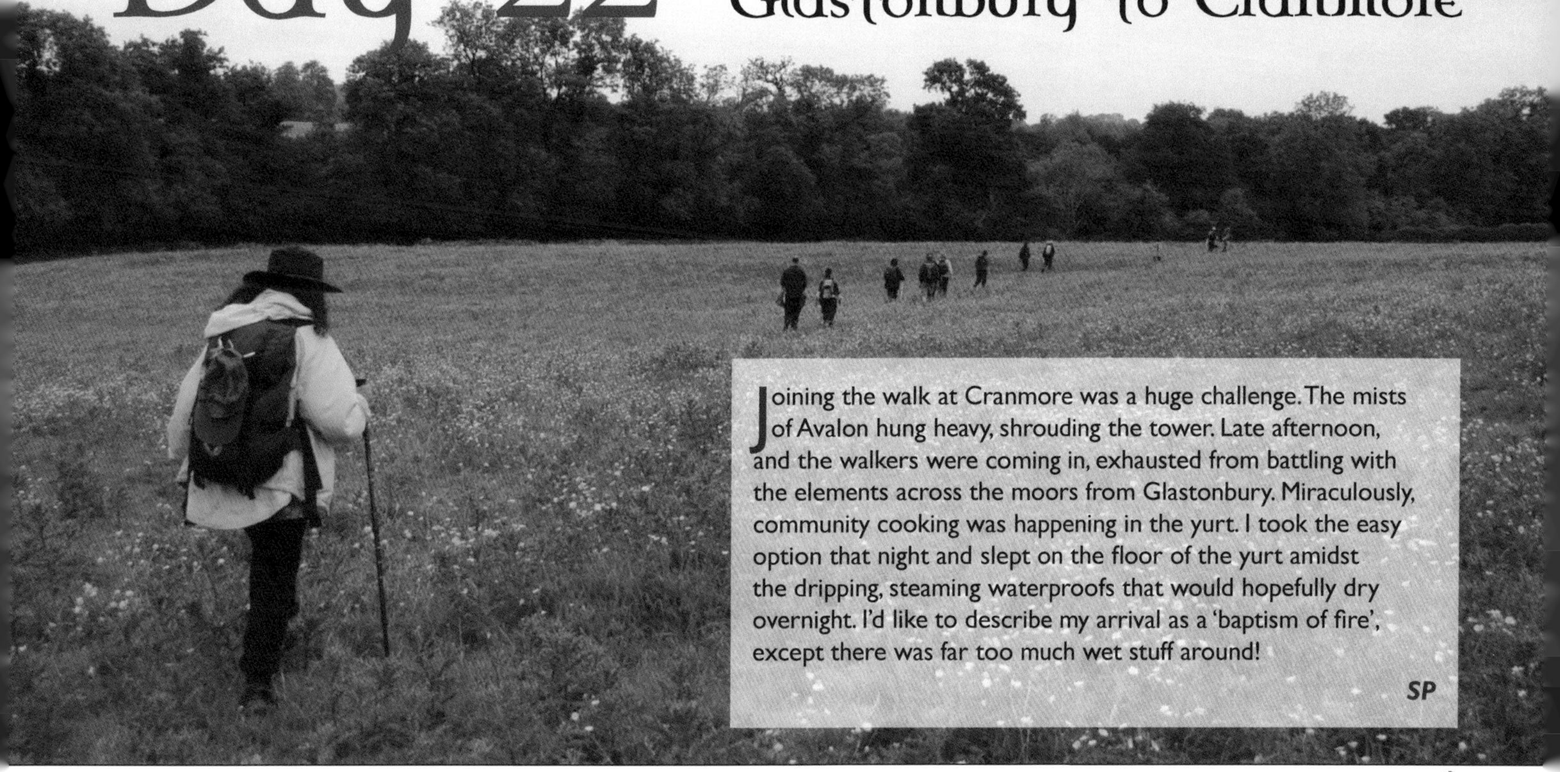

Joining the walk at Cranmore was a huge challenge. The mists of Avalon hung heavy, shrouding the tower. Late afternoon, and the walkers were coming in, exhausted from battling with the elements across the moors from Glastonbury. Miraculously, community cooking was happening in the yurt. I took the easy option that night and slept on the floor of the yurt amidst the dripping, steaming waterproofs that would hopefully dry overnight. I'd like to describe my arrival as a 'baptism of fire', except there was far too much wet stuff around!

SP

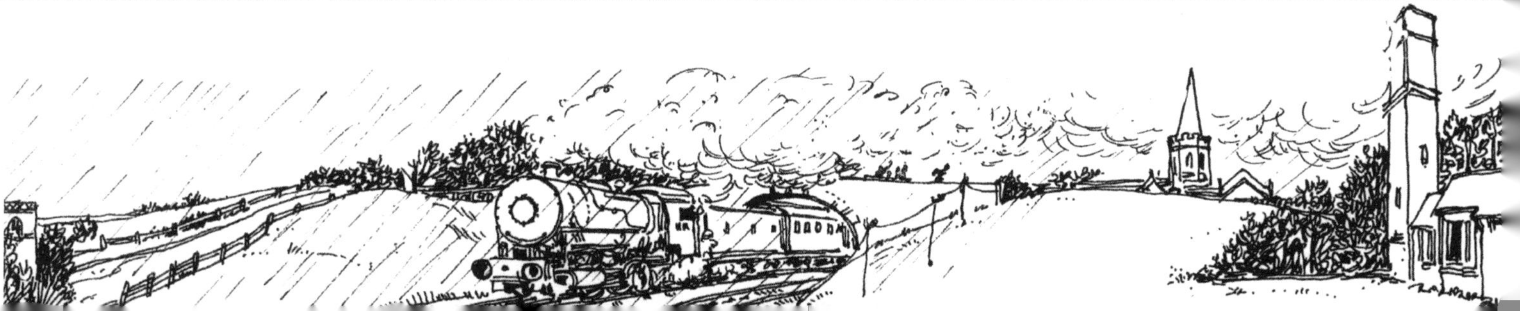

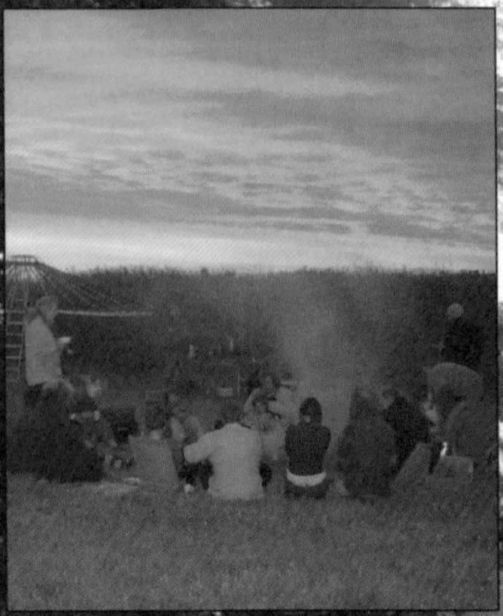

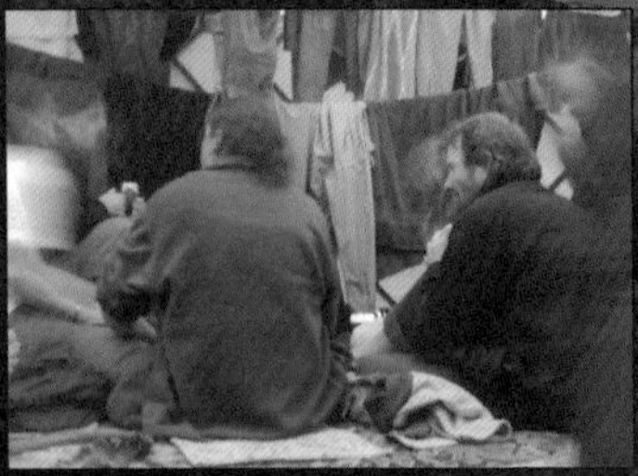

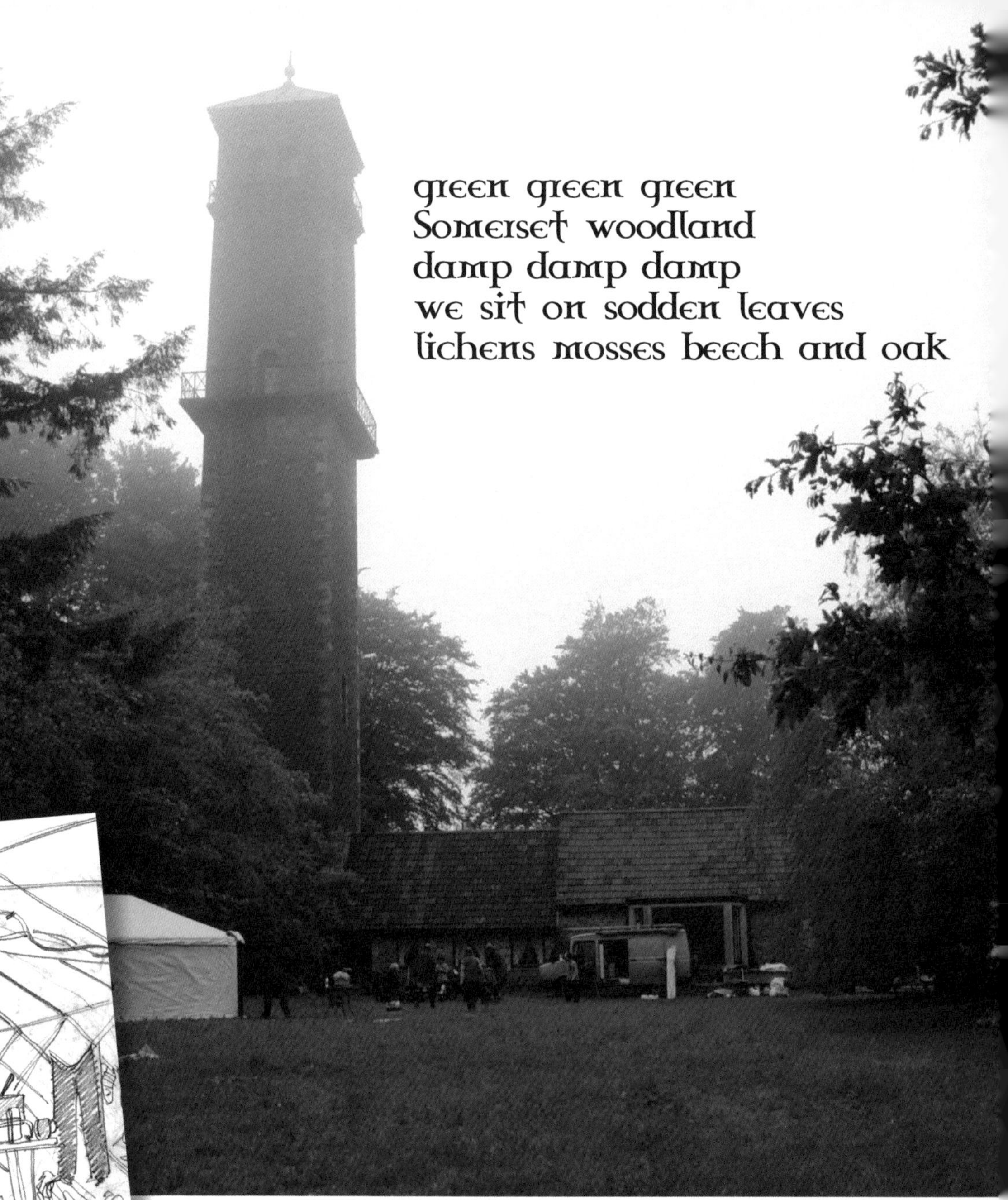

green green green
Somerset woodland
damp damp damp
we sit on sodden leaves
lichens mosses beech and oak

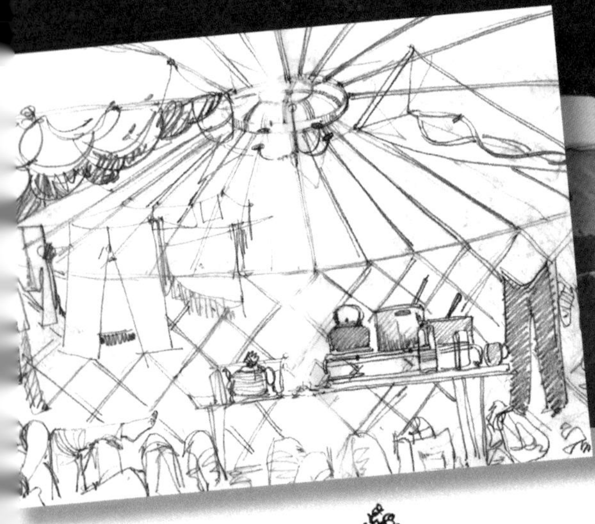

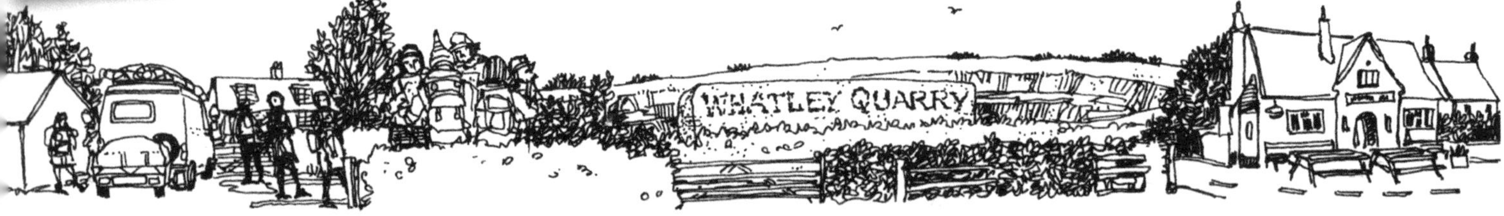

It is so nice to be dry! And warm! Hurrah for a warm fire and a fine day! Dried my boots and sleeping bag in Alex's truck. He is a good kind man. We are camping at Hoopers Pool, near Trowbridge.

It was tough today, especially this morning. In the night a branch fell onto my tent and hit me on the head. It was horrid waking up late after dozing on and off all night with noisy drips of water onto the tent. Chatted with Farhed who gave me a little book on the teachings of Baha Ullah, the Bahai. We talked about humanity, meditation, prayer, love and a personal relationship with God.

Saw a deer running across a field today. We stopped for cider and lemonade at a pub. We left Somerset and entered Wiltshire today. We got lost and had lunch at a different church to the arranged one. Lots of lanes and footpaths today, heavy, claggy mud under foot, beautiful soft barley, a white horse cut in the hill. We sang at Devil's Bed and Bolster stones, in the corner of a bean field. It was nice to chat with the kids today and to achieve a long walk, out of the self pity and low motivation of the morning and into high spirits and celebration of arriving at the next site. Gorgeous red sky tonight. Saw a big wooden sculpture of serpents, St Michael and St Mary.

ML

Nice to sleep in wood. Branch fell on Mel's tent, head. She's OK. Leaf mould all in tent. Damp, sticky pack up. Long day's walk. Graham on 'Albion'. Rhian and Alex map read. Lost but not lost. Called in 'Awakening' for lunch, change, new location church. Devil's rocks. Creamery pong, scum. Sewage plant, pongy. One pint of cider, Farmers Arms. Long day. Late already. Finished dinner. Took wet socks to 'Albion' 10.00.

SS

Walked footpaths across fields for hours today with the enjoyable company of B'anna and Nick. I was struck today by the way all the animals we encounter acknowledge our presence – a dog barks and wags his tail, a bullock runs across the field to see us, cows amble over to a gate, horses look up and may approach, sheep watch from a distance ...

SB

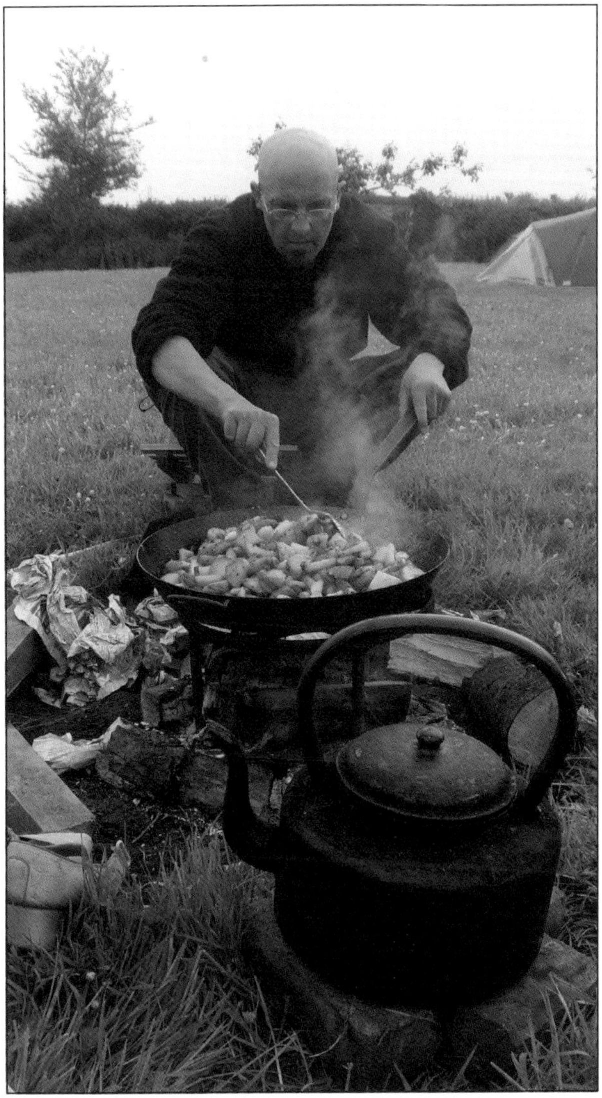

Day 23 Cranmore to Hoopers Pool

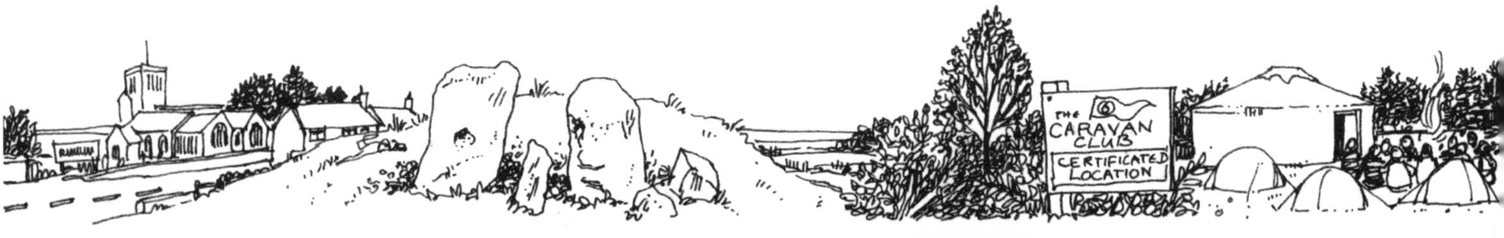

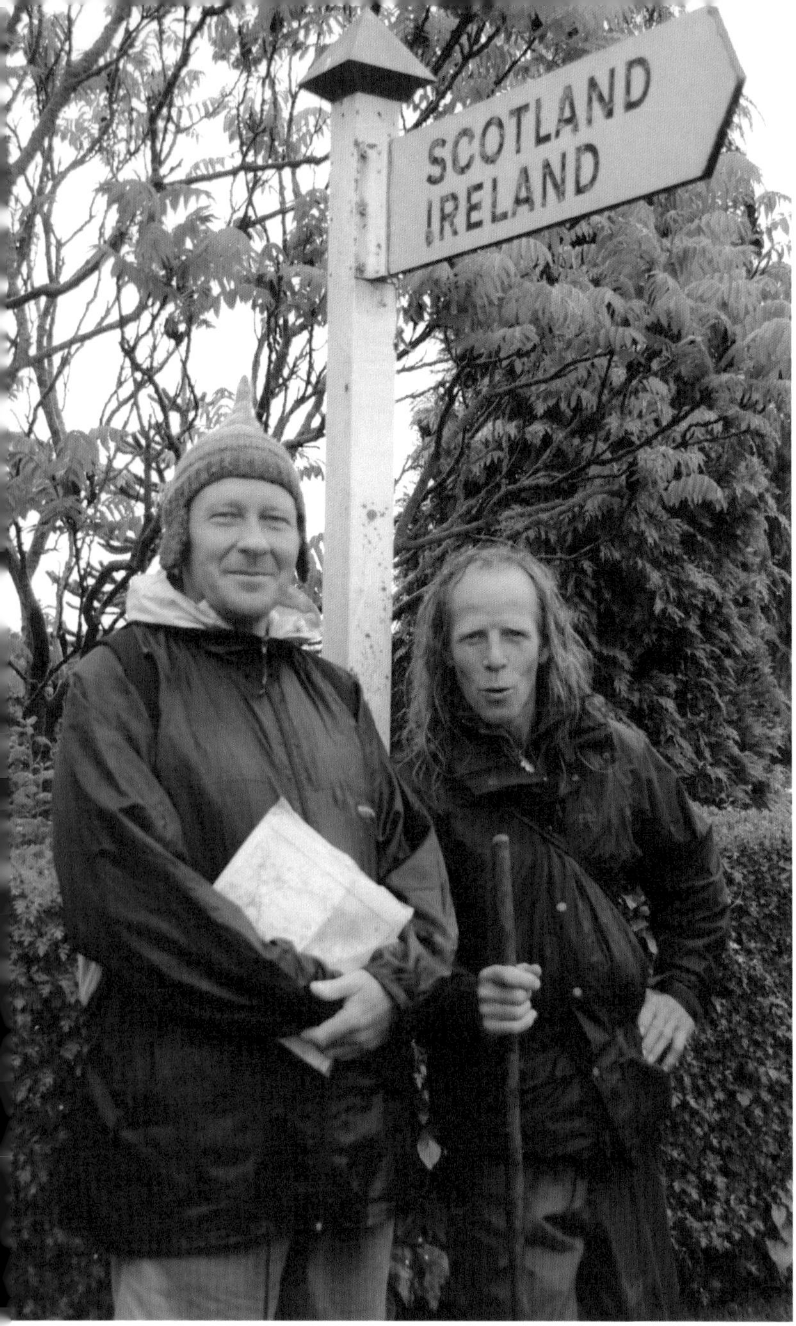

Woke up this morning to find my spirits lifted, which is great! Took down the yurt frame and ended up not crewing as there were so many people wanting to ride. It rained pretty much all day. We walked through Trowbridge and had lunch under a bridge by the canal at Whaddon. There were some little moorhen chicks. We saw a majestic, almost pre-historic looking heron rise up and flap effortlessly to the other bank, on long, languid wings. We saw lots of barges and brightly painted long boats.

Today we passed the halfway point on our journey across Albion. Some of us crept into a wooded copse on a modern housing estate to sing and build a shrine to the crossing of the lines and the heart of our journey. We left a many pointed arrow, tobacco, a spiral, crystals and flowers. It felt magical and bizarre.

We are staying at the Three Magpies, at Sells Green. A lovely evening in the yurt. Graham spoke about Avebury and the connections with the quarter point festivals, Imbolc, Beltane, Lammas and Samhain, and the earth goddess in her different incarnations, birth, maiden, mother, and crone, and how the land and the stones signify these things. We all sat in a circle and listened, then we gave each other foot, head and back massages, sang an earth chant and ate banana rice pudding, made by Nate, in the warm, steamy yurt. What a delicious evening!

The woman at the campsite this morning gave us five dozen eggs and we ate a 66 egg omelette for tea!! I heard woodpeckers today. Life is good. ***ML***

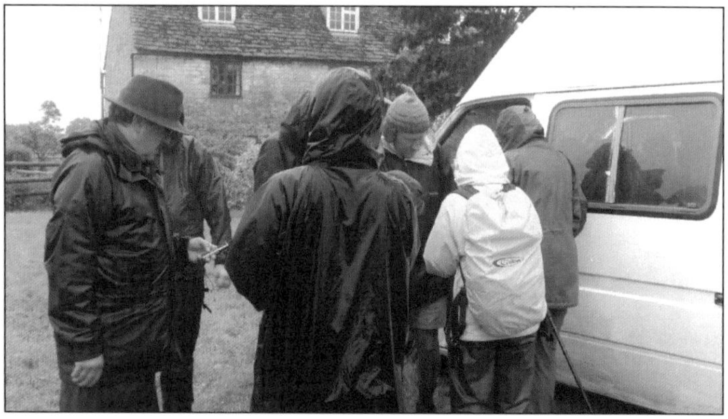

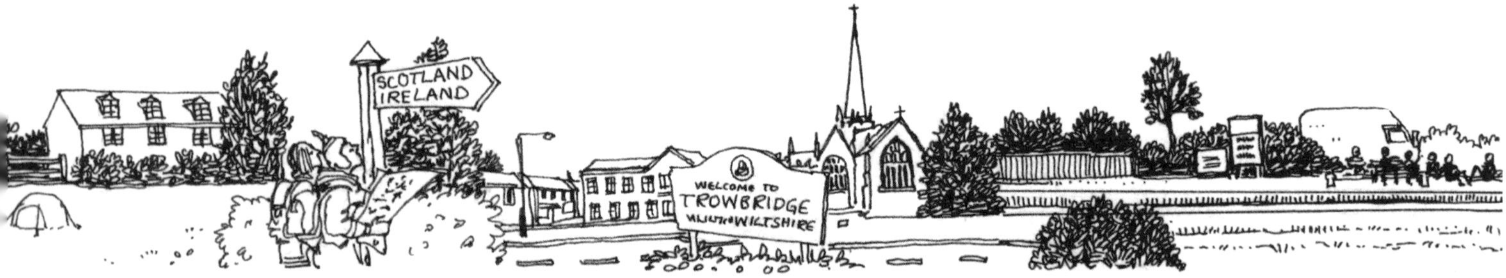

Day 24 Hoopers Pool to Sells Green

six dozen
eggs in this omelette ...
carefully
we manoeuvre
the giant frying pan

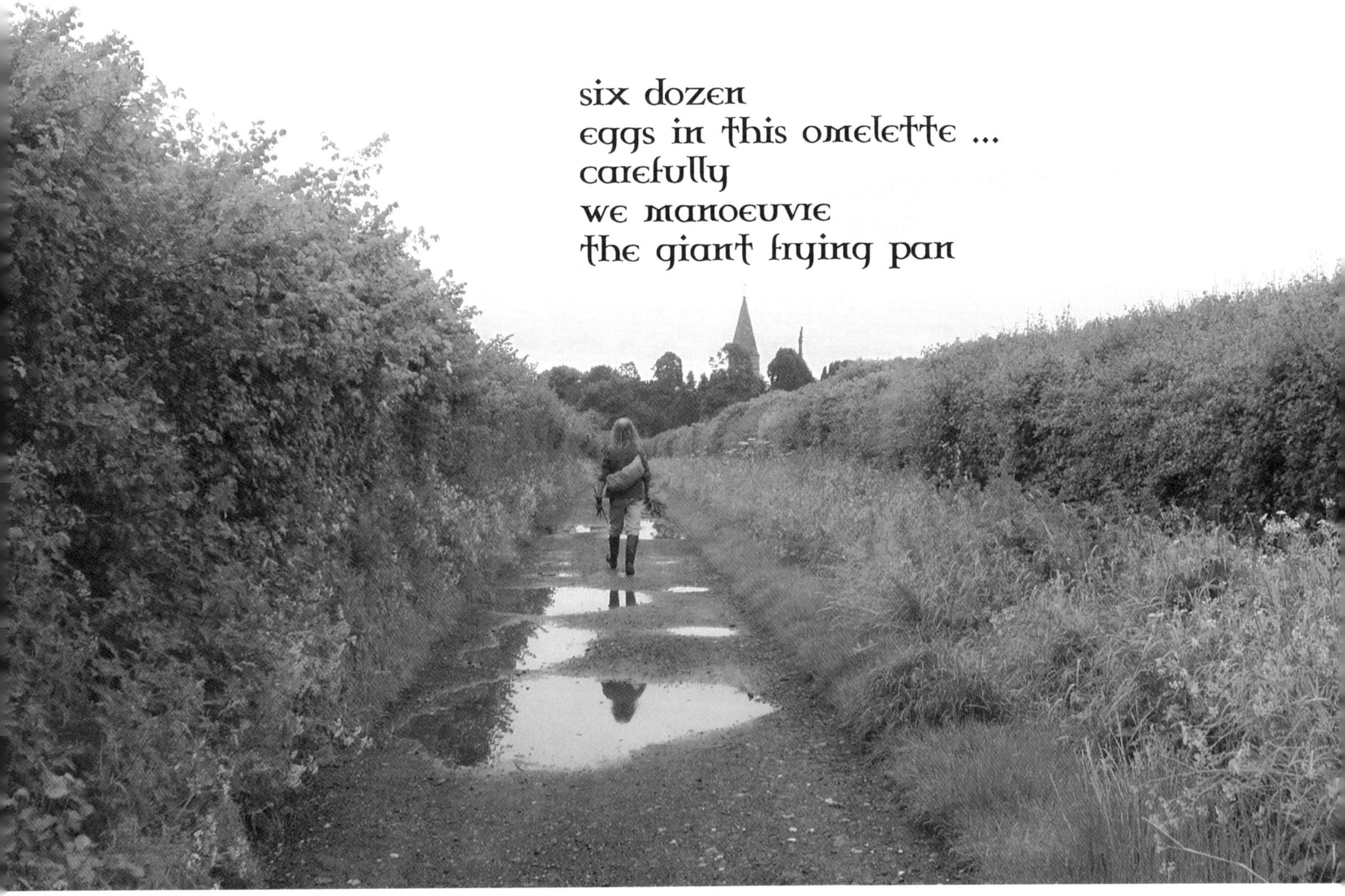

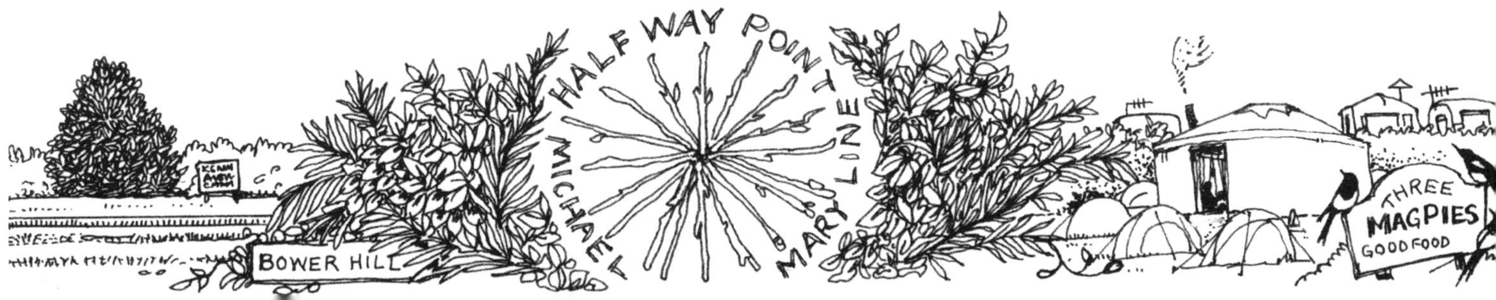

Day 25 Sells Green to Avebury

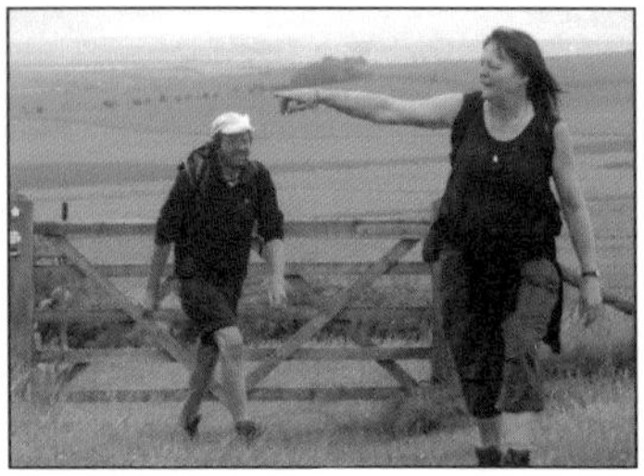

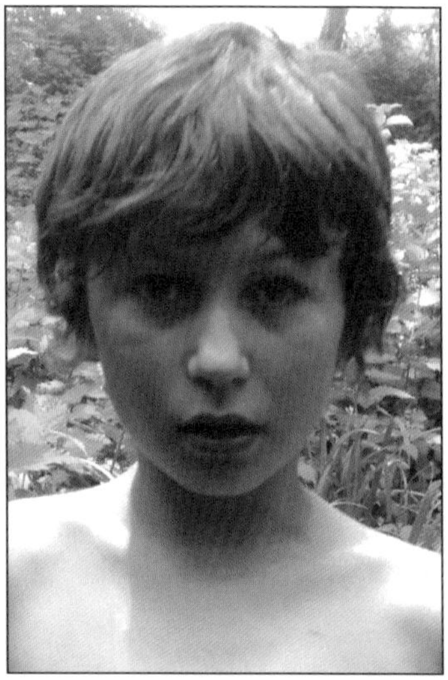

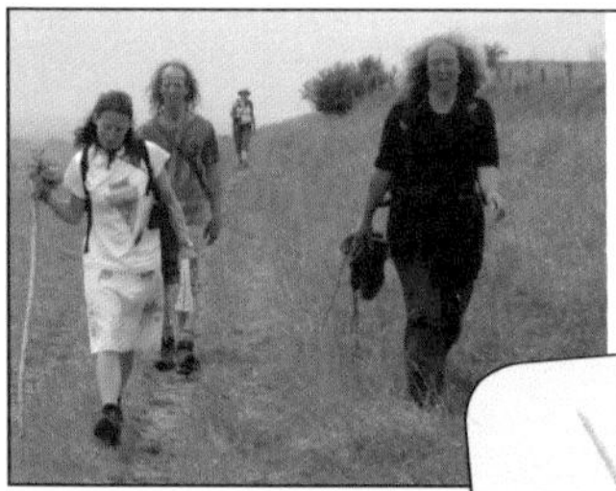

Fantastic day. Oliver's Castle ... the leylines cross there. Then on to Windmill Hill and Avebury. Saw a hare at close range near Windmill Hill. ***RH***

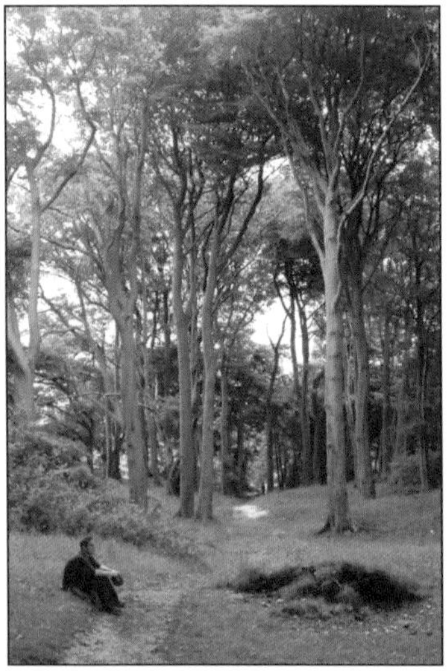

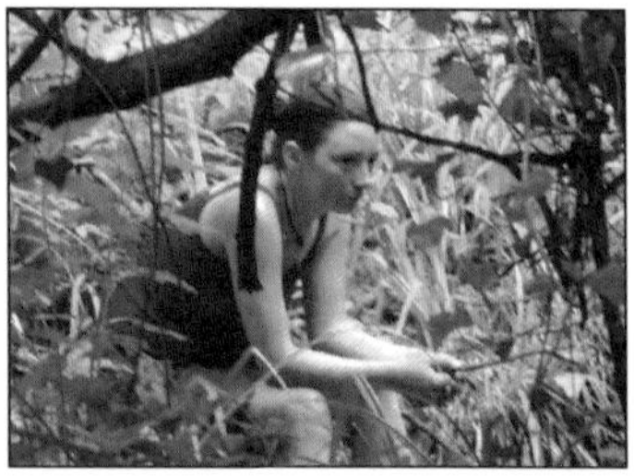

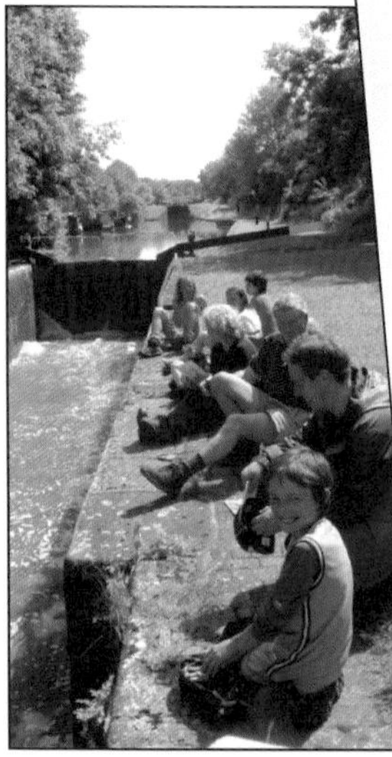

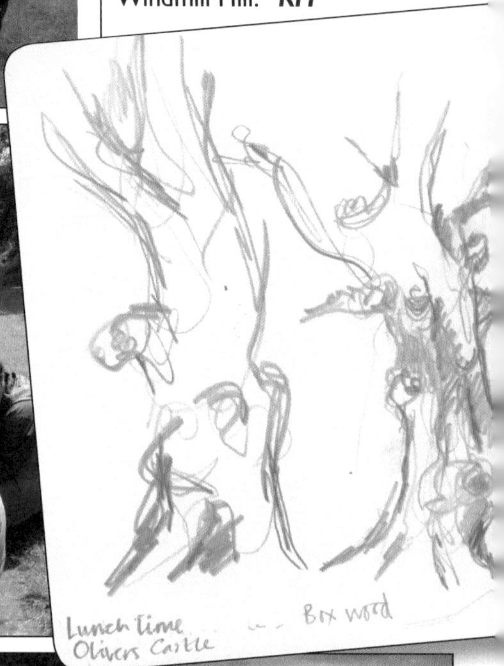

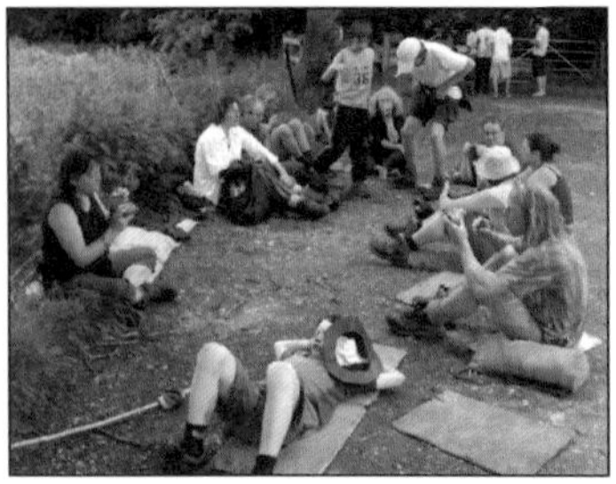

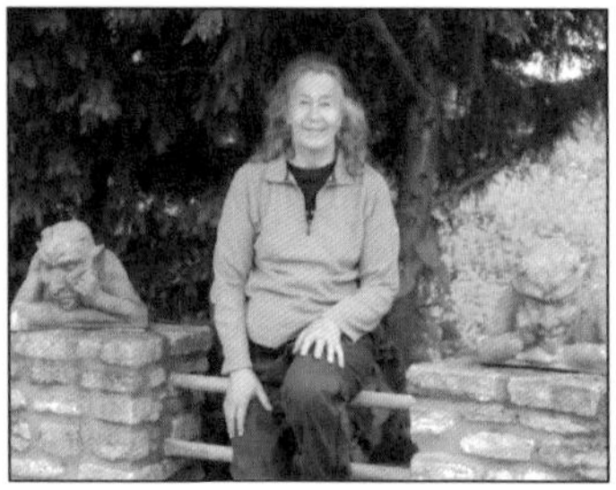

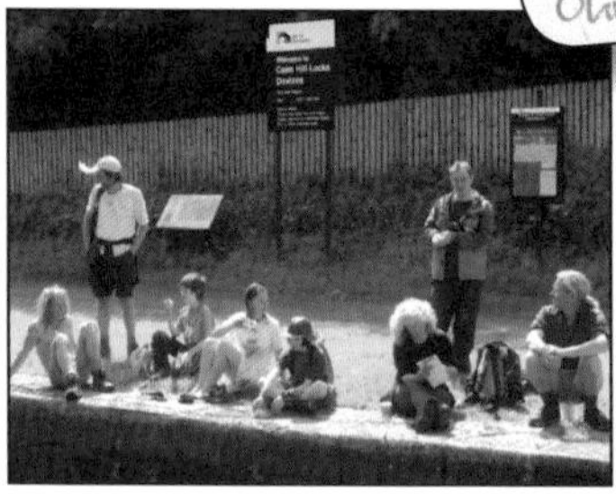

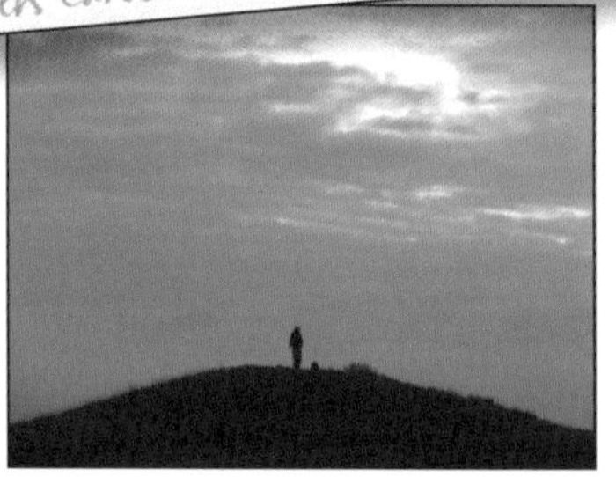

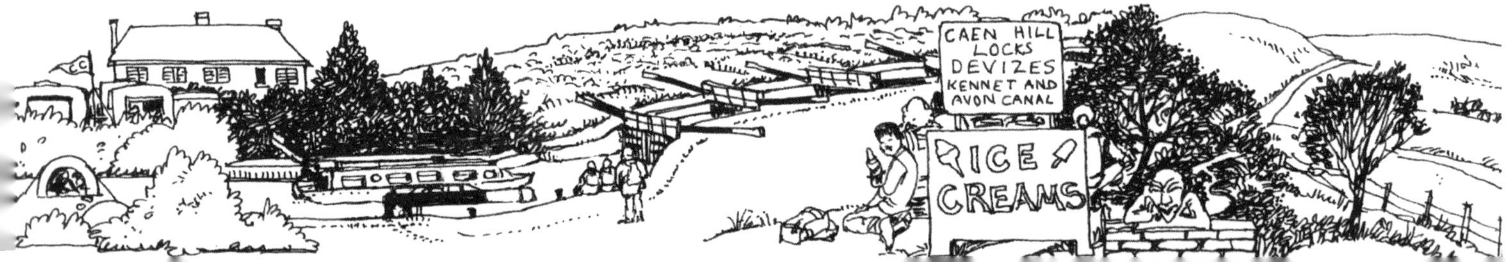

smoke swirls
around the campfire
conversation
swirls around the group ...
I sit there swirling

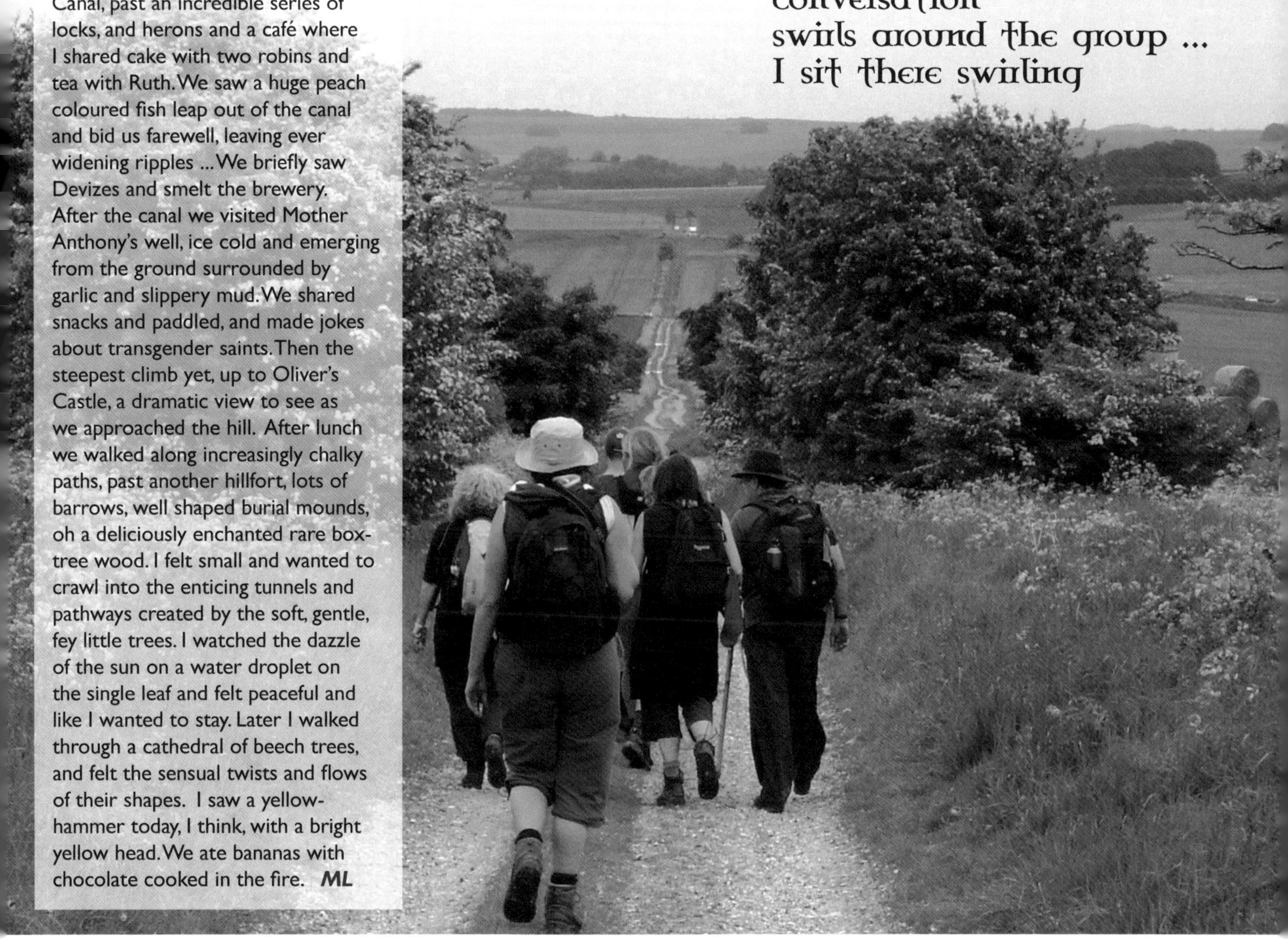

Gorgeous day's walking: along more of the Kennet and Avon Canal, past an incredible series of locks, and herons and a café where I shared cake with two robins and tea with Ruth. We saw a huge peach coloured fish leap out of the canal and bid us farewell, leaving ever widening ripples ... We briefly saw Devizes and smelt the brewery. After the canal we visited Mother Anthony's well, ice cold and emerging from the ground surrounded by garlic and slippery mud. We shared snacks and paddled, and made jokes about transgender saints. Then the steepest climb yet, up to Oliver's Castle, a dramatic view to see as we approached the hill. After lunch we walked along increasingly chalky paths, past another hillfort, lots of barrows, well shaped burial mounds, oh a deliciously enchanted rare box-tree wood. I felt small and wanted to crawl into the enticing tunnels and pathways created by the soft, gentle, fey little trees. I watched the dazzle of the sun on a water droplet on the single leaf and felt peaceful and like I wanted to stay. Later I walked through a cathedral of beech trees, and felt the sensual twists and flows of their shapes. I saw a yellow-hammer today, I think, with a bright yellow head. We ate bananas with chocolate cooked in the fire. ***ML***

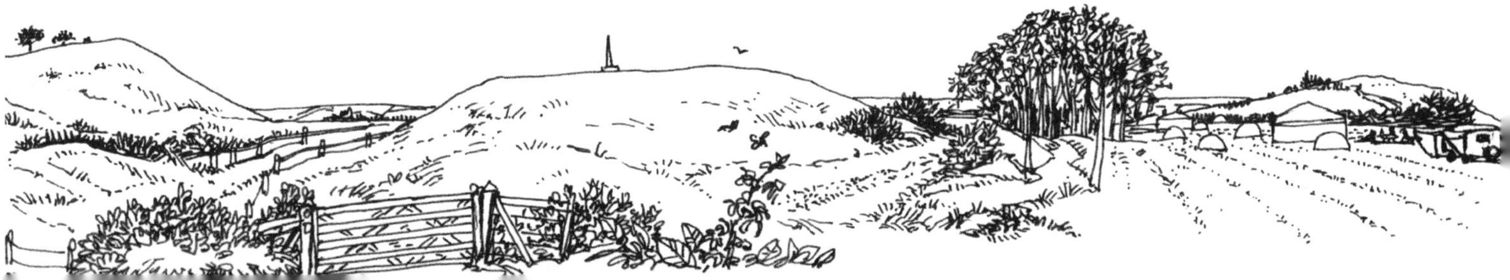

night on the
ancestors' hill – I wake
to starlight
waning moon … misty dawn
tranquility

Ian came and brought a gorgeous cake he had made in the shape of Silbury Hill – dear sweet man! Did a fire show after tea. Nate gave me the opportunity to have a go. It was fantastic to spin the wire wool basket and send showers of sparks spraying all around me. B'Anna gave me a gorgeous necklace made from a shell found on the beach in California. Dear sweet Nate and B'Anna are leaving tomorrow. They will be sorely missed.

We had a very hot sweat tonight, amazing! Feel so grateful and real and me and right. Had fun today and feel refreshed.

ML

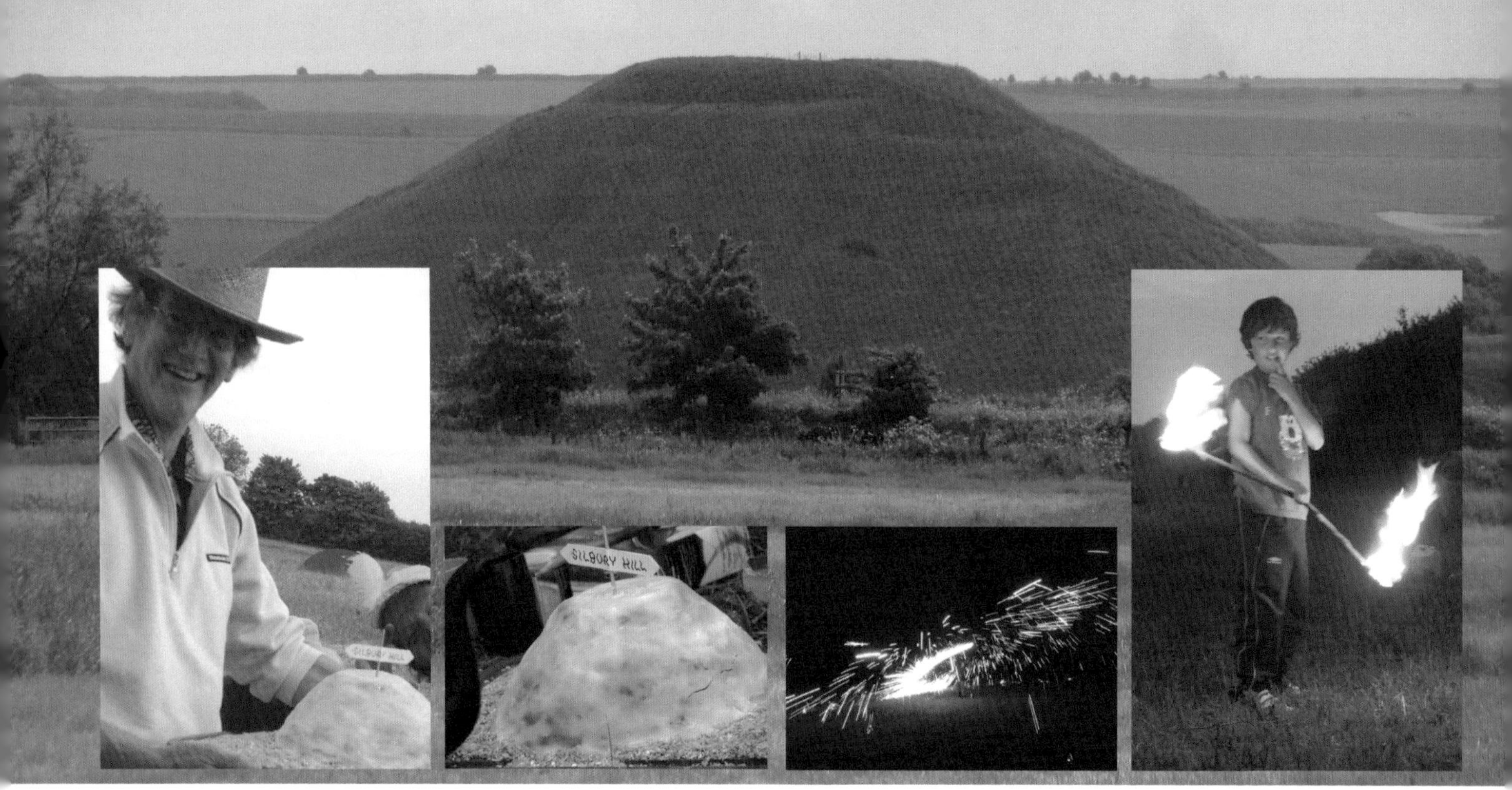

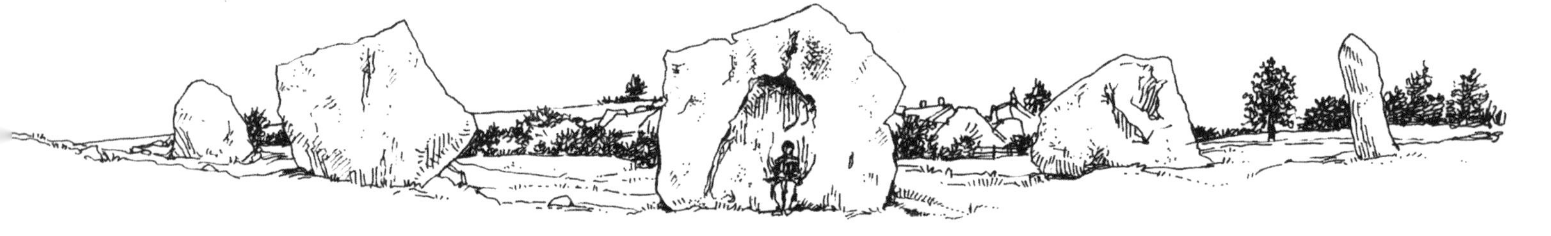

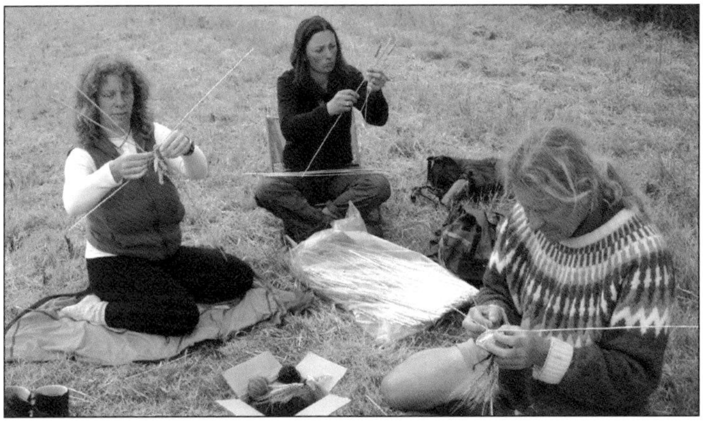
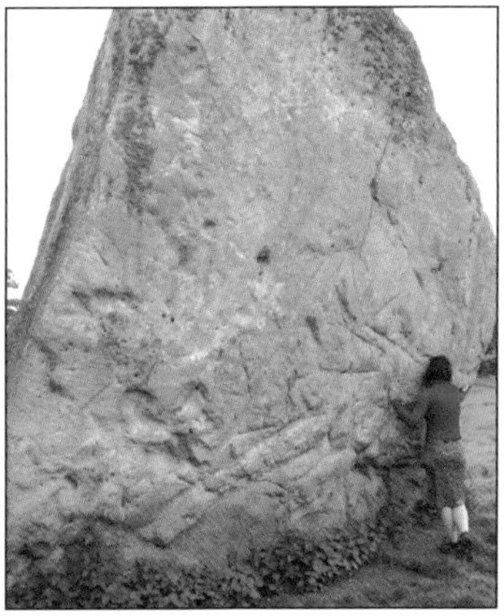
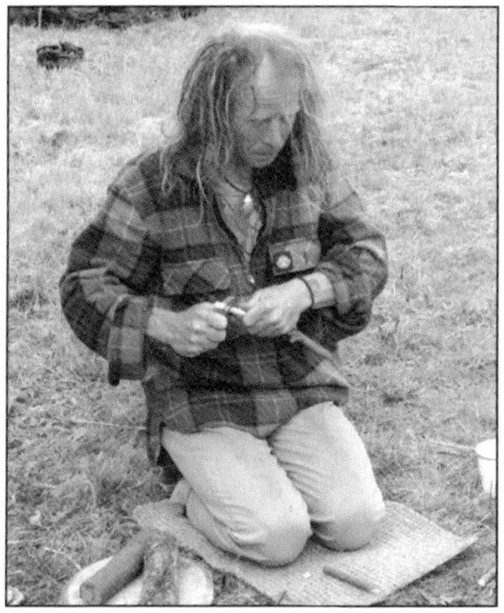
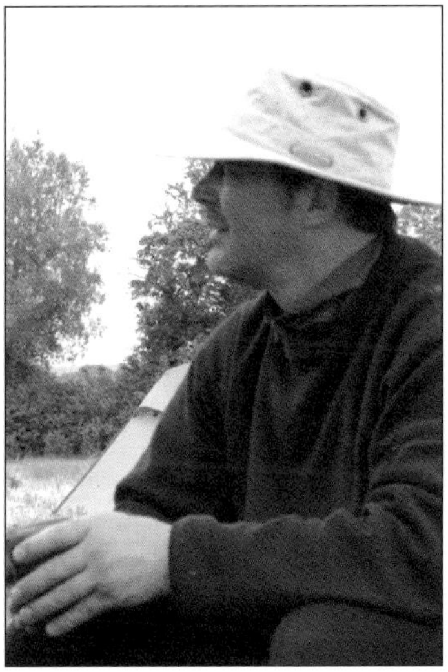

Followed the Kennet River through Avebury and on down to West Kennet Long Barrow. Had a wash in the river on the way! Walked back along the Avenue. What a place! ***RH***

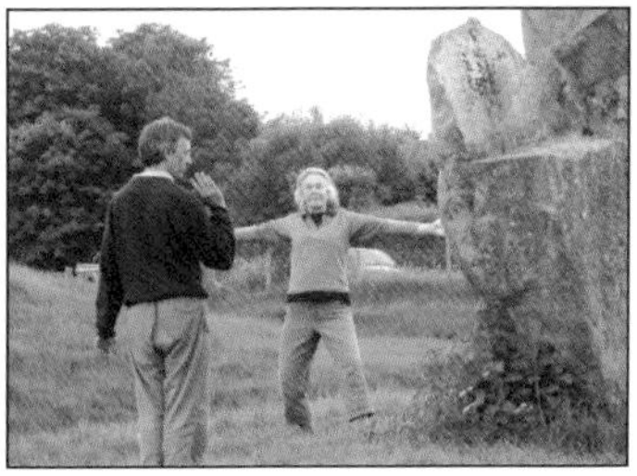
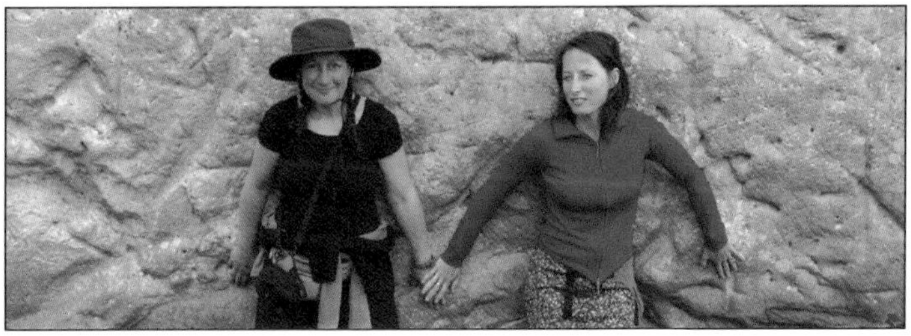

In the evening I walked up to Windmill Hill. The setting sun threw an incredible light over the land and I stopped to take a series of photos from a low angle up through the teasels and seed-heads into the chalky sunset. As I walked through dusk's half-light, I was surprised by the sense that there were others walking on the path. I turned expecting to see someone. But there was no-one about and despite the odd sensation, I relaxed into a sense of people passing me, heading toward Windmill Hill and contemplated the many folk who must have walked this path since 3700BC ... I am walking on the threshold of a parallel world and the ancestors are all around me. ***SB***

Day 26 Rest Day at Avebury

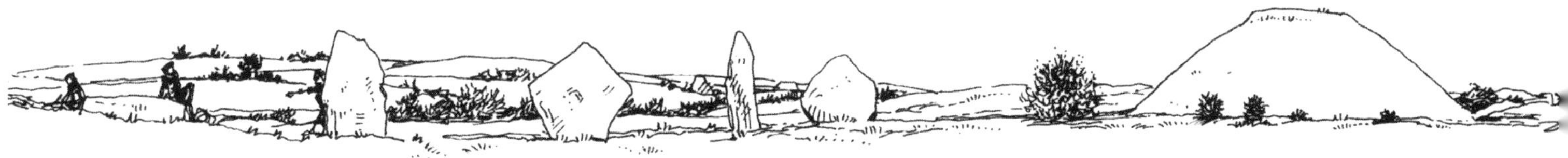

Day 27 Avebury to Ogbourne St George

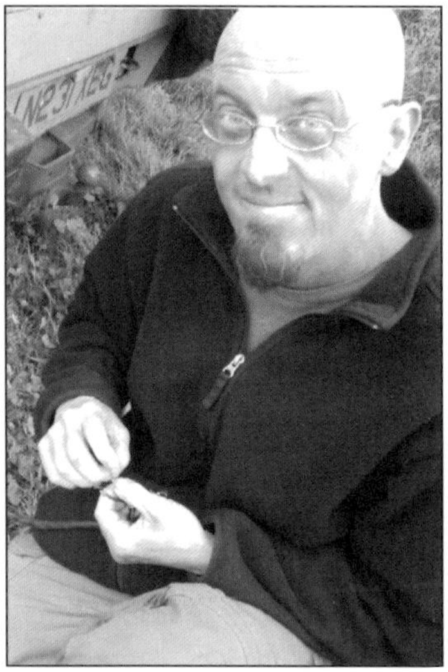

At Ogbourne St Andrew, a crossing point of the leylines near the mid-point of our walk, beside the little rustic village church was a circular earth mound. There I sang a gentle mystical song, while Summer blew soap bubbles into the air as if to encapsulate my sounds into each colourful orb and float them out into the still evening air. Following this we entered the small, peaceful church, where a box of percussion instruments was found in the vestry. We had a fabulous, joyful procession around the church, drumming, singing, beating tambourines and at the end it felt as if we had brought the spontaneous and unsuppressed joys of nature into the church and blown away the cobwebs of Christian solemnity. **CC**

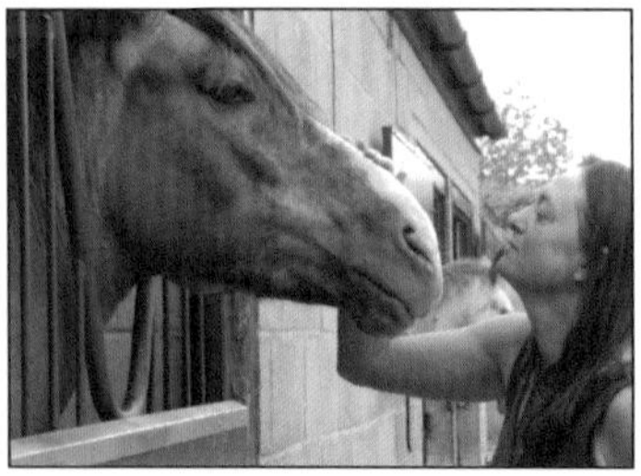

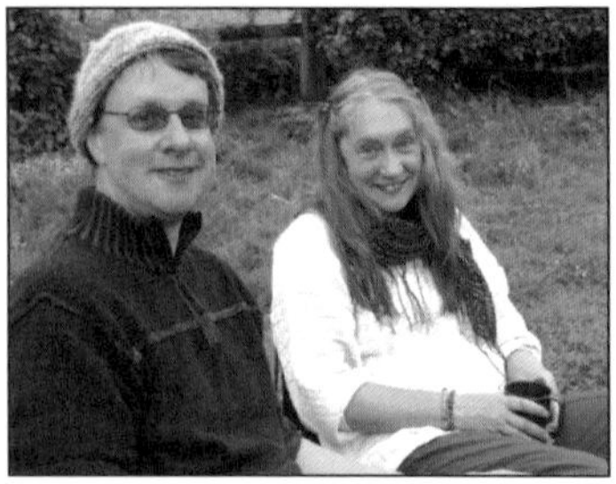

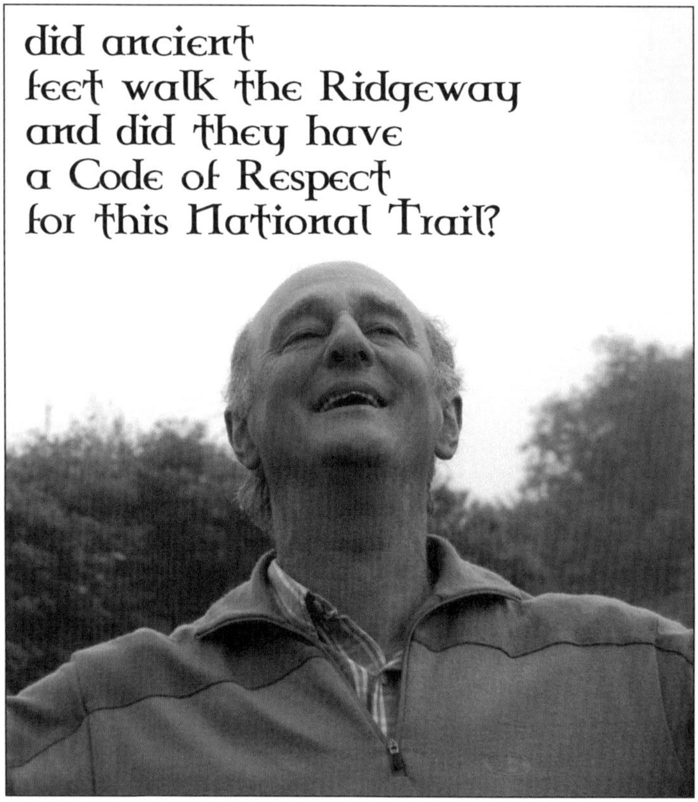

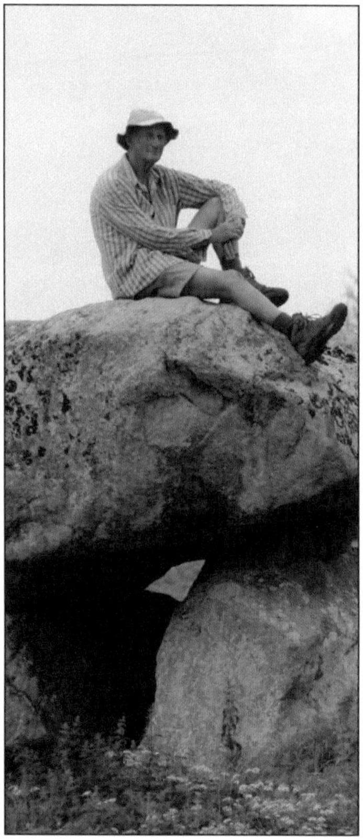

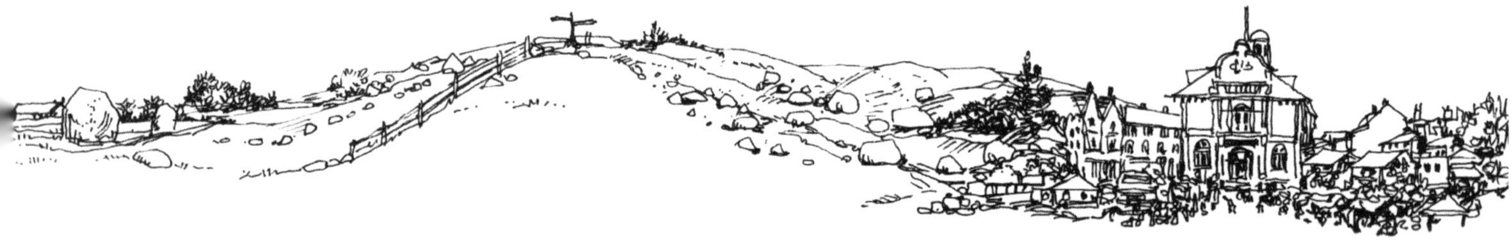

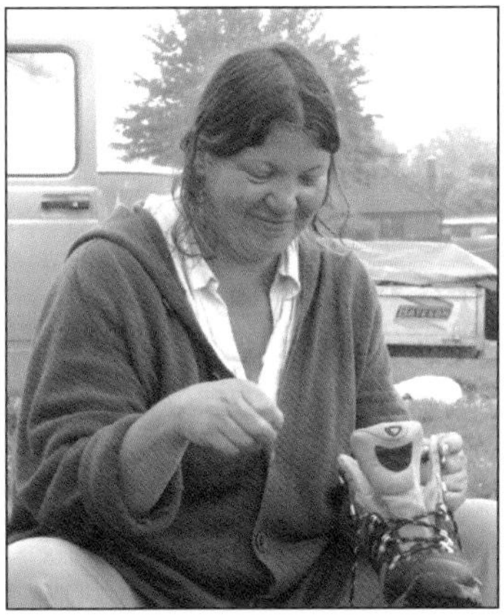

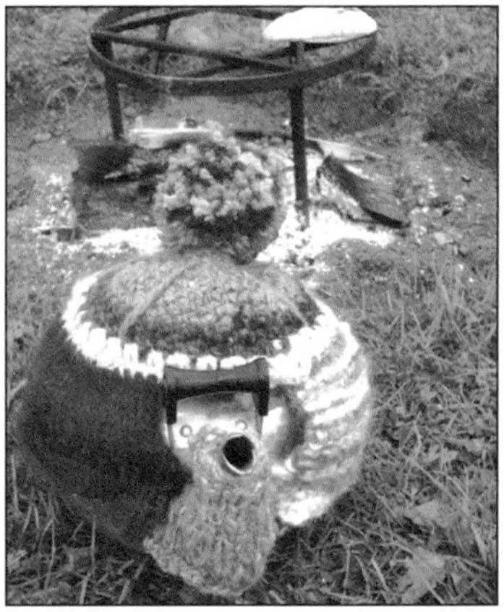

We crossed the M4 today. Gerry had the urge to piss over the bridge onto the motorists below but stopped just in time when he heard his wife calling from Canberra. "Gerry, England is a civilized country!"?! ***SB***

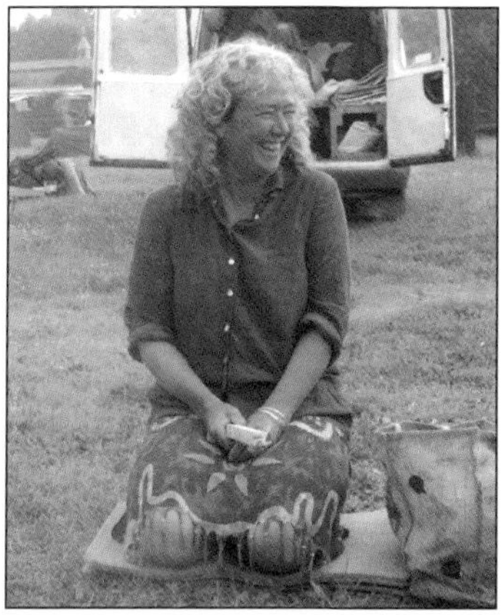

Warm sunny start. Geoff brought me hot buttered toast, before I could get a cup of tea, what about that! He also gave me loads of goodies to share on the walk. He and Julie leave today, with sons Harry, Max and Jim. Ruth also leaves, she was a great member of the community, she helped me make the Pom Pom for the tea cosy which several took part in knitting. She made two or three pairs of knitting needles.

Nice walk through valley of rocks, fields of stones, unspoilt since the ice age. Walked into Marlborough. Giant mound in school grounds like Silbury Hill. The school was on half term, so it was ok for us to go in and see. The security man asked us if we would like to see the Folly inside the mound. Wow! It was like a little summer house, three sections all open arched as one room and all the walls were lined with shells of all shapes and sizes, totally amazing. Half pint of 6X beer in the Green Dragon with Graham early afternoon, Marlborough. Og River, plus several hamlets with Og at the beginning. Another barrow in churchyard. Sat while Carolin chanted. Noisy camp site, main road. Horses' field with jumps and chickens. Scrumpy with dinner. ***SS***

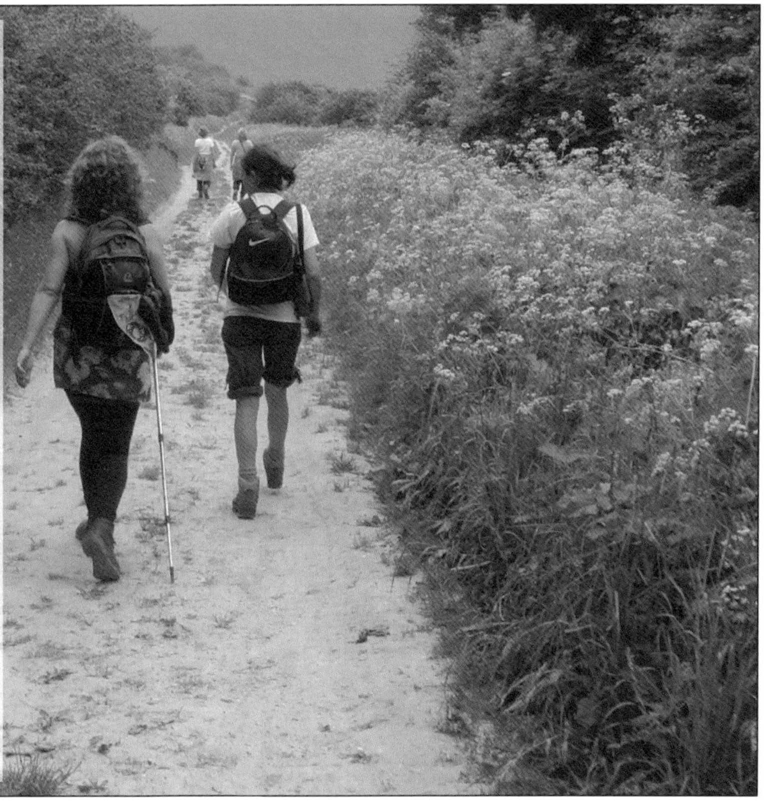

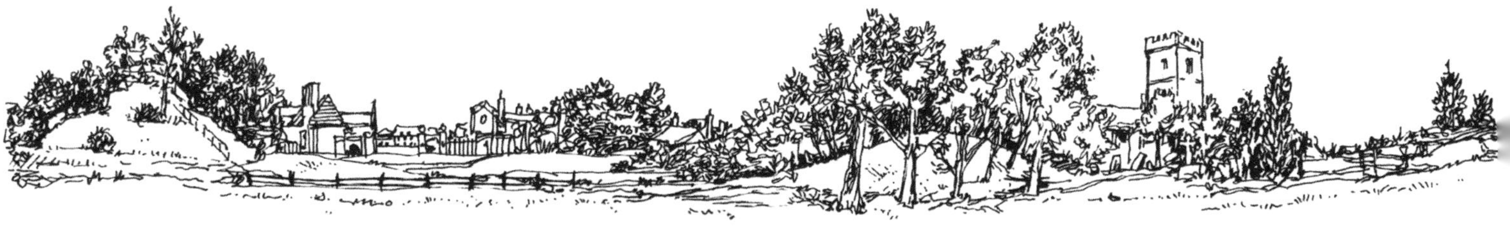

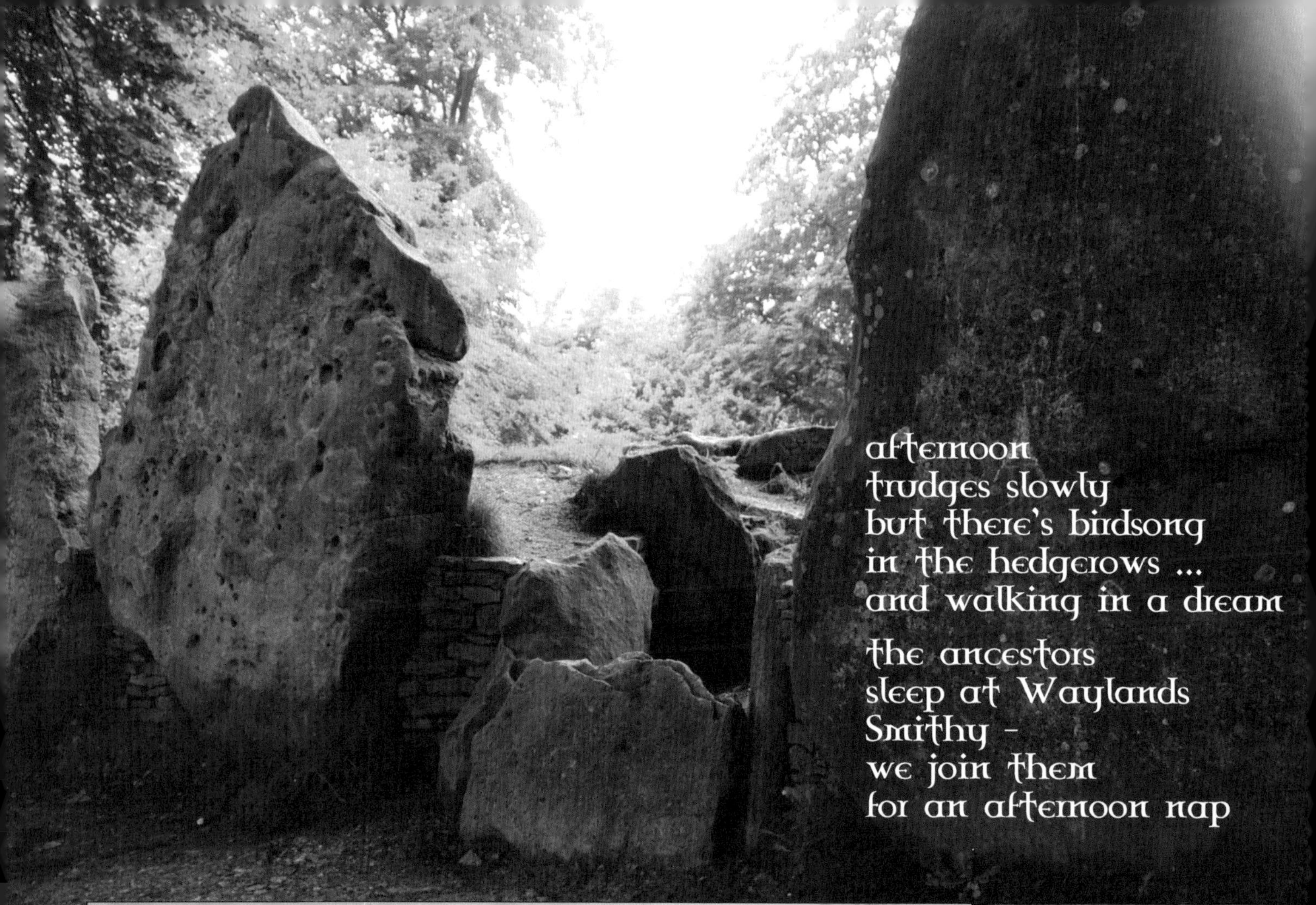

afternoon
trudges slowly
but there's birdsong
in the hedgerows ...
and walking in a dream

the ancestors
sleep at Waylands
Smithy -
we join them
for an afternoon nap

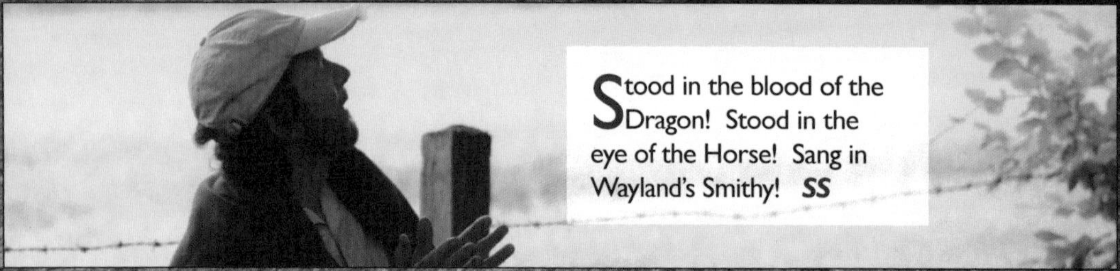

Stood in the blood of the Dragon! Stood in the eye of the Horse! Sang in Wayland's Smithy! ***SS***

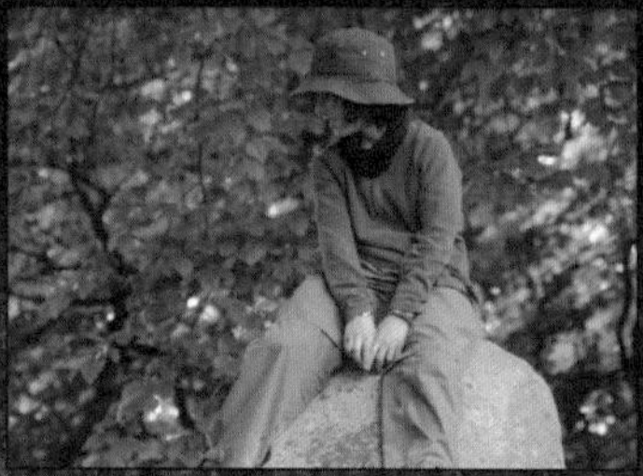

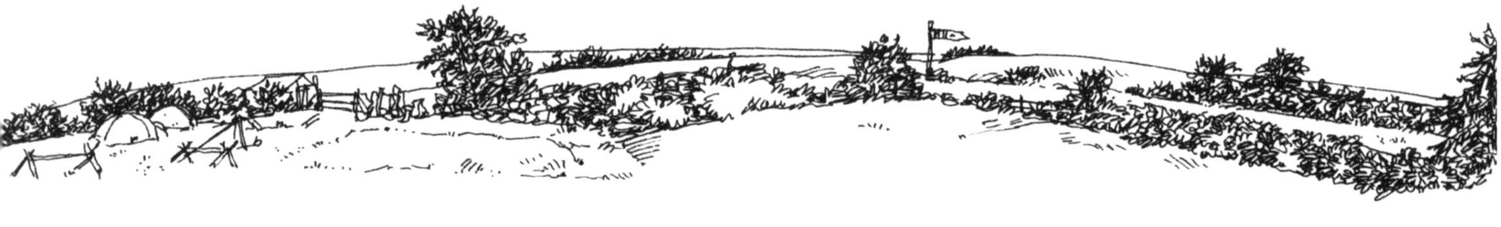

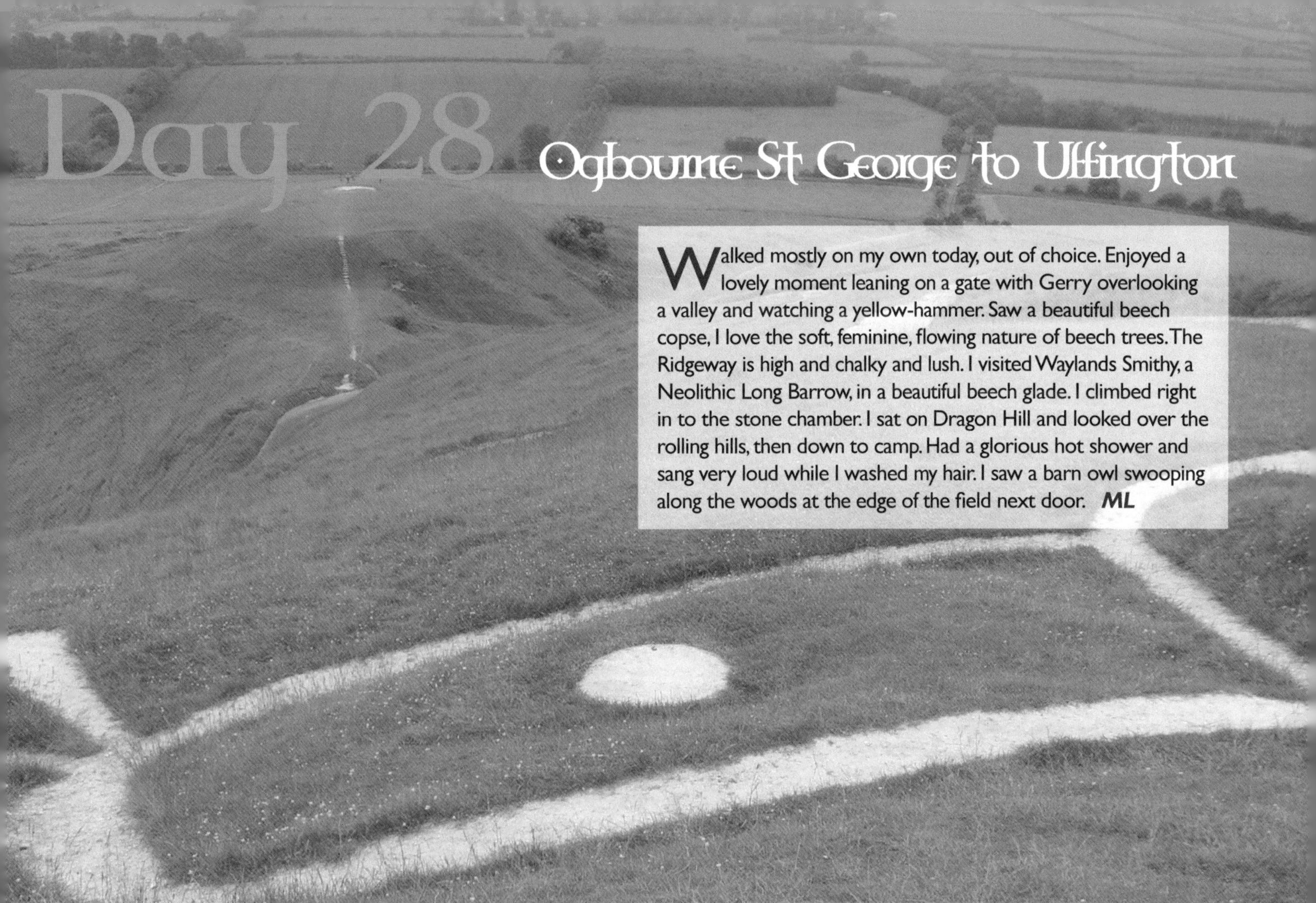

Day 28 Ogbourne St George to Uffington

Walked mostly on my own today, out of choice. Enjoyed a lovely moment leaning on a gate with Gerry overlooking a valley and watching a yellow-hammer. Saw a beautiful beech copse, I love the soft, feminine, flowing nature of beech trees. The Ridgeway is high and chalky and lush. I visited Waylands Smithy, a Neolithic Long Barrow, in a beautiful beech glade. I climbed right in to the stone chamber. I sat on Dragon Hill and looked over the rolling hills, then down to camp. Had a glorious hot shower and sang very loud while I washed my hair. I saw a barn owl swooping along the woods at the edge of the field next door. ***ML***

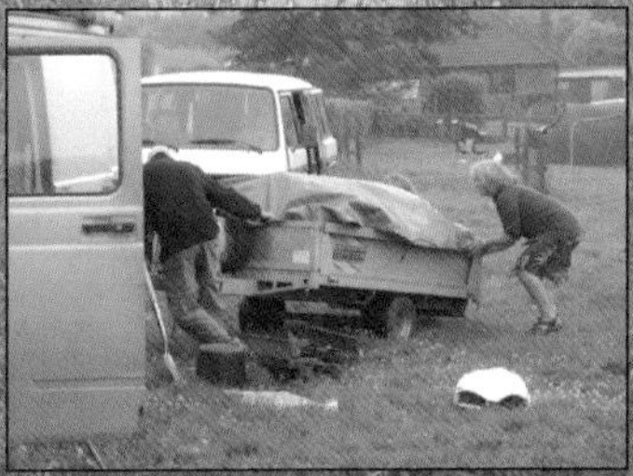

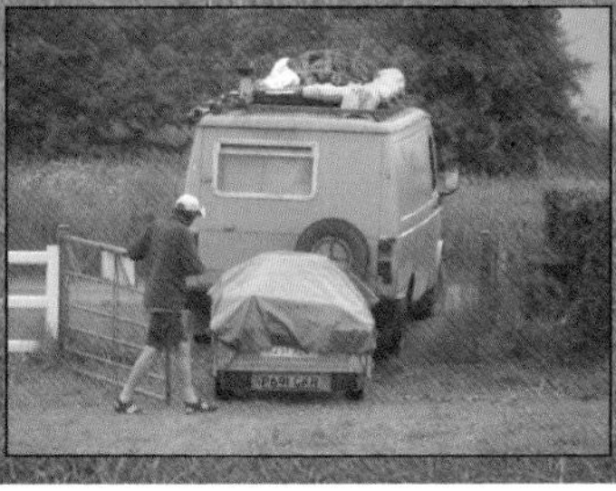

I was a part-time pilgrim, joining a group of strangers at Avebury and for ten days getting to know my fellow pilgrims and walking the ancient Ridgeway to Ivinghoe Beacon. I had few expectations except to walk the length of the path, which is part of my daily life and landscape as I walk my dog up Whiteleaf Hill every morning. How was I to know what would unfold? ***JH***

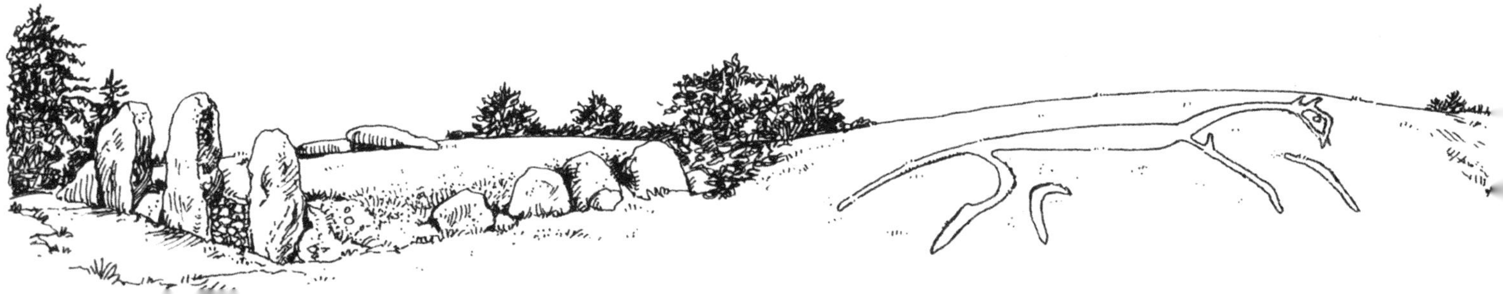

Day 29 Uffington to West Illsley

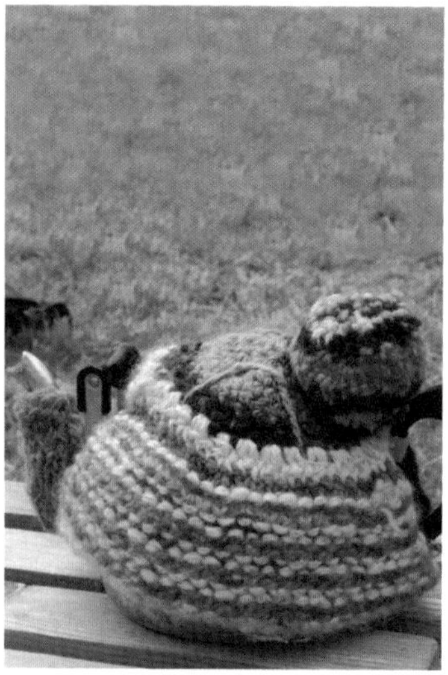

A damp evening ... we went to the village pub for a while encountering the strange energies of a couple of locals ... we shared reading stories around the table ... then I left to go to bed ... this rough patch of sacred ground not a good campsite ... intermittent rain at night but I stayed dry ... then it came on continuous in the early morning ... stood in water brewing up for breakfast and retreated to the tent to write ...

GJ

the afternoon
greys - mist veils
a distant
power station -
veil between two worlds

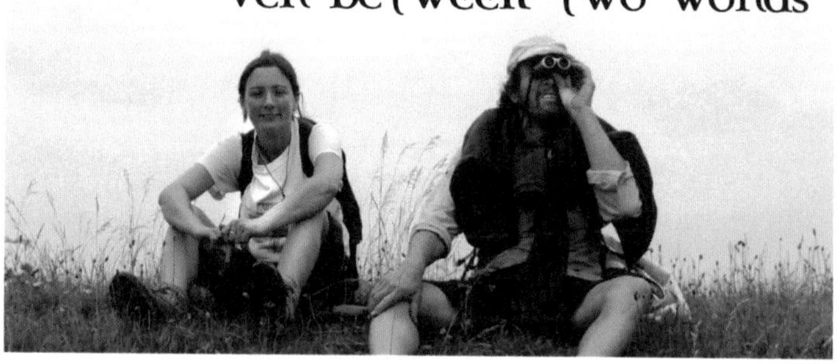

A bit of a grim campsite tonight. We're in some farmer's yard pitched next to rusting farm vehicles. The earth is churned up with tyre marks and there are big orange slugs everywhere. Oh ... and of course it's raining! The atmosphere has been contemplative today; thick grey skies look just fantastic against the yellow and umber crops. There were also lots of red kites overhead and there's a stunning black Freidland horse in the next field. The weather forecast is looking wet for the next couple of days. ***SB***

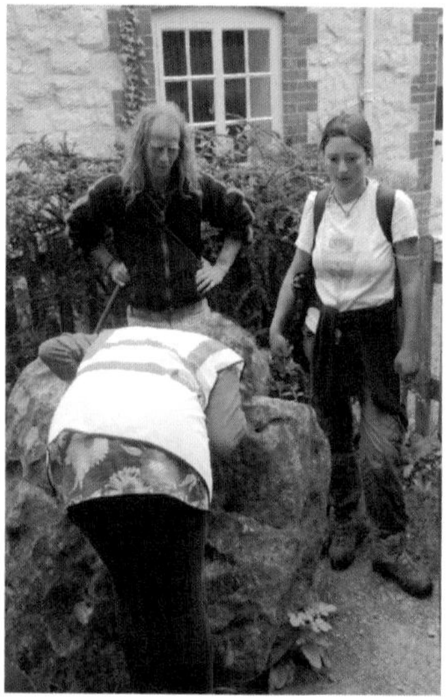

We walked more of the Ridgeway today, I felt tired but happy and quite sociable. I borrowed Alex's bird book. Saw a pair of red kites today, they glide so softly, their tails are angular and their wings curve backwards and they are big! They were gliding over a valley called the Devils Punch Bowl. I also saw partridges, a yellow-hammer, a great tit and a whitethroat. I visited Scutchamer's Knob! A suspected burial place of the Saxon king, Cwichelm, which has been sadly desecrated. Also I went to the Blowing Stone, a huge saracen which sits in the front garden of a cottage, and has several holes in it, one of which can be blown like a didge. Summer blew it really well. It was great to walk and share with Summer today.

Tonight we went to the village pub 'cos it was raining after a delicious dinner. We all sat round a big table, lit a candle in the middle and read a story to each other "White Buffalo Calf Woman" by Ken Carey. It was a great story. Came to bed early tonight, need some extra sleep. We had a bit of sharing around the fire. ***ML***

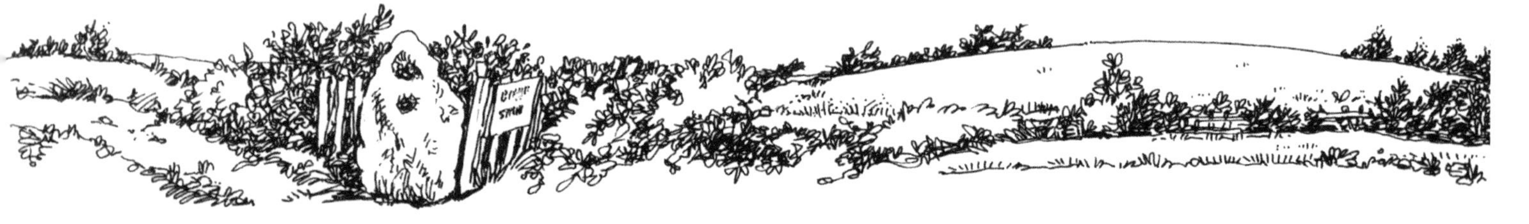

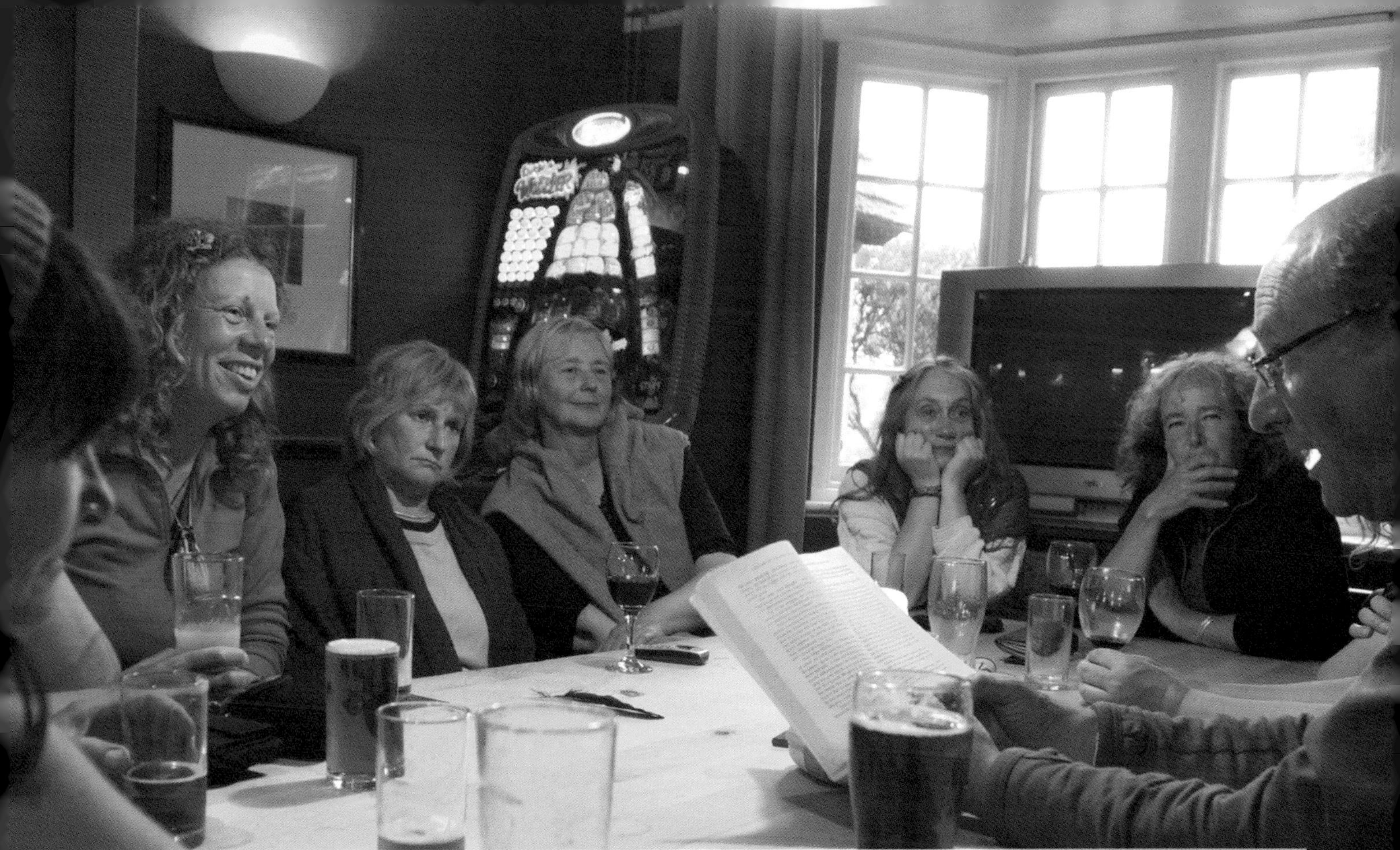

Must do something about peeing in the night: yogurt pots are good especially in wet times. Neither wet or dry start. Said goodbye to Lois, Keiran and Carl. Carolin left for a couple of days R and R. Marion started Yoga Mantra for the day. Om Vardahnam Namah. Crews today: Lynne, Jane and Gerry in 'Awakening'; Rhian and Justine in 'Albion'. Nice walk. Good hill to start. Blow Hole in giant flint boulder, used by King Alfred to summon his troops. Now in the front garden of a little cottage, quite remote. Walk along Ridgeway. Another large Iron-Age hill fort. Lunch. Yummy! Continue on ridge. Obelisk to a lord. Knob: burial ground, big part of it robbed now, horseshoe shaped. Saw first red kites, skylark on fence-post. Home by 4.00, about 12 miles. Farm, rough ground. Great dinner. Went to pub. Read story, White Buffalo Calf Women. Everyone took a turn in reading, passing round the book and Gerry's glasses. The story rang bells in me, must take note, spiritually then love. Nice little fire moment. Lynne giggled with two voices! Quite freaky! Such laughter had by all. Raining, good night. 10.35. ***SS***

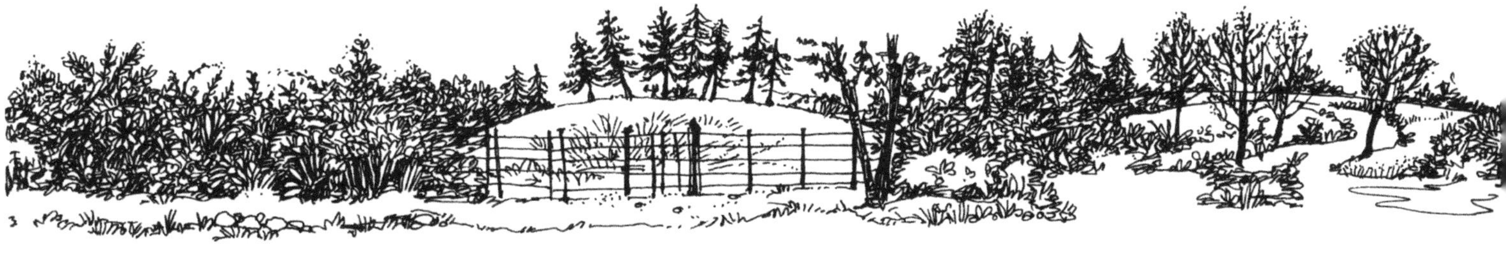

Stories in the yurt: Norfolk Songlines. Warm, steamy and very cosy. ***RH***

It rained *all* day and *all* last night. I woke this morning to find my tent in a pool of water that had run down the slope. Slugs were crawling all over the outside of the tent and even up the inside of the flysheet. Amazingly my little tent kept the water out! When I got up I put on my swimsuit instead of clothes and washed in the rain behind rusted farm vehicles. I was cheered on from Lynne's steamy van where the pilgrims were crammed in eating breakfast. ***SB***

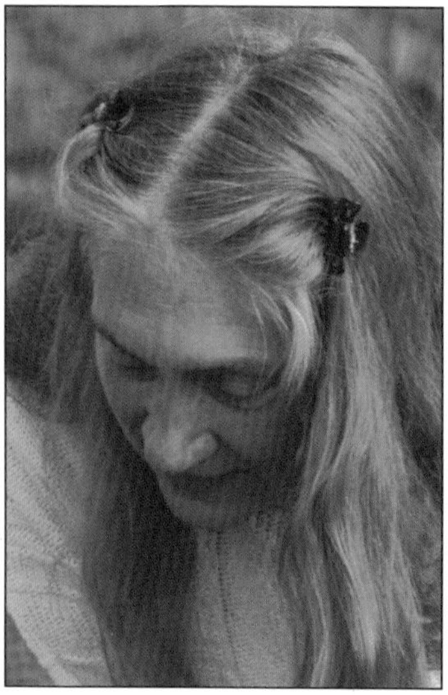

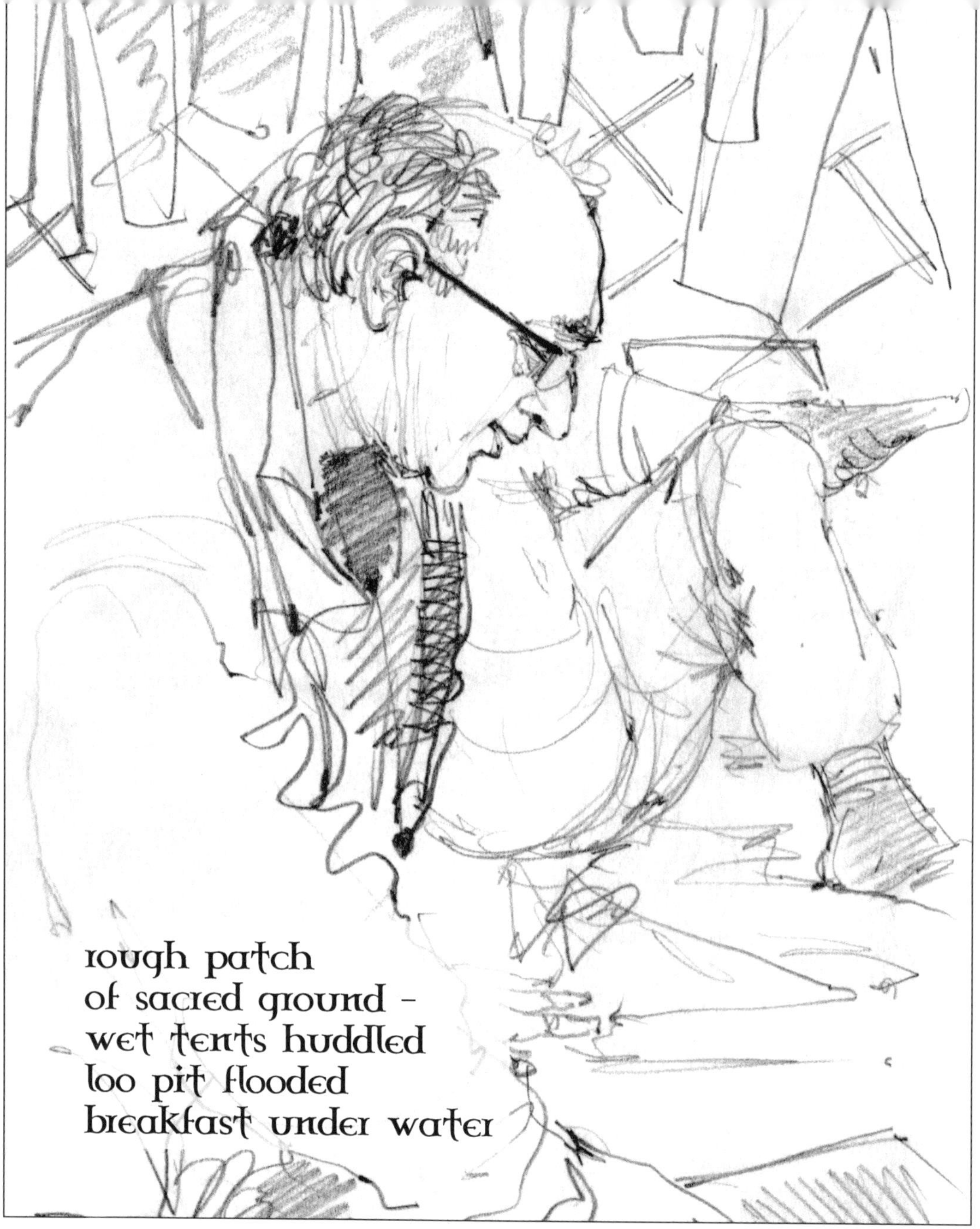

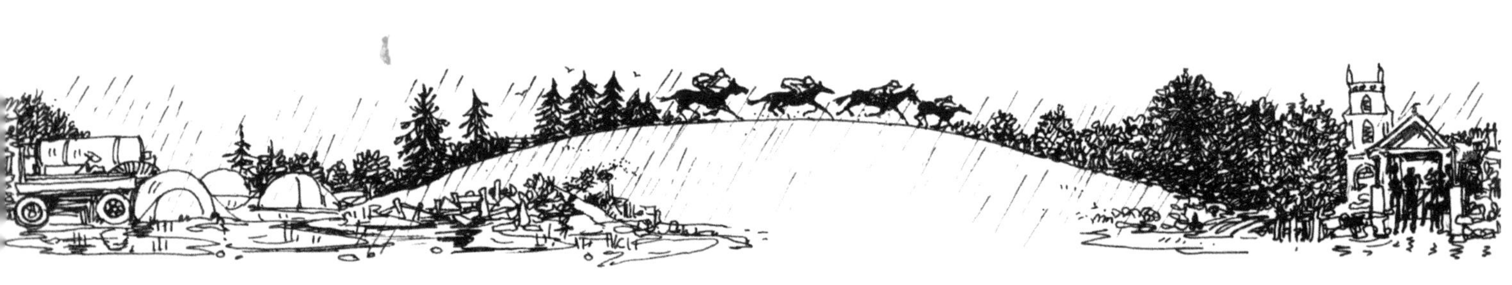

Day 30

West Illsley to Little Wittenham

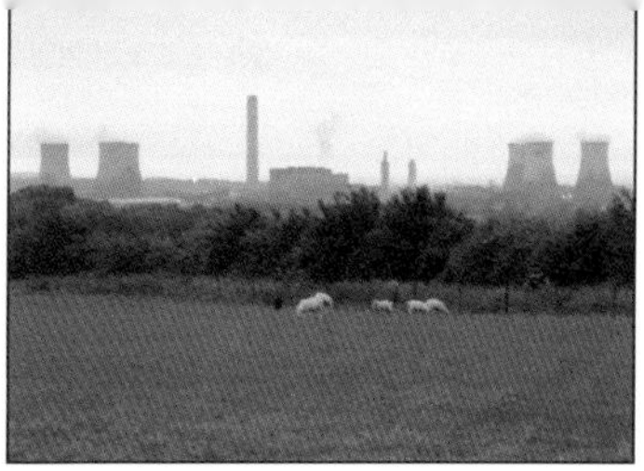

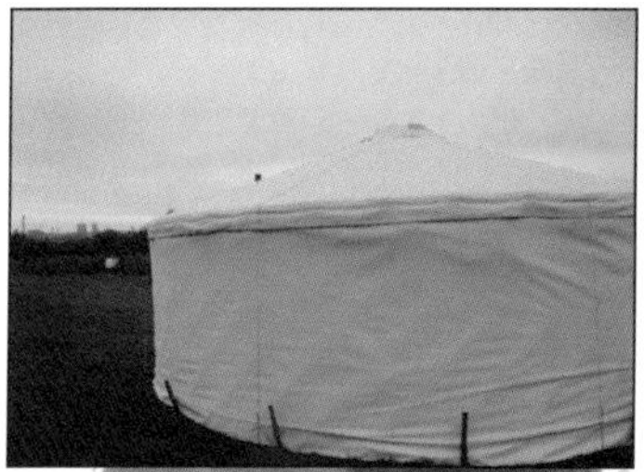

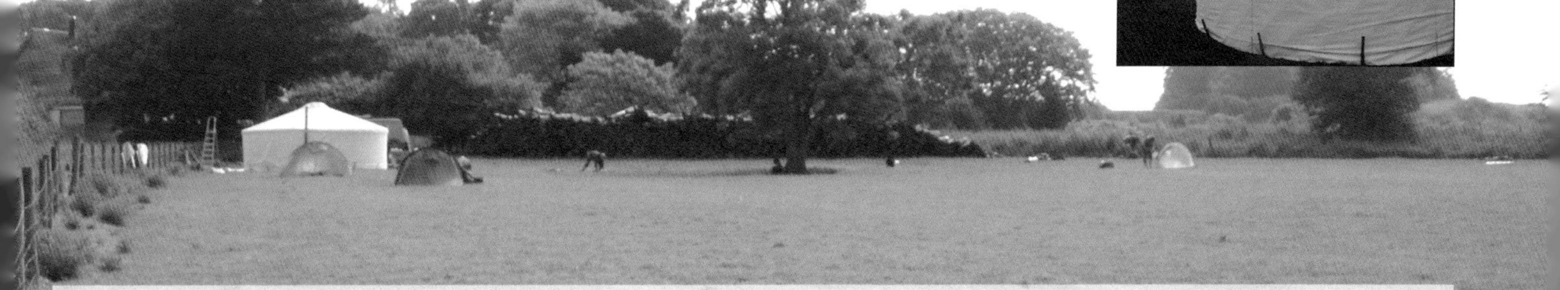

We are back in Oxfordshire, somewhere near Didcot. The place we are staying is a field attached to an eco-education centre. Tonight the sky is deep, deep red. The cooling towers of the power station silhouetted against the vermillion.

It has been a tough day weather wise, raining pretty much non-stop. It takes much more energy to pack up in the wet. I have felt happy today, looking forward to seeing Poppy and Emma and Paul hopefully at Rougham. Didn't see much scenery today as I was mostly looking at the ground trying to keep the rain from my eyes. We made a fast pace, reaching the lunch stop at Blewberry at 11.30!! We only stopped once for a quick huddle under a bush to eat some nuts. We saw racehorses galloping. Alex saw a hare bounding up and through some long grass.

The funniest thing of the day was seeing Sarah emerge into the pissing rain, from her tent, wearing nothing but her swimming costume!!

I played guitar as we ate porridge in Lynne's van, and Jane began to cry at my "beautiful music"! We also sang a bit of Pilgrim's Blues. Lots of singing in the rain today. Had to knock on someone's door to get help to find our last footpath.

Lovely evening in the yurt, we got home early and ate yummy pasta tea, followed by cake and custard. Then stories: Hugh Lupton's book about walking the Peddars Way, beautifully read by Graham, Lynne and Gerry. I would like to walk the Peddars Way ...

Saw lovely baby ducklings this morning, one was all yellow. We sang and toned under a huge road bridge, it sounded fantastic. In the afternoon we stopped at the "Bear at Home" pub, for a lemonade, it was snug and I welcomed the opportunity to dry my clothes under the powerful hand drier in the ladies! There is a drying room here and I have put my boots in it overnight. I have got a cold today. ***ML***

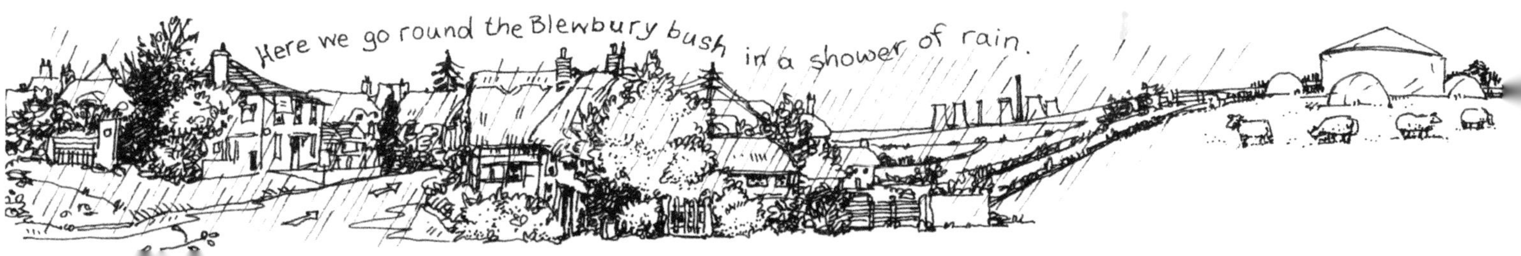

Day 31

Little Wittenham to Christmas Common

It was a very long walk today, especially toward the end when we tramped past a massive pig farm to the top of a long and steep hill. A cyclist passed us at about ¼ mile an hour on his tortuous way to the top. All bedecked in colourful lycra, sunglasses and a go-faster helmet he seemed faintly ridiculous but half an hour later all became clear as he came screaming down the hill at about 50 miles an hour.

It is Gerry's 5th birthday (five years since his op) and when we arrived at our site for the night there were decorations and balloons and a cake to celebrate. Rhian had cooked some more Chicken in the Woods and it was really delicious.

Again we are camped on the edge of the escarpment and have amazing views over the plains and the spectacular Didcot power station. All evening, red kites have been circling low over us. ***SB***

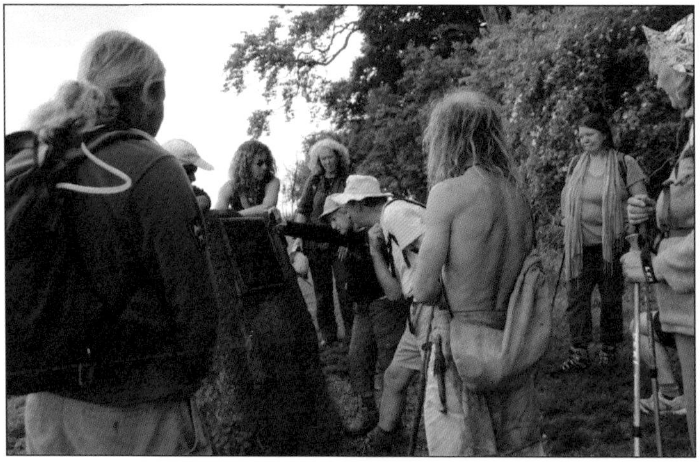

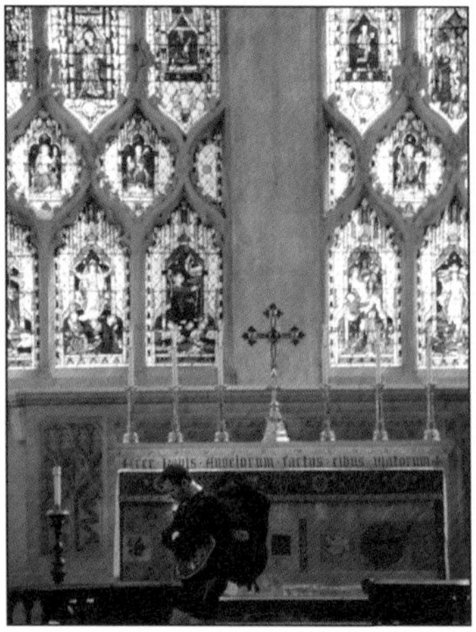

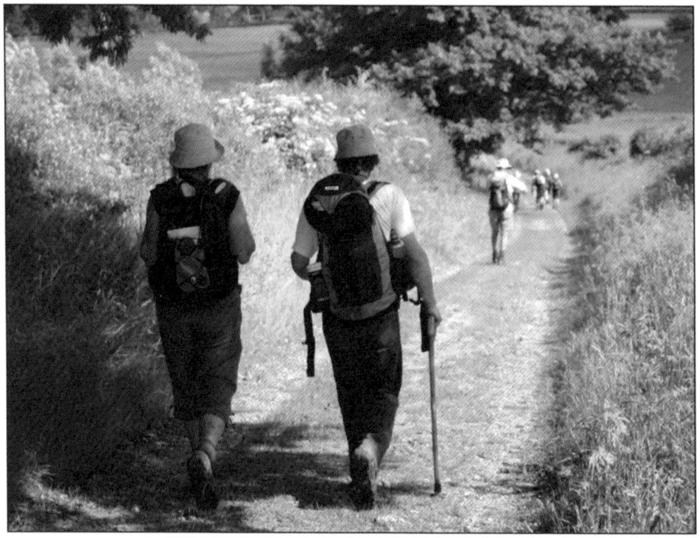

Watlington Hill with yew tree grove. The red kites soaring and swooping down so low. Went for a walk in the dark ... tawny owl and glowing bracket fungus ... so dark in the yew woods! ***RH***

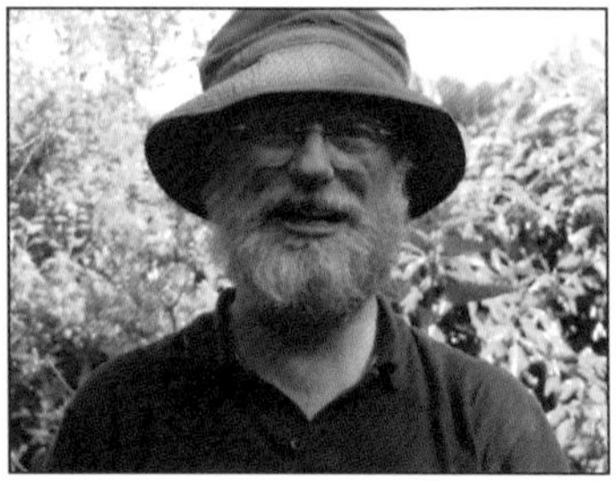

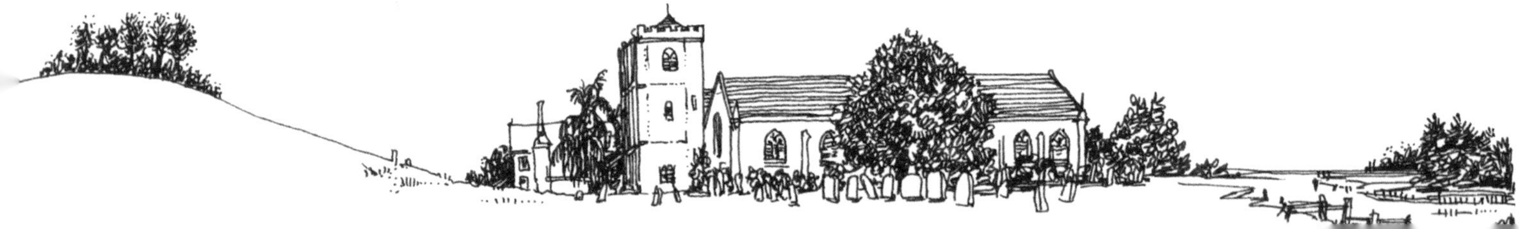

where we walk
is flooded - we splash
and gluk
through muddy
bridleways and footpaths

walking deep
in dark damp woodland ...
a sunken
bridleway ... pierced
by a shaft of sunlight

red kites
circle the campsite
sharing
the celebration
of re-birth in this place

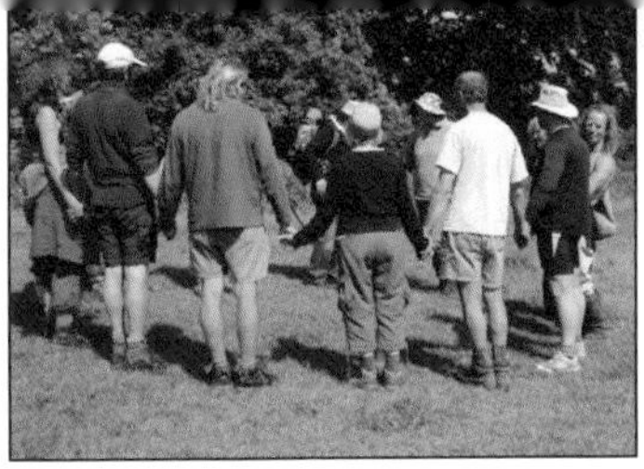
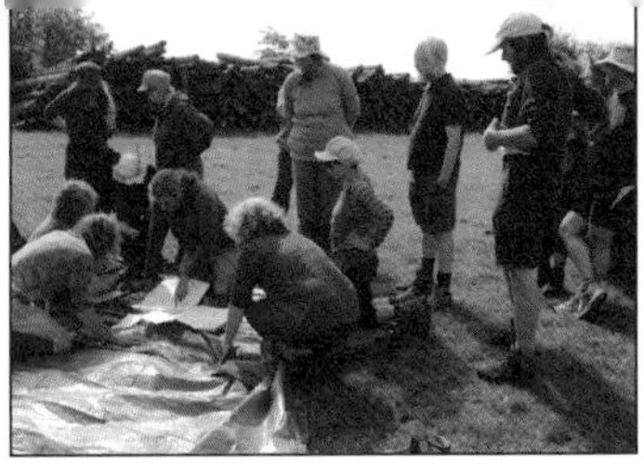

A long long day, deeply satisfying, celebrating the fifth anniversary of my heart surgery with a long long walk. We crossed the flooded Thames and Thame on bridges. At Dorchester Abbey we sang Dona Nobis Pacem and I lit candles of thanksgiving. And on and on through flooded muddy bridleways ..."Where I walk is flooded ... SPLASH!"

Walked on through Brightwell Baldwin on bridleways and lanes ... wet patches and nettles ... I felt wobbly with a back injury ... Sasha took my pack and Sarah gave me water and raisins ... we found a magical bridle path sunken deep into the woodland by the feet and hooves of centuries ... in this dark damp woodland a single gleam of sunshine ... *GJ*

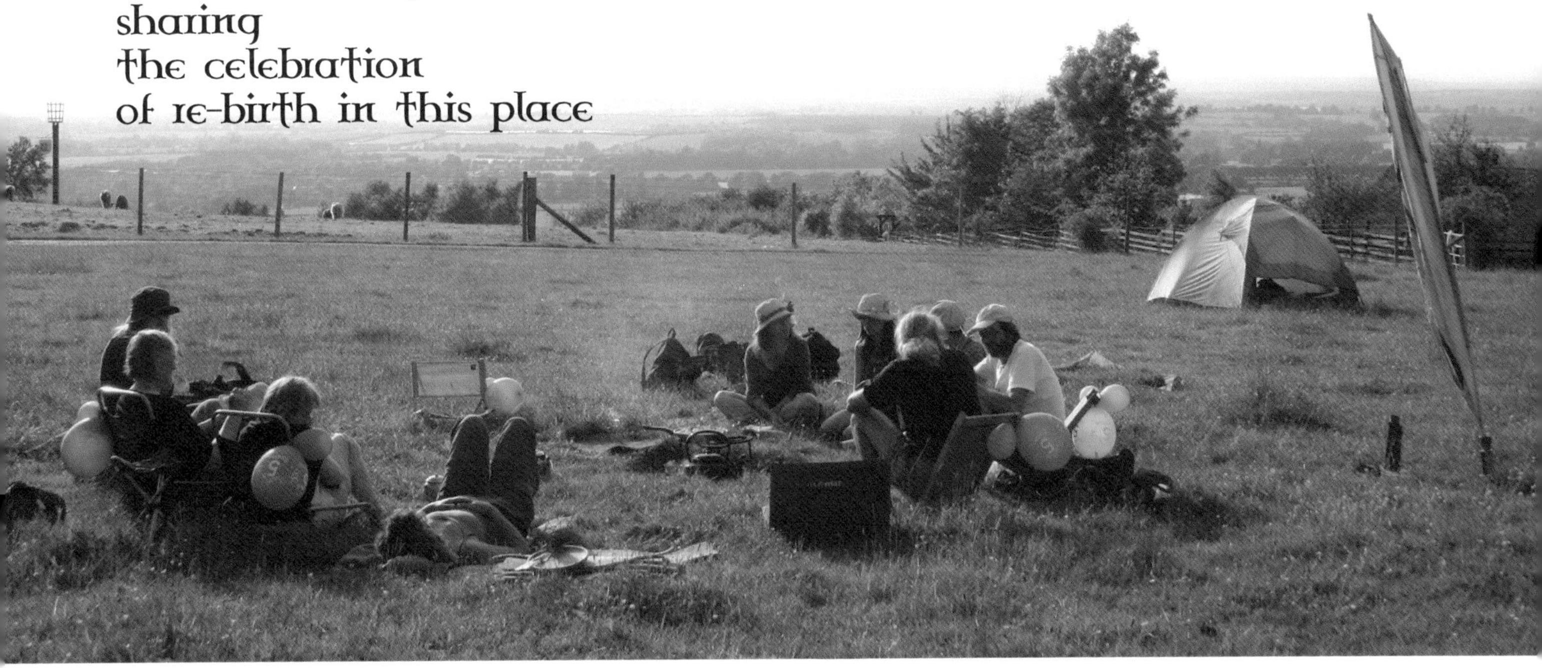

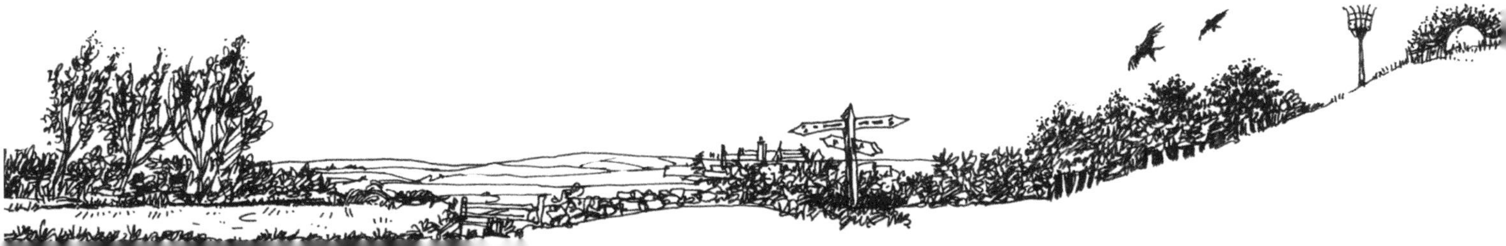

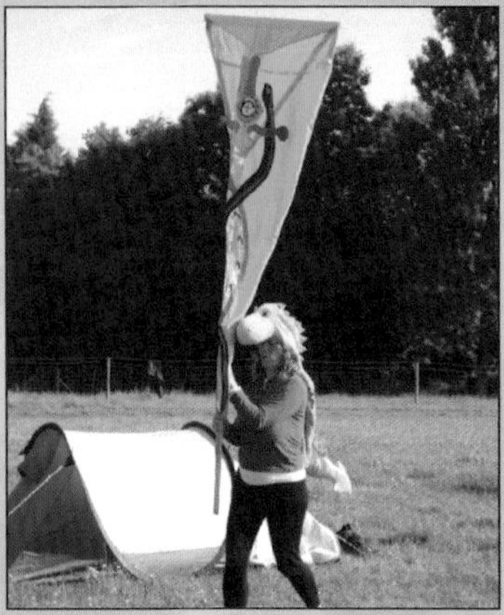

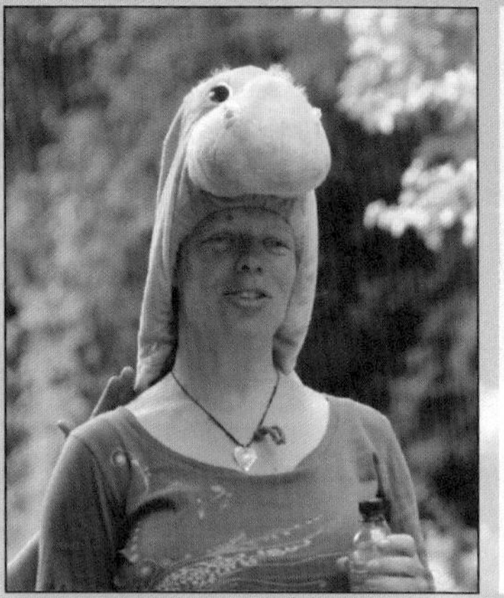

Sunny morning, clarity of decision, not to walk but to crew, feeling the lethargy and stiffness of yesterday's long day ... did the shopping in Princes Risborough with Lynne and Sasha ... served lunch for walkers at a crossing of the Icknield Way ... then to the camp site at Little Kimble. Slept for an hour needing to heal with the earth and sun, cooked dahl on the fire enjoying the rest and space of the campsite, Rhian brought me wild thyme and we sang it ... "The Wild Mountain Thyme" and Sarah sang an Irish song to my delight ... later our sharing circle and talked by the fire, Summer left with group hug, fell asleep with the new moon ... ***GJ***

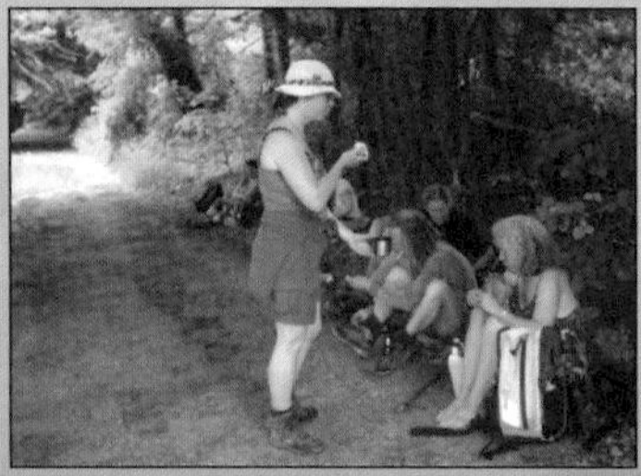

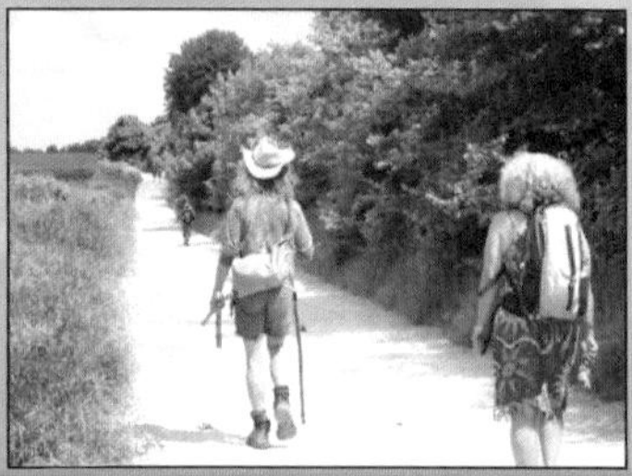

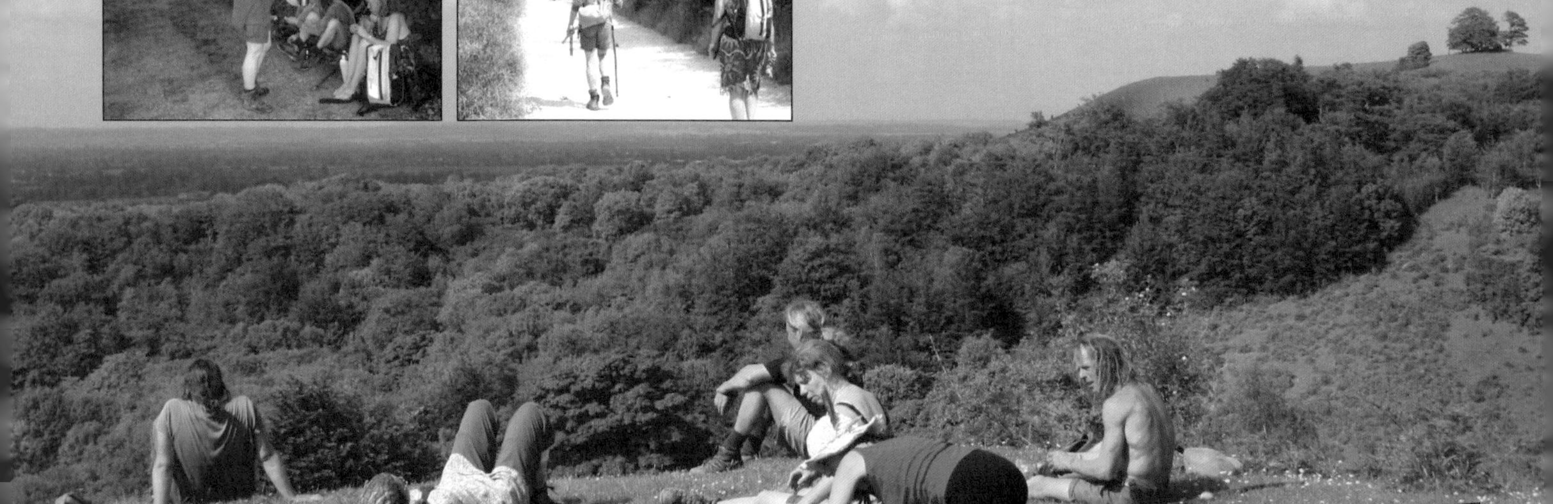

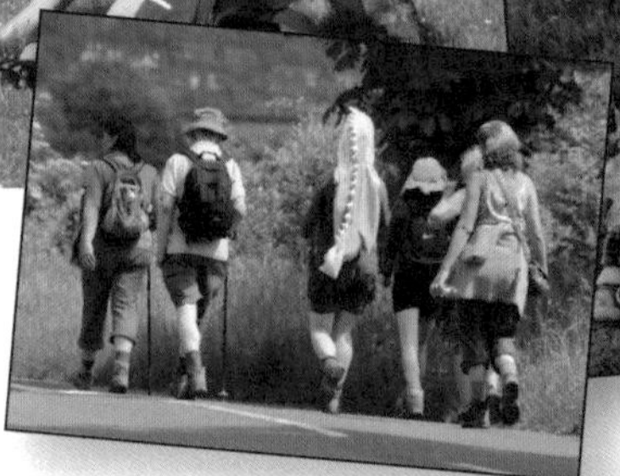

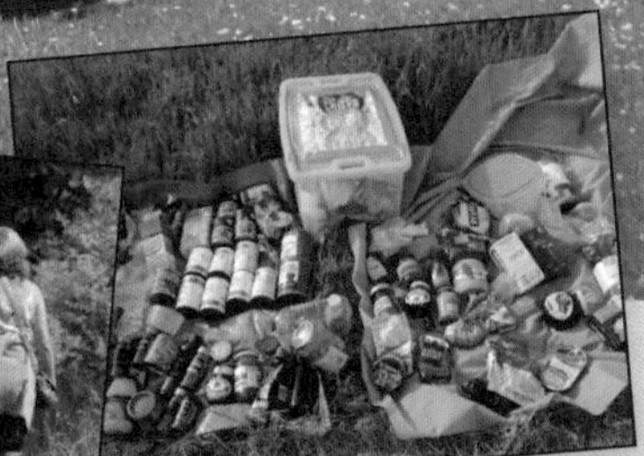

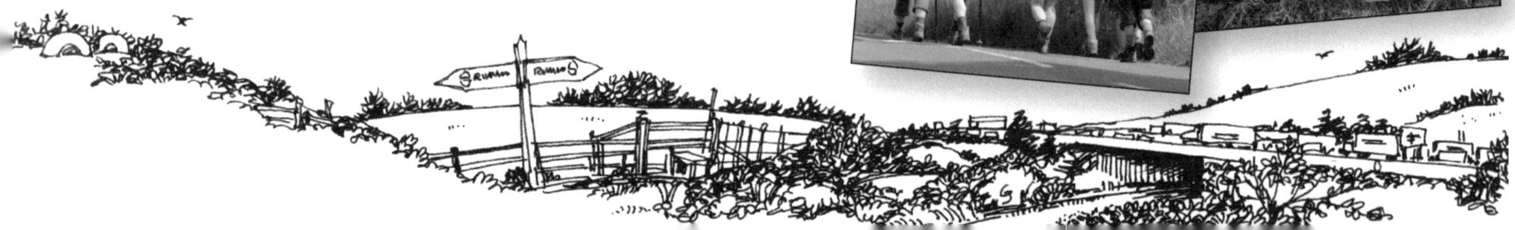

Day 32

Christmas Common to Little Kimble

falling asleep
watching the new moon
set
through the tent door
waking to starlight

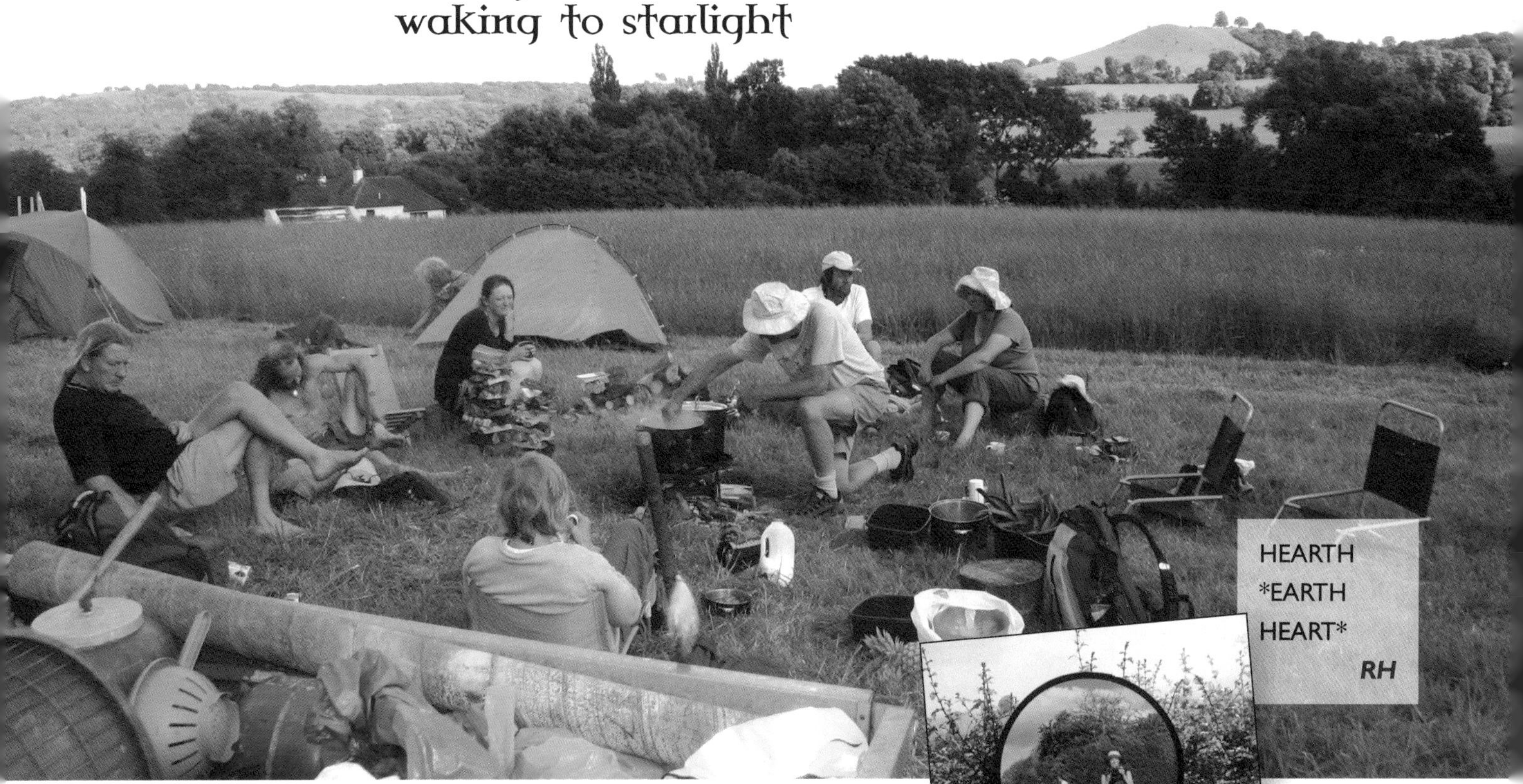

HEARTH
*EARTH
HEART*
RH

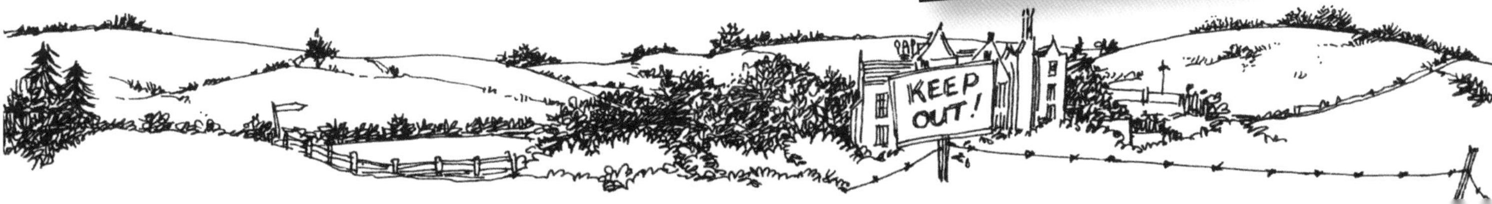

Day 33

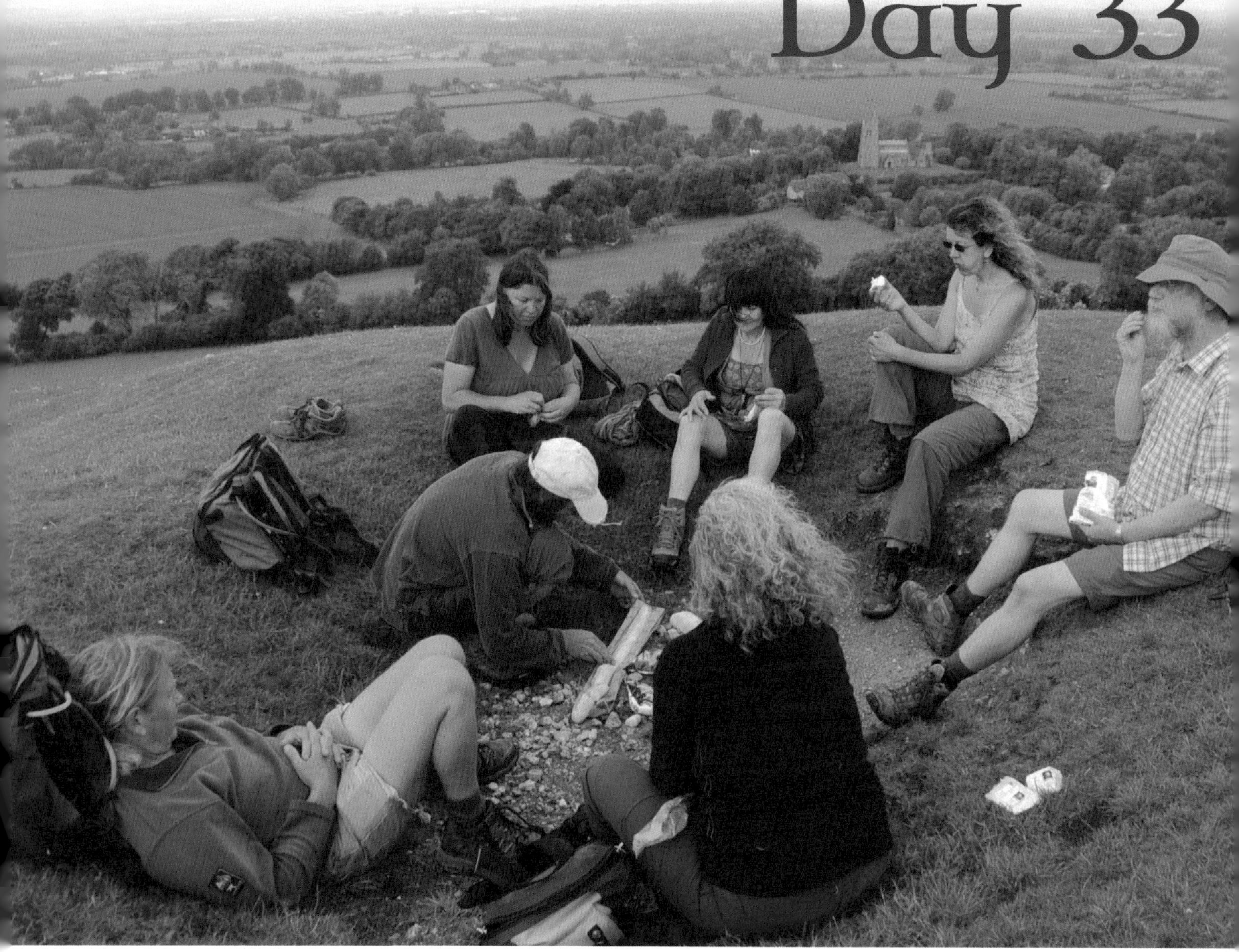

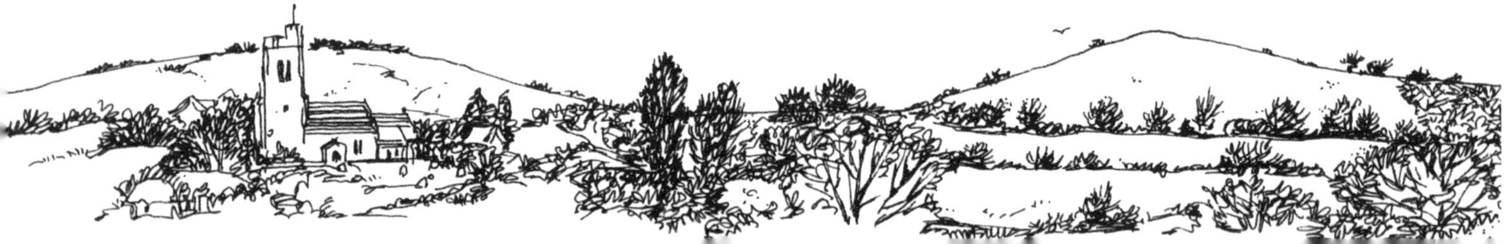

Rest Day at Little Kimble

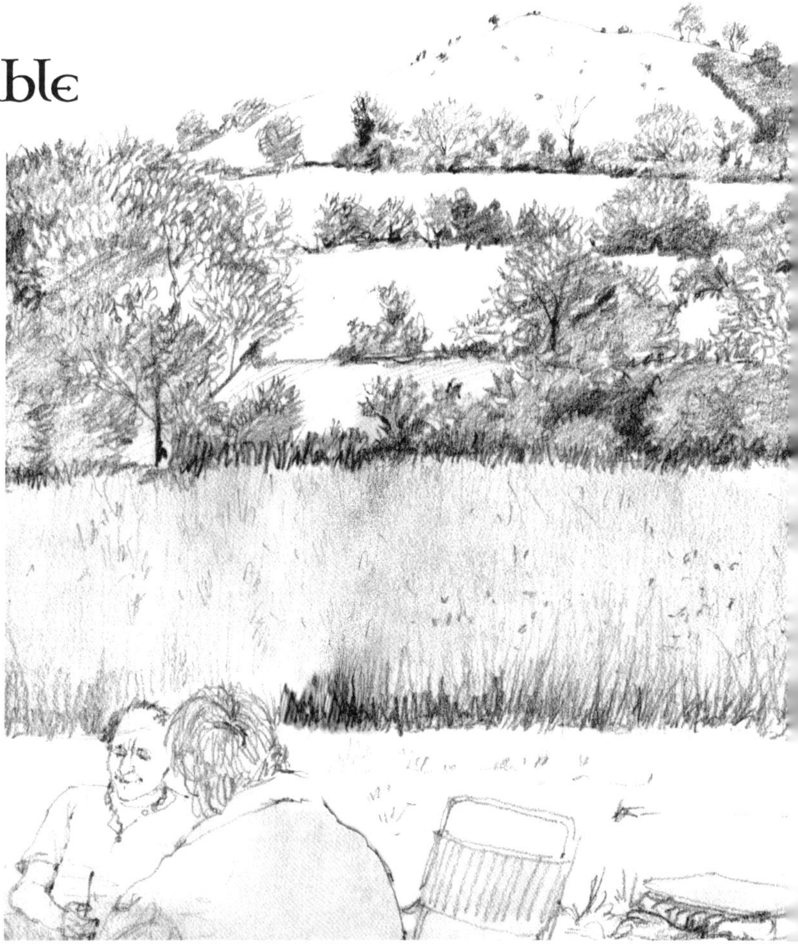

This place is surreally full of old lawn mowers and thousands of rusting lawn mower components. It also has this most picturesque meadow, full of thigh high wild flowers, in which we have the great privilege to be camping.

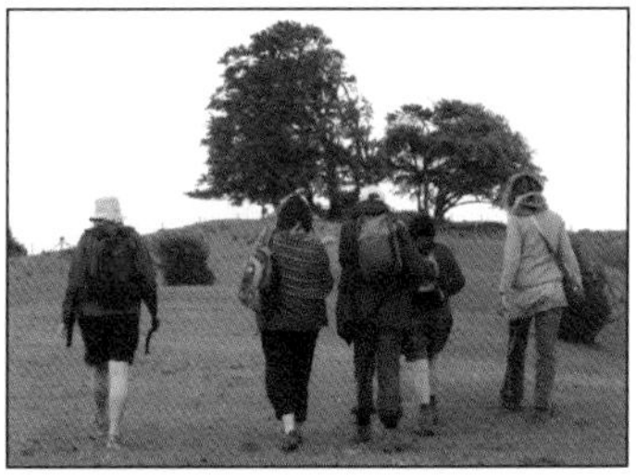

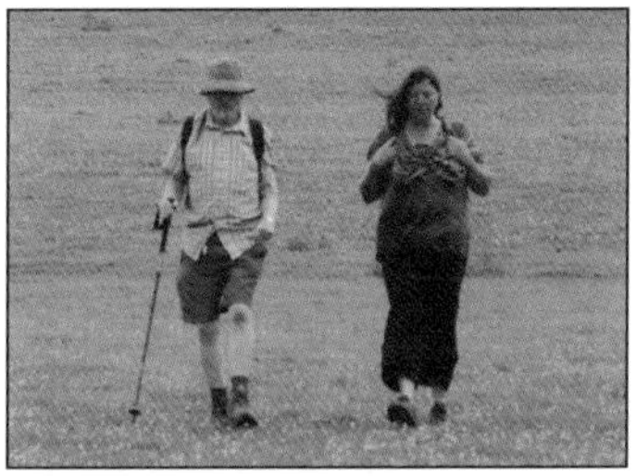

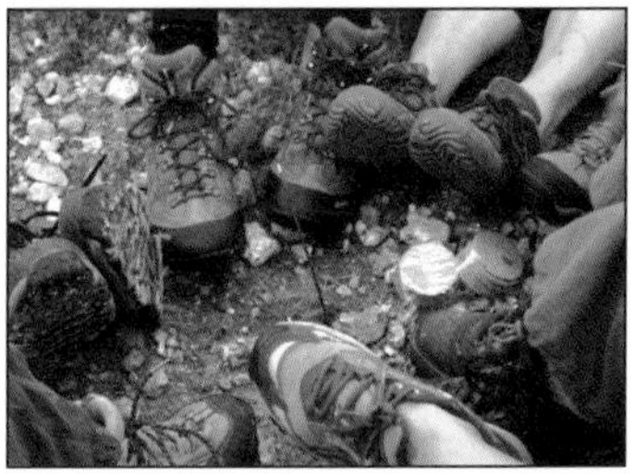

In the afternoon we took a walk up Beacon Hill and had a picnic at the top watched by the CCTV cameras from the boundaries of Chequers. We walked up to the fence and J told us tales of doors that open in the hillside to release security services like Arthurian sleeping knights. M had a good story of a Greenpeace demonstration that had involved dressing in black and ascending Beacon Hill in thousands. S had a piss over the boundary fence, next to one of the many notices that warn of impending arrest and imprisonment ... a simple act of morale-building defiance! ***SB***

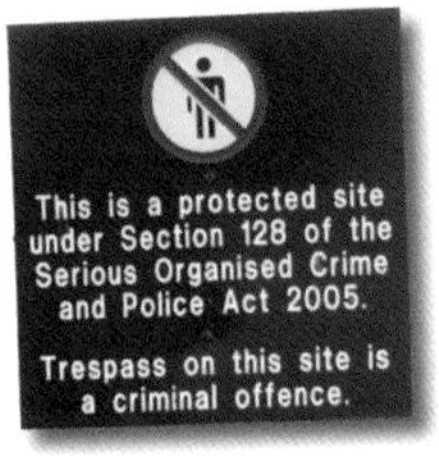

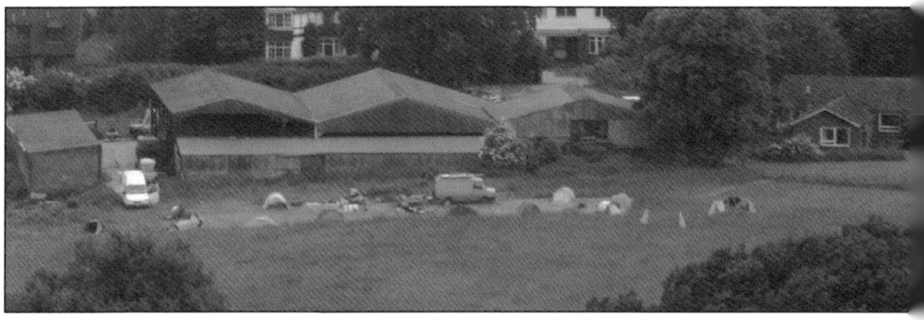

friends leaving
the walk ... moving on
the group shrinks
consolidates ...
walking on ... moving on

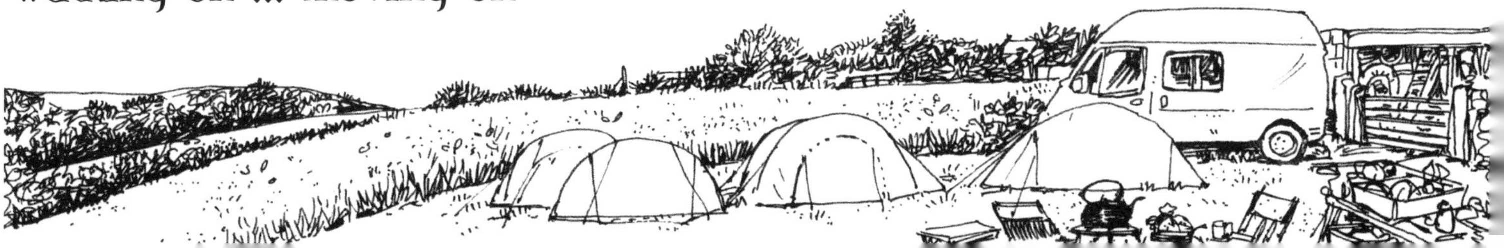

Day 34 Little Kimble to Ivinghoe

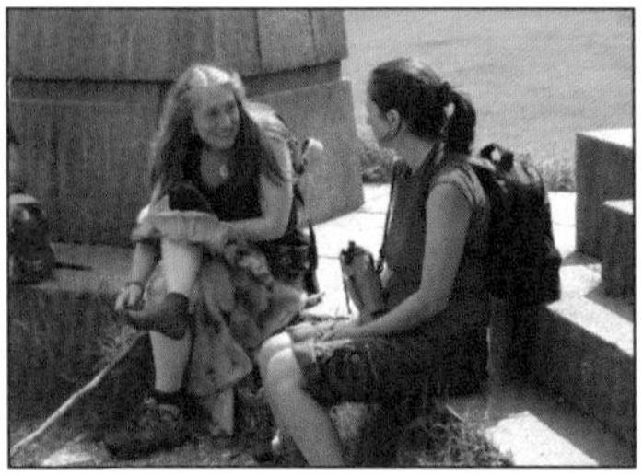

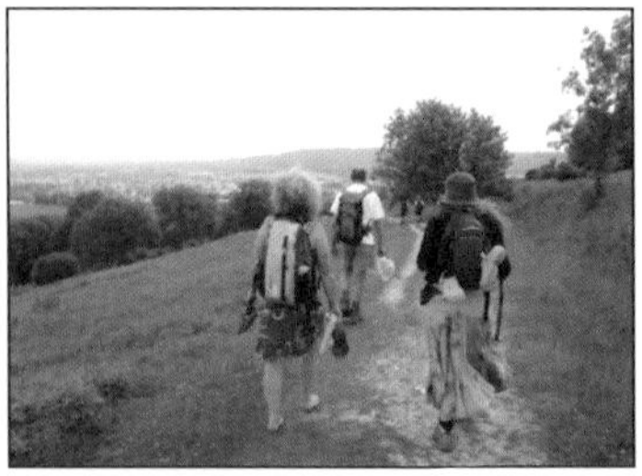

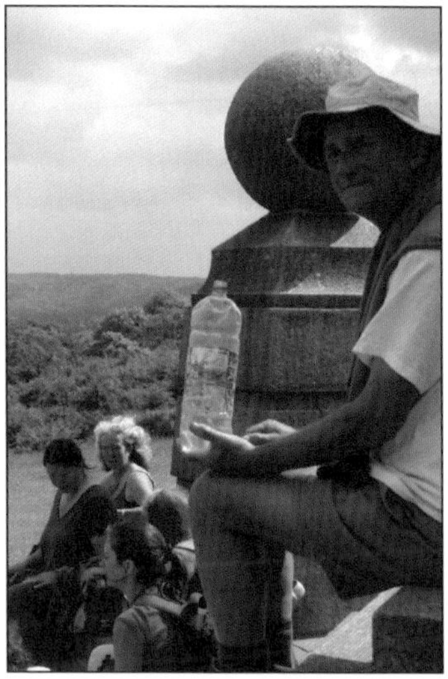

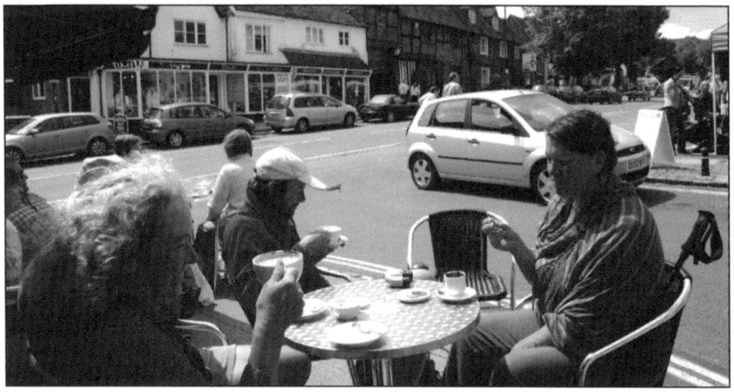

Saturday
morning ... Wendover
market
sunshine ... jazz band
coffee – pilgrims delight

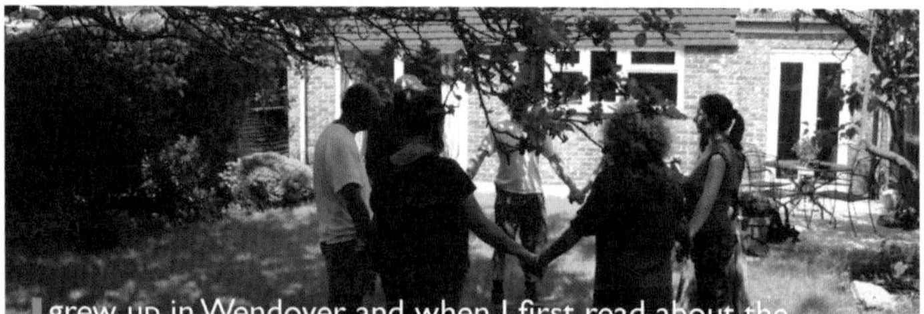

I grew up in Wendover and when I first read about the Michael Line – back in 1972 – I soon realised that it passed through my zone. Two years later I set out on my first trek down the line to Glastonbury. Ever since then I've had a vision of it becoming a great pilgrimage route so I'm thrilled to be involved in Awakening Albion because it feels like some kind of manifestation. But this year I'm about to move from here to the end of the line down in Cornwall! So as we all enter Wendover today I'm on poignancy overload. I ask my fellows if they'll support me in something. My Dad died in 2006 and, before I can move, his house has to be sold. I race ahead to the house then ... gulp ... there's a prospective purchaser standing outside! I introduce myself and splutter: "Any minute now a bunch of people are going to come round the corner – they're walking from Cornwall to Norfolk and we're just going to be in the back garden for two minutes!" "Wow" she replies. As the raggle-taggle gypsies appear so does the estate agent – in a white trouser suit! The house-viewing proceeds as we briefly stand in a circle. I silently thank this land and my parents for all they have given me in 55 years. Then we file out and move on. As Buckinghamshire has been my home for so long I'm really sorry that I couldn't have been more hospitable – circumstances did not permit. But it still feels extraordinary that this suburban back garden has become one of many stopping off points between Carn-lês-Boel and Hopton! The sacred has truly been brought into the everyday! *JMH*

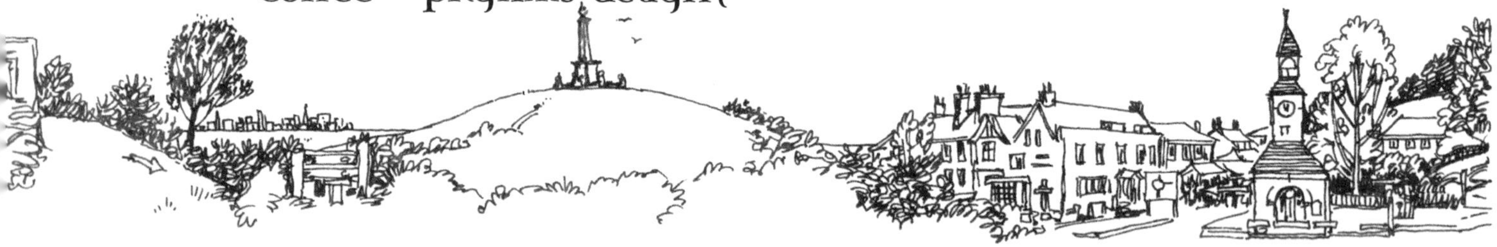

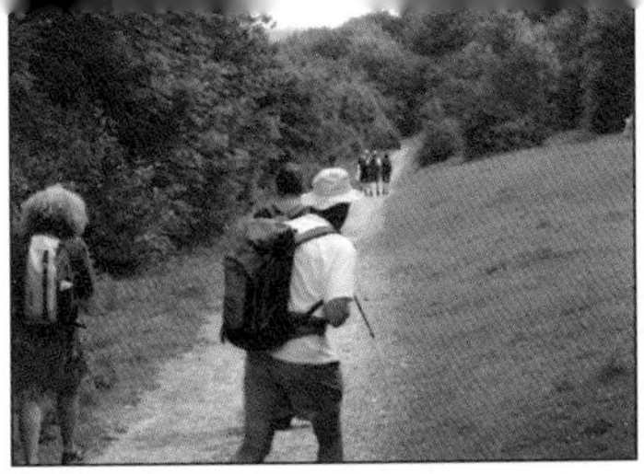

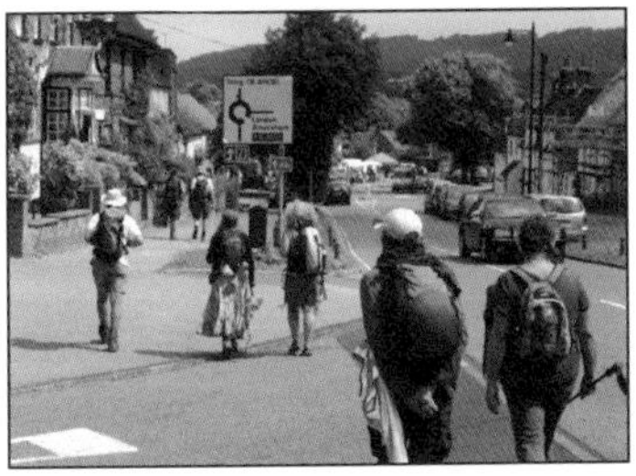

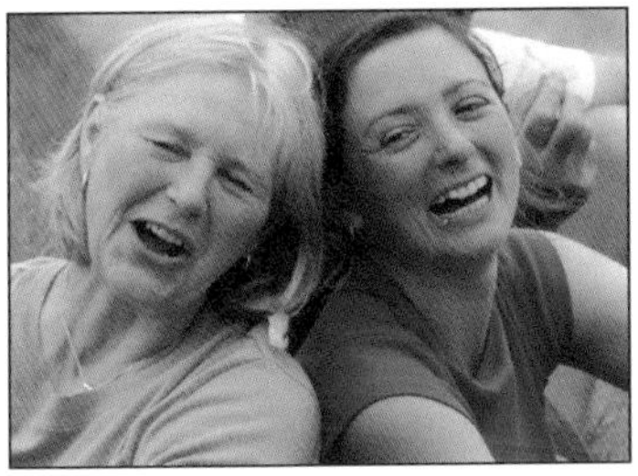

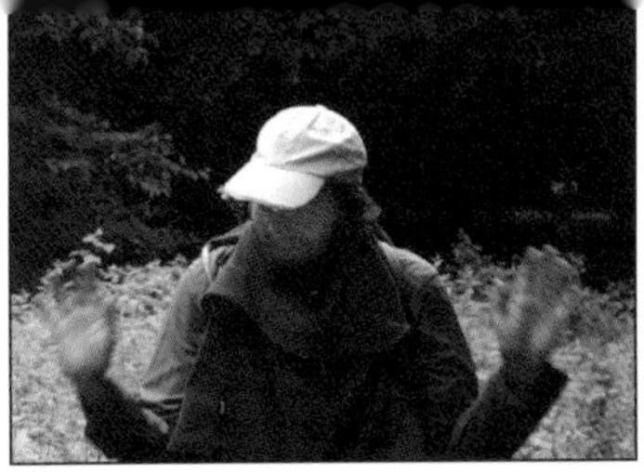

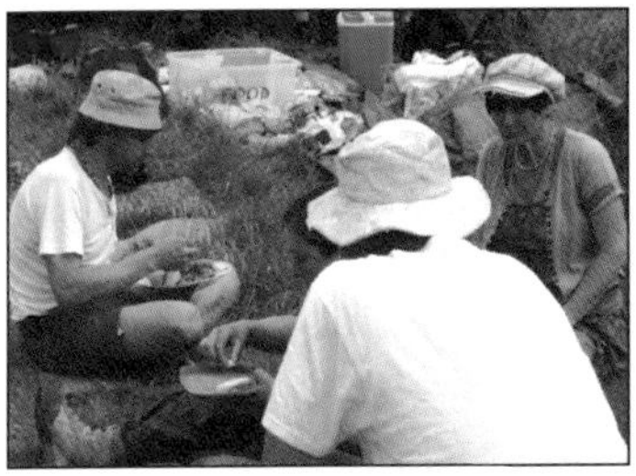

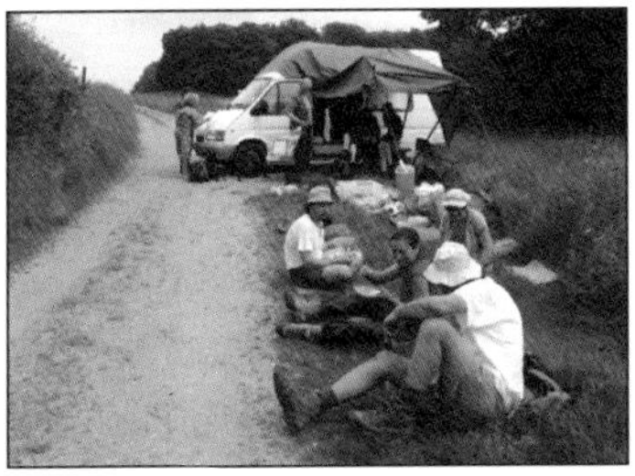

Dry. Nice take down. Latte coffee/hot chocolate, jazz band, market, interesting. We sat at table outside and enjoyed the moment. Jonathan's parents' house up for sale, we visited, had pee in garden while prospective buyers were being shown, I was not aware of them at time! We held hands in a circle and sang our song in the garden and took photos before setting off again. Lost in Wendover. We must have walked about 2 miles before we realised we had gone the wrong way, nice detour. Yes, we were lost for a while ... Long walk. Lunch 1½ hours late. Great lunch, made by Marion and Lynne. Ridgeway walk to Ivinghoe Beacon. Incredible vistas, views, along the way. Met Gerry near the Beacon. We often bumped into Gerry in the most unusual places. Met Graham in woods on the way to the camp site. Justine left. Dixie arrived. Justine's partner Graham came with beers for dinner. Sarah P's two daughters came to visit. Jonathan left after lunch. Elderflower fritters, made by Marion, mugwort tea with honey. Ian visited, he came brimming over with beer, wine and Very Special Dragon's Eggs in a Beautiful Basket. Camp by pond, you could hear the carp jumping. You could also hear and see the lights of a pop concert going on in the valley. So tired. Night! ***SS***

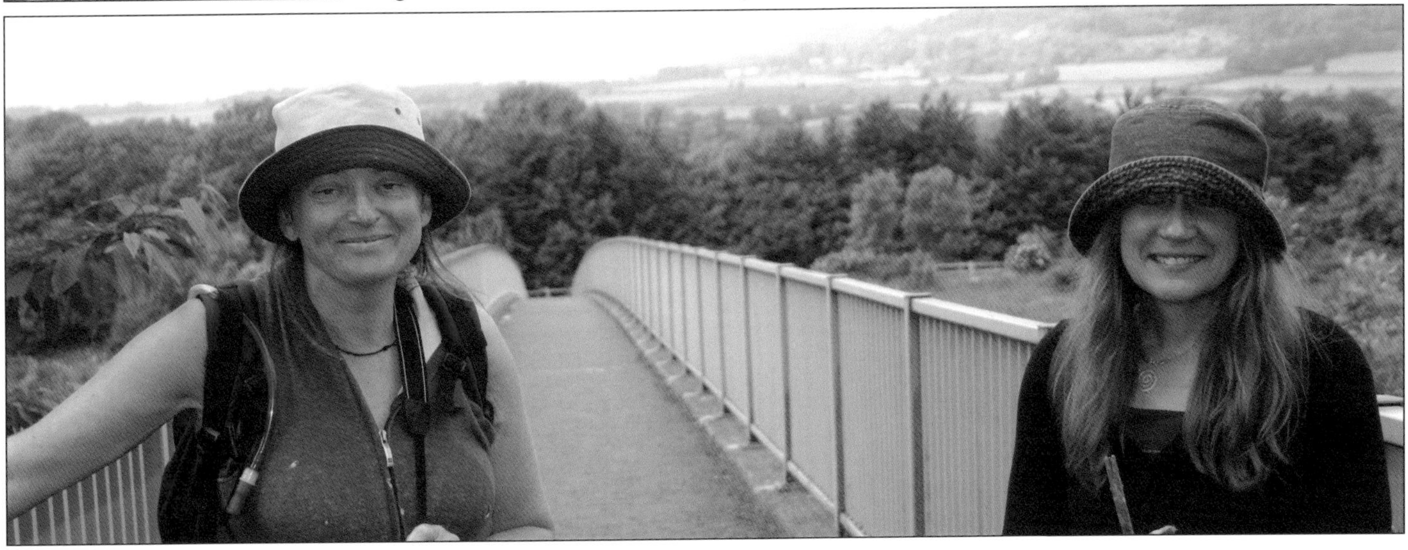

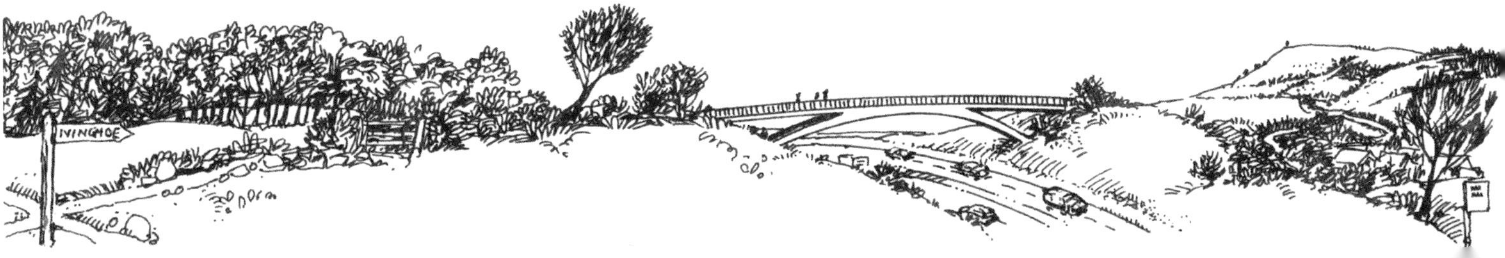

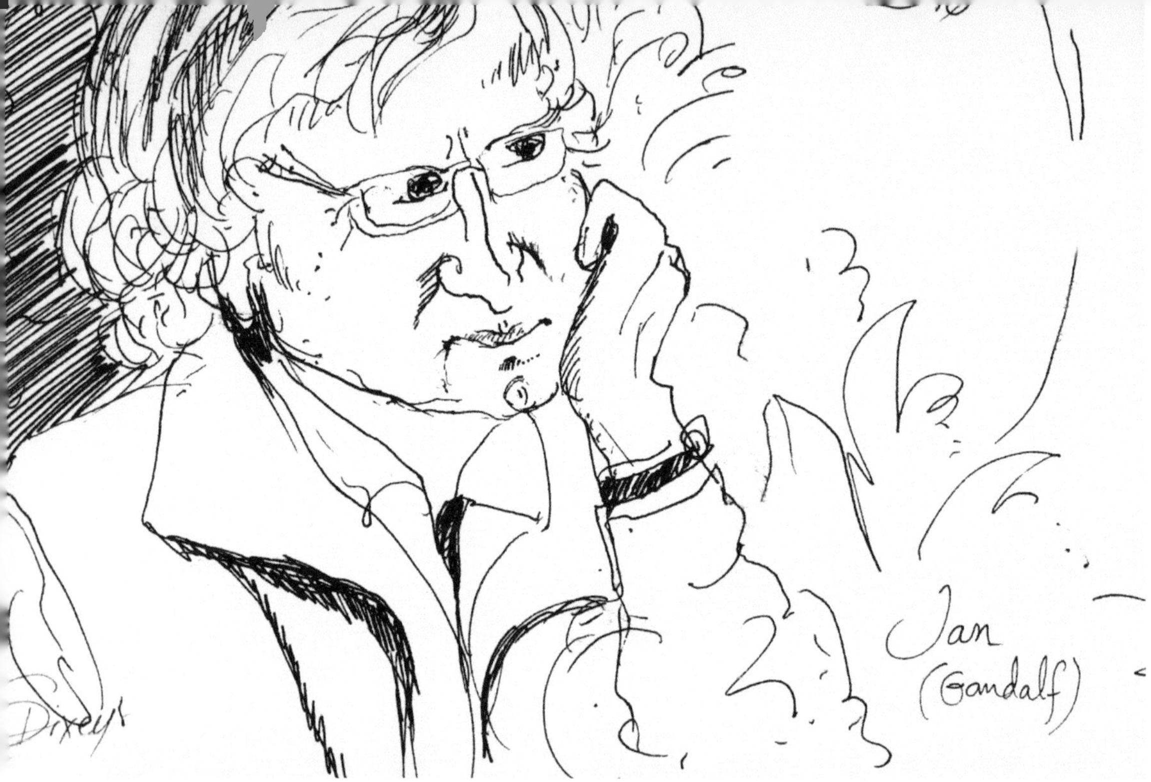

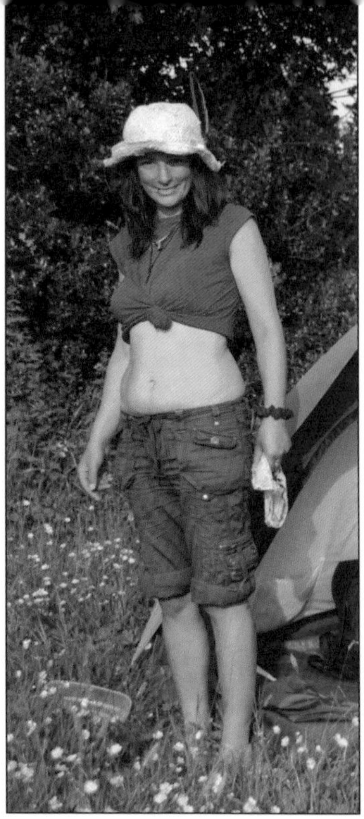

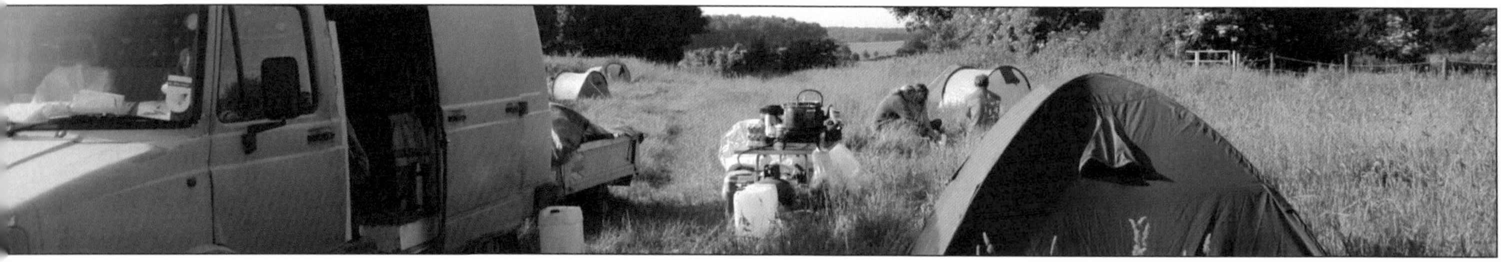

Dry morning. Tea in bed. Up 7.40, porridge then coffee. Nice calm take down.

Jane said goodbye. We are eleven strong. Alex returns tonight.

Lovely walk through morning. Grassy slopes, wooded pathways, across golf course and common. Just wonderful. Lunch 2.00.

After lunch, quite tough. Lots of tarmac walking. Really pounds feet. Last mile on footpath. Lots of sunshine.

I am the Pilgrim Archer. Placed many arrows today. Feels very significant!

Camp on common ground. Lots of noise, next to Luton airport. Church singing.

Sasha and Dixie cooked dinner. Very tasty.

Very tired. Had sharing. Still tired. Early night. I can hear one or two around fire but I think I'll stay here.

I think Alex is back. Lynne and Sarah P went to fetch him. Bed 10.15. ***SS***

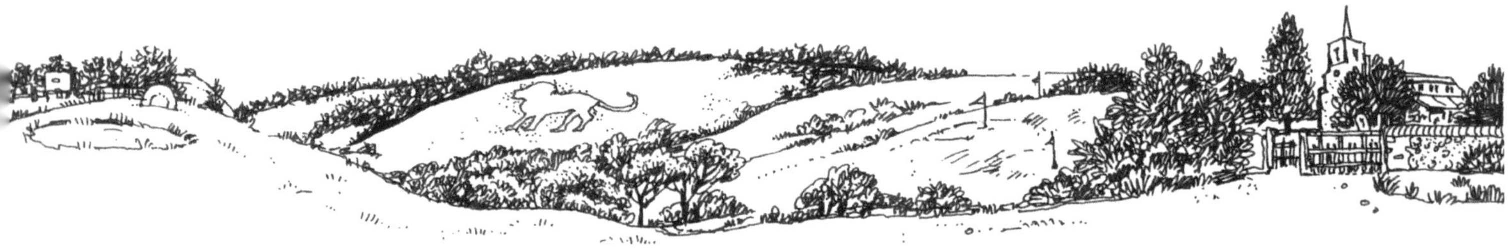

Day 35 Ivinghoe to Chiltern Green

Am looking out on a field of golden buttercups and a dark line of trees, capped with the last embers of a glowing red sunset. This evening I watched two deer, playful, pushing and nuzzling each other, ambling up the set aside land in the field next door. There are pheasants in the fields here.

Some of us are camped on the other side of the track on the common ground. The people are so friendly here in the cottages, one family has opened their home to us, so we can go in for showers. We are not far from Luton, you can see and hear the planes taking off from Luton airport.

It was hot and sunny all day today. I walked barefoot for a while, feeling the mud between my toes, the grit on my heel, through magic woods. I dipped my feet in a pond. Lynne saw tadpoles and a newt. I saw a stoat run across the road today too. We wondered at some incredible ash trees, a huge single trunk and also some multiple pollarded trunks. Lovely lunch in a cool churchyard and an afternoon pause in the shade of a young oak on a green, grass bank following a long pull up a hot tarmac road.

Crossed the A5 and the M1 today, hundreds of people hurtling along in cars. We stood on the bridge and waved. Lots of people slowed down when they spotted Sarah with her camera in a high vis vest!!

Delicious organic dinner cooked by Dixie and Sasha. I am enjoying seeing new people arrive and relax. Jane left today. It was sad to see fly-tipping today. ***ML***

common ground
evening deepens
waning moon
campfire sharing
milky tea ... dragons eggs

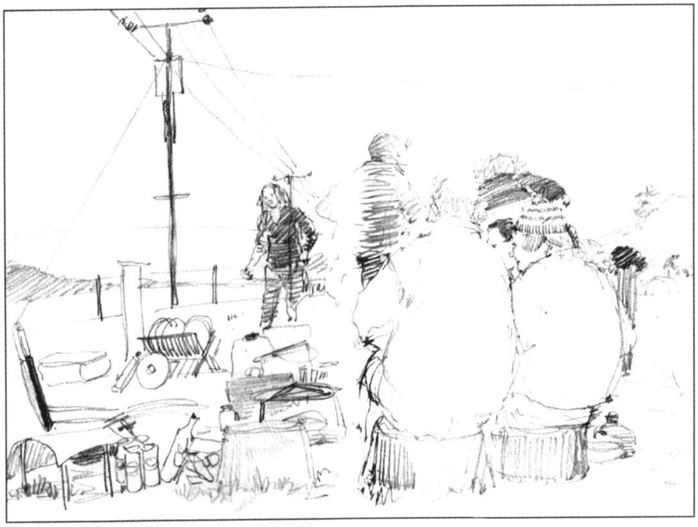

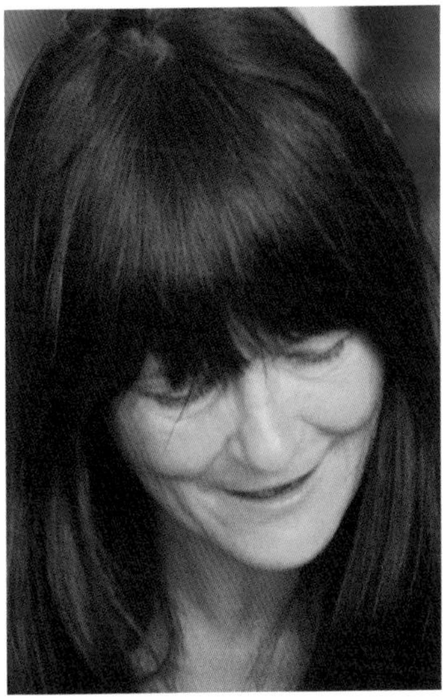

We passed a lonely emu in Whipsnade Zoo, navigating the boundary on the off chance ... we crossed a motorway junction ... a place that nobody ever goes ... the traffic rushes past. It feels desolate, empty ... a non-place.

Aeroplanes coming in and out of Luton dominate the landscape. For me, flight is miraculous and these planes make happy sounds ... in the distance a church choir reminds me it's Sunday. ***SB***

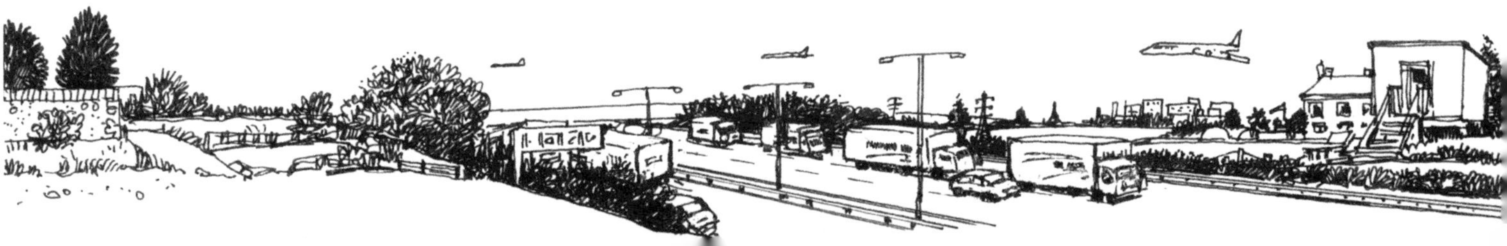

Day 36 Chiltern Green to Graveley

Gorgeous sunshine all day! This morning I felt homesick and tearful first thing. Porridge and watching the black dog, Flash Boy, from the cottages, in the middle of our singing circle, helped me feel happier. I enjoyed driving 'Albion' with Sarah today, we found the site easily, a farm at Graveley, near Stevenage. Tim and Jenny are our hosts and their little dogs Dot and Poppy, mother and daughter.

I sawed logs in the hot sun, we borrowed a bicycle, it is fun to ride around the track, to the toilets. Carolin came home today. I sunbathed, lazed about, played guitar, gossiped in the shade lying on my sarong, with Lynne. After supper we picked strawberries and ate them round the fire with cream and sugar. Amazing!!

I took a chance at trying some healing. I felt really moved to lay my hands on Dixie, and I asked God to heal her, I opened my eyes and let it all drift up on the smoke, Graham was playing a song on his whistle. ***ML***

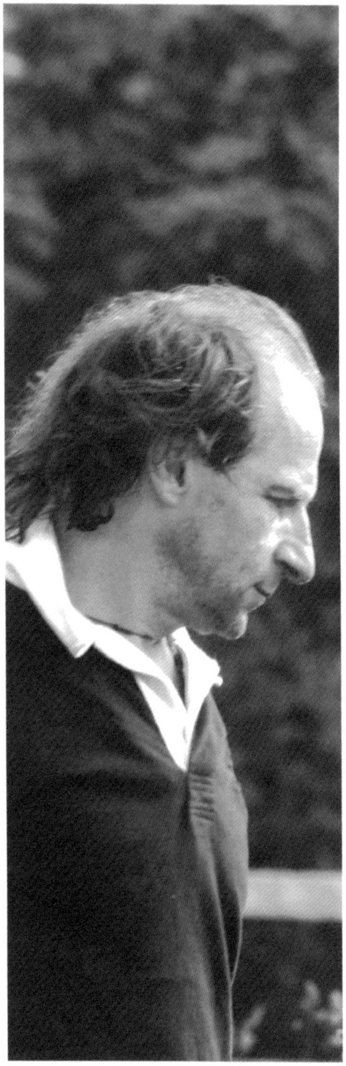

Nice sleeping on the common. Local folk very kind, some of us went and had shower in their home. Gentle pack up and breakfast. Porridge, made with oats or rice, sultanas, milk, nuts, what one can find at the time, followed by coffee. Paparazzi today with Marion and Sarah 'C'. It's a Lou Reed day 'Oh, such a perfect day ...' a timeless song written in the late sixties or early seventies. Forget-me-not field. Sunshine, blue skies, fluffy white clouds, wonderful colours, fields, woods, trees, footpaths, bridleways. All manner of ways. Arrows galore, made of coloured paper, flowers, twigs, plants and other materials, stones, and chalk ones. It was the first day that I didn't place any arrows myself as I walked with Marion taking pictures and filming, which meant being at the back of the walkers. Twisted giant oaks, giant beeches. Orchids. Water-Cress Farm. No cress for sale but we bought choc-ices. Ginger beer over ice. Releases in hay field! Numbers to count, 1-12-24-36 etc ... this was to do with taking pictures at certain places and gaps apart from each shot. It will become clearer when Sarah 'C' edits and makes her movie of the walk, which everyone will get a chance to see. Buttercup lined path, oh so pretty. Rabbit wire, digger madness, rabbit warren along path, seems like a huge colony, mega damage! Strawberry picking after dinner. Unripe gooseberries. Bicycle ride to the loos lent to us by our host. Outdoor dressage arena next to camping area. Our host's daughter was practising her dressage skills while we were there. Lou Reed!!! ***SS***

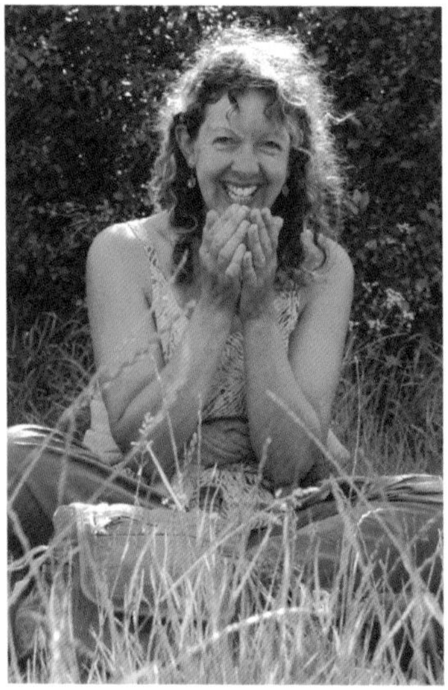

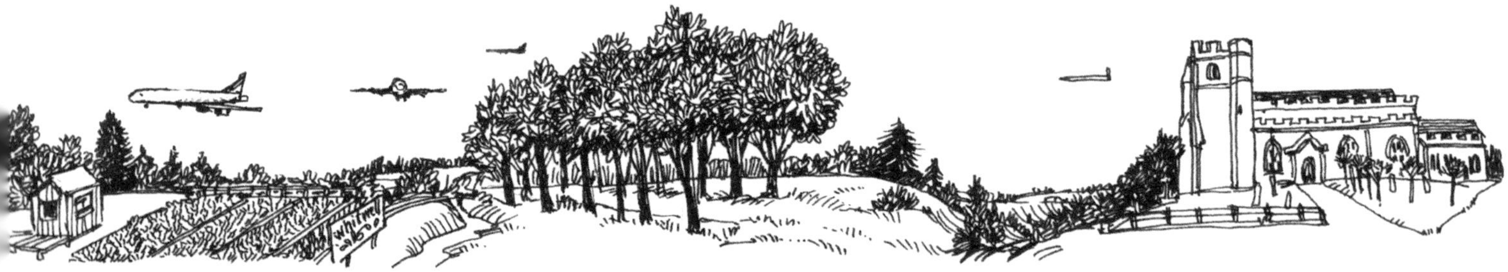

This morning I woke in a field of buttercups with four Arab horses looking at me. At breakfast the children from the house next door joined us around the fire, like little faeries. Today I was crewing with Mel. We drove to our next campsite and met up with the owner Tim. I dug a fire pit and we collected some jerry cans of water and unloaded the kitchen. And that was it. We lazed around for the rest of the day!. ***SB***

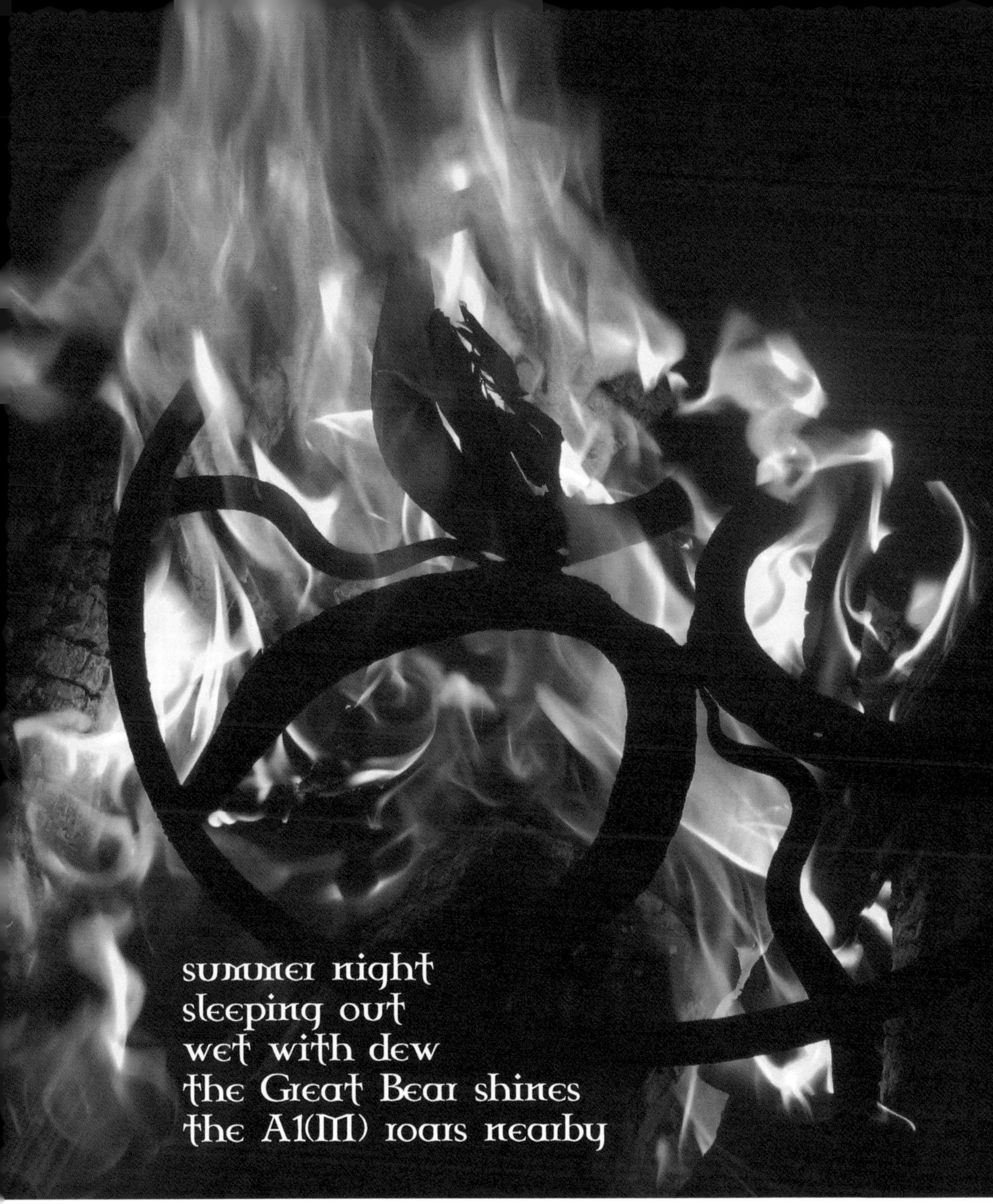

summer night
sleeping out
wet with dew
the Great Bear shines
the A1(M) roars nearby

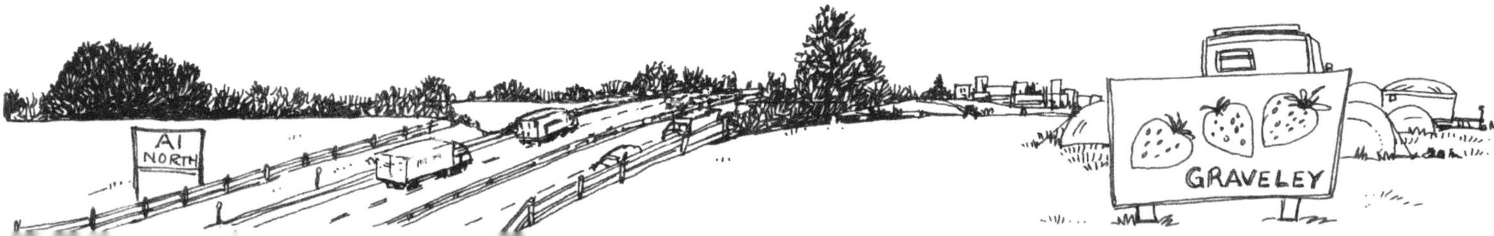

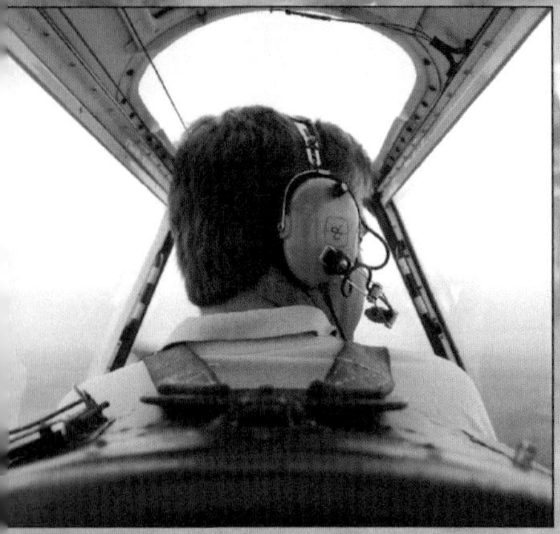

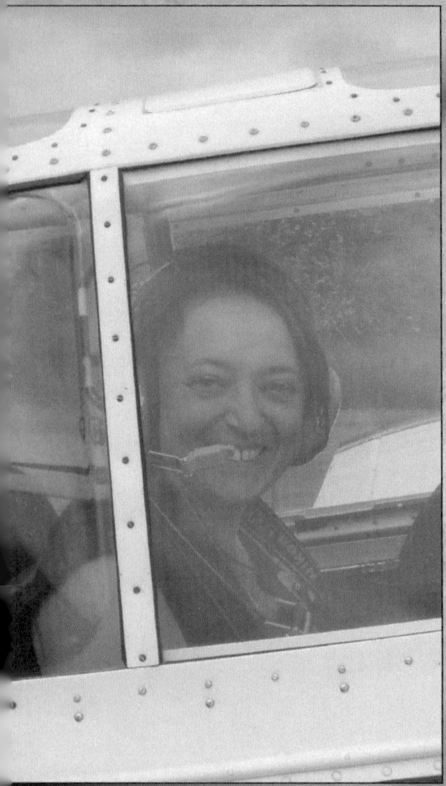

This morning Tim, the owner of the land, said he had a surprise for us. As we set off we found him waiting in a small aircraft next to a grass runway and offering one of us a flight. The rest of the group encouraged me to go as I had a camera and could film it so they could all see it later. A generous offer indeed! Tim let me fly for a bit. I was struck by the sensitivity of the joy stick, just the tiniest touch and it moved left, right ... climbed, dived. We even did aerobatics, first climbing to 2000ft. It was the weirdest and most intense feeling and what amazed me most was that Tim could still control the plane whilst doing them! I took 400 photos! ... what a treat, I love flying and was incredibly touched that the group encouraged me to take the flight. The rest of the day was a lovely walk through long summer meadows. The rape seed flowers are nearly gone already and the seed heads are heavy and there are buttercups everywhere and now too some cut fields as the hay making begins. But all day part of me still remained at 2000ft screaming 'OhMyGod'! ***SB***

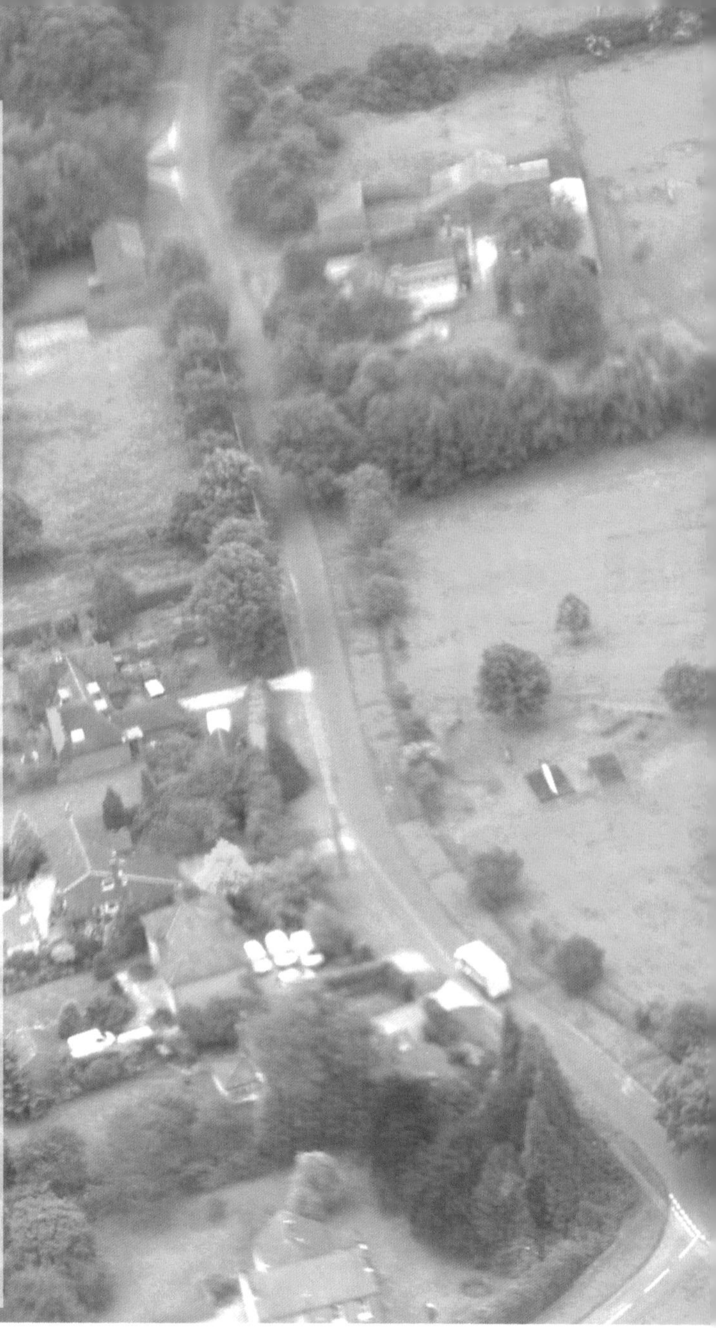

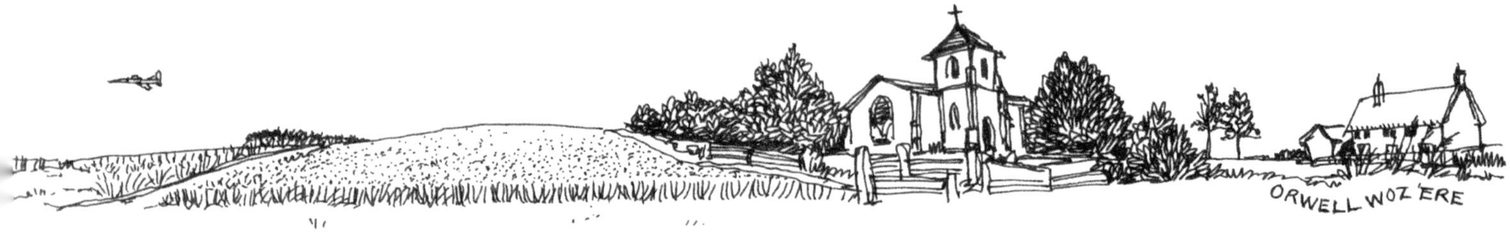

Day 37 Graveley to Therfield

Beautiful sunshine. 6.00am. Open tent, sunsoak until 7.20. Up for tea. Back to bed. No! Kind of! After tea, usual breakfast. Plus marmalade on toast. Yummy! Crew day, Albion with Lynne. Marion leaves after Take Down and Set Off. Carolin takes her to the station. Carolin is using her car so she can continue the journey until she is strong enough to walk. Arrive at new site 10.20 am, Fox and Duck pub. Lynne books herself in for the night. We camp in the beer garden at the rear. Set up kitchen, dig fire pit, loos in pub. Sawed logs, lunch in pub. BLT+$J_2 0$. Made fire. Wrote yesterday's experience. Lynne read extract from *The Sun and the Serpent*, 'Awakening' van very late arriving. Only ½hr before walkers, don't know why. Helped Gerry prepare and cook dinner. I mainly chopped and peeled. Great dinner. Had circle sharing, OK, talked about meat! Then went to the pub for a pint of Ruddles. Graham, Mel, Rhian and me. Back to the fire, all in bed except Carolin who was having a 'Wee-Nippy-Sweetie', I also joined her. Then to bed. 10:30. ***SS***

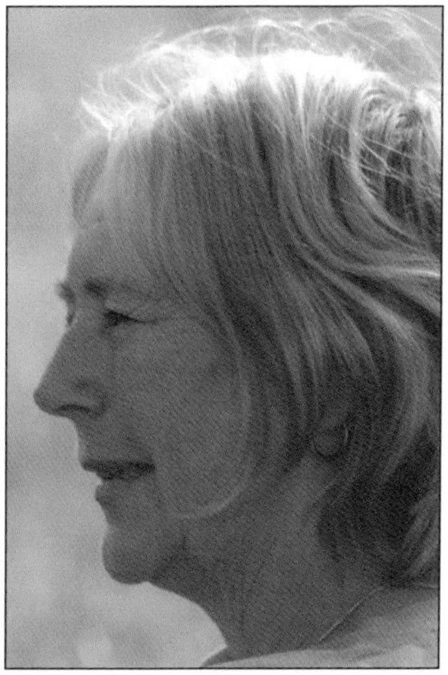

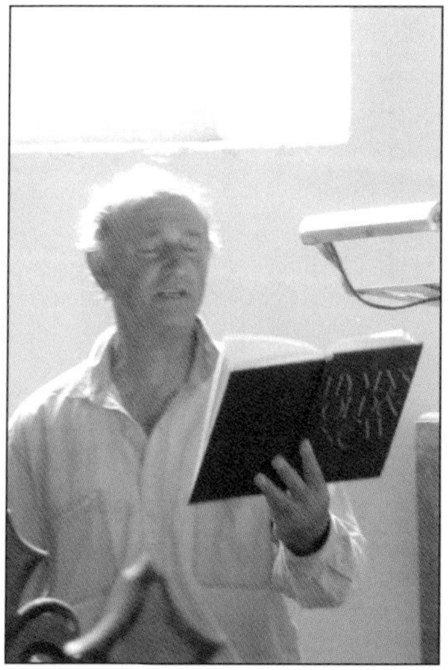

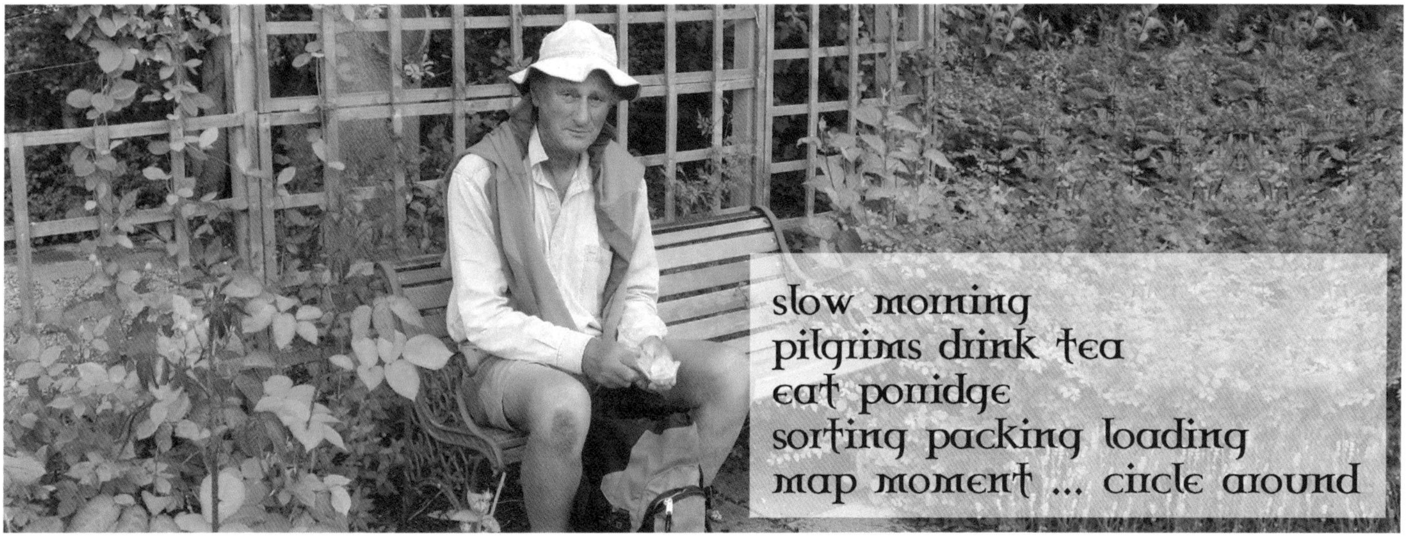

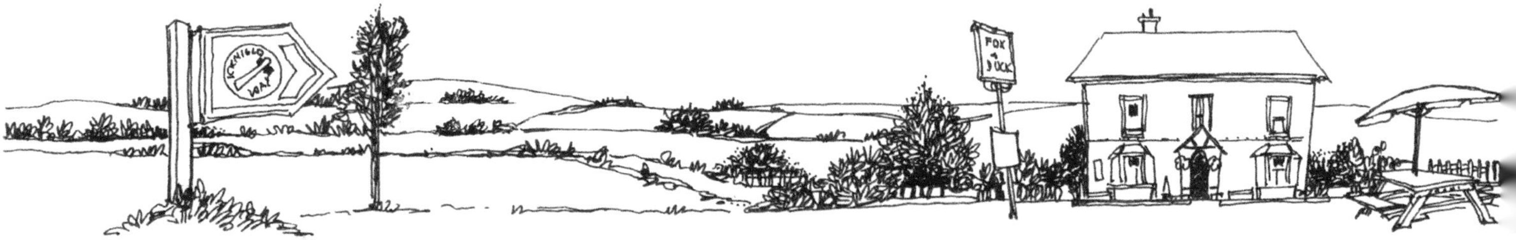

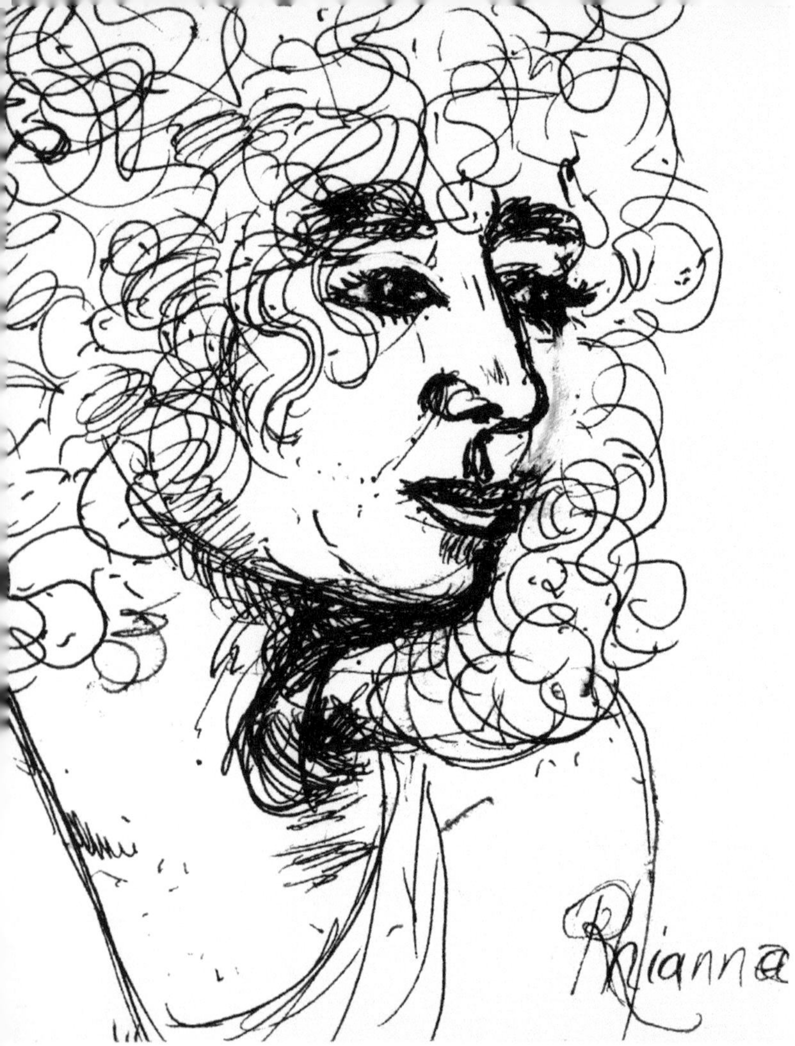

Day 38

What a great day! Think it may be a bit late, sat up talking round the fire with Graham, about plans and ideas and hopes and walking and people and places.

We visited Royston Cave today, bang in the town centre. After a coffee at "Wedgies" coffee shop we descended a few stone steps, and a steep damp corridor, under the street to the cave, with its amazing chalk carvings extensively explained by our 81 year old guide. I felt intrigued by the mystery and magic of the cave and wondered about the secrets held and ceremonies performed there. The connection with the Freemasons made me think of my Grandad, Douglas. I wonder who he was and regret not trying to know him better.

Lovely walking this afternoon, on more Icknield Way, through fields and meadows. We visited Ickleton Church and saw oak pews with beautiful dragons, and learnt about the chorister who lost the plot and set fire to the church in 1979, revealing 12th and 14th century paintings underneath the top coat of paint.

After tea we ate chocolate, 100%, bitter, Green and Blacks and Dixie's lovely homemade almond and brazil nut chocolate, and talked about Freemasons, King Arthur, sacred geometry and sex. We laughed and had fun. What a rich day! ***ML***

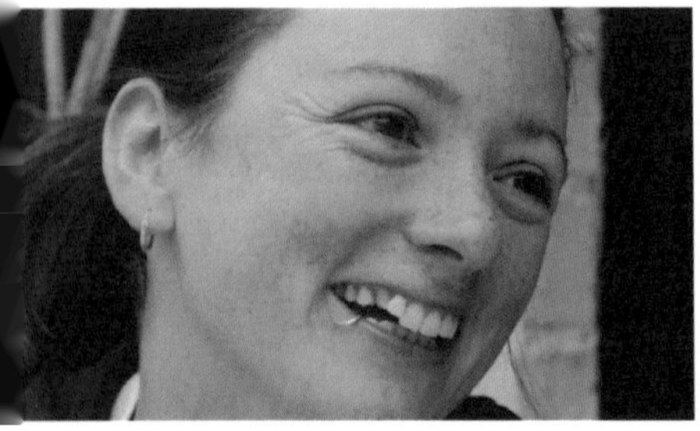

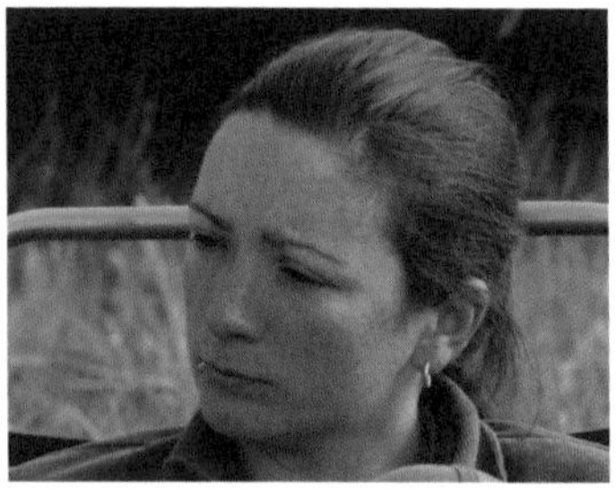

early morning
partridges walk the camp ...
a pheasant
perches on the grey van ...
lo the hunter is asleep

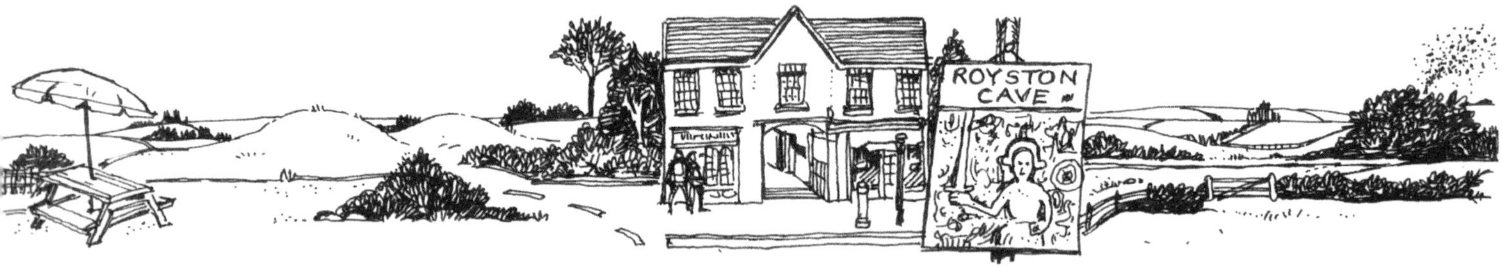

Therfield to Lt Walden

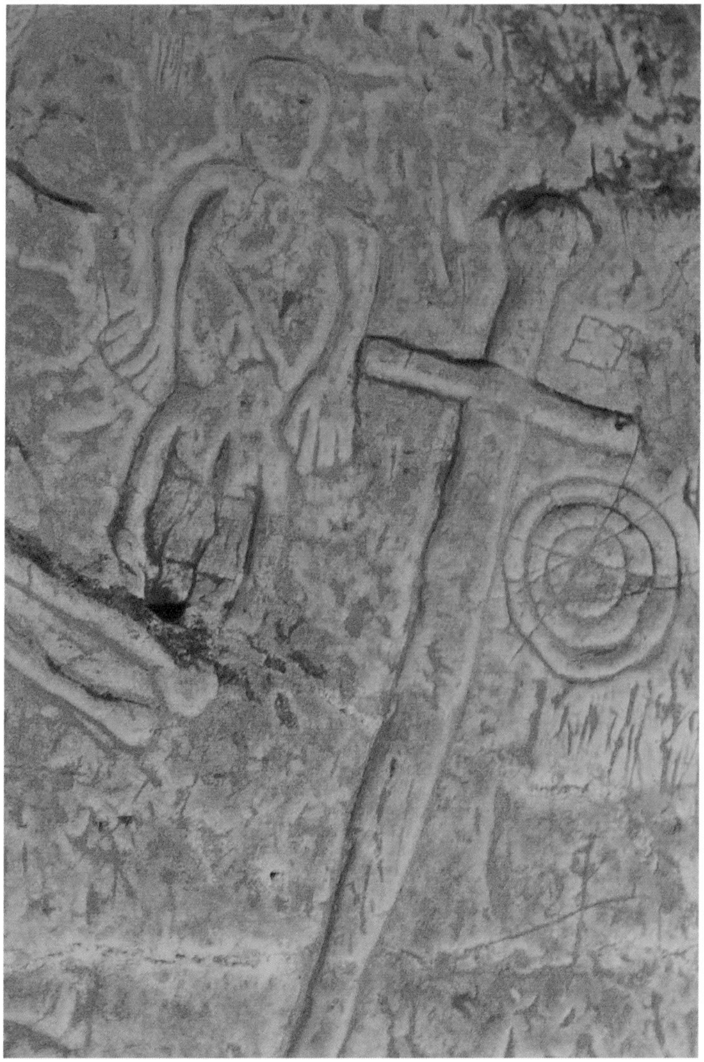

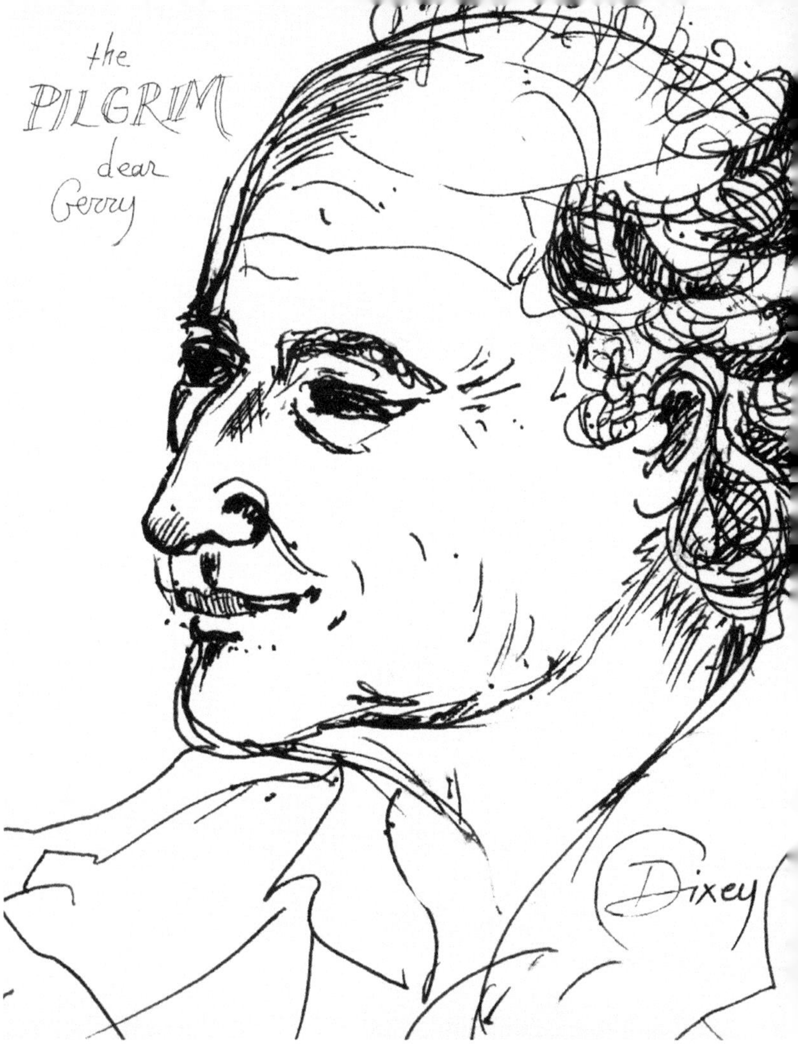

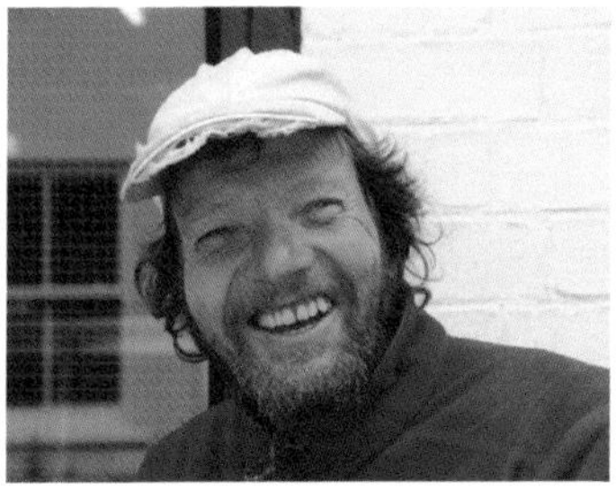

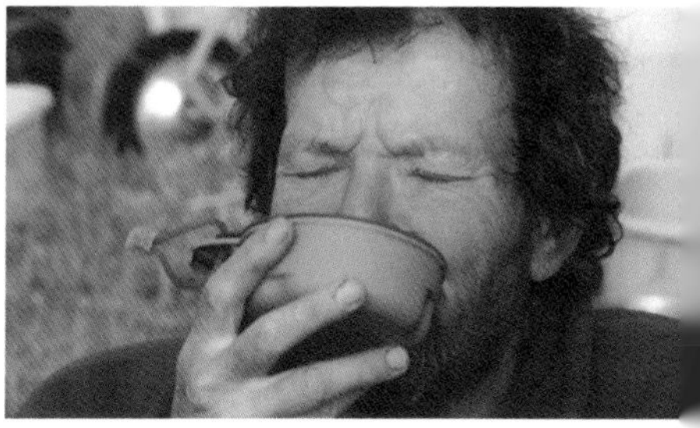

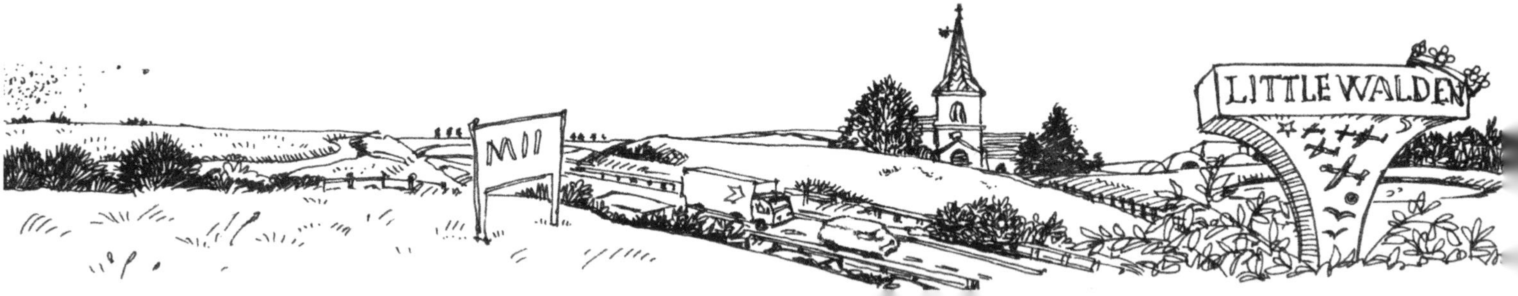

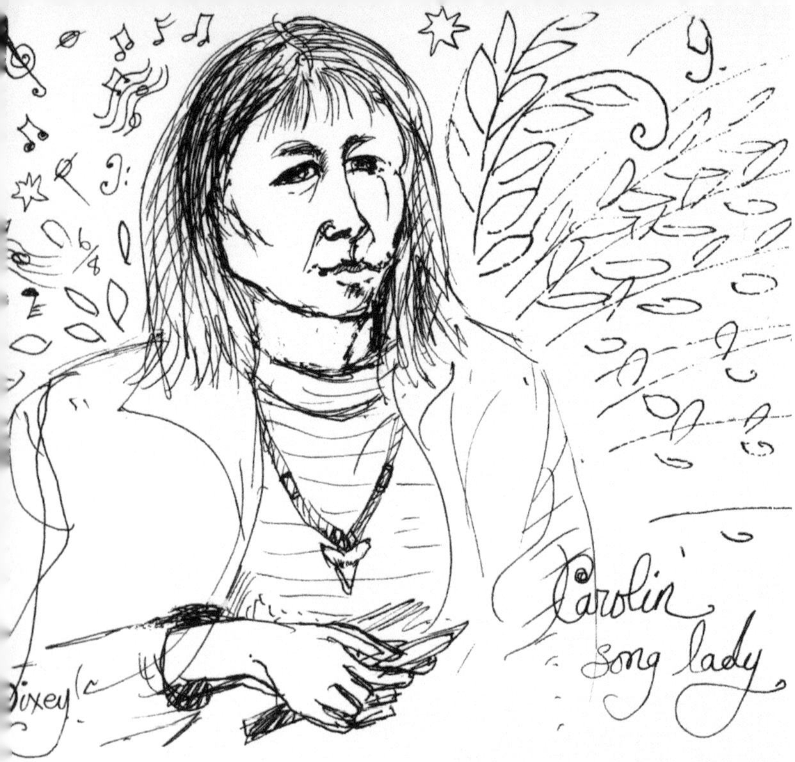

Day 39

Lt Walden to Carlton

Brrr ... it's cold tonight, I'm in bed with my hat on. We are near Newmarket, at Carlton. I had a lovely time with the small herd of cows in the field next door. They all came to the gate where I stood and sniffed me with their wet noses and licked me with their long tongues, I looked in their gentle eyes and felt so sad for all the horrible things which people do to cows. I still feel sad now. Good walking today, felt positive and happy. The wild roses were beautiful in the hedgerows. We had lunch under an old wooden market cross in Balsham. We ate pasties in another village and walked through fields of wheat. It rained today and the long grass was so wet. I saw a fledgling rook on his first visit out of the nest, clumsy and ungainly, with long gangly legs, anxious parents swooping to divert my attention, at Great Chesterford churchyard. ***ML***

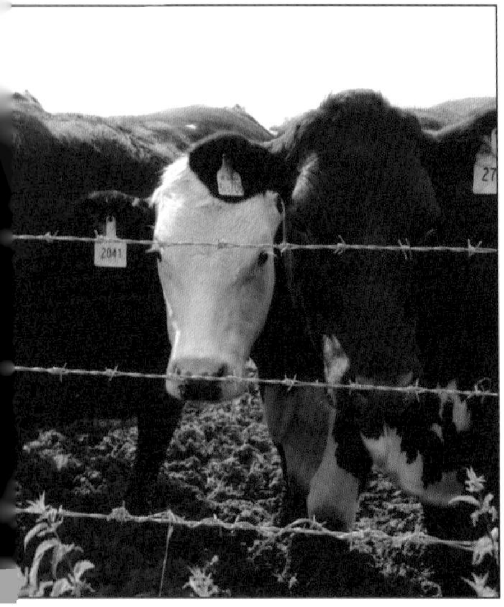

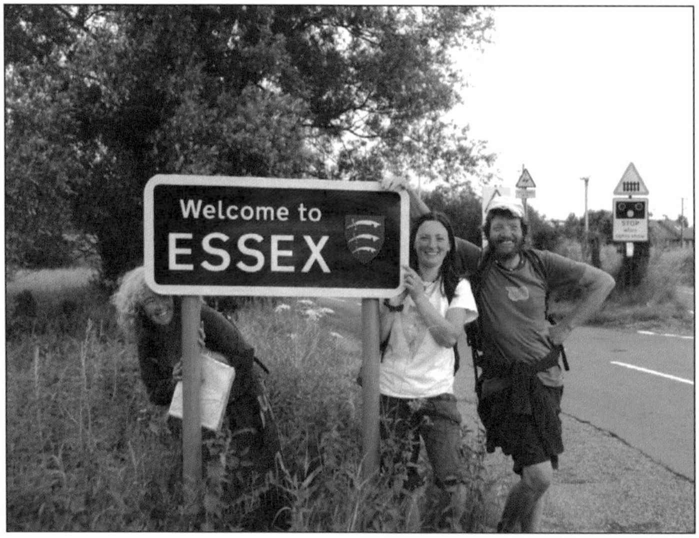

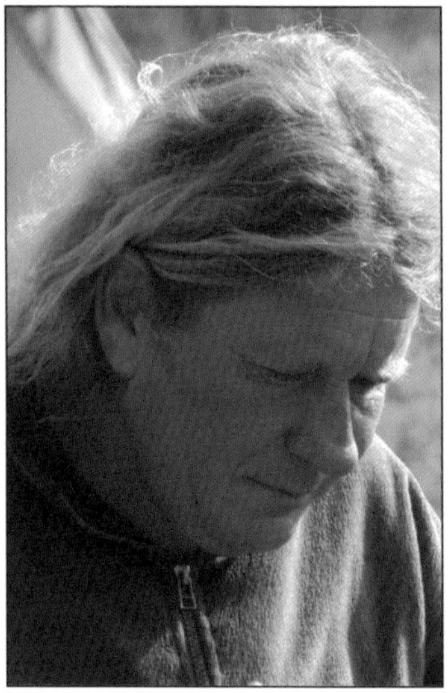

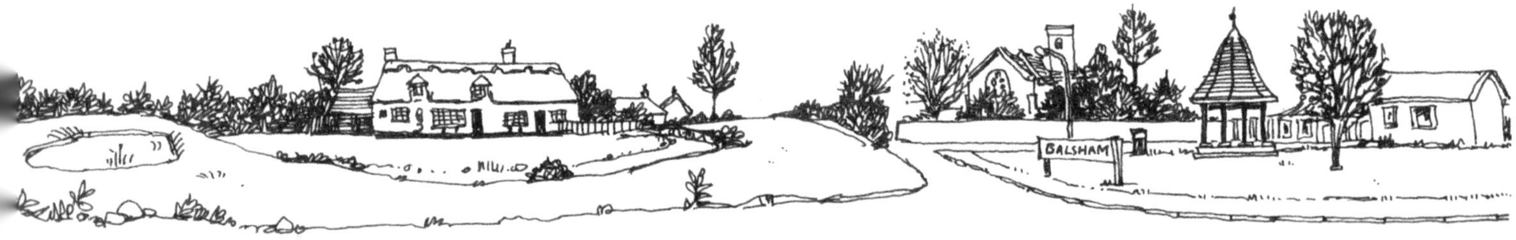

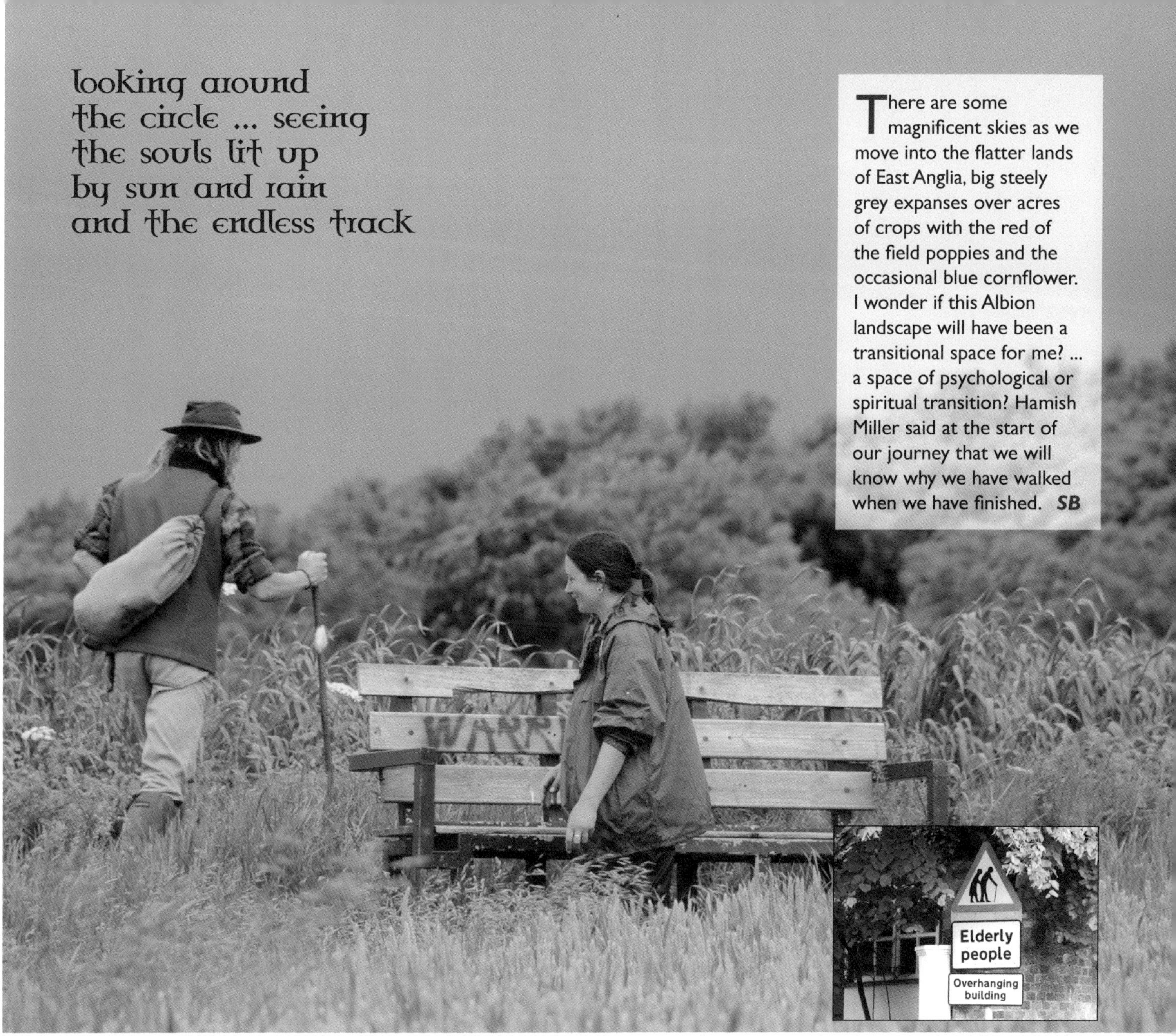

looking around
the circle ... seeing
the souls lit up
by sun and rain
and the endless track

There are some magnificent skies as we move into the flatter lands of East Anglia, big steely grey expanses over acres of crops with the red of the field poppies and the occasional blue cornflower. I wonder if this Albion landscape will have been a transitional space for me? ... a space of psychological or spiritual transition? Hamish Miller said at the start of our journey that we will know why we have walked when we have finished. ***SB***

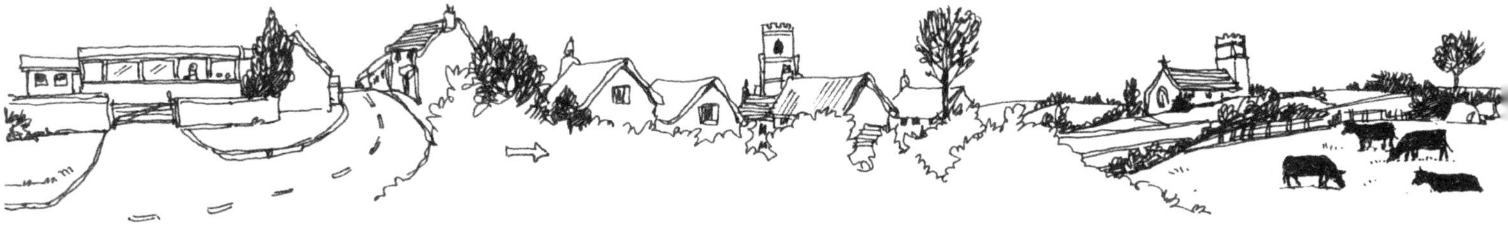

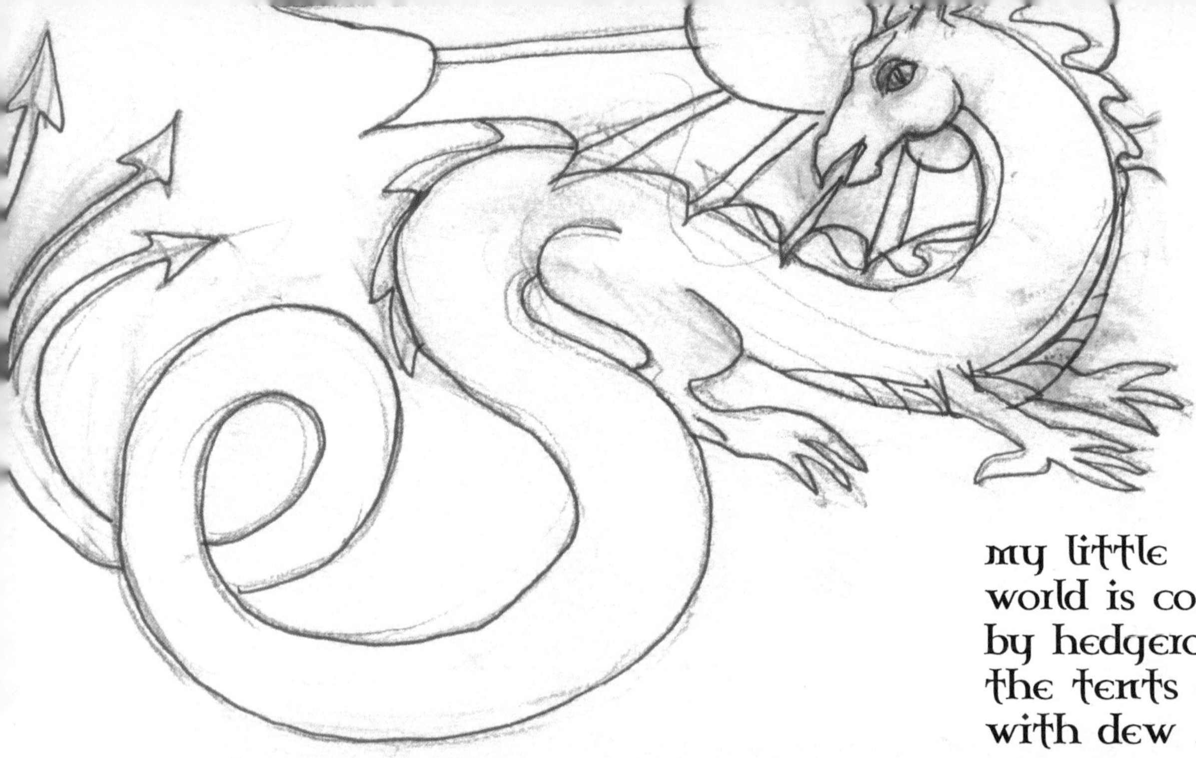

my little
world is contained
by hedgerows ...
the tents are wet
with dew ... the sun rises

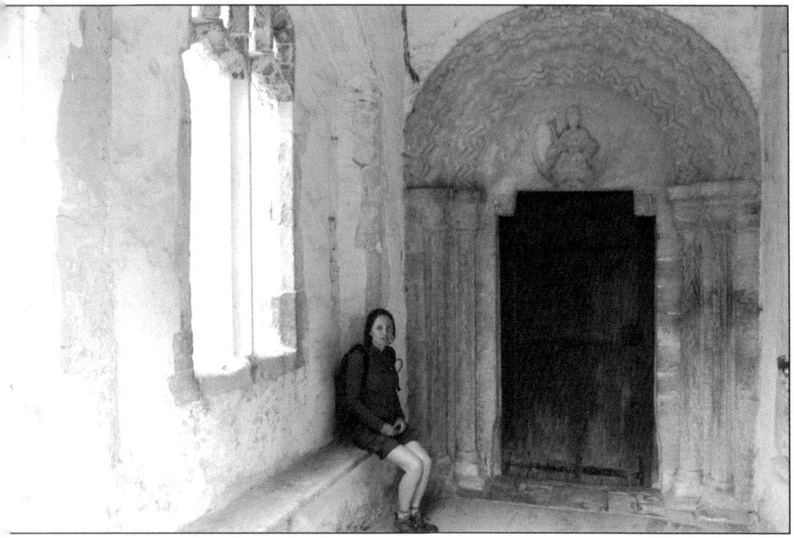

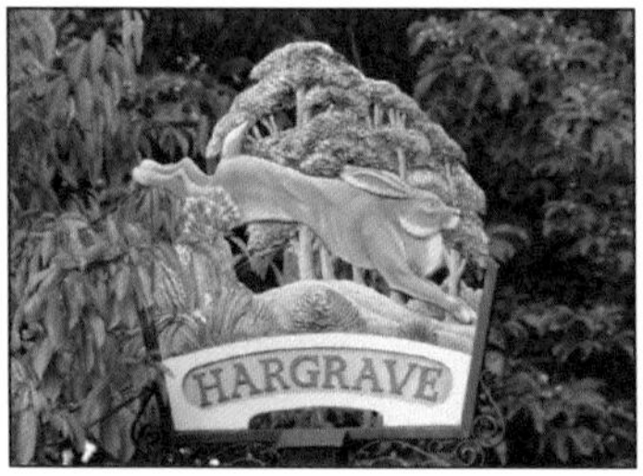

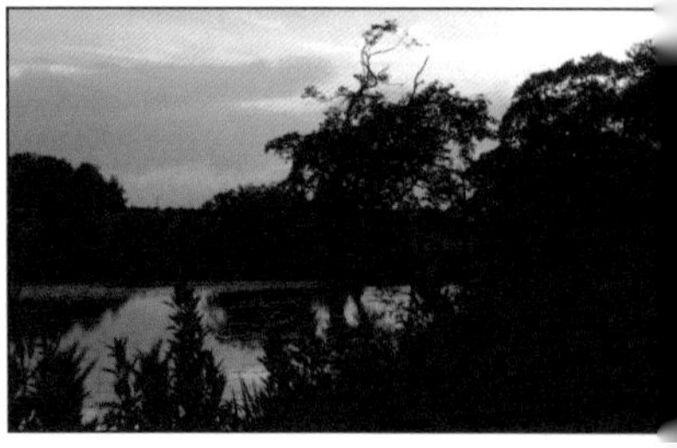

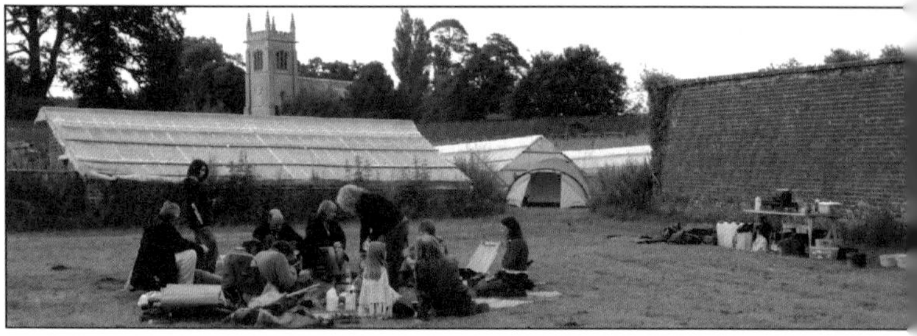

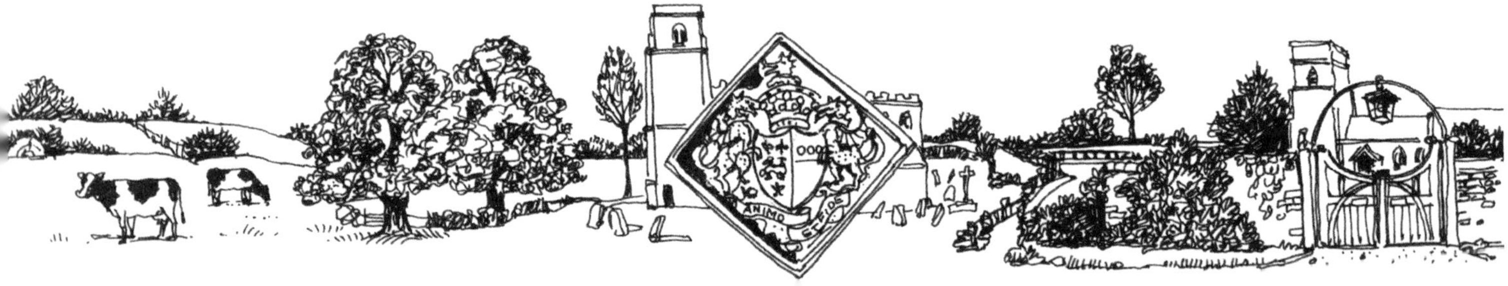

Day 40 Carlton to Ickworth

We are camping in the walled garden of the very beautiful Ickworth Park. This is National Trust land, we are so lucky to be able to camp here. We are sheltered on two sides by Victorian red brick walls, the land slopes gently down to a clear lake, where geese, ducks, moorhens and coots swim amongst the lily pads. Behind is a vineyard and apple orchard, mistletoe grows on the twisted branches. In the adjoining garden is an old summer house, with huge sash windows, and double glass doors, the floor tiled in patterns. There are some beautiful trees here, oaks, elms, redwoods, beeches and willows. I was driving 'Albion' today, crewing with Steve, it was great to come into the park, and drive past all the beige day visitors, like a gypsy. I saw six goldfinches playing, pecking at the bricks, swooping and twittering to each other. I enjoyed working hard, digging the fire pit and taking the turf out in one piece, my hands were covered with earth and I felt happy, safe and content. The morning was sad and harsh. After the walkers left, men came and took cattle away in a big truck. When Steve and I went up to the big sheds to fill the water butts, we saw cows, crammed indoors, push their noses under the gap between wall and ground. I glimpsed a hood, the white of an eye. Then I saw lying in the yard, a big black cow, eye staring, dead. It was so shocking, so stark. I cried at the injustice, the awful treatment of the beautiful, placid, gentle creatures and for the indignity of the dead cow. We visited the church at Kirtling, with its paintings of dragons and the tomb, carved with stone dragons. The incongruent mix of beautiful stone, wood, cloth craftsmanship and the chaotic mess of calor gas heaters and junk propped up randomly. I helped to cook curry for tea. Carl, Kieran and Aiofe arrived tonight. ***ML***

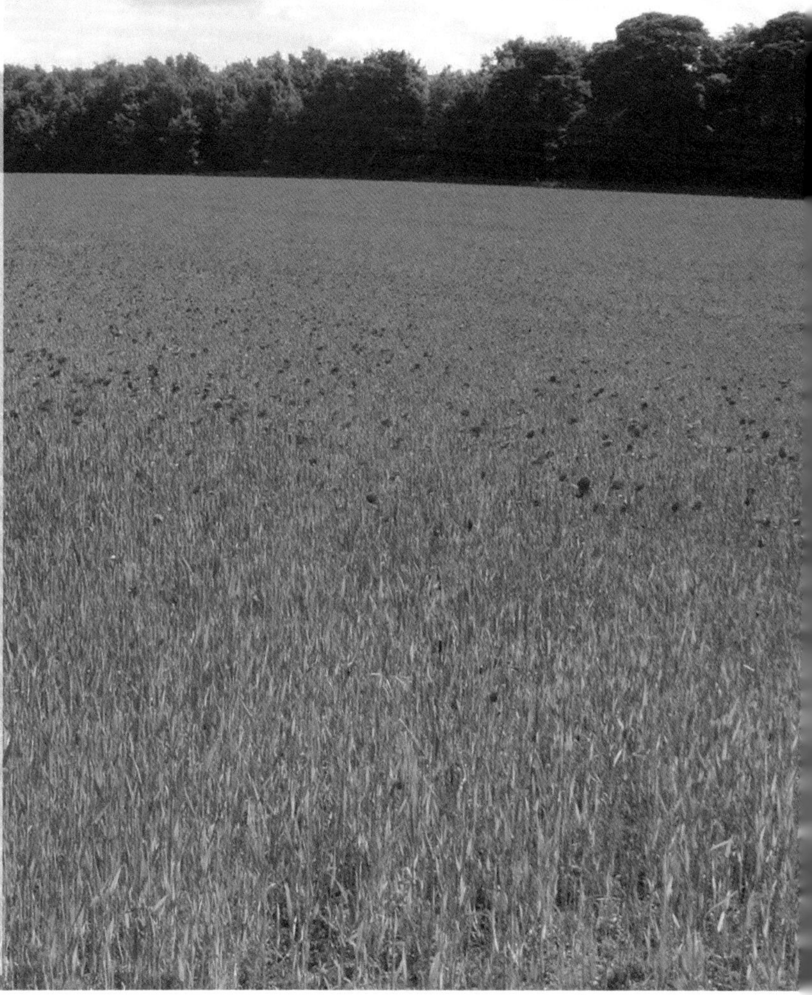

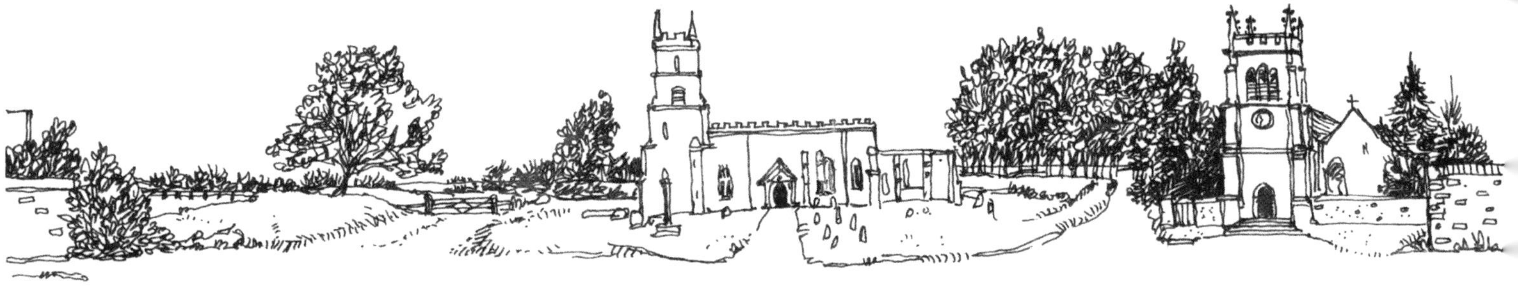

Day 41 Ickworth to Rougham

I had a powerful experience at Bury St Edmunds, when the Michael and Mary lines came to a 'kissing point' in the grounds of the old ruined Abbey. Here, going right down the nave of the ancient Abbey, the lines came together, very nearly touching, but not crossing, along the whole line of the nave before separating once more to travel their own route. This made me think of Gibran's poem *On Marriage* with its image '... the strings of a lute are alone/Though they quiver with the same music'. To represent this idea of being alone, but quivering with the same music, which the Michael and Mary lines demonstrate so beautifully as they weave in and out of each other through the countryside, we created a lovely dance, making an arch of joined hands along the line through which couples would dance and kiss. **CC**

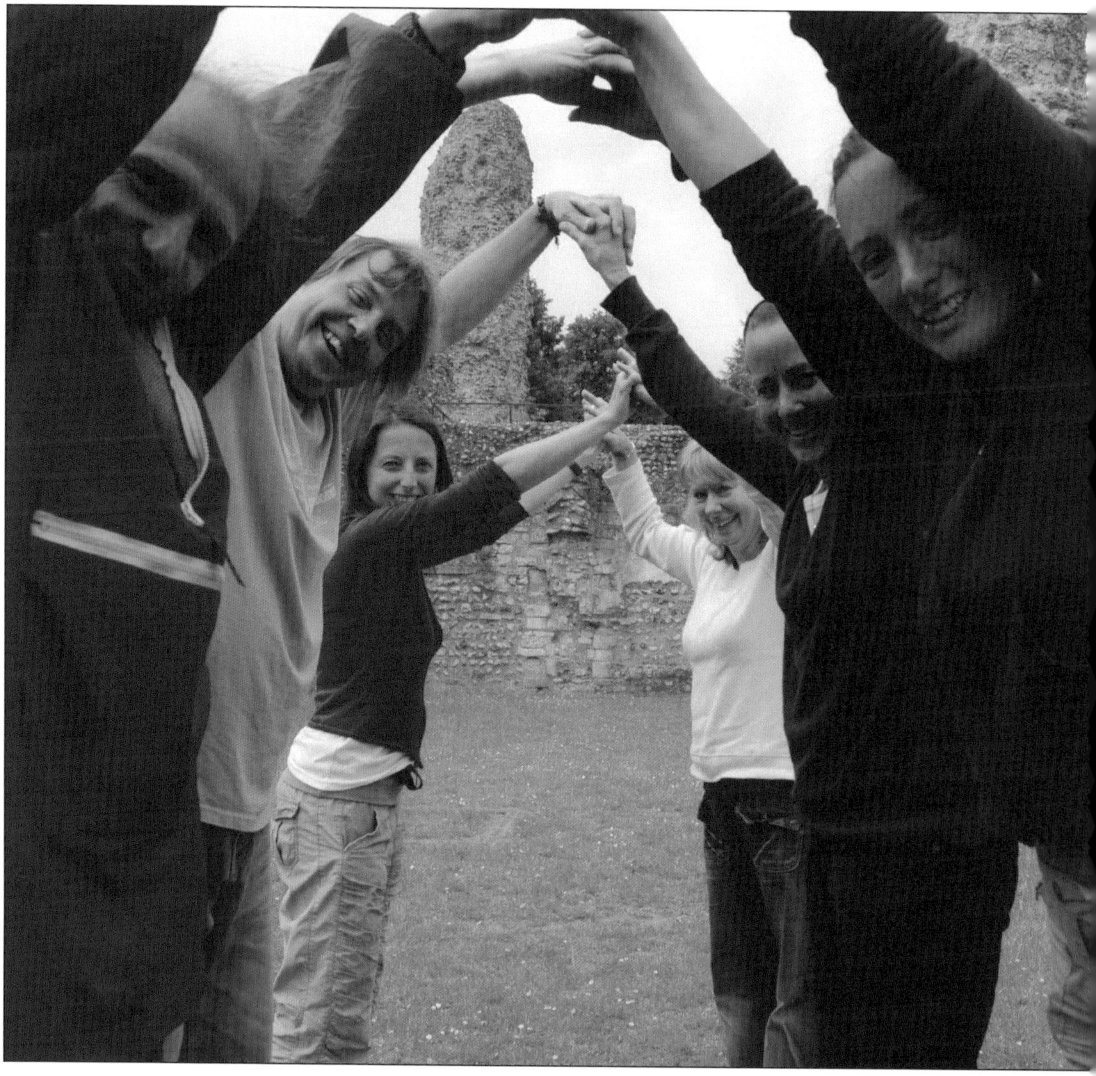

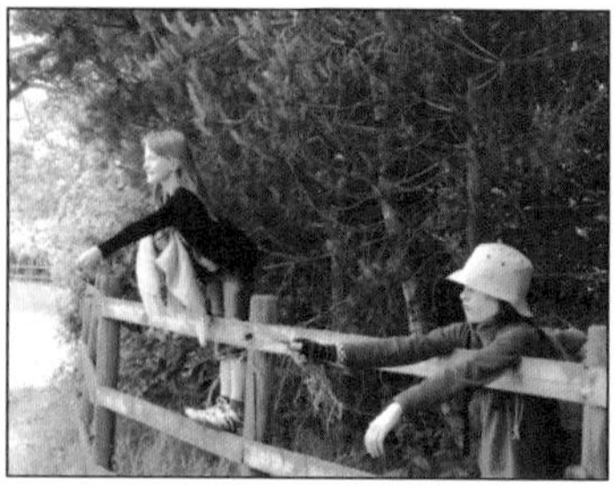

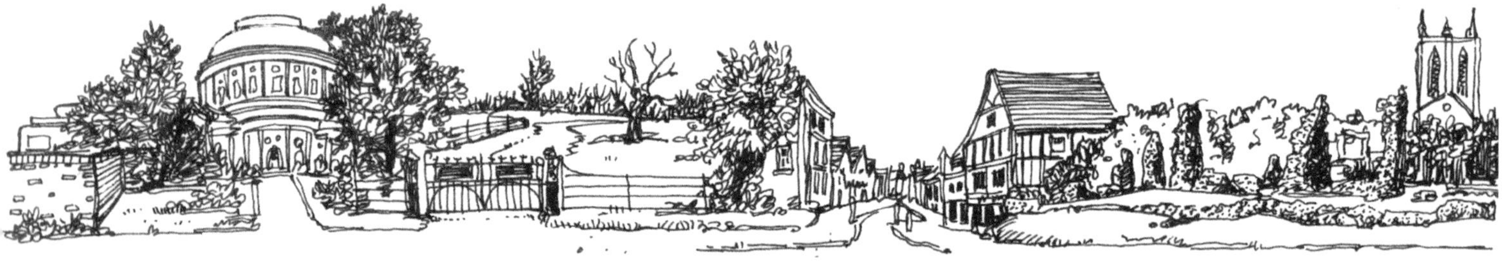

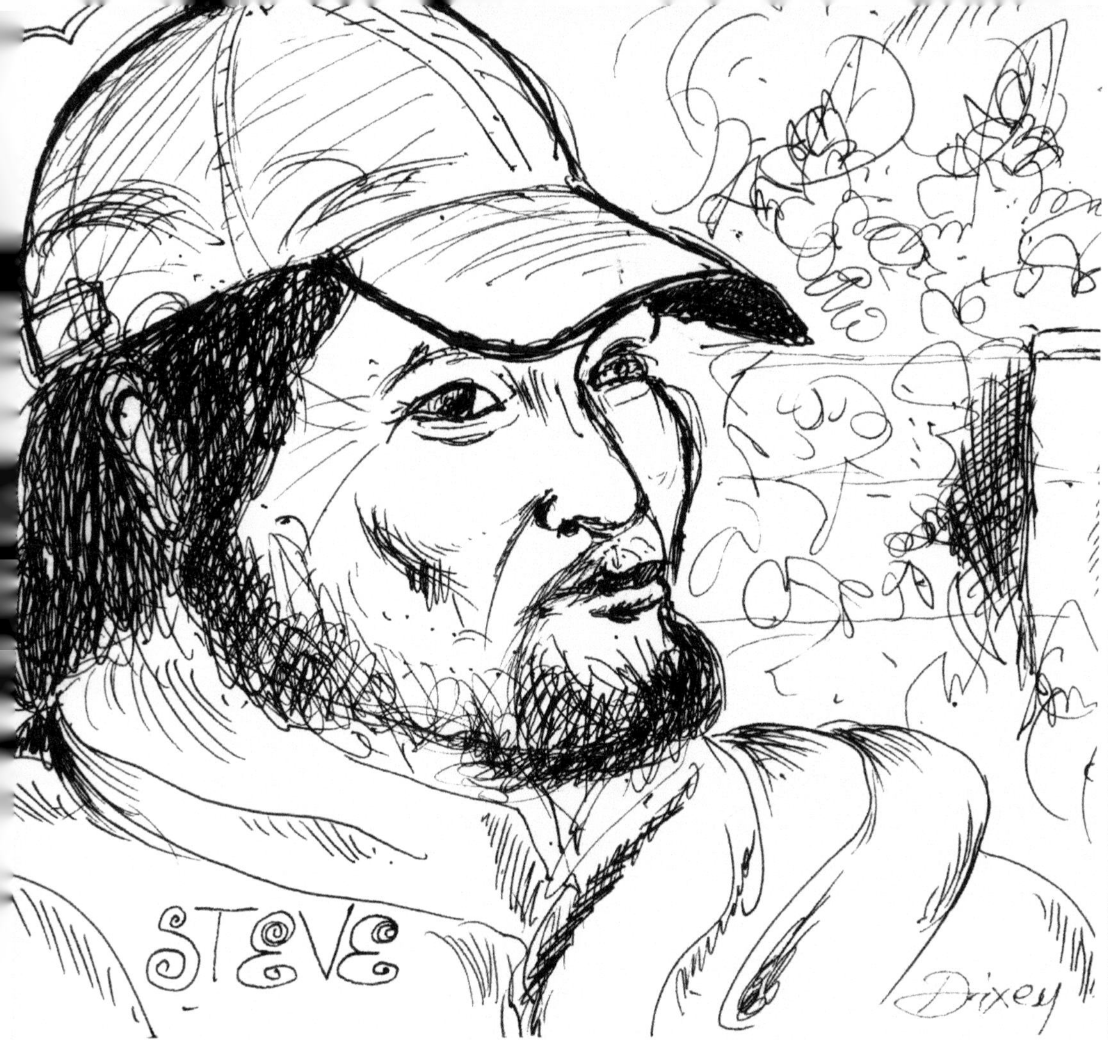

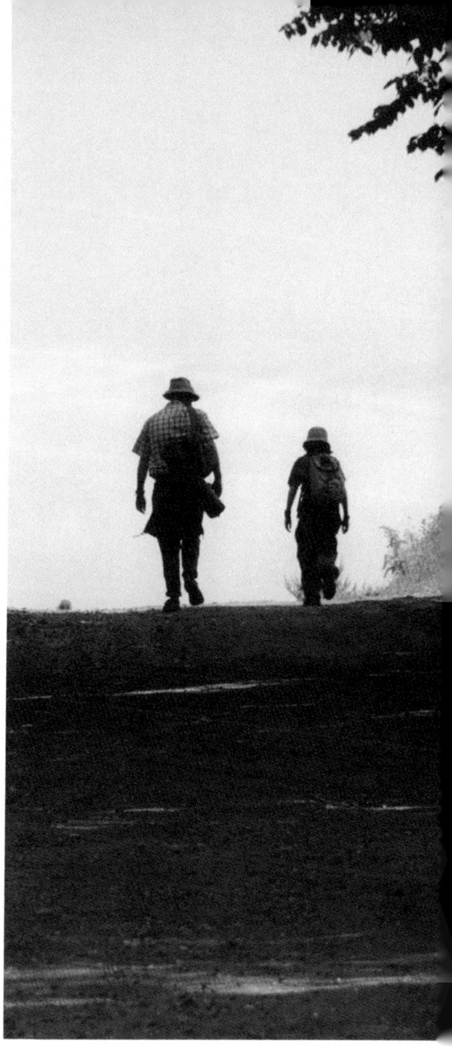

his eyes are dim
his great heart forges
ahead
he lays arrows
for us to follow

I am a visually enhanced person from today, that's what Geoffrey called me. This came about from our wanderings today, after explaining my visual impairment he said "Steve, you are not visually impaired, you're visually enhanced!" because I look closer to things and listen a lot more closely and sense things a lot more than ordinary folk making myself really into the moment etc … and not feeling lower about myself than others which I must confess that I have spent the last 35 years doing, until today. So as from today, I am no longer a visually impaired person but a visually enhanced person. Wow, I feel great! Thanks Geoffrey!!! ***SS***

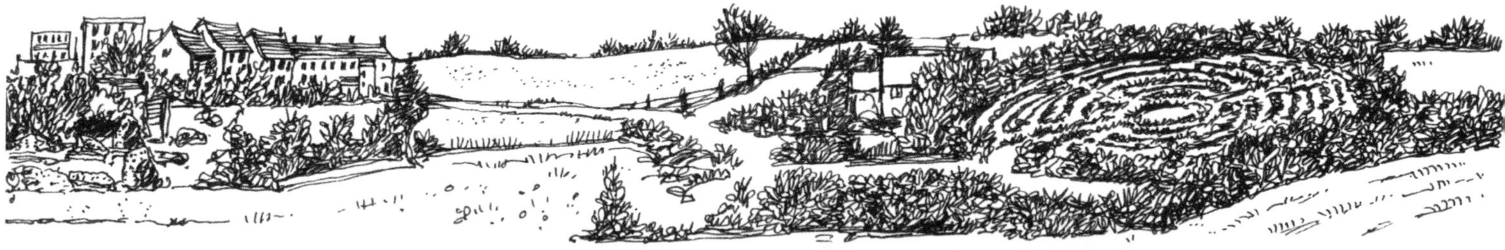

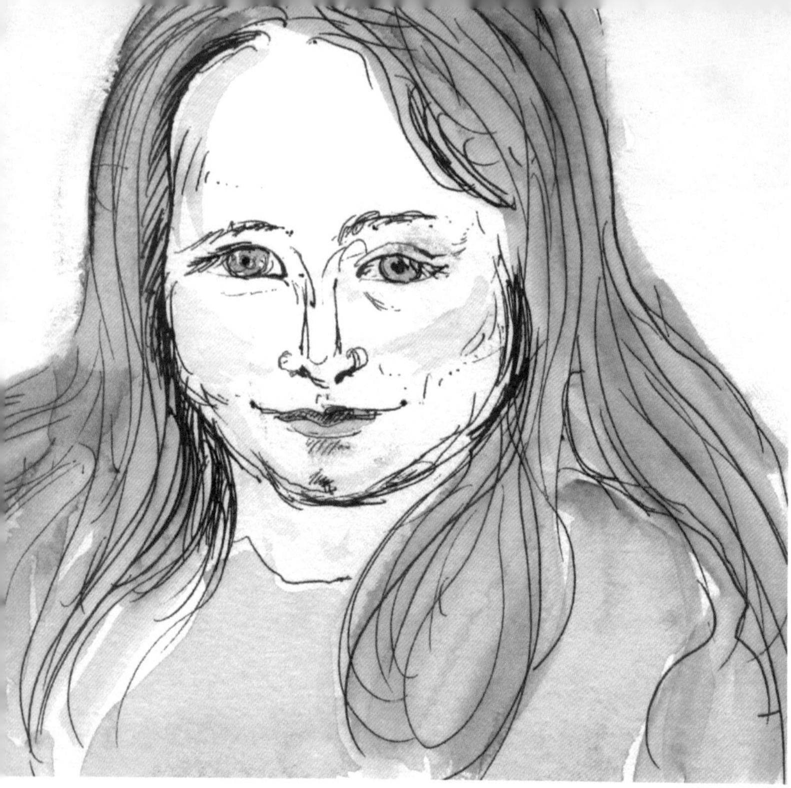

This is the start of the final week of the walk. We're having our rest day in the substantial and beautiful garden of Clare. She has turned a bean field into an oasis, or perhaps a refuge, and has built a labyrinth at the centre of the land. Last night I did my laundry and this morning, a supermarket run with Lynne. I had a sleep in the afternoon and awoke to a camp full of new and returning faces. How very different from the small party of four walkers who were keeping the dream alive in the middle of the week. I hear a gong?!

Presumably inviting me to walk the labyrinth, have a pipe ceremony ... (how does that work for non-smokers?) ... and then a sweat lodge ... what a privilege. ***SB***

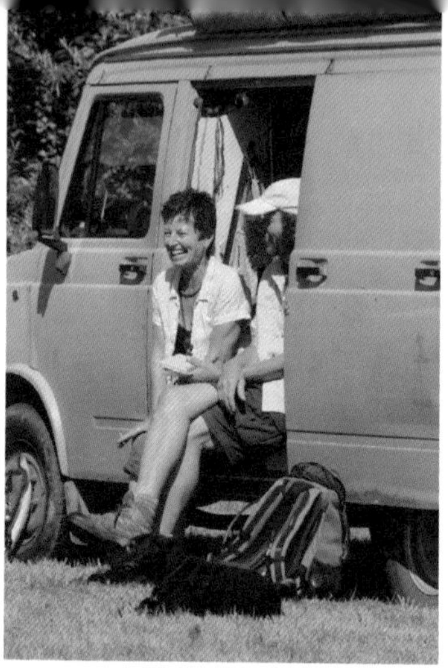

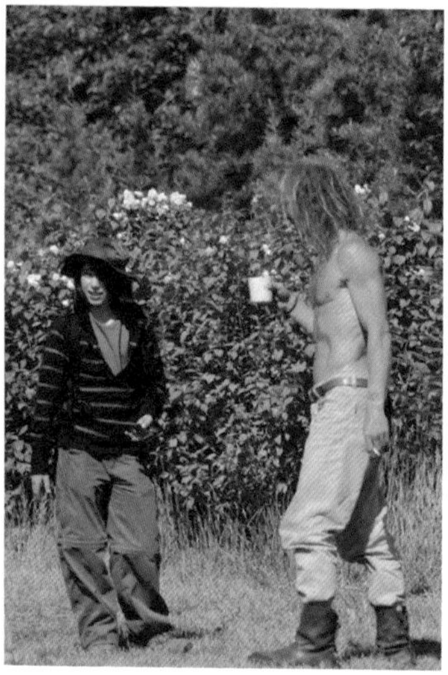

And so we walk
we walk together and alone
through the green of Albion
each step a gift...
birds, small and large,
dart and soar,
singing beauty into our hearts
as over airy hills
and through lanes
      secret with damp growth
and lush decay
across meadows jewelled with
                                        flowers
by flowing water,
      still water
and by great trees
rooted deep and strong,
high branches swaying, leaves
                                        dancing,
      reflecting
such Grace
      under the sky
we walk
till there is nothing left
only a humming nowness
in the bright moment

DB

Day 42

Rest Day at Rougham

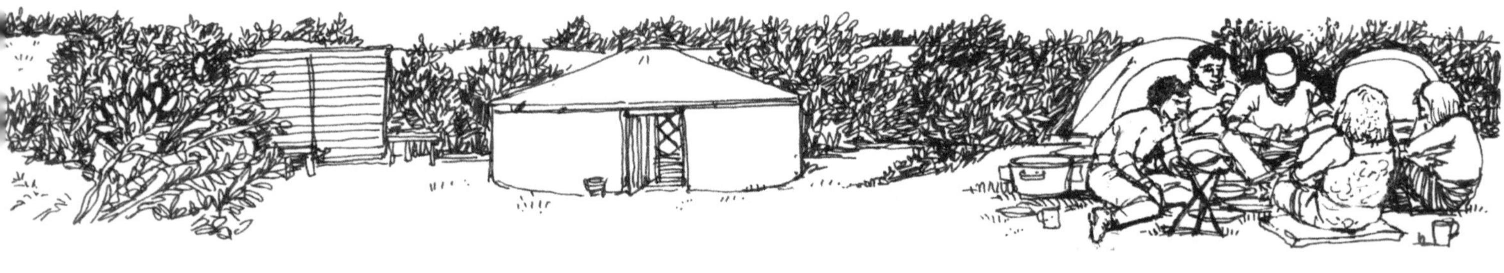

grey afternoon
sitting on mossy
tree trunk
listening
to the wind's song

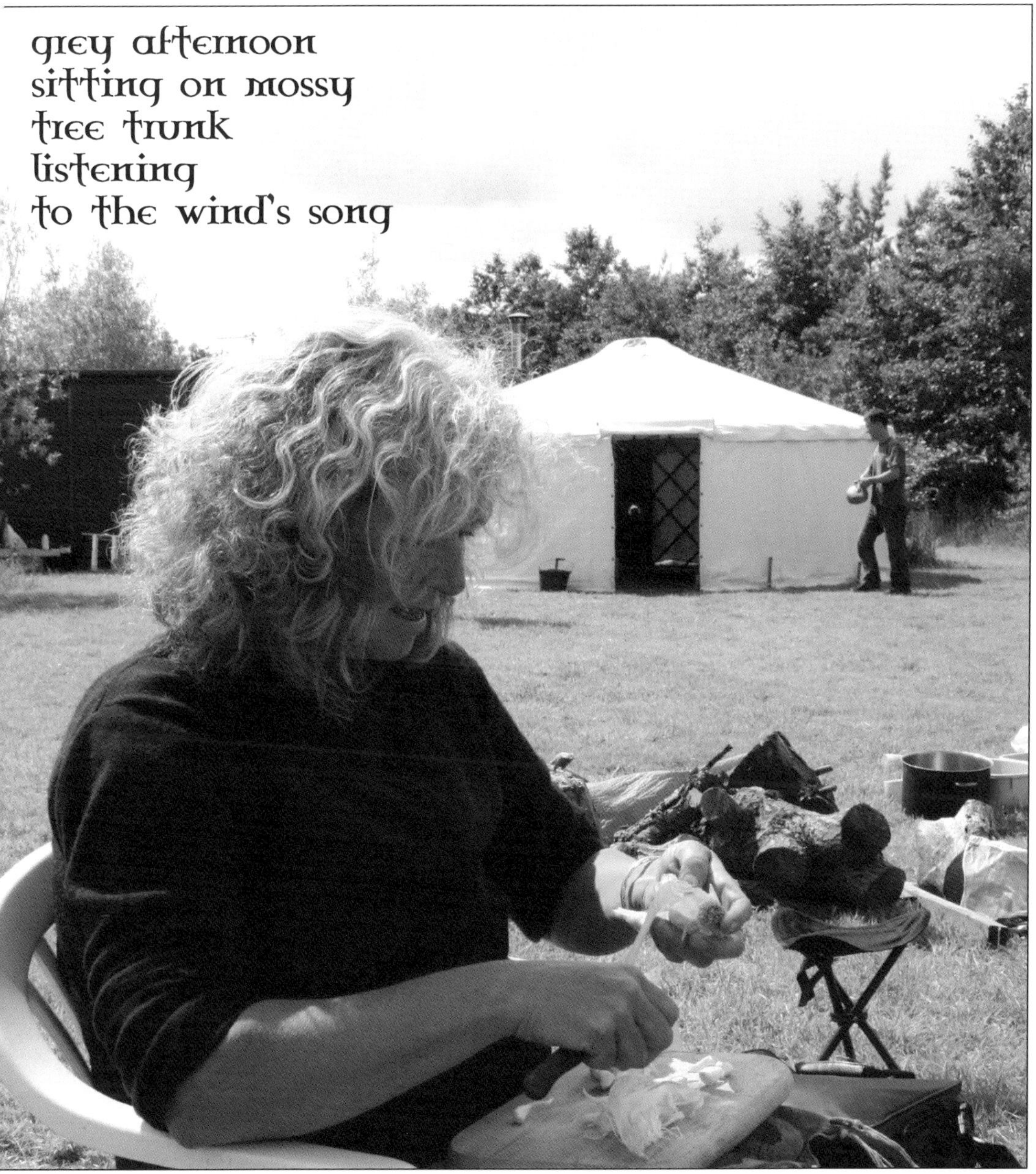

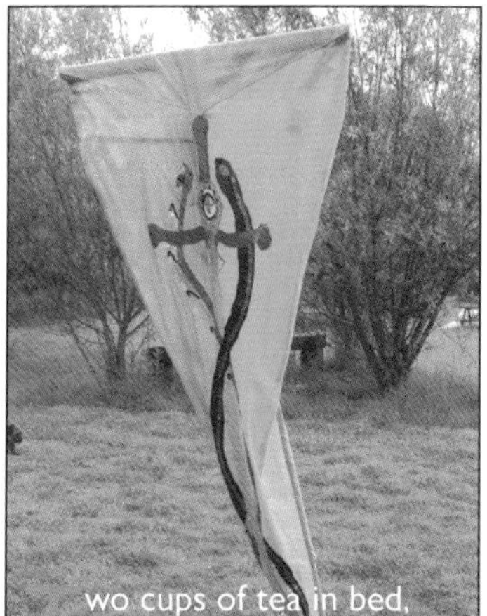

Two cups of tea in bed, sunbathing naked until 9.30, breakfast, porridge, fried egg on toast, bacon butty and three coffees. Wow! Meeting at 11.00 about New Jerusalem – Fields of Albion. Then Tessa and Kim and Cal and other pilgrims turned up. Chilled out. Circled in the afternoon. Planned sweat ceremony, Alex's pipe and Native American Indian Tobacco grown in Norfolk with herbs and spices. About 24 of us did the ceremony, we walked the labyrinth to its centre where we passed around the pipe while Alex performed the ritual and then entered the sweat lodge, 17 did the actual sweat. Very late. 1.00. Just ate two pieces of liquorish. All's well! Fantastic really! *SS*

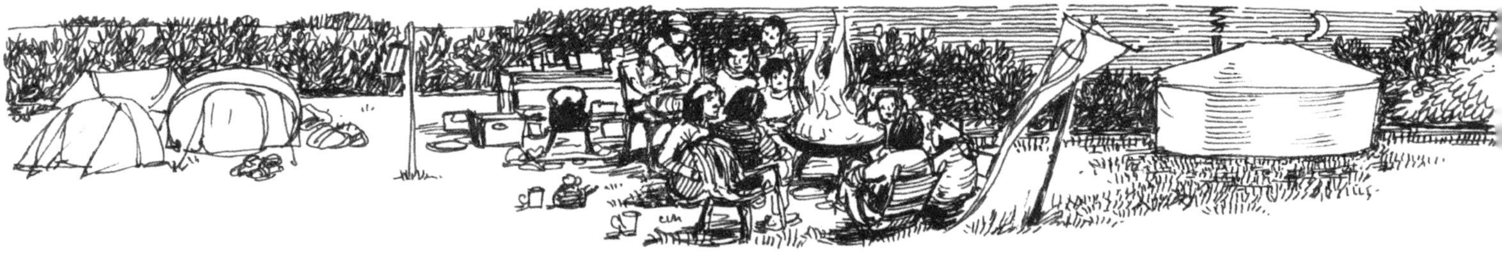

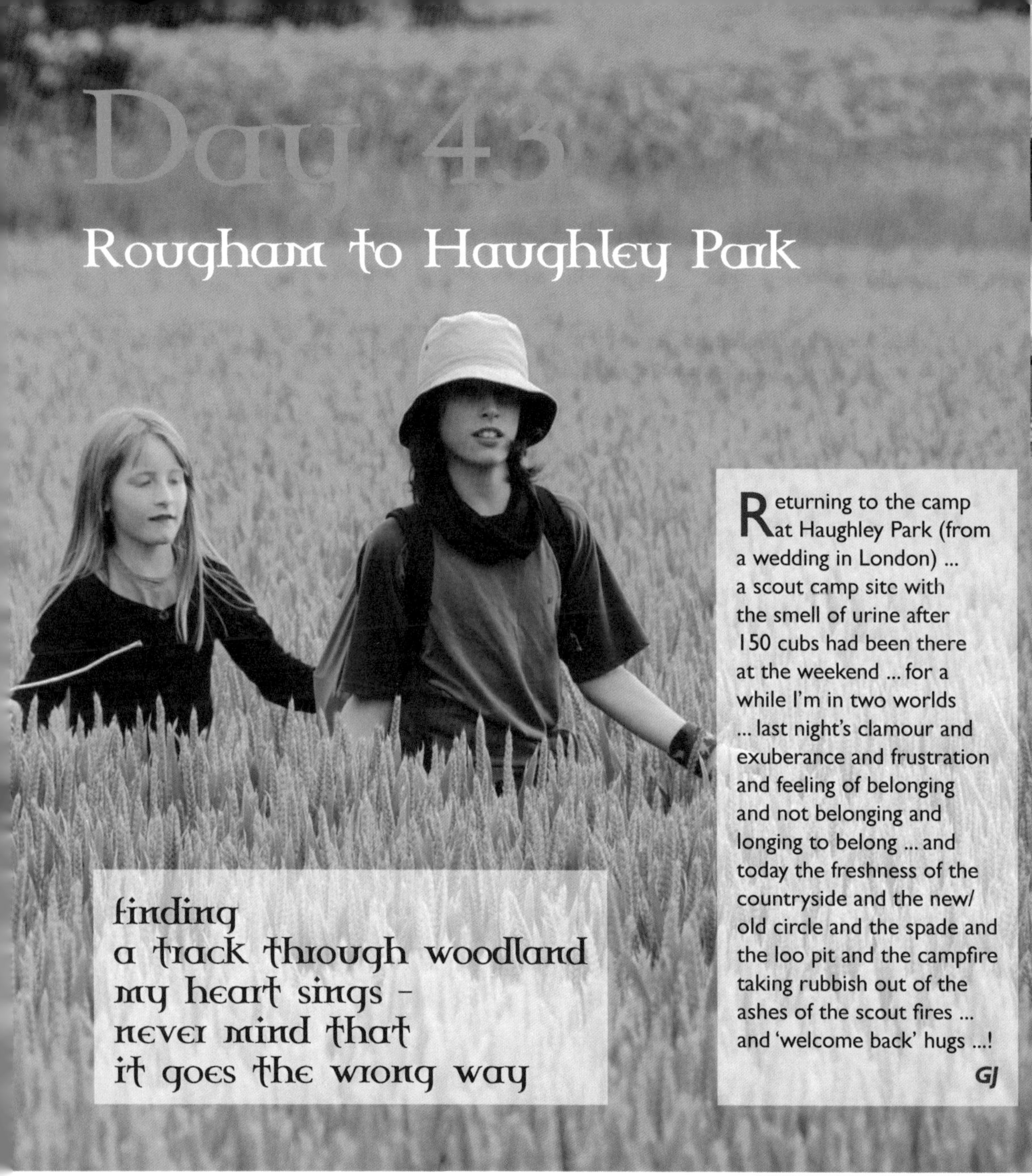

Day 43

Rougham to Haughley Park

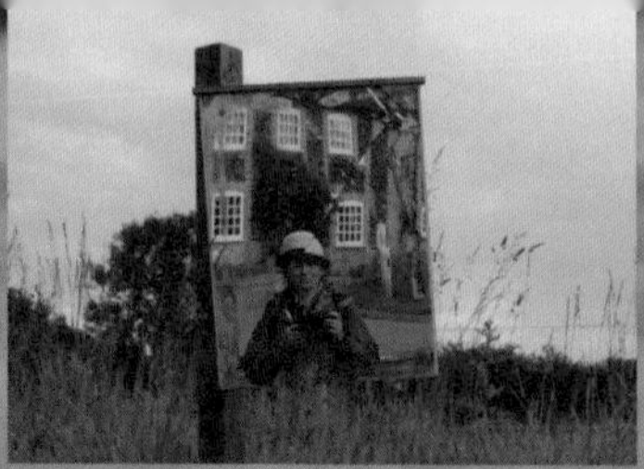

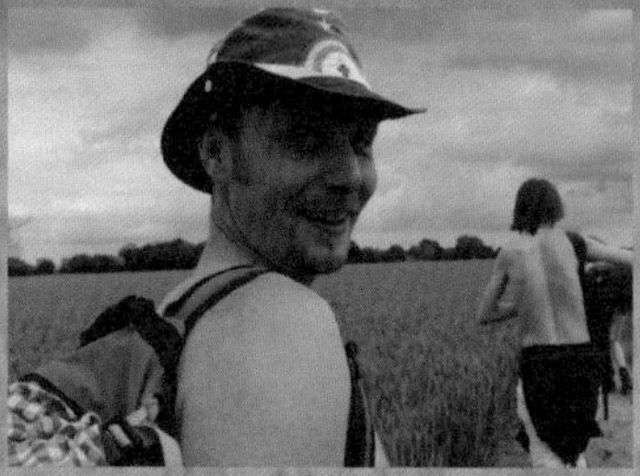

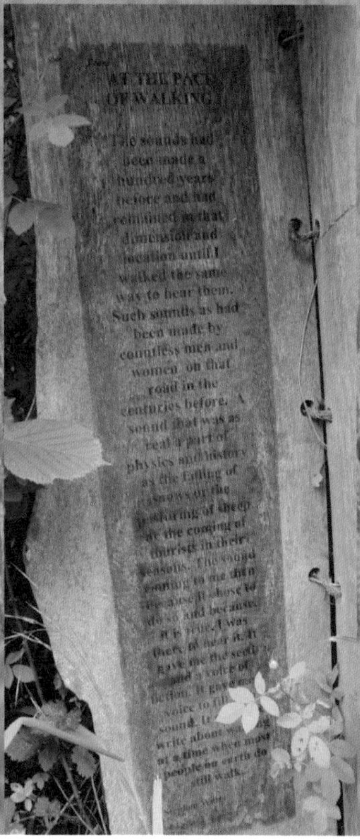

finding
a track through woodland
my heart sings –
never mind that
it goes the wrong way

Returning to the camp at Haughley Park (from a wedding in London) ... a scout camp site with the smell of urine after 150 cubs had been there at the weekend ... for a while I'm in two worlds ... last night's clamour and exuberance and frustration and feeling of belonging and not belonging and longing to belong ... and today the freshness of the countryside and the new/ old circle and the spade and the loo pit and the campfire taking rubbish out of the ashes of the scout fires ... and 'welcome back' hugs ...!

GJ

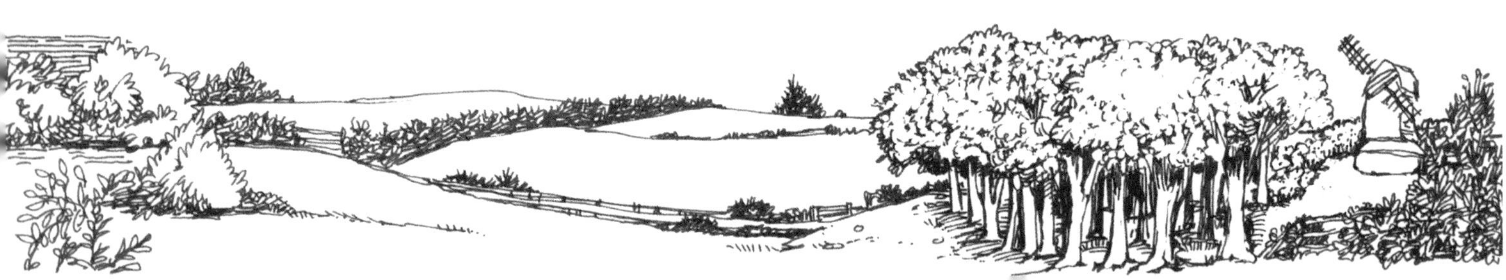

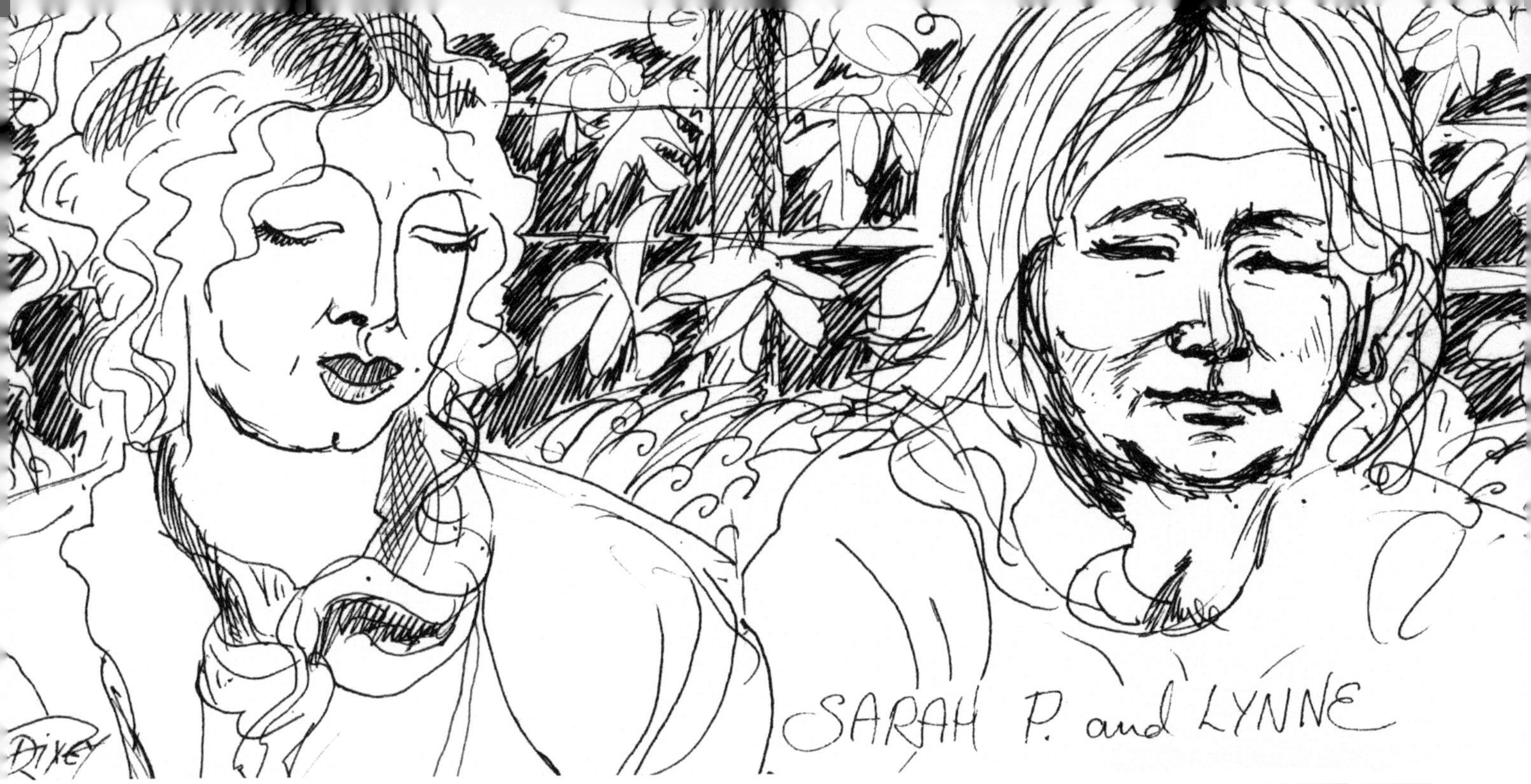

Another amazing day of pilgrimage! Tonight we are camping in the beautiful Haughley Park, the place which hosts the "Weird and Wonderful Wood Fair". The view is beautiful, a big, low, bright moon, almost full, against a deep, blue sky, with misty white clouds. The parkland trees, grown to their full potential, their lovely shapes. There are a lot of sheep baa-ing, they were shorn today.

It has been lovely today to find my way with Poppy. It has been great watching her figure out what community is about, and to let go of the world of chaos outside. I admire Poppy for finding her own way.

We walked through fields of corn and barley, Poppy fell in some holes and we laughed. We visited Bradfield Wood, ancient coppiced woodland, with ash and hazel. How inspiring to think those amazing trees have provided wood for hundreds of years. We walked into Woolpit, and visited the church, with dragons and dogs and fantastical creatures carved on the wooden pews. We crossed the busy A14 today, I can hear the crazy traffic droning on.

After a lovely tea, we listened to Graham read the last part of a Norfolk Songline, and Poppy soaked her feet in warm water. Some people saw deer, hares, foxes, treecreepers, black caps and buzzards today. Poppy and I saw heartsease and poppies and cornflowers. I feel right back in the day and happy to be right where I am. It is lovely to be part of a community, and to feel people's care and support.

ML

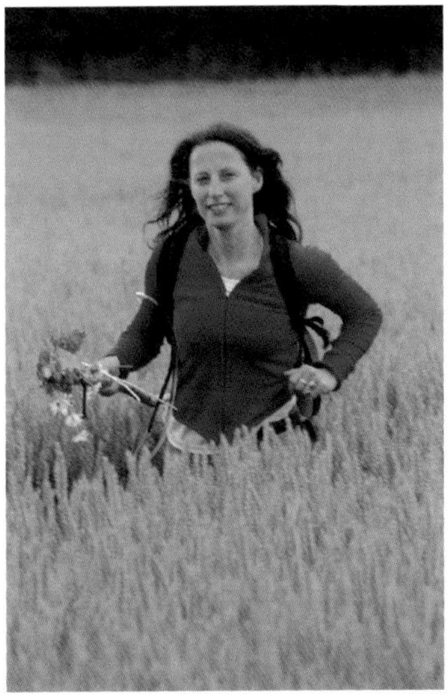

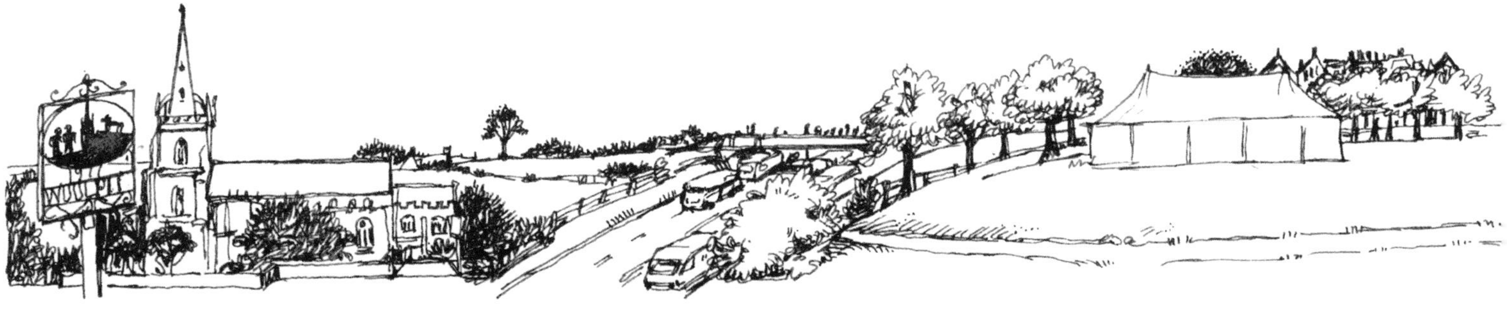

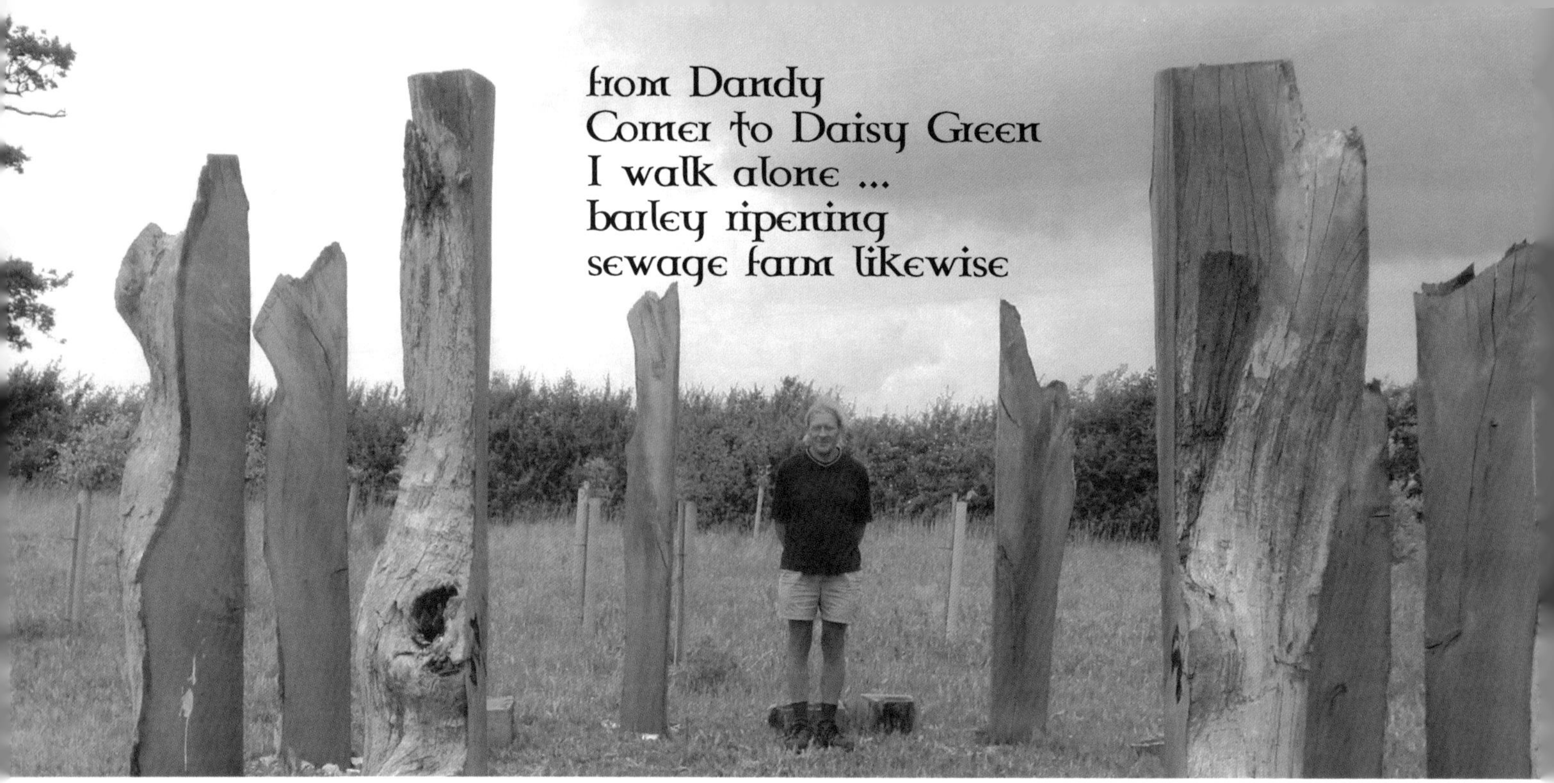

Dry start no sun but OK. The drone of the A14, so tough for the local inhabitants. Dan and Rhian had the maps and I had neon coloured paper arrows made by Mel's daughter Poppy. New idea, elevenses, coffee/tea. So around 11.00 Albion turned up with said stuff and biscuits. Before this we had to make our way across a rapeseed field in full bloom and about 4ft high. It was so tiring, we took it in turn to lead the way like swimming breaststroke for about 10 strides and then step aside for the next path maker. Dan and I took it in turn at the front to do most of it. We were very oily all over after exiting the field. Two large white horses. Coffee break, before Albion arrived we shared nuts, fruit, cheese, bread and chocolate. We walked past our next place of interest a wood henge by about a mile before realising our mistake, when we asked a chap in a Land Rover where the wood henge was, he kindly gave us a ride in the back of his truck to the henge. The henge was made from a single very large tree split into eight sections. There was also a wicker figure of Mother Earth Goddess in a sitting position about 6ft tall and 10ft long. Wild elements. Great lunch. Police turn up during lunch. Lynne chats with them. All's well. We come across white-line painters. Rhian asks if they had any spare chalk they could let us have and they gave us two sticks which are about 6in long and about an inch thick, they use chalk to mark the road. We used it to draw arrows. Walked through Thornham Magna estate, woods/park to Andy's and Sam's home where we next camp. Got lost a bit, met Christine and Melody on route who had directions to the house. They have come to rejoin the group which is growing, now in high twenties. Great dinner, butter bean curry with melon and banana salad. Yummy! Rhubarb-ginger fruit juice. Thick yogurt and biscuits followed by several bars of Green and Blacks chocolate. Peace Pipe with host Andy. He's off to Glastonbury festival in the morning. I'm on Albion with Alex tomorrow. Sore feet. Hips ache. Tired. 10.25 I'm in bed, as usual, doing this. Several people still up chatting. Ben Plats-Mills, Linda Rodgers and others. Good night. ***SS***

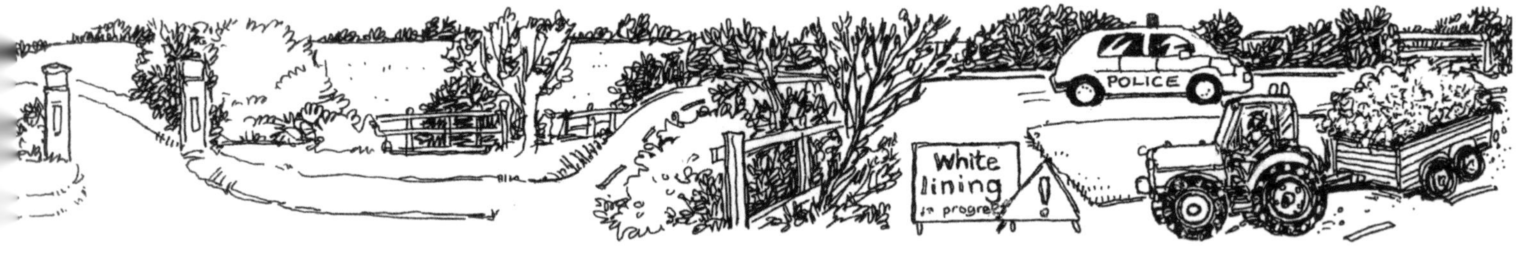

Day 44 Haughley Park to Thornham

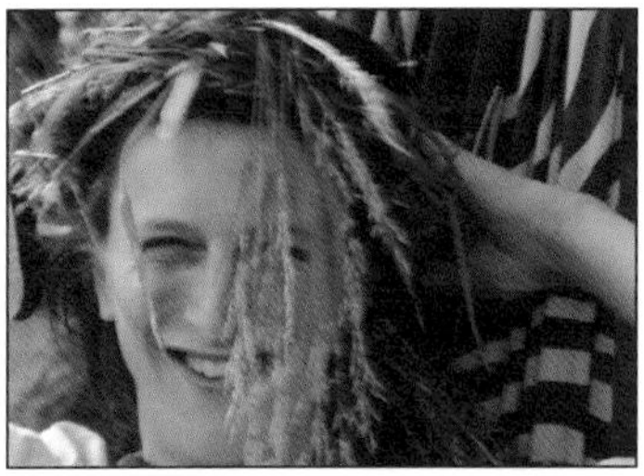
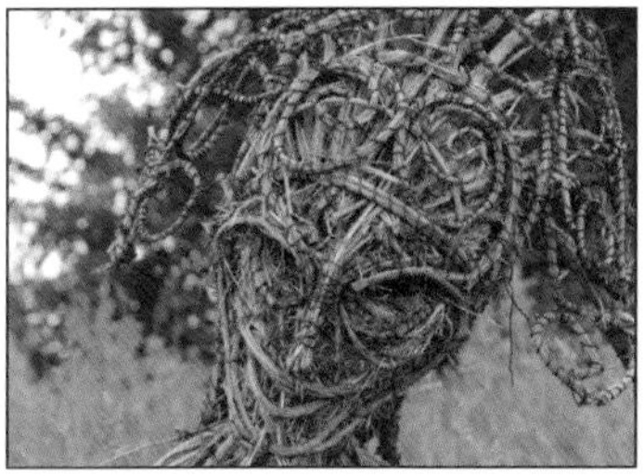
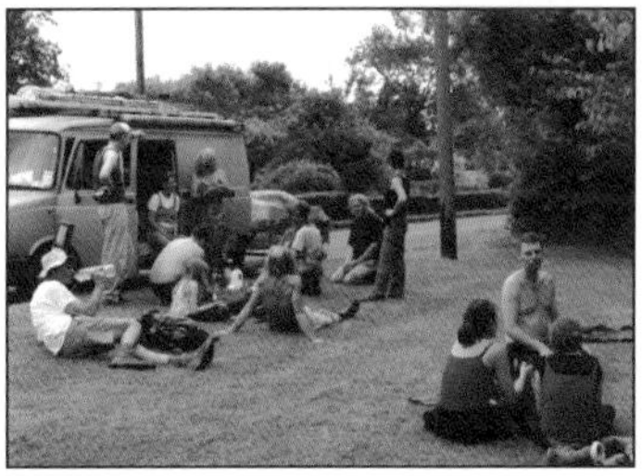

The march across Britain has become a leisurely stroll as we move toward the end of the walk, easy and happy through the abundant skyscapes of East Anglia. The van, unusually, met us for morning tea. We lounged about a wooden henge and generally had a very relaxed day. All is well - - - full moon in Scorpio. ***SB***

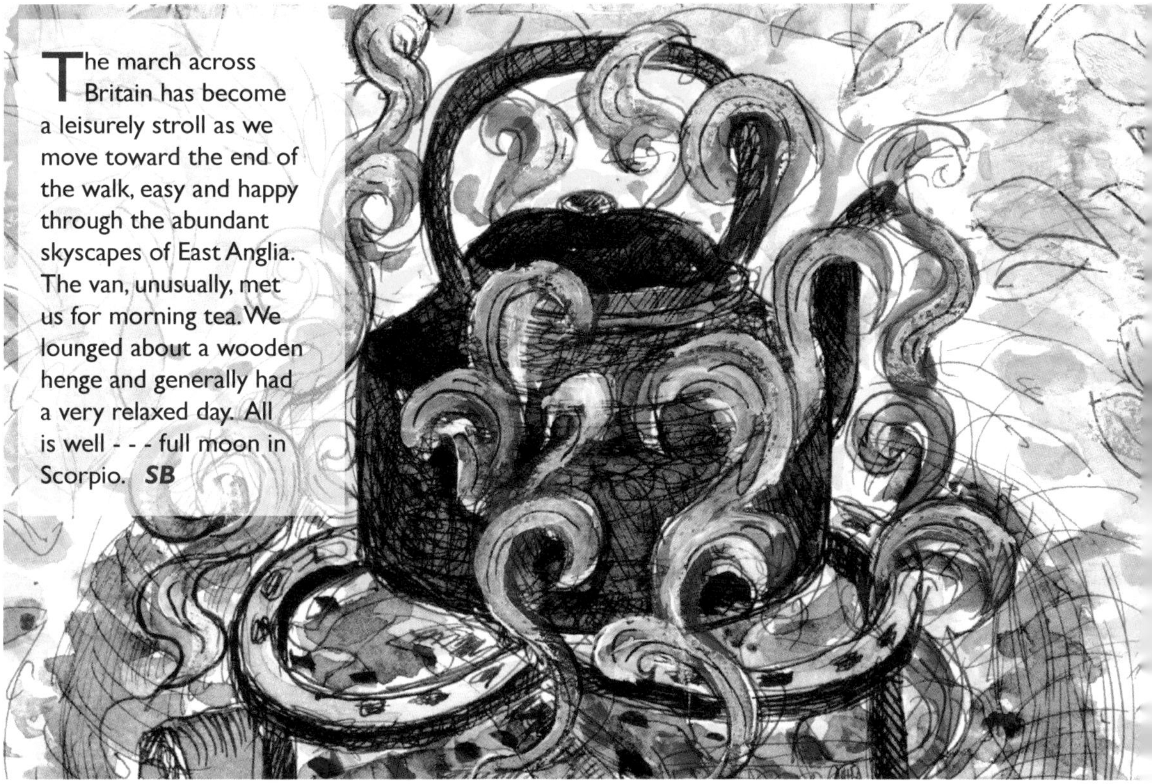

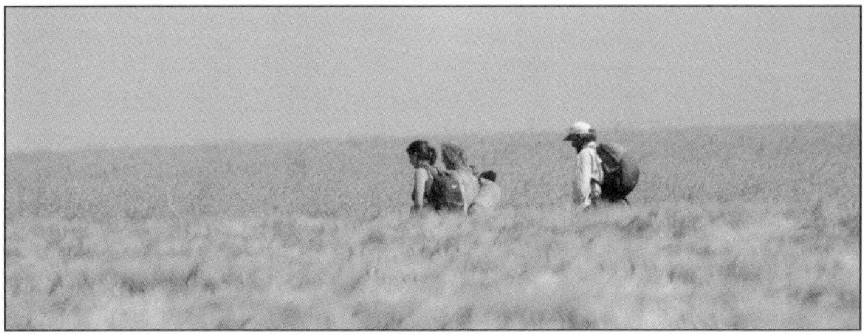
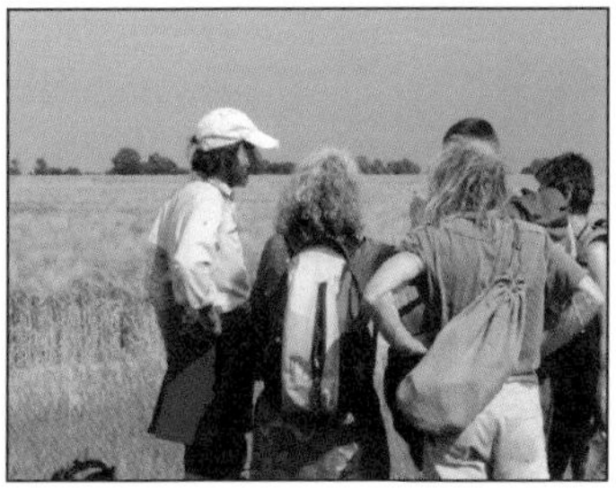
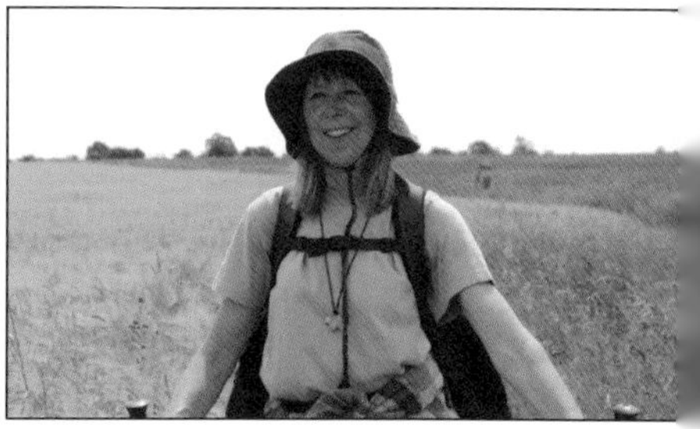

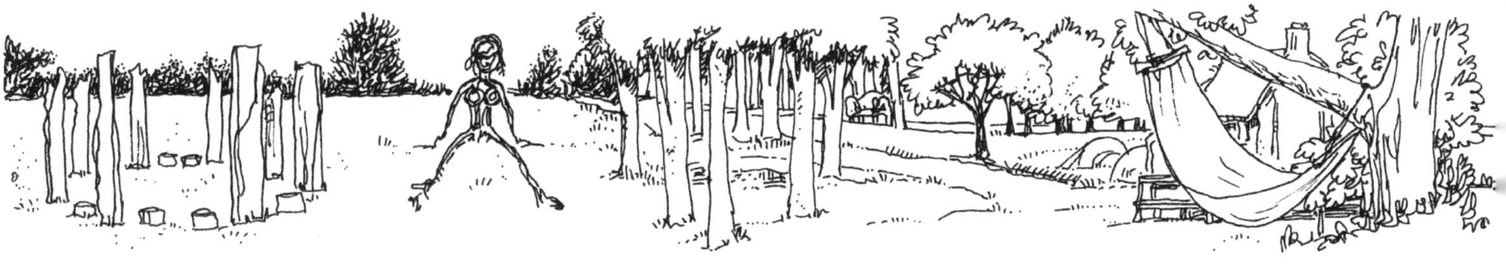

Day 45 Thornham to Weybread

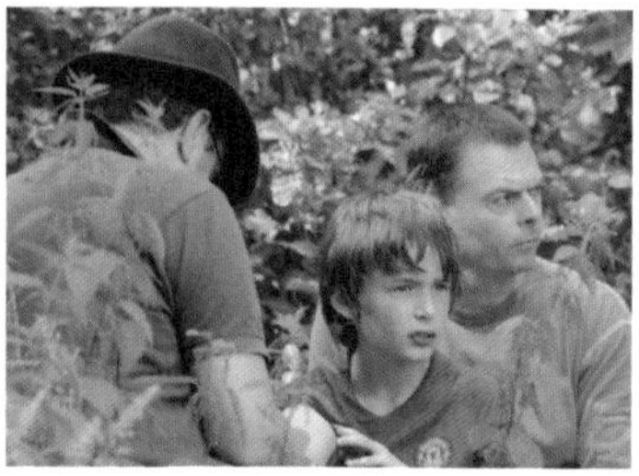

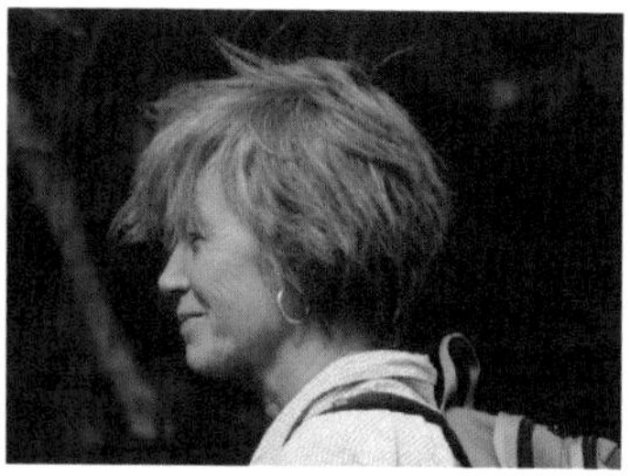

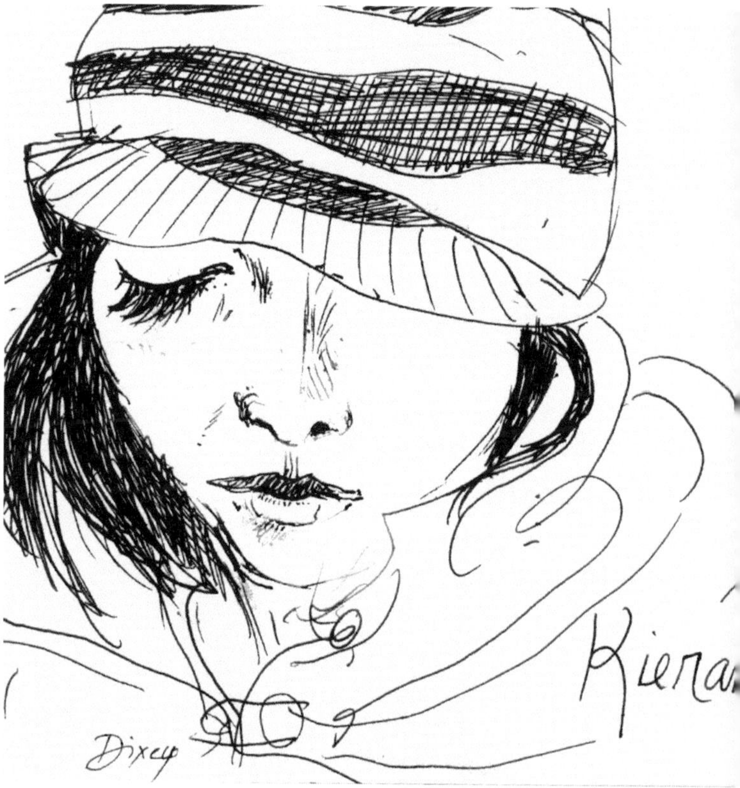

Weybread night
wind in the trees
rain
on the tent roof
snuggling into the earth

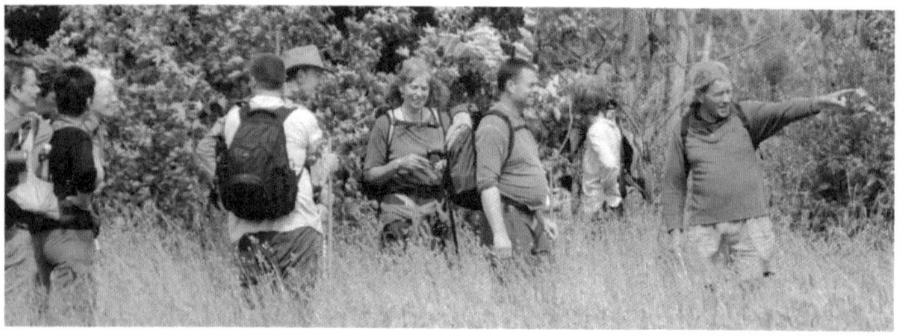

Started the day bleary eyed in an English country garden, dirty pots, blooming flowers ... we sang in a small church at Thornham Parva ... walked along Topsy Turvey Lane and some footpaths, I was at the rear talking to Carolin and Sarah ... sang in Eye Church and I bought a new shirt in the church shop ... lunch at Hoxne Bridge where St Edmond was killed in 870 ... muddy river wading with lots of delighted and delightful squeals ... footpath along the River Waveney ... there are pink cottages and thatched cottages in Suffolk ... a long afternoon across country which turned out to be Graham's home country which he was pleased to share with a few of us ... Rhian and I had cider at the village pub to finish this long satisfying day before going in to the camp at Orchard Cottage, Weybread.

GJ

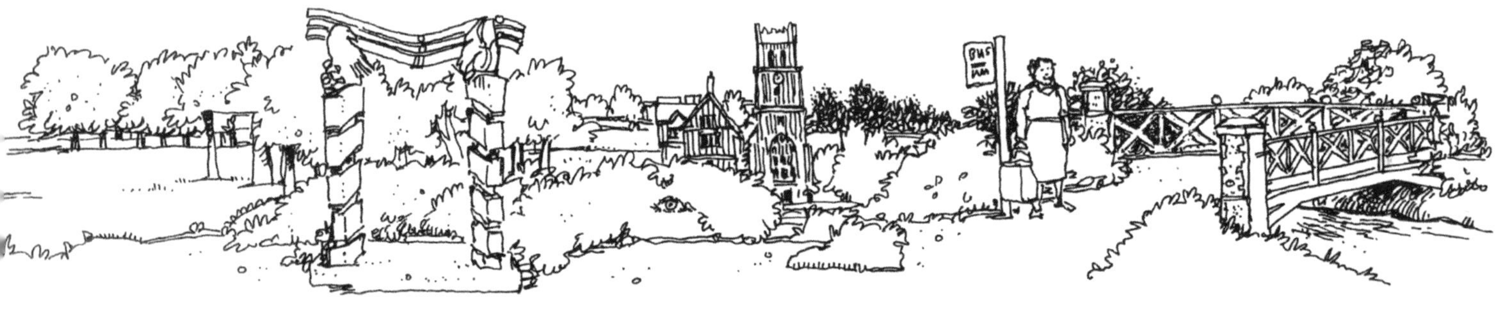

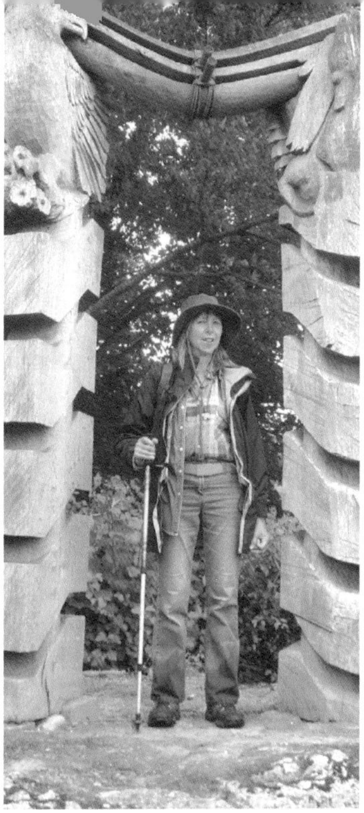

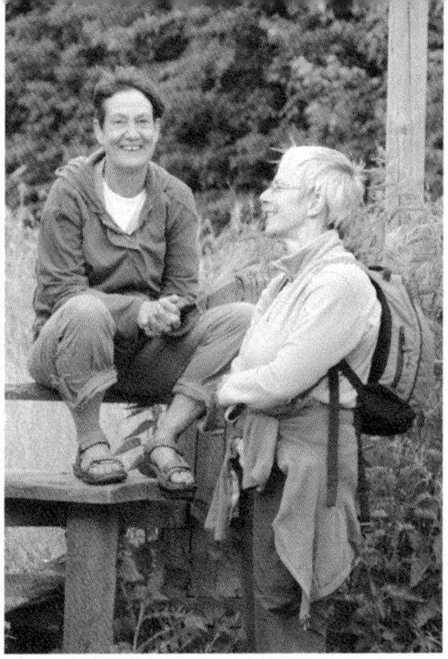

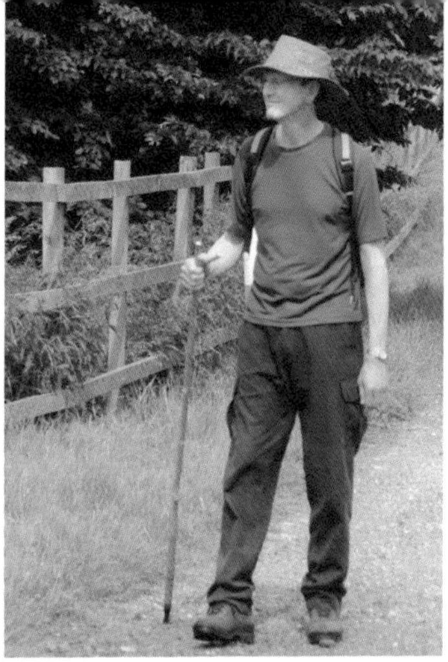

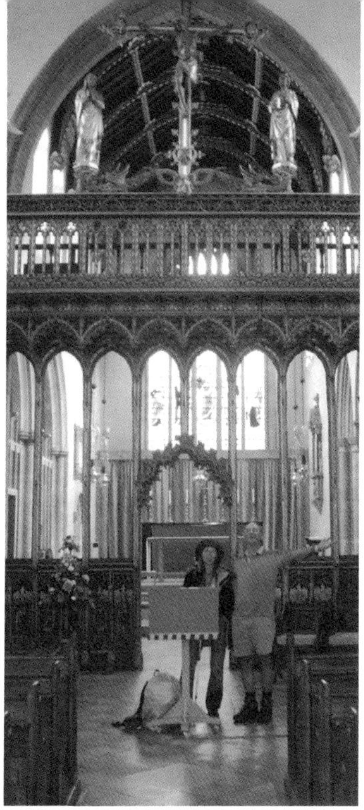

Another great moment was in Eye church, Suffolk, singing with Gerry loudly and enthusiastically "And did those Feet in Ancient time walk upon England's mountains green" – the rousing hymn 'Jerusalem', based on William Blake's visionary verses. It made me ponder whether we were indeed treading an ancient sacred pathway walked upon by Joseph of Arimathea and perhaps his young nephew Jesus.

CC

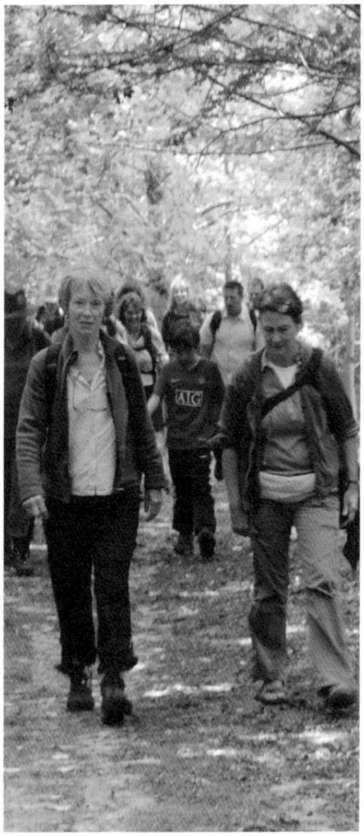

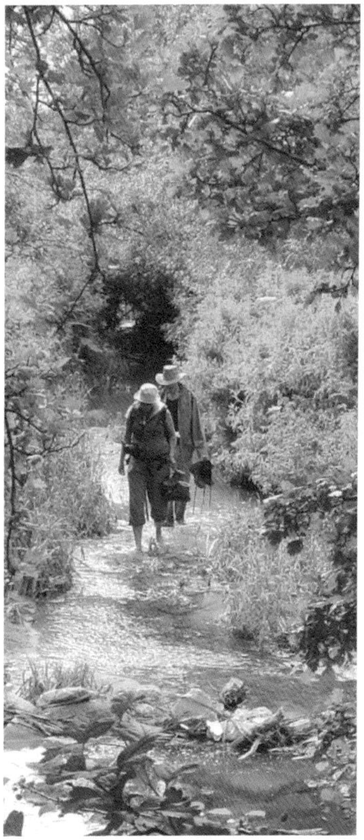

It was a long walk today through beautiful fields and water meadows. We spent a longer time than usual in the churches we visited. One was especially beautiful, the Church of St Peter and St Paul in the village of Eye, another had a thatched steeple! Carolin and Gerry sang in them all and we continued to sing and dance as we walked on toward the coast with warm feelings of community and optimism.

SB

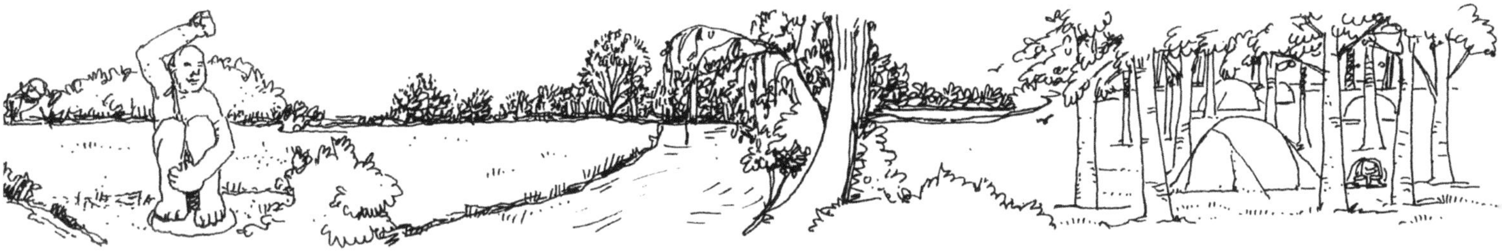

Day 46 Weybread to Barsham

What a cool day! We are camped at Barsham Old Hall, a groovy self-sufficient place, with chickens and a barn where we have built our kitchen. We used teamwork and a jacket potato as a distraction for the other birds, to herd an errant chicken back into the pen. We had a look at the river Waveney but decided against a swim 'cos it was cold and muddy. Nick is sleeping high up in the tree house. Tonight twelve of us walked across the fields to Geldeston Locks Inn, for folk night. Lots of cool people were outside playing guitars, fiddles, pipes, whistle, flutes and drums and singing. I danced with Dano, it was great fun; Spanish, Irish, dancing low down, twirling and twisting. I danced slow and fast and chaos and flowing and lyrical, barefoot till my feet hurt, which could be a mistake 'cos there are about 20 miles to go tomorrow, but it is so great to dance! We walked back in the dark, by the light of the rising, orange moon, through the field with the sign which read "Bulls in field", bit alarming!! We all

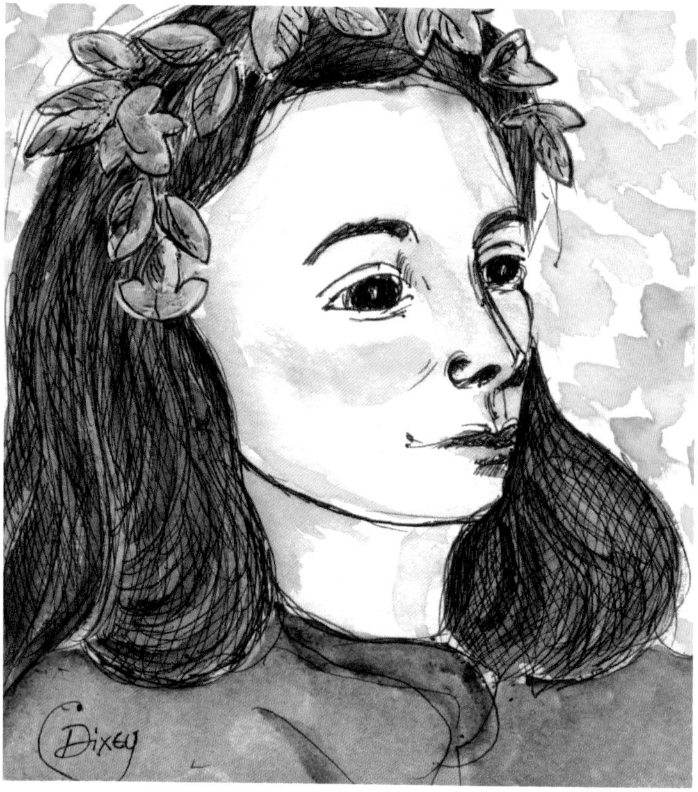

sang on the way too. I saw bats swooping over the river. Walking today I saw ladybirds and a big hairy caterpillar, and two hares. We stopped in a beautiful, simple little church, of Mary Magdalen, in Withersdale. Cal and I climbed up to the balcony and sang notes, long notes in the white painted church room, almost like a meeting house. We were met by 'Albion' for a coffee break, rugs, tea, coffee, cake, brownies and biscuits laid out at the edge of the field. Delicious!! We visited South Elmham, ruins of a possibly Saxon Cathedral and I was moved to tears, tuning into the pollarded, ancient hornbeams, so rugged and sinewy, with cascading green flowers. For a while I walked slowly, alone and barefoot, then through a grove of tall poplars, blown by the summer wind. Rustling. We walked through some beautiful old meadows today, ancient hedgerows thick with different species of plants, and over Ilketshal Common, where we saw a wild maned black and white horse tethered without water or shade. We walked past Ringshall Eco-Study Centre, where Education Otherwise have a straw-bale house. I have had fun today. We had council to plan for our last night tomorrow, it was going on so long and getting so detailed, so I whispered "Pub! Pass it on ..." to Graham, and gradually the Chinese whisper went round the circle. Jan, Alice, Sasha and Dixey came back today. Don't want to acknowledge that it is nearly the end, and feel very happy and in the moment. ***ML***

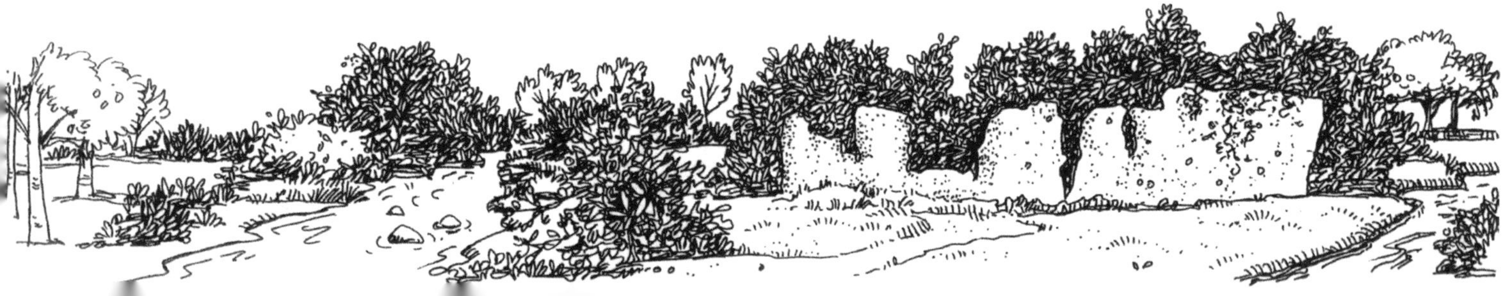

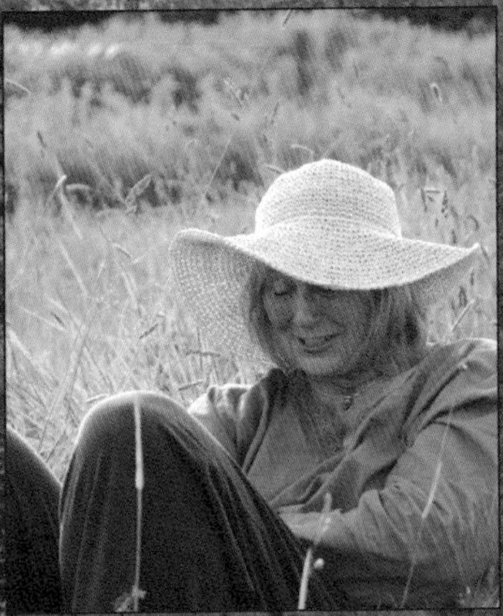
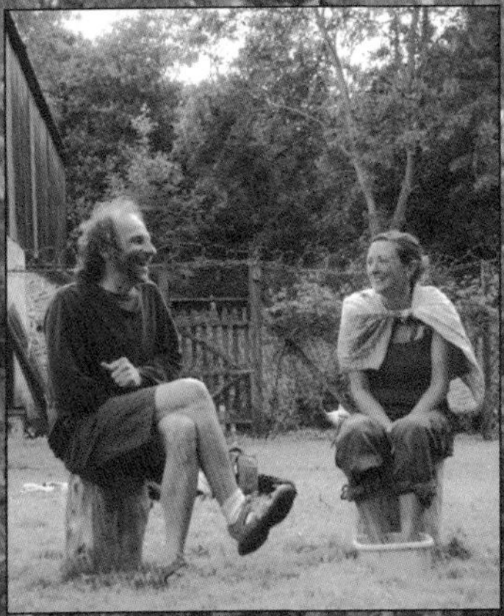
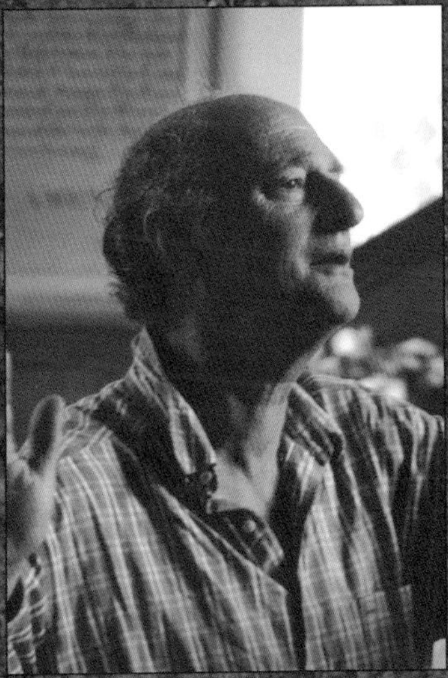
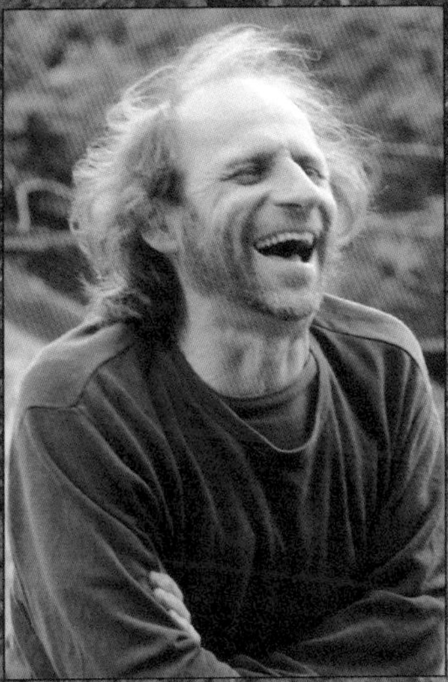

church of
St Mary Magdalene -
feeling
the weight of silence
we sing it into life

evening lingers
footpath darkens
heart unlocks -
outside the pub
a fiddler plays

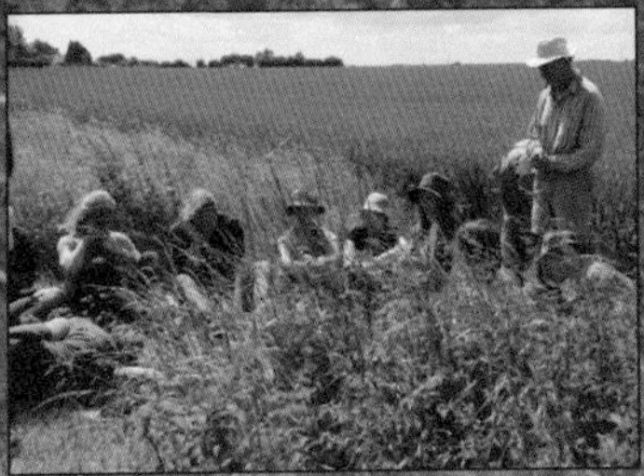
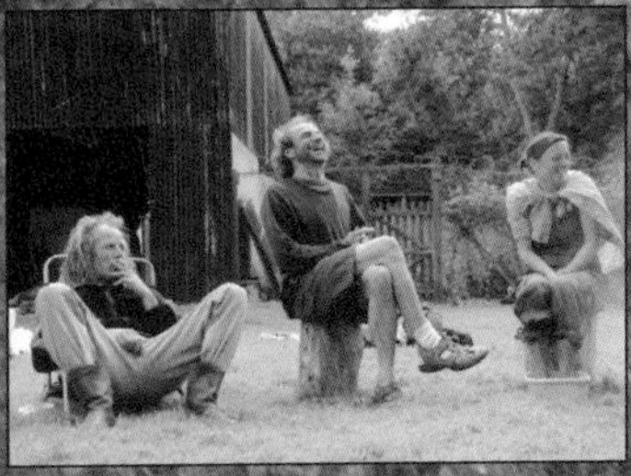
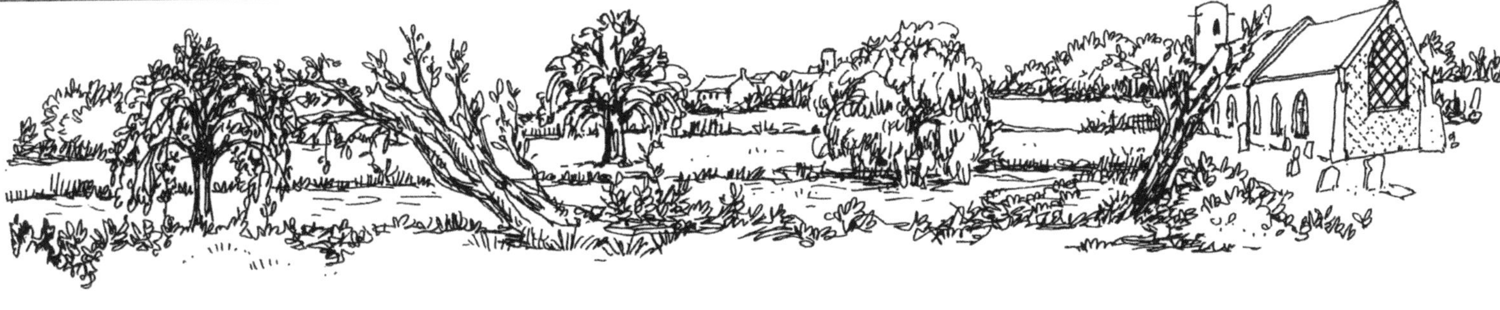

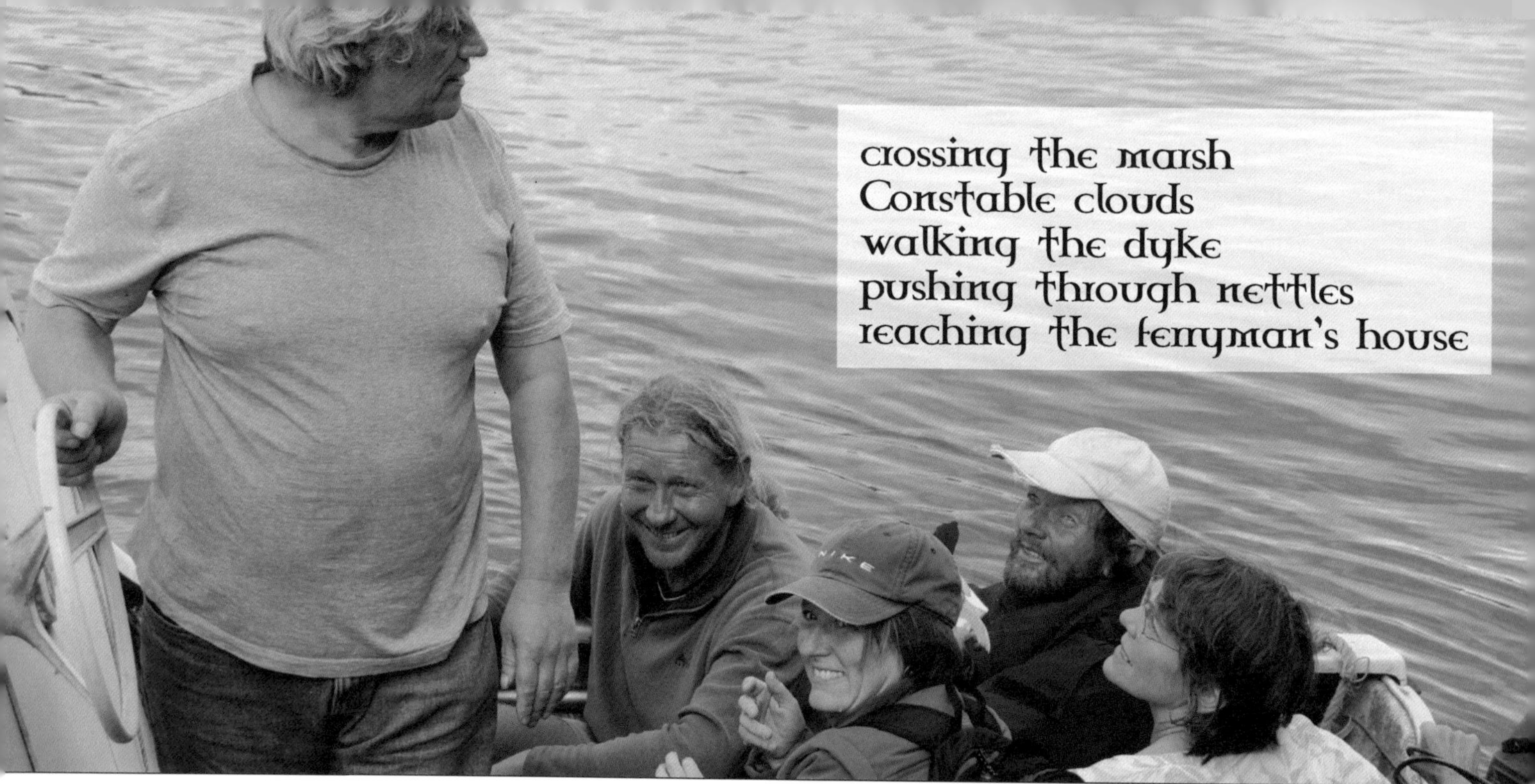

Crossing the marshes necessitated a winding route as we searched for the right path. A land of myth and fable indeed ... we balanced across beams over dykes, under bridges, crashed through nettles, until we reached the ferryman's house where we lay on the grass and drank tea and brandy. The ferryman told us tales of crossings that ended in drownings and people swept away by the current. This certainly built up the tension before we climbed aboard his tiny boat to be ferried to the other side. ***SB***

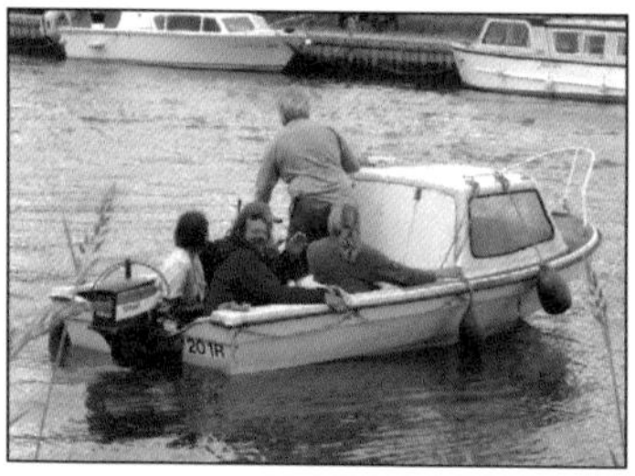

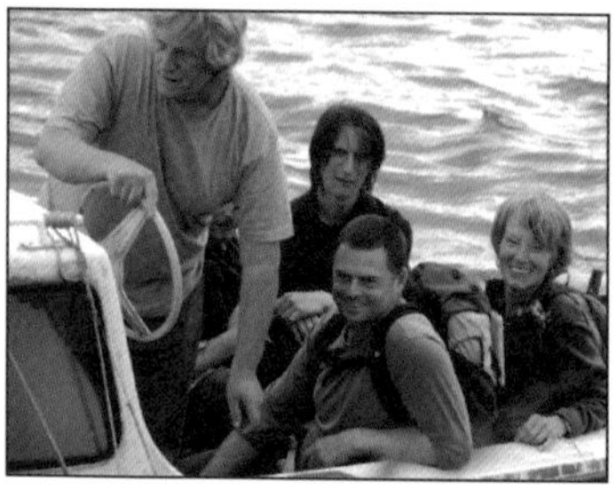

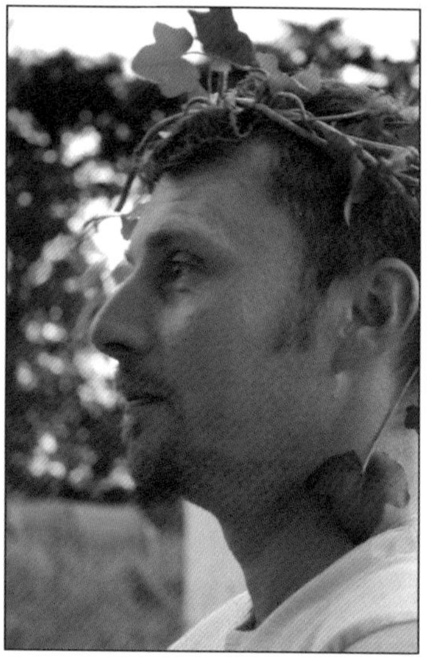

Day 47

Barsham to Somerleyton

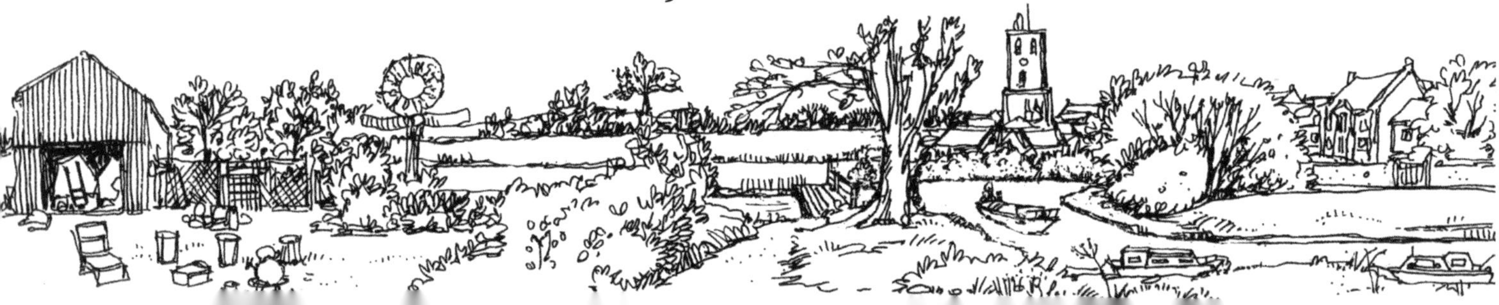

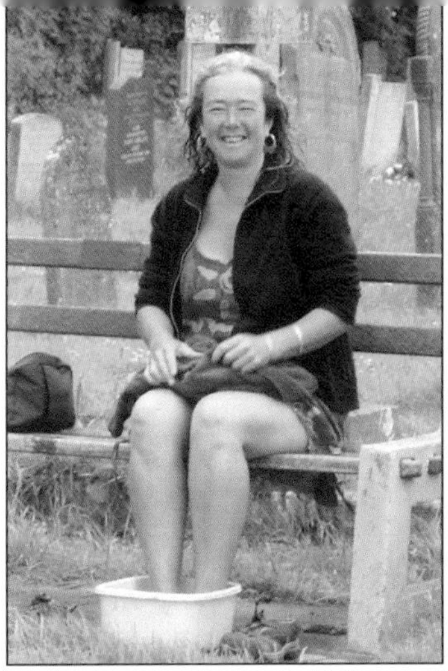

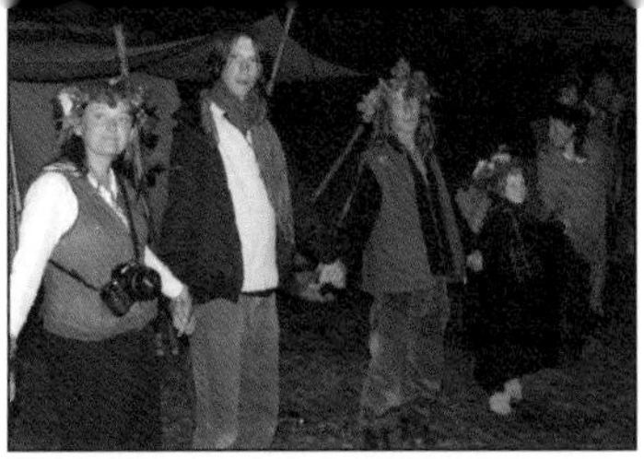

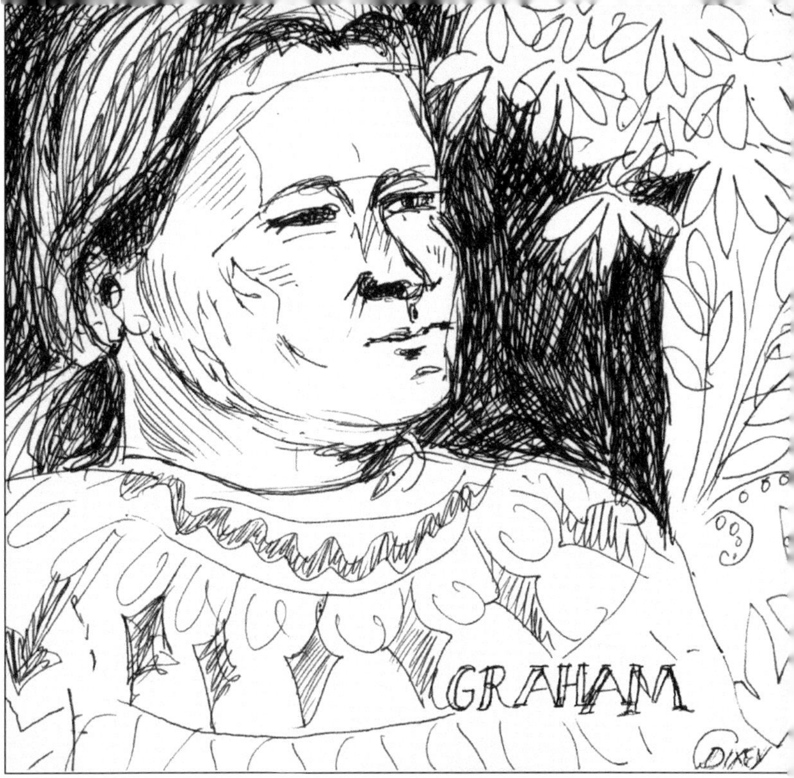

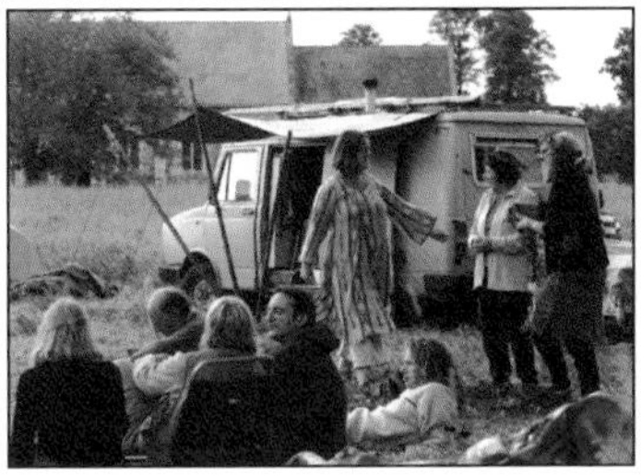

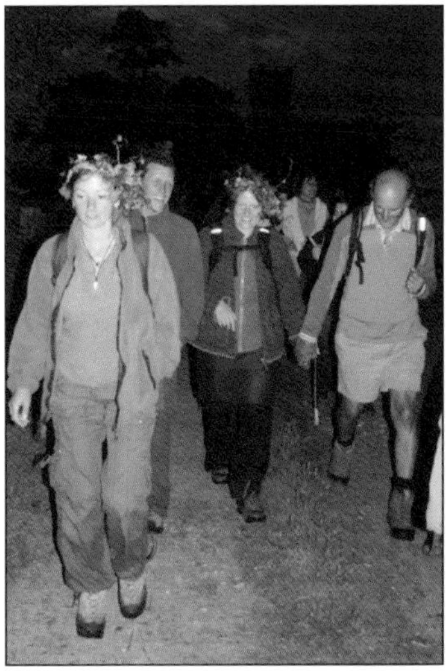

Drops of rain ... striding ahead ... crossed the marshes ... feeling fit ... smelling the sea ... smelling the end of a great journey ... led the way through thistles and nettles to the ferryman's house ... John Ferryman gave us tea, then brandy, told us stories of sinkings, eventually took us across the River Waveney in a wobbly little boat ... and so to Somerleyton, walked the last two miles to camp at St Mary's Church, arrived very high singing Dona Nobis Pacem ... elated and exhilarated ...! ***GJ***

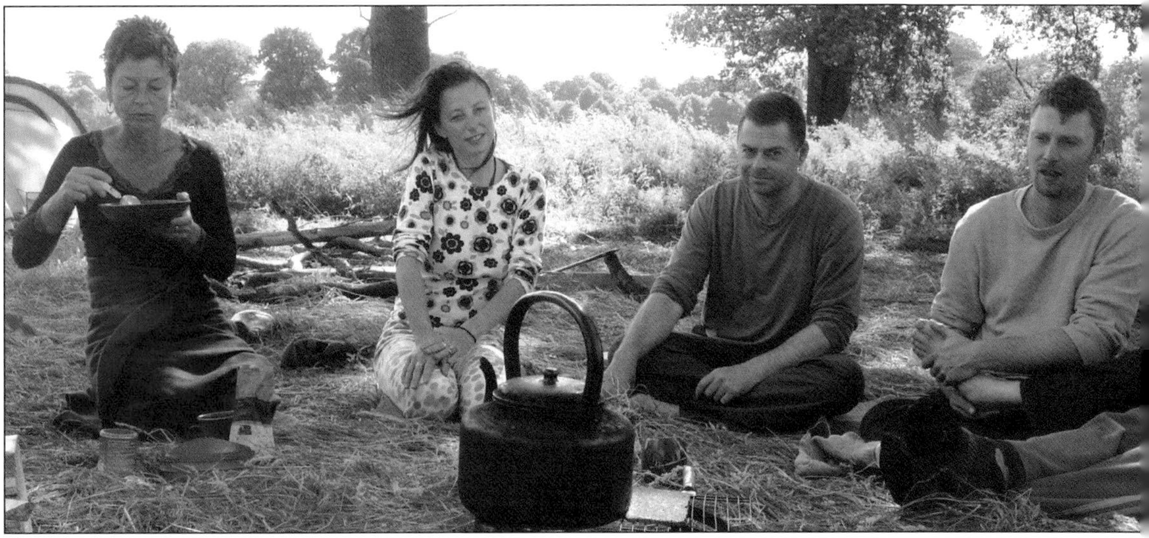

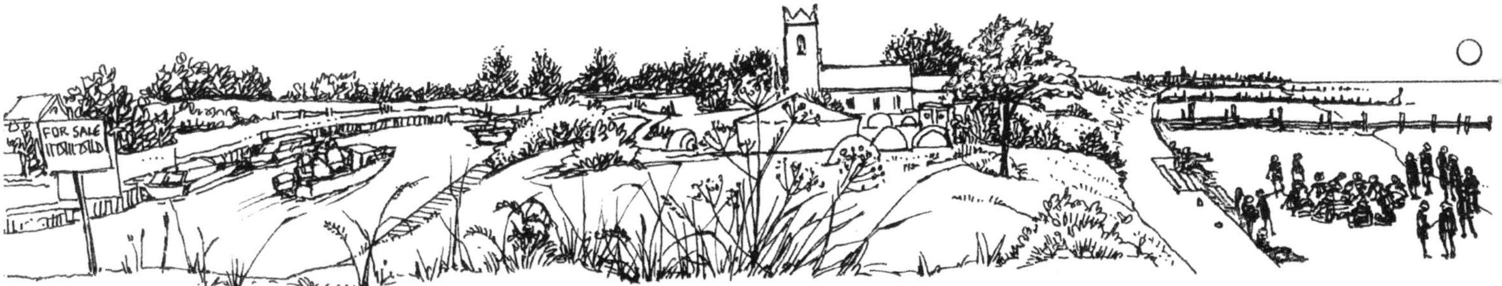

Day 47/48 Somerleyton to Hopton

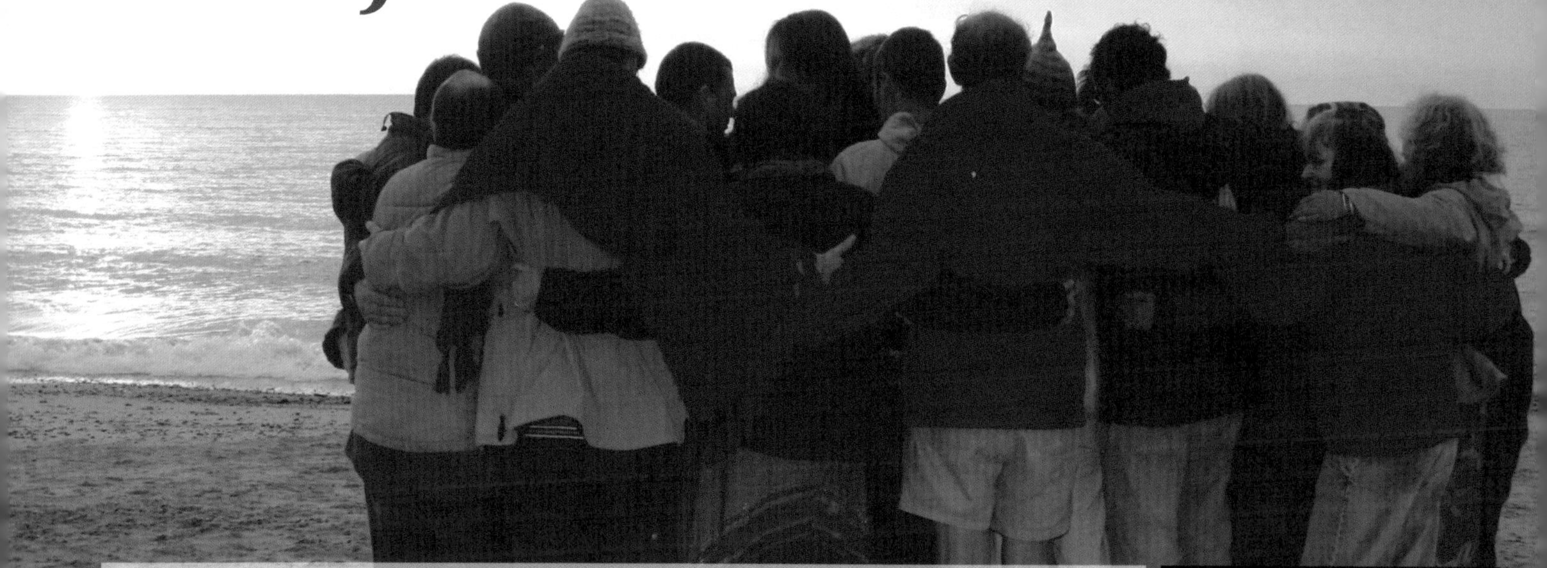

After dinner we set off for Hopton. It was odd to process past bungalows and mocking drinkers from the holiday camp pubs. We met at the church, waiting for others to catch up. I started a circle, humming and felt happy to know the tribe would join together. We walked the final leg of our journey in silence.

I have walked across our land. Coast to coast, west to east, along the line. Once on the beach I stripped naked and ran into the sea, cold and liberating and alive as a big orange moon rose over the clouds. As Alex began to make sacred fire I began singing "Earth my body, Water my blood, Air my breath and Fire my spirit", gradually others joined and as the ember glowed, the tinder caught, the fire roared, we circled and sang. The moment of Solstice round the fire, huddled together, hot chocolate, sugary treats, the sky in the east lightened. We gathered in little groups, sang, and Ed played guitar, improvising silly songs and dancing on the sand as the sun rose.

I gathered our core nine walkers and we held each other and sang, then widened the circle to draw in the rest of our gathered extended tribe. I felt moved, and sad and full of love.

ML

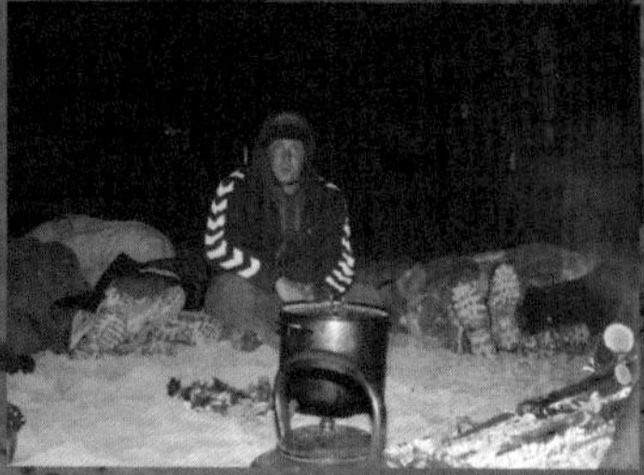

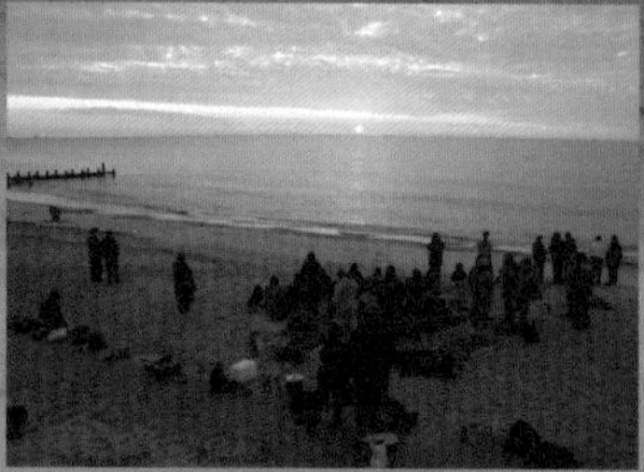

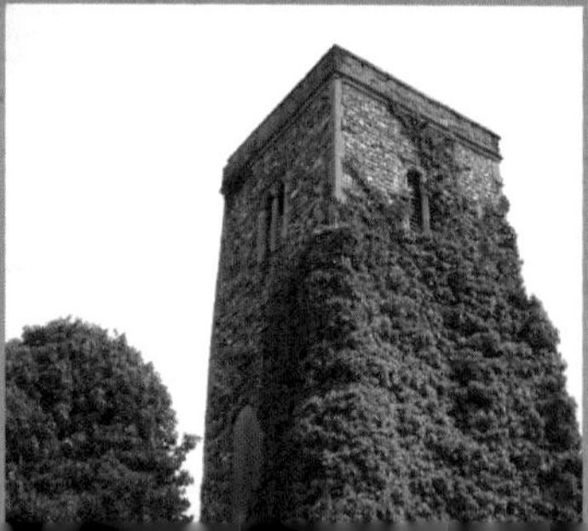

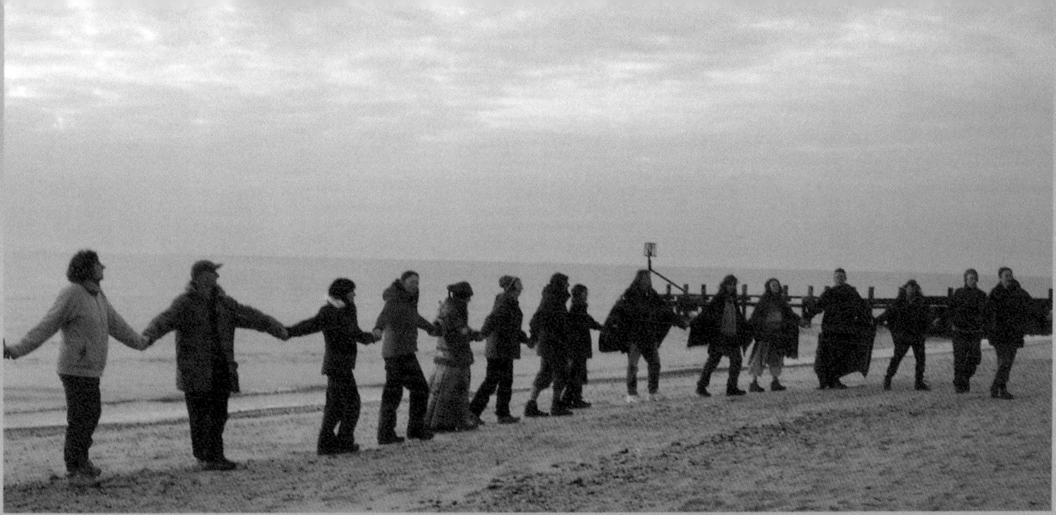

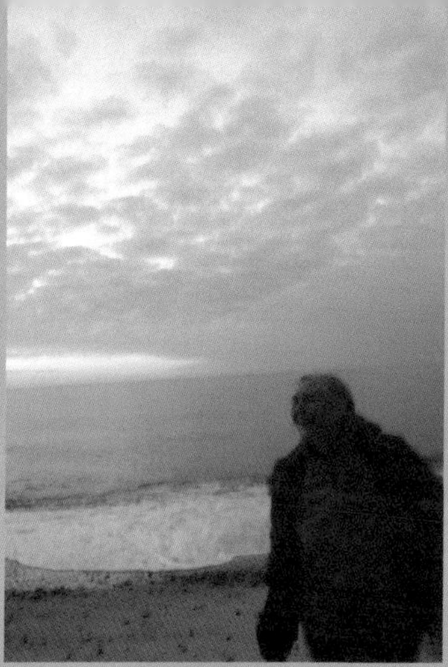

Hopton
churchyard ... midnight
hand in hand
silent pilgrims walk
down to the moonlit sea

snuggled in
the sand lulled by
wave thump
moonlit ... firelit
friends silhouetted

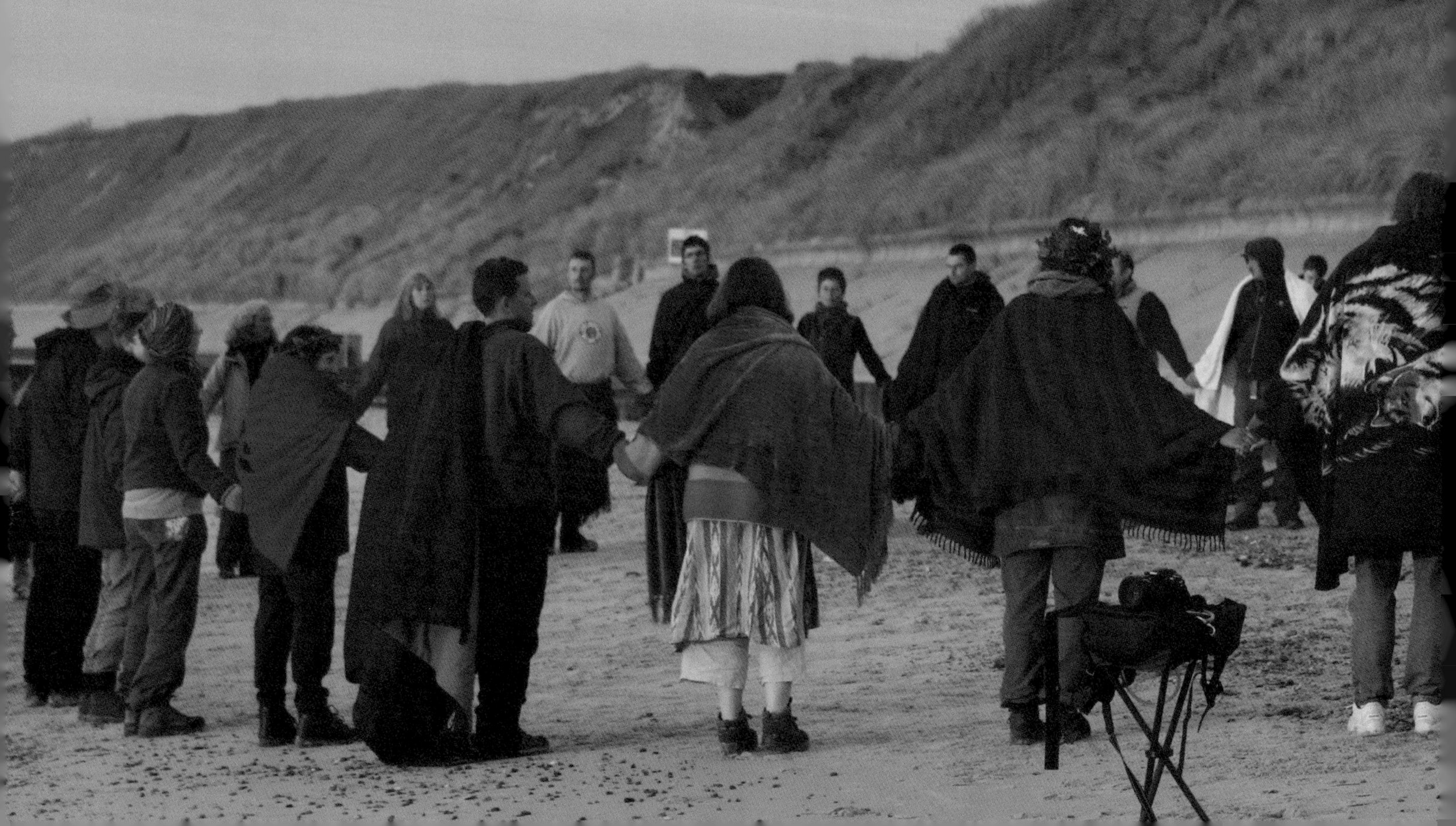

Day 49

Somerleyton

last call for
cups of tea ... last fire
last circle
last song ... last hugs
it's time ... pilgrims please

beyond
the kissing gates
of Suffolk
a rough footpath
stretches ahead

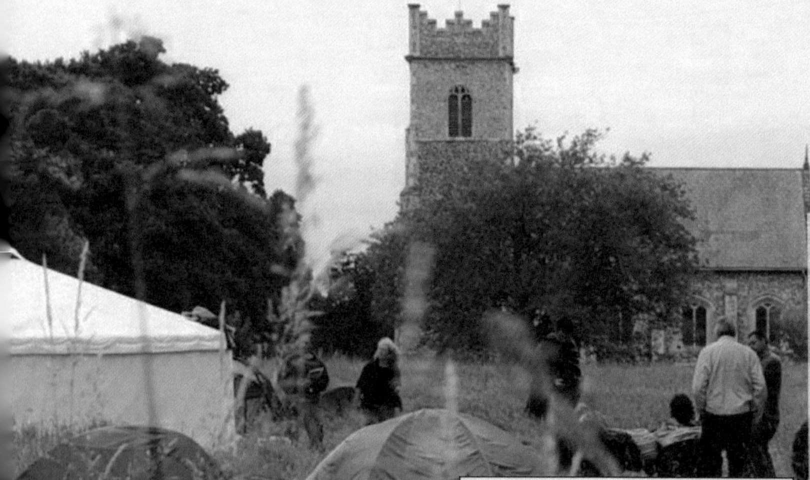

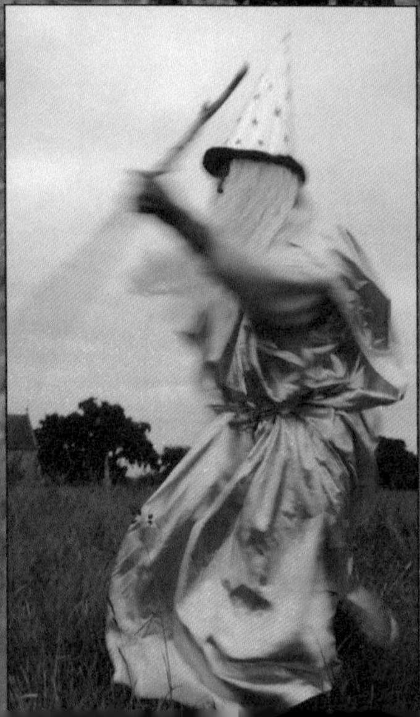

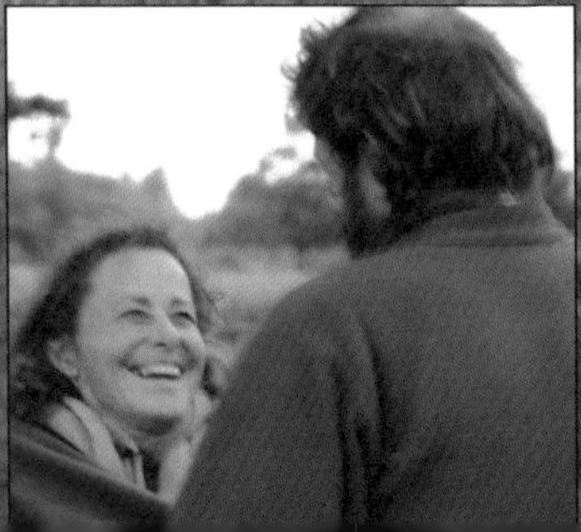

Last day of waking up with the community. Tea and porridge round the fire, I sat under the oak tree and wrote in my journal. We began to say our goodbyes and to disperse. We held a ceremony; those of us who walked all the way passed a garland of daisies over each others heads, and then Gerry placed it round the fire. Our final circle was so moving; we sang our song, "Where I walk is holy", everything was packed away, the final fire pit was filled, we sang the Celtic Blessing and hugged and kissed and cried our goodbyes. My amazing tribe of friends, I will never forget you ... ***ML***

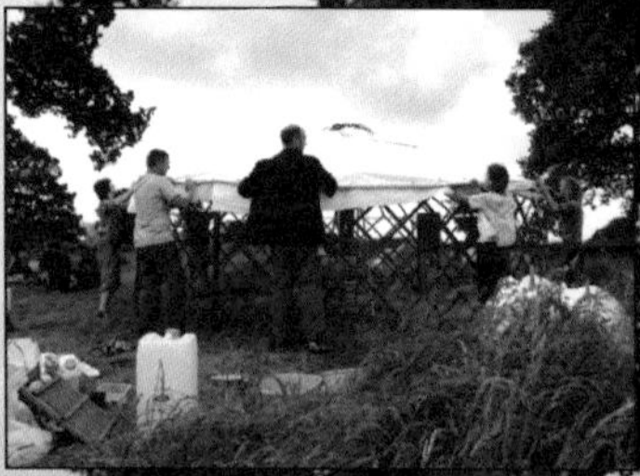

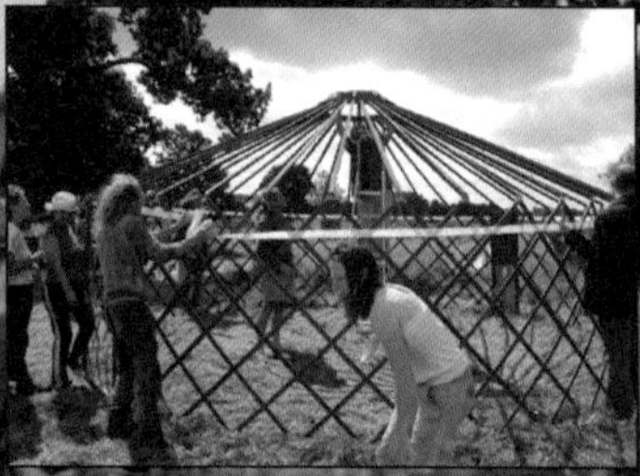

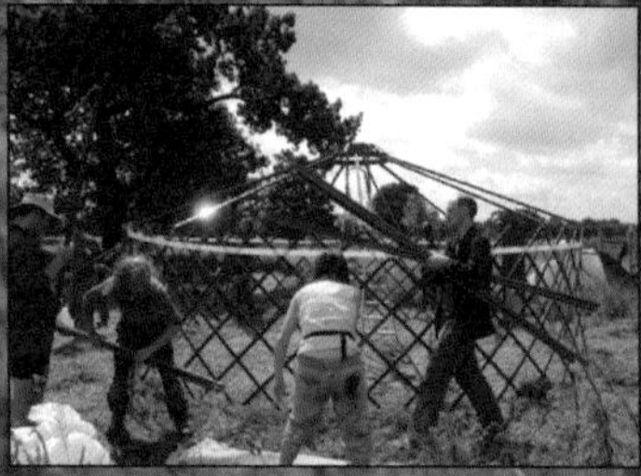

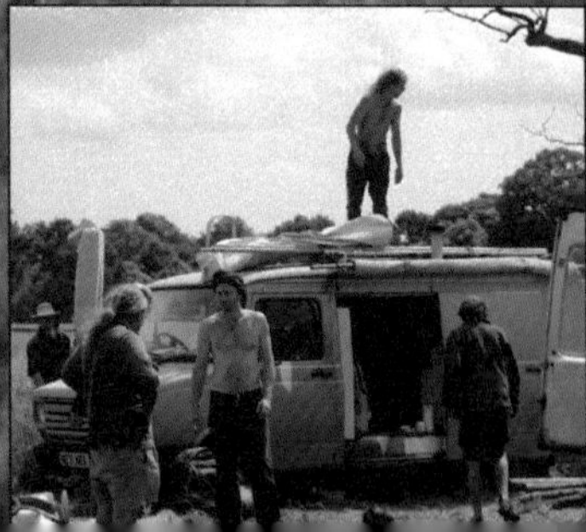

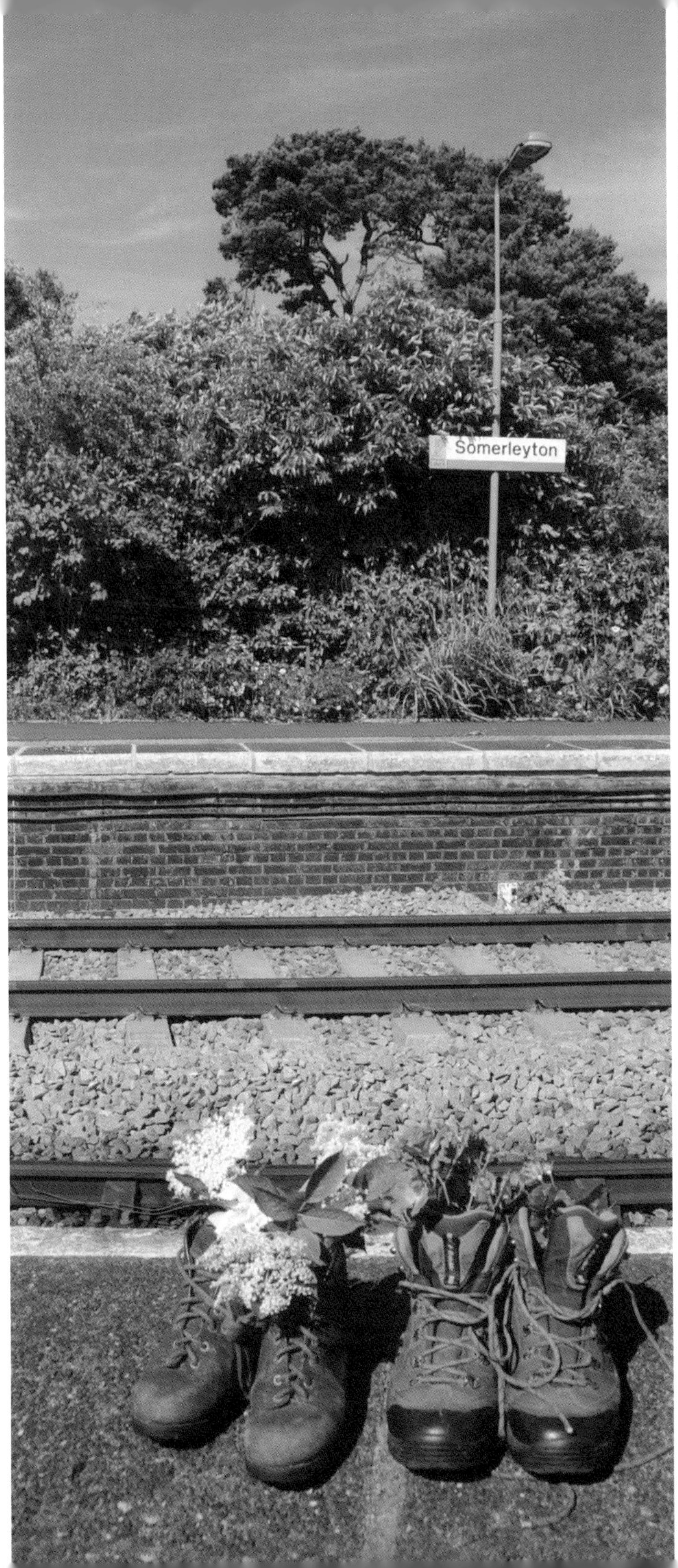

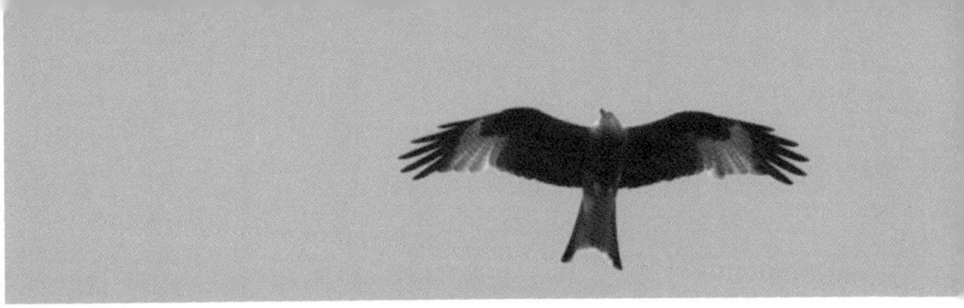

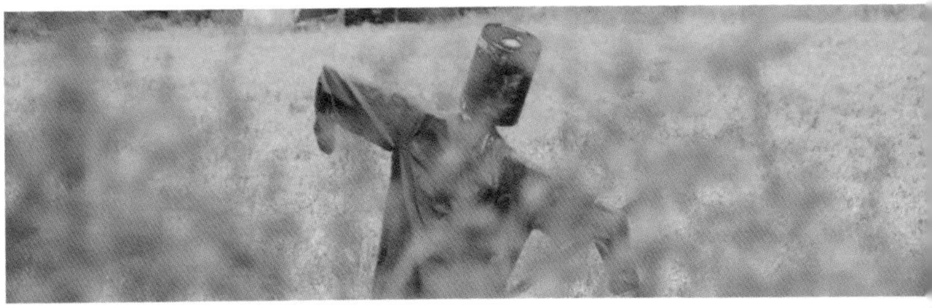

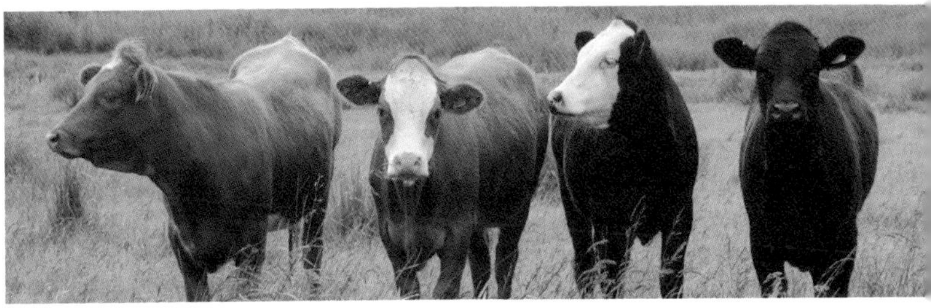

I filled my
lungs with seven
weeks of life -
the open road
the open circle

slow knowing...
fifty days and nights
of rain and sun
and clouds and stars ...
and shared cups of milky tea

in the morning
I miss them - dear
companions -
and the fire unlit
the words left unspoken

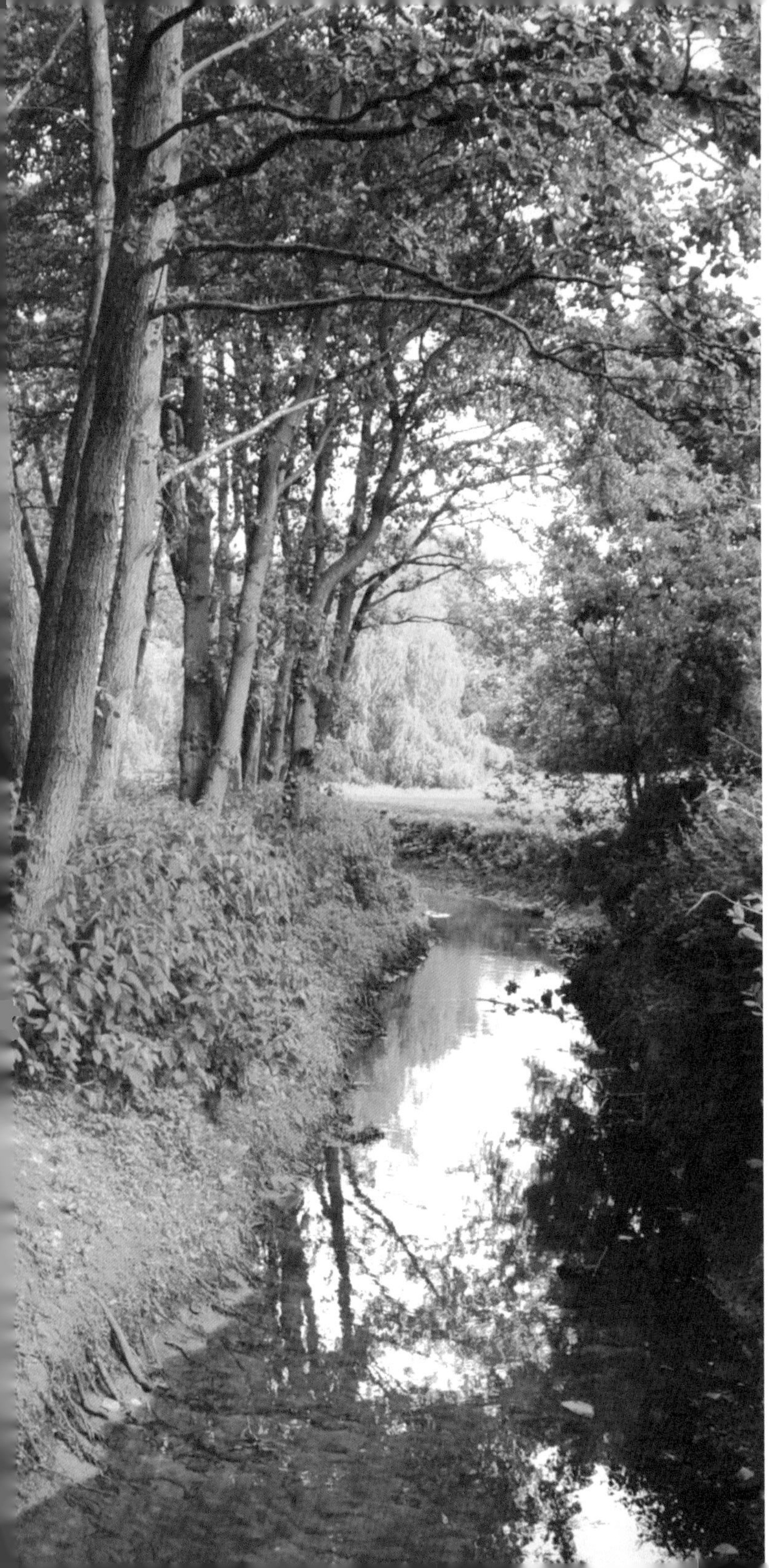

Epilogue

The basic intention was straightforward; to walk the land, celebrating its beauty and witnessing its wounding, whilst also experiencing being in community. The practical reality of the walking schedule rapidly stripped the Walk to its bare bones, as it became obvious that there was little time for extra activities during the day, and that tiredness often precluded evening events. But there was also delight in that very simplicity, the daily practice that evolved. The Walk was also, as one walker put it, very Yang, with little time to be quietly receptive to nature, yet we did it, we made our pilgrimage, and the receptivity was in the walking itself. We delighted in the ever-changing landscapes and slowly shifting seasons, from the primroses and bluebell woods of a Cornish spring, to the hedges full of wild rose and the poppy-filled wheat fields of mid-summer Suffolk.

JGJ

High up above the valley ... the hunting buzzards weave their circles in the air. Circling circling as they have surely done for so many thousands of years here above the valley. And as I stare up shading my eyes against the bright early summer sun I hear the little birds singing and busy in the hedgerows and I think: A thousand years ago did some passing ancestor pause here, perhaps, to eye that hunting hawk. Or listen for a moment to the singing and busy chirping of the little birds.

And did she stoop, like me, to peer more closely at the intricate folded petals and delicate colour of the little hidden violets and breathing deeply of the misty scented mixed perfume of flowers and green things and know that for a thousand thousand years the birds have sung in just this way here in the early summer and in just this way have the buzzards hunted and circled above the valleys and so too each year have the violets bloomed and the smells of wild garlic and greening earth mingled in the great expanding tides of spring and mid summer.

And I watch her, this ancestor of mine as she pauses there, a solitary woman, and I wonder does she watch me too, peering down for this one moment through all the summers of a thousand years, years of her children and her children's children and on and on through all the millenia and changes and turmoil of our passing human cultures to these sad and fearful times when the old great ancient spirit of the land sighs and murmurs in her tranced sleep, from which it seems possible she will never now awaken.

The wind on the hills rustles and stirs the leaves and runs along my cheek, chill suddenly and quiet and I know in a sudden moment of hope and patience and faith that in a thousand years the children of my land and body will still stand here in the spring and pause as she did then and I now. I watch, peering down through all the long years to this future, to this far far distant child of mine, as she too lifts her hand to her forehead shading her eyes against the bright sun peering up and up high above the valley where the hunting hawks on the edge of sight circle in the hazy skies.

Much later when I am home I remember something I have read once and liking it wrote it down and searched for it and found it but I can't remember now who wrote it ... 'Things come home to our hearts and we feel the unbroken line of our national life stretching back into the remote past, and know that it will reach into the far future and that we ourselves are a part of it.'. ***TR***

We started each day in a circle, all connecting before we set out to snake our way across the land. As I walked either solitary or with fellow pilgrims I continued to feel connected to the community with the knowing that our path was the same and we would meet again at the end of the day; also the arrows left by those in front of me kept me in touch and showed me the way. As the days flowed, this connection increased, along with my connection with the land. My consciousness altered and intensified as I gradually became more tuned into the trees, the grass, the sky, the mud, the rain and nature in general, and at each sacred site that was experienced on the way.

The daily routine and rhythms became a very satisfying and therapeutic way of life. Packing everything away, the camp gradually melting until the space returned to its former glory. Then the circle and 'a map moment'. The day's walk, each time a new adventure; what will I see? Who will cross my path? How will my senses alter from one step to the next? Will I get a blister?

At the end of the day, arriving at the camp, with only one thing on my mind: a cup of tea (Earl Grey of course)! Gradually the site becoming home as I orientated to the place, with the focus always being the fire. The fire, to me, was one of the most sacred aspects of my day. It was the centre, the focus, it supplied so much warmth

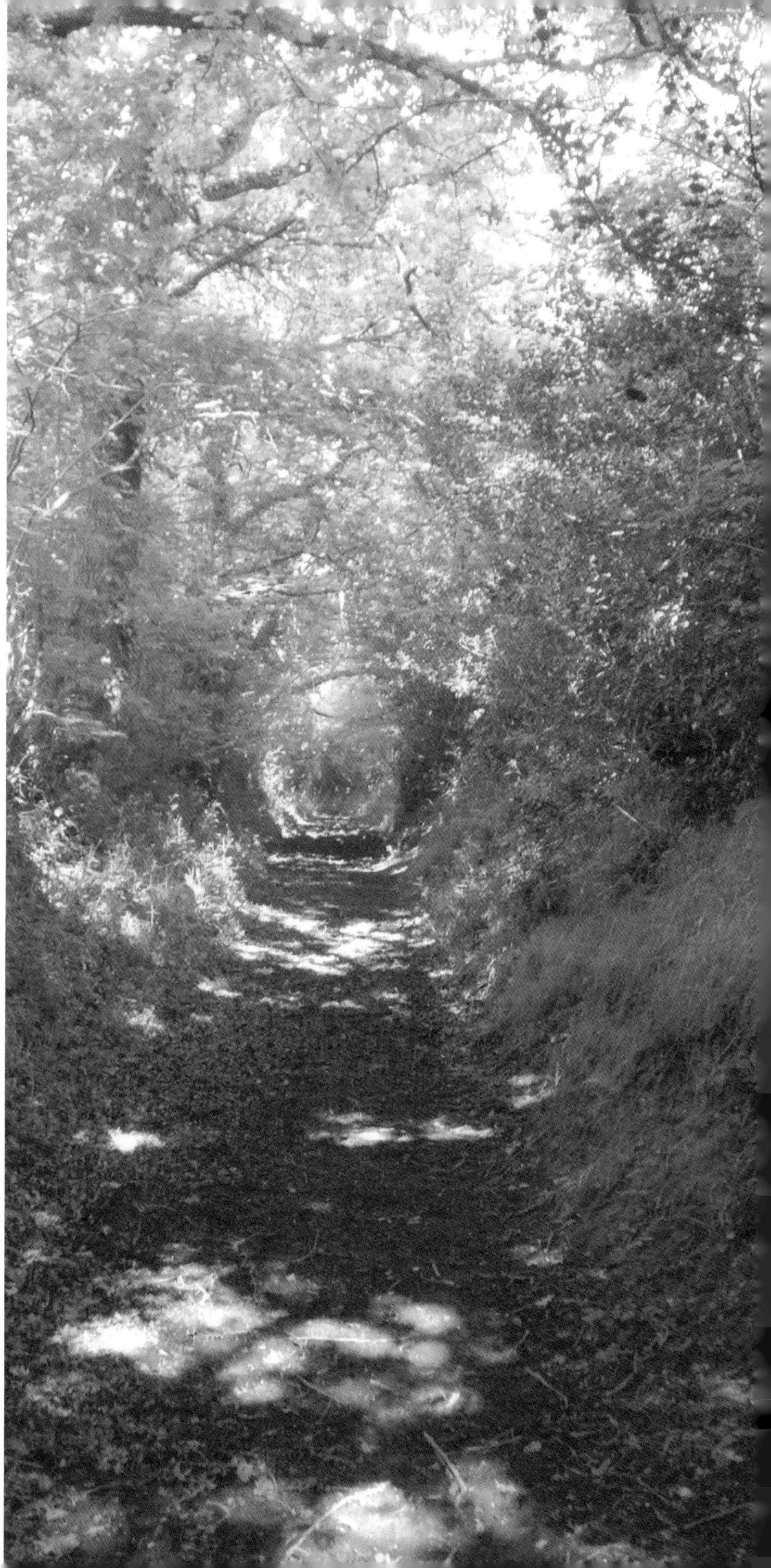

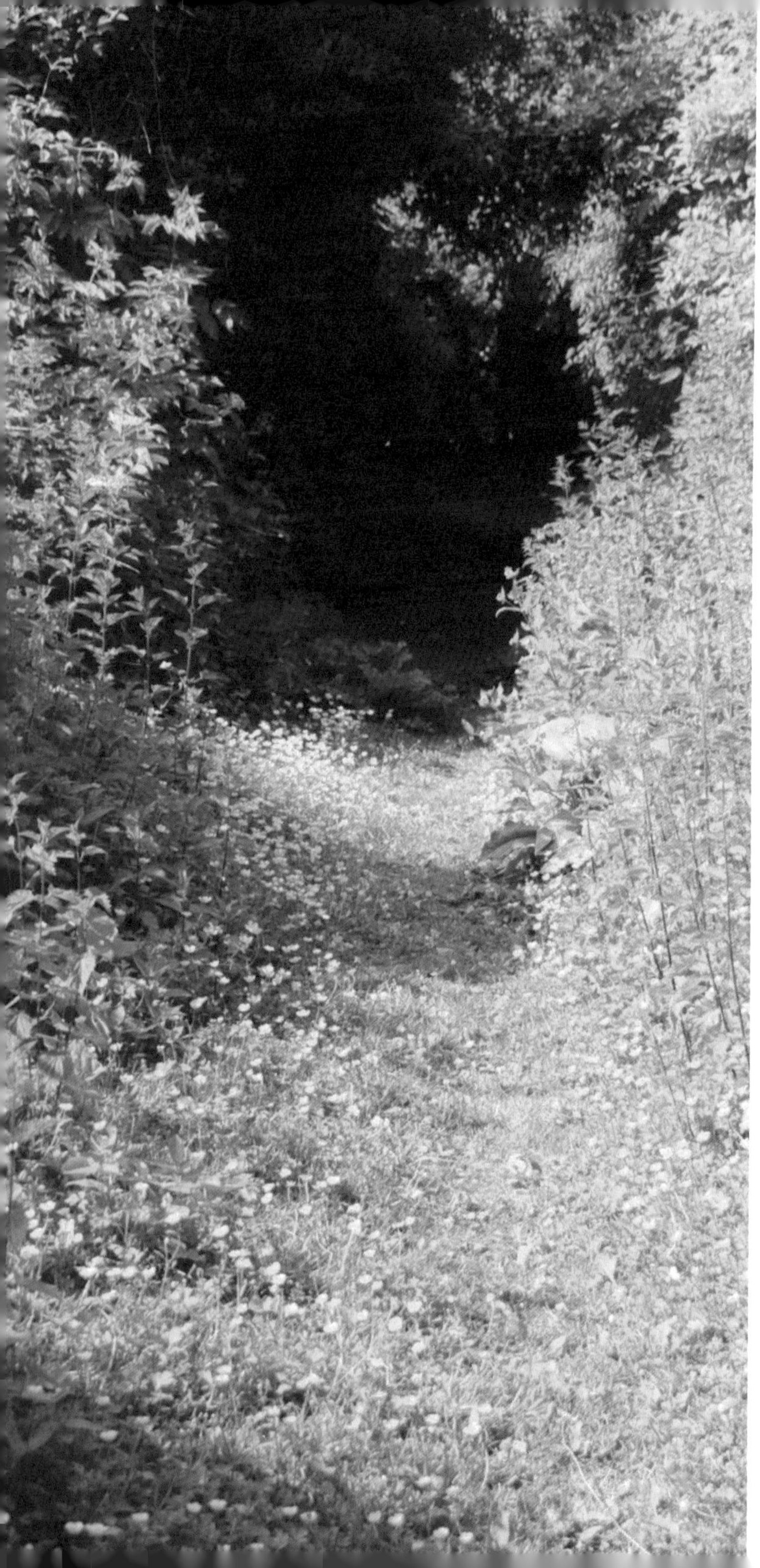

in so many ways, it was often surrounded by laughter, chat, gazing and always accompanied by a big tea-pot. The tea-pot being an important part of the fire experience and always (nearly) full of tea. It kept warm by the fire, sitting snug inside the community crafted tea-cosy. ***JH***

The memorable things about the walk which affected me deeply were the ways that we observed nature changing and growing as we continued on our way. The slower pace of walking allowed us to take in each field of newly planted wheat, each magical bluebell wood, each leaf forming on the trees and as we progressed so did the flowers, crops and trees grow and develop around us. We were able to be part of the turning of the year, to feel part of that growth process and allow our thoughts to slow down to the more gentle pace of the changing landscape.

The shocks came at the times when we were forced to cross roads and motorways and we came up against the frenetic and crazy pace of modern humanity. Sitting round the campfire in the evening, cooking over the flames, and sharing stories and the highlights of the day under the moon and stars, were all factors that grew us into a loving and caring tribe. We were living and walking mindfully, respectful of and at one with our surroundings and with each other. ***CC***

I feel so proud that I walked. I feel empowered and changed and inspired by the experience. I feel that many more adventures are possible. I am very aware of the things which nurture my spirit and the things which don't. I feel a strong sense of responsibility for myself, and only me, I feel better able to let others be as they are. ***ML***

The route we followed was inevitably a compromise between where the Michael and Mary Lines ran, and existing paths and roads. As we walked, sometimes on or near one, and sometimes the other, we explored their energies. We dowsed them on a number of occasions, and even without rods several people said they could feel the energies and the difference between them. At the nodes or crossing points we often made some simple ceremony. ***JGJ***

I was moved on a number of occasions when wild animals would emerge from the woods and just walk nonchalantly past us without any apparent sense of fear. We had become at one with them and therefore not a threat. ***CC***

Highlights for me were at the points when I was singing the intersections of the Michael and Mary lines along the route. At these places I would feel a sense of co-creating with the energies of nature and that the land was filling me with its creative essence, from which a song would be birthed. I would never have any preconception of what song might emerge, but at each point the feel of the place would dictate the mood and style of the music and a spontaneous, wordless flow of sound would come from me. Sometimes the place would feel dark and gloomy and the song would be a solemn dirge and at other times it would be haunting and lyrical, whilst on other occasions it would be rollicking and jazzy. Each place and song was unique in flavour and inspired a completely original, improvised vocal creation. ***CC***

At a rough guess, probably over two-thirds of our pilgrimage was walked off-road. We had contacted county footpath officers prior to the Walk to discover the state of the paths on our route, but it was still a relief to discover that nearly all were clear and well maintained. Indeed many were much more than that: 'another beautiful path!' became a regular refrain. It seems clear that walking the footpaths, bridleways and byways gave access to a secret land, to an unknown and magical country that could not be experienced any other way. These worlds, the green-lined hollow ways, ancient woodlands or chalk ridgeways, are unknown to all but those willing to walk. The narrow country roads too became part of this magical world, for they are but ancient green lanes recently tarmacked, the lesser used of them with the grass breaking through again. While vehicle traffic roared along the motorways and trunk roads, these paths and lanes, mainly used by those who inhabit the local landscape, were the ancient ways of this land. It was a joy to walk them!

JGJ

What has enriched my life is that now on my daily dog walk, in addition to standing at the top of Whiteleaf cross next to the ancient barrow and looking out across the different counties to the familiar sites and scenes, I can now see two, three, maybe four days' walking and I can see the clumps at Wittenham and visualise standing on the top of the hill looking forward to Whiteleaf Hill. I also had the opportunity to share a few moments with some of my companions sitting under one of my favourite trees. I can now sit here as often as I like and feel connected to them and the whole pilgrim experience. For this I am eternally grateful. ***JH***

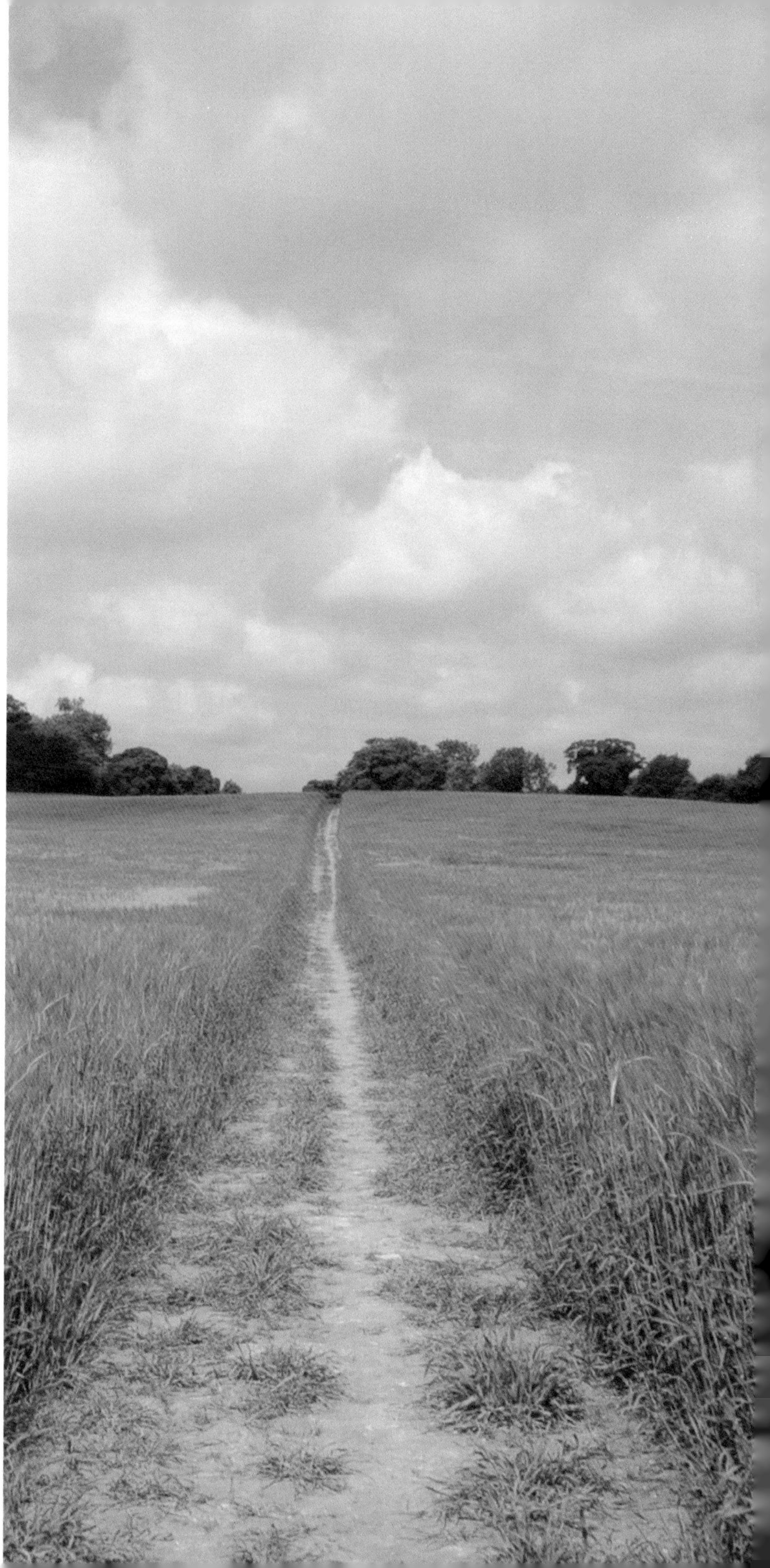

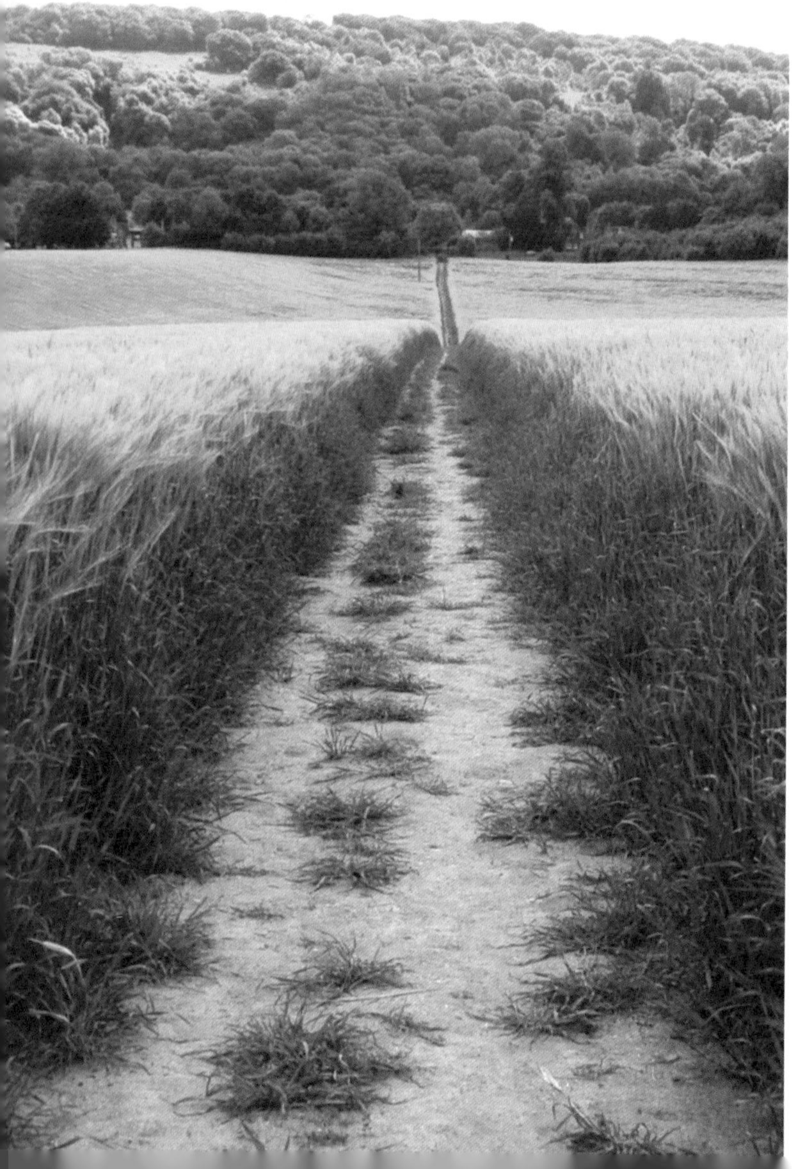

I enjoyed the magic, the ritual, the dance, the singing, the stories, the hugs, the food, the sharing, and the living in community. I enjoyed working hard, being physical, relaxing, stopping, gazing, watching, listening, tasting, touching, and smelling. I valued living lightly on the earth, the openness and generosity of my heart and the openness and generosity of everyone I met along the way. I loved the walking, the physical fitness and challenge, the pull of the hills, the beating of my heart, and the air in my lungs. I loved every leaf, flower, tree, bird, animal, rock, plant, view, river and hill I was lucky enough to witness. ***ML***

Within the busy walking schedule we did make time for our creativity. Carolin and Gerry led us in singing and dancing at many churches and other sacred sites, and we had some memorable drumming and dancing evenings. We carried a yurt sauna with us and used it for sweat lodge ceremonies, where we offered our songs and prayers. Nate made exciting fire sculptures, while Alex created fire itself. Rhian introduced us to gathering wild food, and Graham showed how to make corn dollies. At Avebury Ruth whittled endless knitting needles out of sticks, and we knitted and crocheted our fabulous Awakening Albion tea cosy. Sarah's ongoing film work was astonishing to witness. The lead walkers made beautiful natural arrows to guide those following, while the daily crew made our lunch breaks and homecomings most welcoming. The Walk had a regular visitor, Ian, who invariably brought some unforgettable creation, the Silbury Hill cake, and Dragon's Eggs springing to mind, as well as his final wizardly appearance as Gandalf. ***JGJ***

It was a rare life experience to feel so totally accepted for just being myself. Walking and nature, what a powerful combination. Just being outdoors with a wonderful community; it was so simple, authentic and genuine. What more can one hope for in life? ***JH***

We certainly were a community, the core group of nine who made the whole journey, and all the many others who came and went, walking a week, a fortnight, or more. We walked together through the land, and willingly shared the work, crewing the vehicles, cooking and eating together around the hearth fire, sitting in circle, telling our stories of the day in the evenings and supporting each other. We learnt to work skilfully, generally being packed and ready to start walking by 9.30 each morning. The process of people coming and going throughout the Walk went more easily than some of us expected. There were occasional days of feeling overwhelmed and having to readjust, as numbers went from 15 up to 25 and down again, and this of course affected logistics such as shopping, cooking, and carrying gear in the vehicles, but on the whole the group seemed to maintain its identity and coherence fairly well. We also touched the hearts of many as we travelled. People we met in churches and shops, on footpaths or at our campsites, were frequently astonished and moved at hearing of our venture. Some joined us for a while. ***JGJ***

Along the way sometimes people would stop and ask what we were doing and usually they responded with 'I wish I could come with you' or something along those lines. You could sense their longing for the open road and a purpose beyond the ordinary, something special, the archetypal journey, new sights and sounds of lands newly discovered, a chance to see everything afresh with new eyes.

And to those who gave us hospitality en route, with their land, their gifts of fire wood, wine, milk and shelter, our passing seemed to touch them, perhaps awaken an ancient memory of supporting those who sacrificed something and journeyed for the greater good. And I, in turn, as pilgrim, felt privileged and honoured to be allowed onto their lands and witness their homes for one night, to share in their lives for just a short while. It was a real gift of mutuality and a very healthy exchange. Somehow the land needs us to remember her and travel in this way and the people need to feel that this way of being and moving is possible, natural and honourable, something to be revered, an acknowledgment of effort and purpose which is beyond the everyday. ***DF***

The Walk clearly succeeded in creating an atmosphere of generosity. It was always intended as a not-for-profit venture, and this quality was present throughout, from the work of organising it, the website creation, to the kindness of many of the site providers, the willingness of the walkers to work together, and all those who gave their energy to create this book. ***JGJ***

So how were we walkers affected by the Awakening Albion pilgrimage? Did our walk reflect the significance of acknowledging the landscape and were we all in some way changed and enriched by our experiences? And if so did our own personal transformations affect changes in the earth itself? Many of the walkers recorded their experiences in

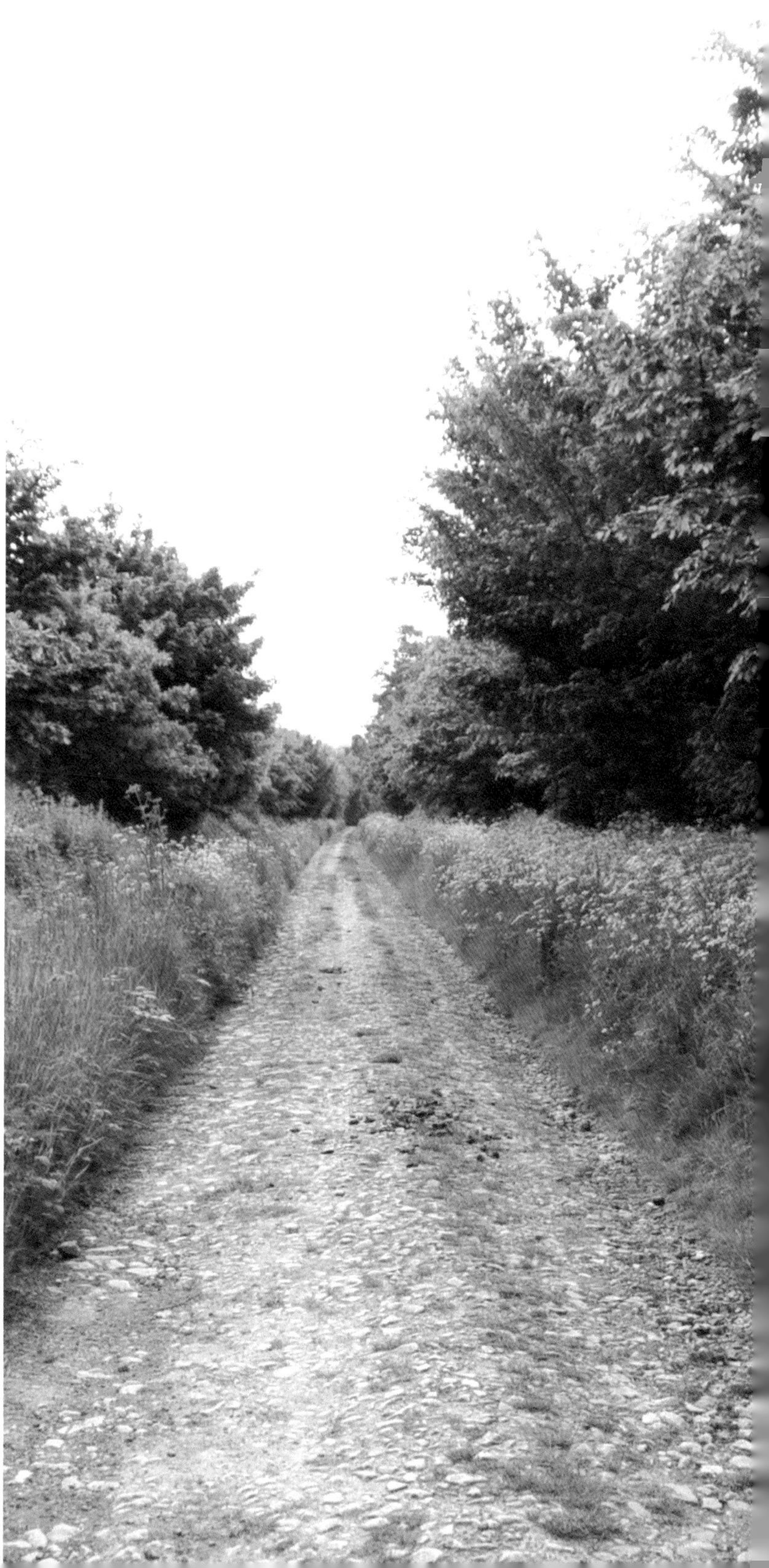

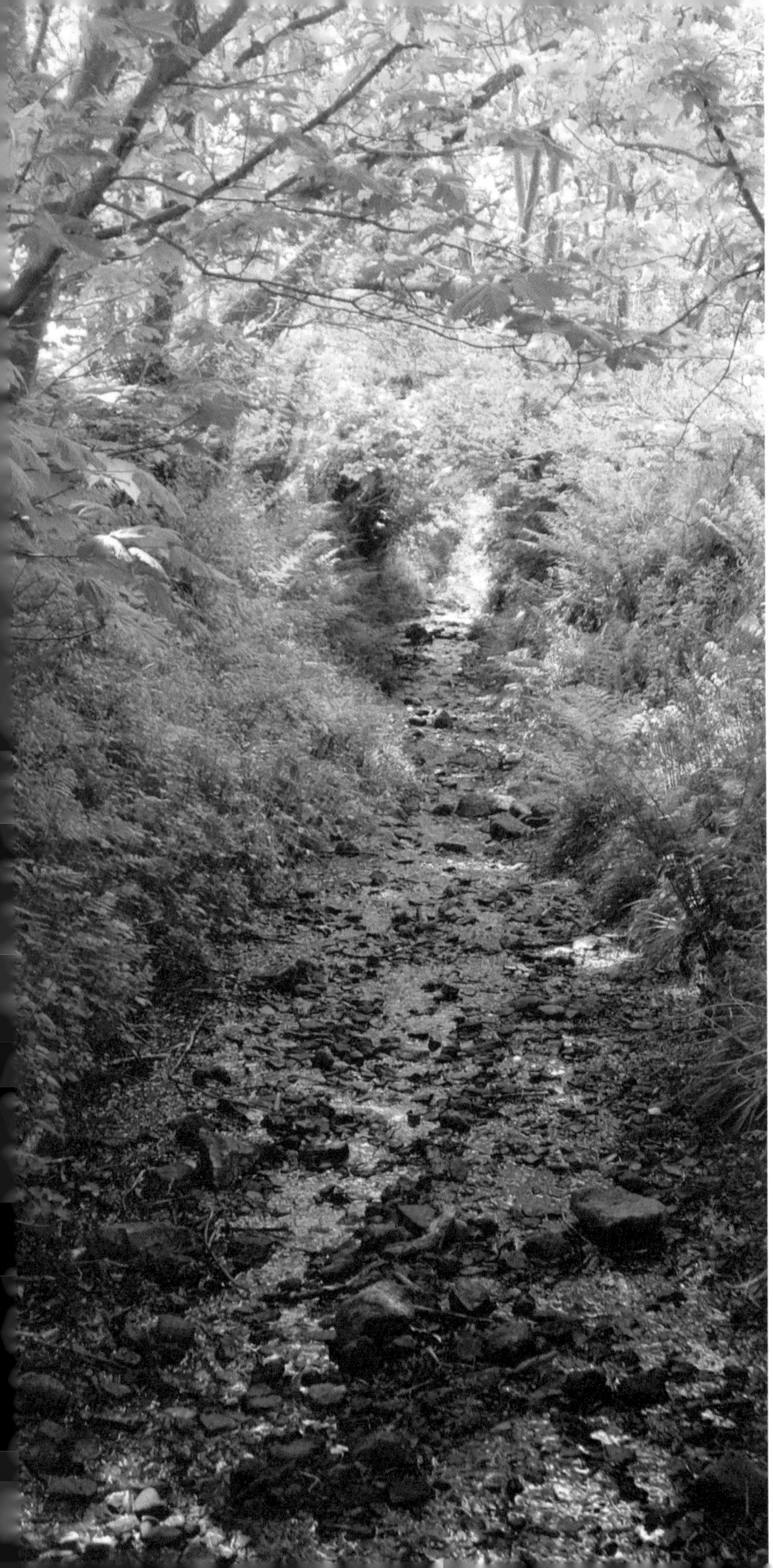

poems or daily journals. I think they show in deeply personal ways how the journey was not just a physical one, but very much a walk of spiritual development and increased awareness. If we can affect our surroundings by the power of our thoughts, then I think it's pretty clear that we have had a powerful transformative effect on the land that we walked. Hamish Miller, who came to see us at our second camp in Cornwall, said we might not yet all know what drew us to join the walk, but that he knew that we and the earth would be profoundly affected by it and he thanked us deeply and movingly for our parts in the "epic journey". ***CC***

For some, the end of the Walk has been hard, returning to our separate lives while still yearning for community. The Walk has acted as a catalyst for change for many of us; some have moved to simplify their lives, others to organise local walks, and for some it has led to explorations of ways to be more fully in community on the land. ***JGJ***

Magical, enlightening, powerful, my life will never be the same again. Returning to my 'normal' life was not a comfortable transition. Feeling a great sense of loss and yearning for my fellow walkers and the community way, but I return with my dreams renewed. ***JH***

I valued the time for contemplation, for connection with God, for the realisation of God's will for me and the power to carry that out.

I loved learning, hearing about and reading about nature, history, geology, magic, myth, legend, food, relationship, community, love, sex, family.

I loved recognising my own strengths and weaknesses and witnessing other peoples'. I loved experiencing the elements, tuning into the power of the earth. I loved the affirmation of my principles and values which I experienced.

I am so grateful for the friendships which were forged during this time. I am so grateful for the opportunities to go, and for everything that implies. ***ML***

I love England and the idea of a walk across the changing landscape sounded very exciting. I was completely surprised by the value of the community that Awakening Albion became then and has continued to be. It was both a challenging and happy time and also a unique experience. And I feel considerably richer from having been a part of it. The legacy of Albion is that increase in personal capital for those who were there, and lucky enough to have walked this land.

GD

As the days went on and meals were cooked and camps were set up and taken down each night, the rhythm of community life became understood and comfortable, and sometimes challenging. People's little ways and habits were witnessed and accepted, any worries communicated through a central sharing after dinner and items of baggage, literal and otherwise, began to fall away, no longer needed. Humour was dared by the shy, and real joys emerged as well as tears, frustrations and lurgies. But we all knew it was part of the process, each one of us on a journey with the self as well as each other and the land. ***DF***

We walked a cross-section of the geology of southern England, a few hundred million years of earth history. The older rocks are in the south-west, and the youngest in the east. Granites form the exciting cliffed coastline of Cornwall and also the uplands of Bodmin Moor and Dartmoor. The canal engineer William Smith developed the science of stratigraphy while excavating the Somerset canals in the 1830s. I wasn't able to see much of the interesting Somerset geology. It rained incessantly; I was often exhausted; and also I was unable to find the geological map in the chaos of the white van, which around that time acquired the name 'Awakening'. Later of course the great Chalk ridge and its flints became prominent in our lives.

GJ

By walking I was amazed by the abundance and diversity of one leafy lane, one small stretch of footpath and the vastness of the trees and greenery which surround us. Seeing and experiencing that directly I realised that what we see depends entirely on what we choose to see and that gave me immense hope. There is an alternative to what we have become accustomed to. We do have a choice. We can change our perception.

Thank you, thank you to all who I travelled with. ***DF***

After presenting the laurels, the final injunction of Gandalf the Brummie to the assembled company was that, having completed the Michael Mary line, the next task was the waking up of Apollo ... by walking the 2500 mile Apollo/Athena line, from Skellig, Ireland to Armageddon, Israel. Once done they would be awarded everlasting life by Apollo. "A piece of cake" I hear you say, and, with a little assistance from William Blake, Albert Einstein, J R Tolkein and Gandalf, we all know, that it can be done, just by ... The Power of Imagication! ***IW***

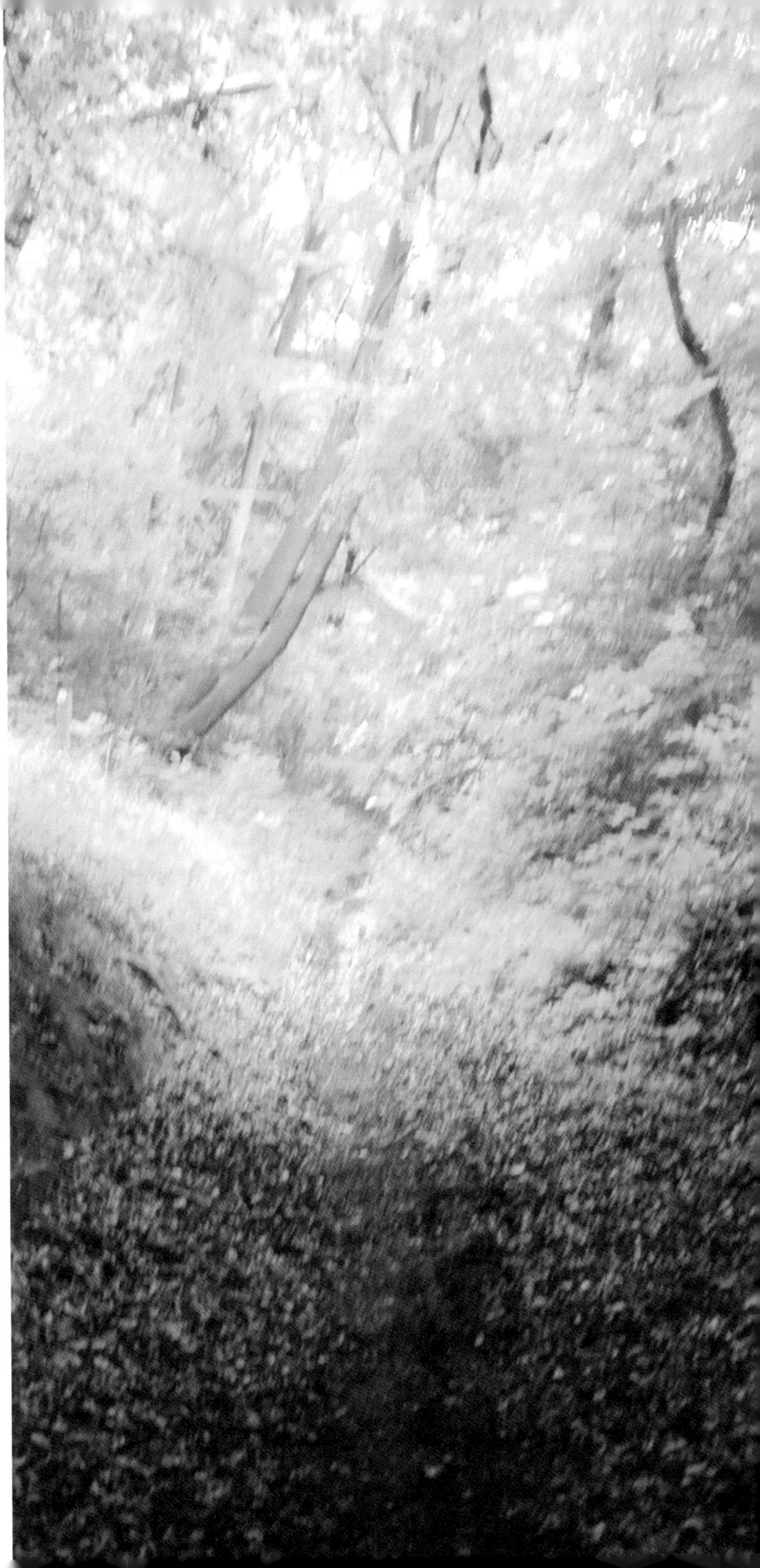

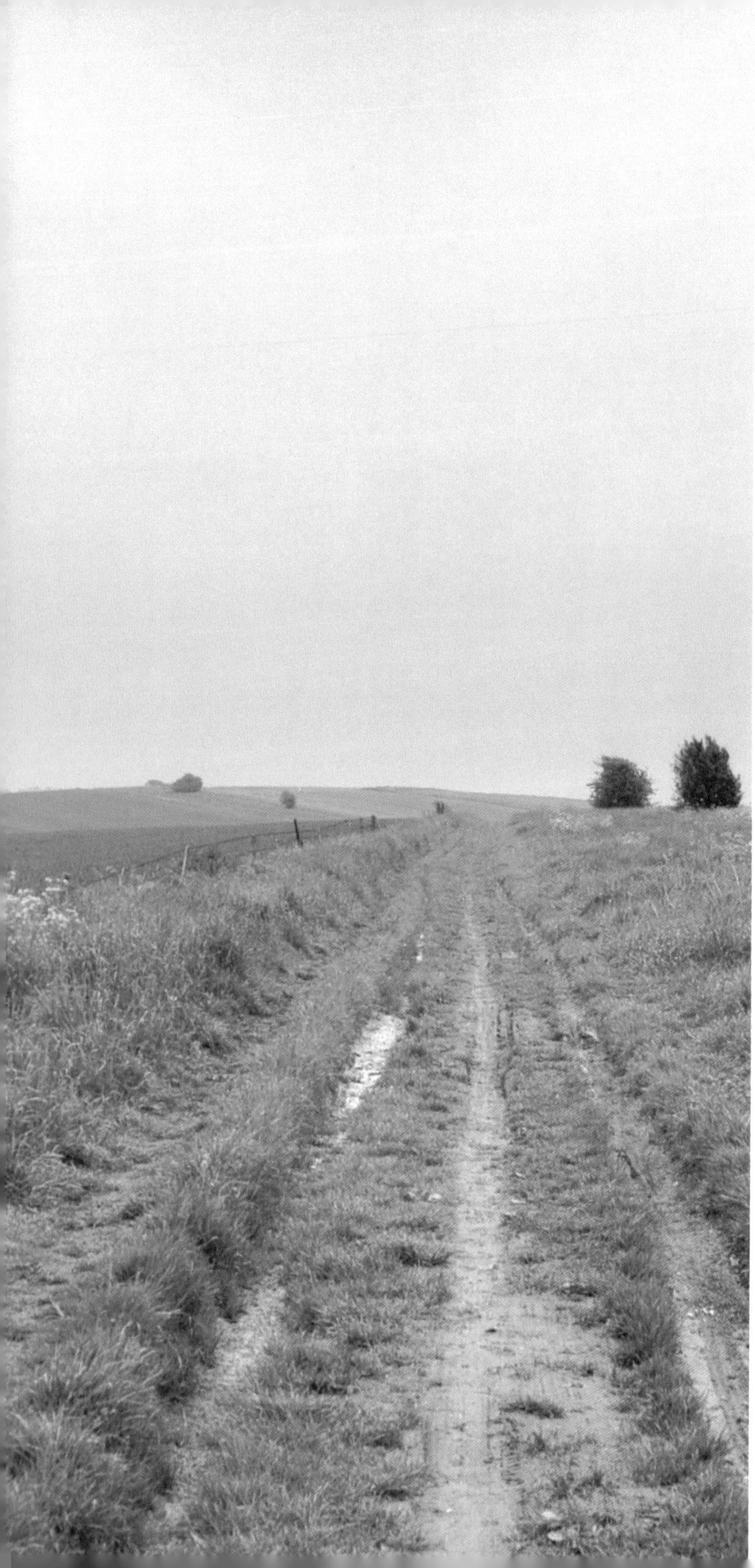

It was exactly seven weeks since our seven week pilgrimage ended when I headed back to Norfolk to celebrate Graham's birthday. Most of those who participated in the walk joined the weekend camp. We went for an afternoon's walk together. Enjoying a summer shower, wading through streams, singing in a church and lying down in fields now harvested. We all spoke at length by phone to Gerry in Australia and learned that co-incidentally as Carolin sang in a de-commissioned church in Norfolk, Gerry was singing the same songs to a gathering on the other side of the planet as he related the tale of our journey.

That night I had a remarkable dream ... I was walking with my fellow pilgrims through a misty landscape. A fantastic flying creature, half bird of paradise, half lizard, (a tiny dragon perhaps?) flew overhead and landed on a tree to my left. I stopped to watch it up on its leafless branch. When I looked down to the path again, the others had walked on and had disappeared into the mist. I knew they had gone and I was walking alone once more. I would continue to travel with my companions in their parallel world but as the threshold between that world of myth and legend and this material world was no longer as accessible, I would not experience that directly anymore, ... I say goodbye for now but as we travel together, I know we will meet again. I felt a great sense of completion when I woke ...

Thank you dearest ones. ***SB***

Unpacking The Dream

Forty miles today,
Driven.
Oil burning, too fast,
Reluctantly studying the straight grey,
Amidst metallic reflection.

As the living green web
Recedes
Into peripheral vision,
Almost unhonoured.

No gathered firewood of the hearth,
This,
As I miss two night stops,
And you ...
And you ...
And you ...

JGJ

Day after day and step after step
I am seeing in my mind's eye the
Hazy mist of bluebells against the tender green light of the beech leaves
The grey old churches with their pagan fonts
and the great granite stones standing sentinel on the land

I am stalking my elder years
Here in the rough high fields
And deep old Cornish lanes
The air is soft but very strong and clear and filled
With the mixed scents of the flowering hedges and the greening trees,
The rich warm milky smells of cows and milking parlours
In the farmyards, full of life and purpose.

Every morning I shoulder my small pack
And take a firm grip of my stick
And stride out feeling the wellness rushing through me and strength in my muscles and legs.
And in front of me and behind me and alongside me, the others all stride out too
My fellow walkers and stalkers
Walking each of them in their own now familiar special way
Strong muscular walking and long legged loping
Light quick steps and bouncing determined ones
Strong legs and big boots, full packs and eyes open, alert and searching

I stare about me as I walk, staring at the ever-lasting passing land,
noting and noticing,
Sometimes, though, I stare at the ground beneath my boots, unfocussed, looking inward to my own thoughts or dreams.
And as I walk stalking my life and the life of the land
My fears stalk *me*
Fears that my body won't hold up
or I will walk blankly touching nothing
But the real fear, the fear that underlies all my thoughts and all my imaginings
is the fear that the land through which we pass is doomed
Perverted at last beyond all hope of awakening.

TR

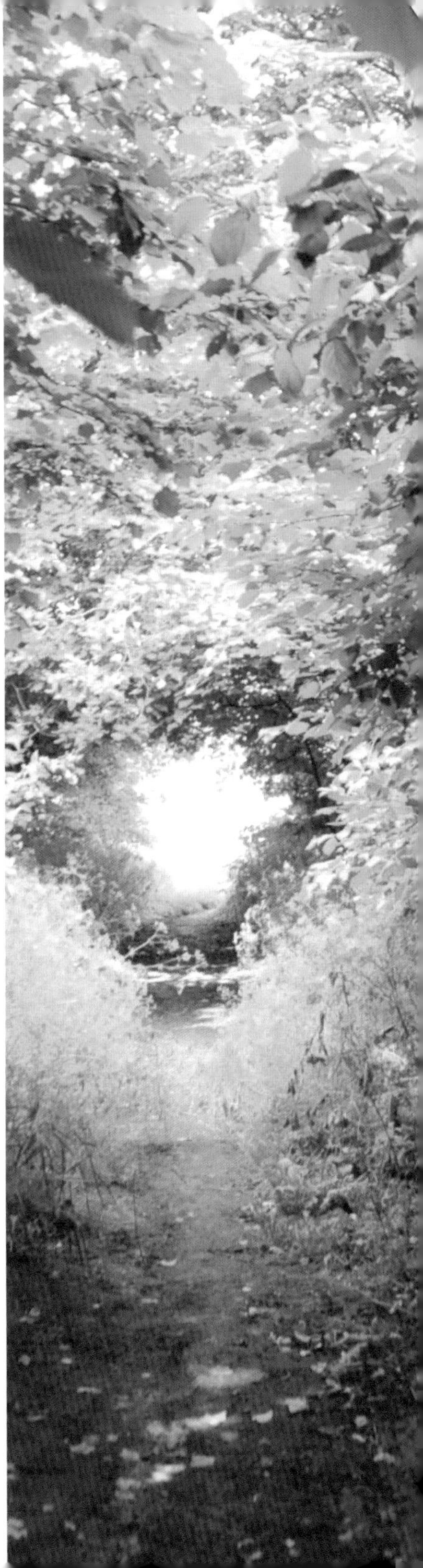

One Hundred Names of Albion

From Carn Lês Boel to Boscawen-un; from Kerthen Wood to Crenver Grove;
From Black Rock to White Alice; from Come-To-Good to Golden Mill;
From Resugga Castle to Menacuddle Well; from Luxulyan to Lostwithiel;
From St Neot to St Cleer; from The Hurlers to The Cheesewring;
From Twelve Men's Moor to Greystone Bridge; from Brent Tor to Peter Tavy;
From Beardown Farm to Piddledown Common; from Blackalder Wood to Little Silver;
From Collipriest to Copplestone; from Wrangway to Netherclay;
From Burrow Mump to Glastonbury Tor; from Hearty Gate Farm to Beardly Batch;
From Doulting Well to Cranmore Tower; from Bulls Green to Whatley Bottom;
From Great Elm to Spring Gardens; from Seymours Court to Hoopers Pool;
From Mutton Marsh Farm to Green Lane Wood; from Bowerhill to Oliver's Castle;
From Furze Knoll to Knoll Down; from Swallowhead Spring to Silbury;
From Avebury Trusloe to Ogbourne Maizey; from Snap Farm to Lammy Down;
From Wayland's Smithy to Whitehorse Hill; from Blowing Stone to Devil's Punchbowl;
From Scutchamer's Knob to Wittenham Clumps; from Day's Lock to Dyke Hills;
From Berrick Prior to Britwell Salome; from Christmas Common to Whiteleaf Cross;
From Cymbeline's Castle to Bacombe Warren; from The Crong to The Twist;
From Tinker's Lodge to Ivinghoe Beacon; from Ringshall Coppice to Dedmansey Wood;
From Luton Hoo to Diamond End; from Almshoe Bury to Damask Green;
From Quickswood to Duckpuddle Bush; from Noon's Folly Farm to Ickleton Grange;
From Raven's Hall to Kirtling Towers; from Genesis Green to Easter Wood;
From Rushbrooke to Drinkstone; from Woolpit to Cotton;
From Dandy Corner to Daisy Green; from Wickham Skeith to Thornham Parva;
From Oakley Park to Hoxne Low Street; from Elmham Minster to St Peter's Hall;
From Beccles Marshes to Somerleyton; from Bloodman's Corner to Hopton on Sea.

Map moment!
Have you got your arrows?
Are your water bottles full?

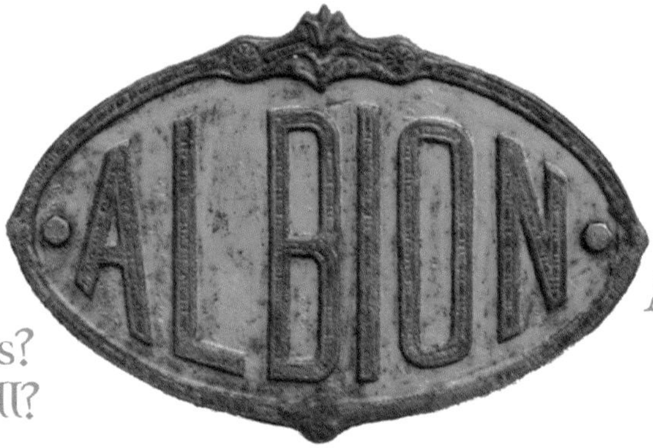

Awakening Ho!
Albion Ho!
Walkers Ho!

LaVergne, TN USA
09 December 2009
1643LVUK00002B